Minds and Machines:
Connectionism and Psychological Modeling

Minds and Machines

Connectionism

and

Psychological

Modeling

Michael R. W. Dawson

350 Main Street, Malden, MA 02148-5020, USA
108 Cowley Road, Oxford OX4 1JF, UK
550 Swanston Street, Carlton, Victoria 3053, Australia

First published 2004 by Blackwell Publishing Ltd

Library of Congress Cataloging-in-Publication Data

Dawson, Michael Robert William, 1959–
Minds and machines: connectionism and psychological modeling /
Michael R. W. Dawson.
p.   cm.
Includes bibliographical references and index.
ISBN 1-4051-1348-0 (hardcover : alk. paper) – ISBN 1-4051-1349-9
(pbk. : alk. paper)
1. Connectionism.   2. Cognitive science.   I. Title.

BF311.D345 2003
153–dc21   2003005918

A catalogue record for this title is available from the British Library.

For further information on
Blackwell Publishing, visit our website:
http://www.blackwellpublishing.com

Contents

List of Figures

List of Tables

Chapter one

The Kids in the Hall

It is noon on a beautiful March day in Edmonton, Alberta. At King Edward Elementary School, a group of schoolchildren aren't playing outside in the sunshine during the lunchtime recess. Instead, they form a crowd in a dark hall that is only illuminated by a small, bright flashlight resting on the middle of the floor. They are acting like scientists, and have in hand pencils and index cards for recording their observations. The focus of their scientific interest is the behavior of two small Lego robots that are navigating through the hallway. Both robots look like tiny tractors from outer space. Motors turn two large wheels at the rear, and a smaller front wheel turns as a robot steers through the hallway. Two small red LEDs shine like headlights mounted on the front. A thin, flexible barrier surrounds each robot, looking like a flexible hoop or shell.

One of the robots wanders down the hall, away from the flashlight, bumping into dark baseboards. As it comes into contact with the wall, it stops and does a short gyrating dance. Sometimes this causes it to point towards the light, but soon it steers itself to point in another direction. On several occasions, the students have to scramble out of the way of an approaching machine. The second robot spends more time bumping into the flashlight. When it is steering, it slowly moves in and out of the pool of light that the flashlight provides.

These students have had some experience building and programming other Lego robots as part of a weekly science fair club. They understand the function of the components that they can see on the moving robots. However, they did not construct these two machines. Their task was to try to figure out why each robot behaved the way that it did. By inspecting their movement, could the students come up with a general story about the program stored in each robot, about how each robot sensed the world, or about why the robots seemed to be different?

When they observed the robots behaving independently, their previous experience was evident. Many of the kids wrote down observations like "One likes the light and the other one likes the dark." Nevertheless, some students came up with theories that far exceeded my programming abilities. One suggested that one of the robots "thinks when stops, figures out things, searches for dark." The complexity of their theories – or at least the complexity of the programming that their theories required – increased dramatically when they observed the two robots moving at the same time: "They want to get away from each other." "The black robot likes to hit things and the green robot likes people." "Together they attack things."

It is later that same week. University students in an undergraduate psychology course find themselves with pens and index cards in hand, facing the same task as the kids at King Edward Elementary School. The undergraduates have a strong technical background in the science of behavior, but have had no previous experience with Lego robots. Many of their observations of robot behavior lead to proposals of very sophisticated internal mechanisms, and of complex relationships between the two machines: "The turquoise robot seemed to be the smarter robot. It first began to move in a circular motion, but seems to be able to adjust its behavior according to the behavior of the black robot." "They must be sending sequence information to each other." "Turquoise keeps trying to attack Black." "Now Turquoise moves to where the flashlight used to be." "Turquoise seems to be more exploratory, directed." "The robots took turns moving. One moved, while the other remains stationary." "Turquoise hesitates until Black hits the light. Turquoise then follows Black off to the right."

The apparent complexity of the robots' behavior is, perhaps surprisingly, not evident in their internal mechanisms. The two robots are variations of one of the vehicles described in a classic text on *synthetic psychology* (Braitenberg, 1984). The two LEDs are part of a pair of light sensors that measure the brightness around them. Each light sensor is connected to a motor, and the motor's speed is determined by the light sensor's signal. In one robot, the light sensor on the right of the machine drives the right motor and the left sensor drives the left motor. In the other robot, the connections between light sensors and motors are crossed so that the light sensor on one side sends a signal to the motor on the other side. The barrier surrounding the robot, when pushed, depresses one of four touch sensors mounted on the body of the robot. When any one of these sensors are activated, the motors are stopped, and then a reflex is initiated in which the two motors run backwards and then forwards at randomly selected speeds for a short period of time. These mechanisms, and only these mechanisms, are responsible for one robot preferring the dark and the other preferring the light, as well as for any apparently sophisticated interactions between the two machines.

1.1   Synthetic vs. Analytic Traditions

When asked to describe and explain robot behavior, both sets of students were facing the situation that makes scientific psychology difficult. The only given is the external behavior of a complicated system. The internal processes that mediate this behavior cannot be directly observed. The challenge is to infer plausible and testable theories of these unknown internal processes purely on the basis of what can be seen directly. "How do we represent information mentally and how do we use that information to interact with the world in adaptive ways? The problem persists because it is extraordinarily difficult, perhaps the most difficult one in all of science" (Paivio, 1986, p. 3).

In spite of this difficulty, psychology has made many advances by carefully observing and analyzing behavioral regularities. For example, psychology has developed many detailed theories of the intricate processes involved in visual perception. These theories can predict minute aspects of behavior with astonishing accuracy, and are also consistent with discoveries about the underlying structure of the brain.

However, some researchers would argue that in spite of such success, psychology and cognitive science in general requires alternative research strategies. There is a growing tendency in cognitive science to adopt a radically different – and nonanalytic – approach to understanding mental phenomena. This approach is evident in research associated with such labels as synthetic psychology, behavior-based robotics, or embodied cognitive science (e.g., Brooks, 1999; Pfeifer & Scheier, 1999). This research is based upon the general assumption that theory building in cognitive science would be better served by synthesis than analysis.

Practitioners of embodied cognitive science would not be surprised that the students came up with theories that overestimated the complexity of the two robots. They would also predict that these theories would become more and more complicated as the scene being observed became more complex as well (e.g., by containing two moving robots instead of just one). According to synthetic psychology's "law of uphill analysis and downhill synthesis," a theory created by analyzing a complicated situation is guaranteed to be more complicated than a theory created using the synthetic approach (Braitenberg, 1984).

One reason for this is that when we observe complex behavior, we have difficulty determining how much of the complexity is due to the mechanisms of the behaving agent and how much is due to the environment in which the agent behaves. For the kids in the hallway, the problem is to decide how much of the behavior is explicitly programmed, and how much is the result of both static and dynamic environmental variables. It seems that we have a tendency to attribute more intelligence to the behaving system than might be necessary.

Embodied cognitive science proposes that simpler and better theories will be produced if they are developed synthetically. In the most basic form, this is done as follows. First, a researcher decides on a set of basic building blocks, such as a library of primitive operations. For the two robots, the building blocks were the sensors, the motors, and a relatively simple programming language developed by Lego. Second, a system is constructed by organizing these building blocks in a particular way. For the two robots, this was done by physically situating the sensors and motors in a particular fashion, and by writing elementary code to convert sensor readings into motor speeds. Third, the system is situated in an environment, and its behavior is observed. For the designer, one of the interesting questions is whether the observed behavior is more surprising or interesting than might be expected given what is known about how the system was constructed.

If these three steps are followed, then there are two general expectations. First, because the system is constructed from known components, the researcher should have an excellent understanding of how it works. Second, when the system is situated into an environment, the interaction between the system and this environment should result in emergent phenomena. These emergent behaviors will be surprising in the sense that they were not directly intended or programmed into the system. The net result of all of this is (hopefully) a better and simpler theory of the complex behavior then would have been the case had the theory been created just by analyzing an existing system's behavior.

This book falls into two main parts. Chapters 1 through 8 explore what is meant by the term "psychological model." After reviewing the general rationale for modeling in psychology, we will discuss a wide variety of different approaches: models of data, mathematical models, and computer simulations. We will see that these can be viewed as falling on different locations on a continuum between modeling behavior and building models that behave. This will lead into a distinction between analytic and synthetic approaches to building psychological theories. This discussion ends with an example of connectionism as a medium that can provide models that are both synthetic and representational – but whose representations must be discovered by analysis.

Chapters 9 through 13 attempt to provide some basic concepts that will enable the reader to explore synthetic psychology using connectionist models. We consider what can be done with three general connectionist building blocks: storing associations in connection weights, using nonlinear activation functions, and creating sequences of decisions. An attempt is made to show that even some very old and simple connectionist architectures are relevant to modern psychology. Some techniques for analyzing the internal structure of a connectionist network are provided. A website of supplementary material for this book (www.bcp.psych.ualberta.ca/~mike/Book2/) provides free software that can be used to generate connectionist models.

Chapter two

Advantages and Disadvantages of Modeling

2.1 What is a Model?

In science, phenomena that are difficult to study or to understand in their own right are often approached through the use of models. The kinds of models that are used are as diverse as science itself. In biology, model organisms are used to study processes that cannot be easily measured in humans. In engineering, models of physical structures are tested in wind tunnels. Some might argue that physics is concerned with the development and testing of mathematical models of physical systems.

Even within a single discipline, one can find a bewildering diversity of model types. For example, in psychology, computer simulation models have been created for many cognitive phenomena (Boden, 1977; Feigenbaum & Feldman, 1995; Grossberg, 1988; VanLehn, 1991). Mathematical models have been used to study human perception, learning, judgments, and choice (Bock & Jones, 1968; Caelli, 1981; Restle, 1971). Statistical models have become the primary tool for expressing relationships between variables (Lunneborg, 1994; Pedhazur, 1982; Winer, 1971). Model organisms, such as the long-finned squid *Loligo pealei*, have been used to help understand the generation and transmission of nervous impulses (Hille, 1990; Levitan & Kaczmarek, 1991).

A famous philosophical passage highlights the perils of defining even the simplest of terms: "Consider for example the proceedings that we call 'games'. I mean board-games, card-games, ball-games, Olympic games, and so on. What is common to them all? – Don't say: 'There *must* be something common, or they would not be called "games"' – but *look and see* whether there is anything common to all." Given the diversity that we have briefly noted above, the term "model" could just have easily been used to demonstrate this point! Wittgenstein went on to argue that there was only a family resemblance between members of a category. "For if you look at them you will not see something that is common to *all*, but similarities, relationships, and a whole series of them at that"

(Wittengstein, 1953, p. 31^e). The features that constitute these similarities and relationships change as different members of the same class are compared to one another. What kind of family resemblance would we find among the members of the class "model"?

Intuitively, a model is an artifact that can be mapped on to a phenomenon that we are having difficulty understanding. By examining the model we can increase our understanding of what we are modeling. "A calculating machine, an anti-aircraft 'predictor', and Kelvin's tidal predictor all show the same ability. In all these latter cases, the physical process which it is desired to predict is *imitated* by some mechanical device or model which is cheaper, or quicker, or more convenient in operation" (Craik, 1943, p. 51).

For it to be useful, the artifact must be easier to work with or easier to understand than is the phenomenon being modeled. This usually results because the model reflects some of the phenomenon's properties, and does not reflect them all. A model is useful because it simplifies the situation by omitting some characteristics. "Any kind of working model of a process is, in a sense, an analogy. Being different it is bound somewhere to break down by showing properties not found in the process it imitates or by not possessing properties possessed by the process it imitates" (Craik, 1943, p. 53). Similarly, "the word model may be used instead of theory to indicate that the theory is only expected to hold as an approximation, or that employing it depends upon various simplifying assumptions" (Braithwaite, 1970, p. 269).

While a model can imitate a phenomenon, it need not resemble it. "Kelvin's tide-predictor, which consists of a number of pulleys on levers, does not resemble a tide in appearance, but it works in the same way in certain essential respects – it combines oscillations of various frequencies so as to produce an oscillation which closely resembles in amplitude at each moment the variation in tide level at any place" (Craik, 1943, p. 51). Similarly, Galileo revolutionized science by using geometry to represent physical quantities like velocity and acceleration that do not themselves resemble lines or angles (Haugeland, 1985).

Of course, consistent with Wittgenstein's notion of family resemblance, none of the claims made in the preceding paragraphs apply equally well to every model. For instance, some models are less analogous than others. The properties of the ionic channels in one model, the giant axon of the squid, are expected to correspond perfectly to the properties of the same channels in the human nervous system (Kuffler, Nicholls, & Martin, 1984). Similarly, some models, such as the scale models of structures that are tested in wind tunnels, have much stronger resemblances to entities in the real world than do other kinds of models.

One property that does seem common to all models, though, is the notion of predictive utility. A model is used to generate predictions that can be used to test the validity of a theory. The model is used because in some sense it provides an easier or faster route to prediction. Later in this book we will see that the many different kinds of models available to psychology can be used in a variety of ways, and that in some sense it is not correct to describe the models of synthetic psychology as providing "predictive utility." Prior to embarking on that much longer discussion in later chapters, let us first turn quickly to considering some of the advantages and disadvantages of using models in general.

2.2 Advantages and Disadvantages of Models

Modeling in psychology or cognitive science is associated with both advantages and disadvantages (e.g., Lewandowsky, 1993). In this section, we will consider three general advantages of modeling. However, after each of these three advantages, we will follow with a discussion of associated disadvantages. Models are like fine knives with which you can create gourmet meals, but with which you can also cut your fingers.

2.2.1 Rigorous specification of theory

"Theory in a field as immature as psychology cannot be expected to amount to much – and it doesn't" (Royce, 1970, p. 17). There are many reasons for skepticism about the quality of psychological theory. Some researchers have argued that psychologists, envious of physics, attempted to develop quantitative theories without first laying a proper qualitative foundation (Kohler, 1975). Others would argue that whenever psychological theories are expressed verbally, they are necessarily vague and imprecise. There is also a long tradition in experimental psychology of being extremely wary of verbal data (Ericsson & Simon, 1984). It would not be surprising if there were an accompanying wariness of verbally or informally stated theories.

   How do you make theories better? Many researchers would argue that this is accomplished by translating an informal verbal theory into a formal mathematical expression or into a working computer simulation. "Even deceptively simple models can benefit from the rigor of simulations" (Lewandowsky, 1993, p. 236).

2.2.1.1 Precision of terms

There are several reasons why the process of formalization is useful. First, it adds precision in specifying theoretical terms. An informal theory can be full of references to terms with vague definitions like "memory" or "attention." Many academic debates emerge because different researchers use the same terms in different ways. In a formal model, conceptual terms have to be carefully operationalized in order for the model to work. This forced precision enables theorists to communicate their ideas to others less ambiguously than would be the case if the theory were communicated as an informal statement.

One interesting historical example of this can be found in experimental aesthetics. One of the main goals of this discipline was to measure subjects' responses or preferences, and to relate these measurements to properties of the works of art or other objects that were presented (Berlyne, 1971). In this field, it has proven difficult to specify both properties of stimuli and properties of preferences. For example, the Gestalt psychologists introduced the notion of "goodness of configuration" with their Law of *Prägnanz* (Kohler, 1975). According to this law, we perceive organized patterns instead of isolated elements, and we actively organize these patterns to make them "good."

Unfortunately, the definition of good in the Law of *Prägnanz* was particularly vague: "psychological organization will always be as 'good' as the prevailing conditions allow. In this definition the term 'good' is undefined. It embraces such properties as regularity, symmetry, simplicity and others" (Kohler, 1975, p. 110). Berlyne (1971) revolutionized the field with formalization, in particular by characterizing stimulus properties numerically using definitions of complexity and redundancy that were taken from mathematical information theory. Berlyne took the same approach to the notion of preference, formalizing emotion in terms of arousal. Berlyne's approach led to extremely vibrant studies of aesthetics by experimental psychologists in the 1960s and 1970s. The renaissance of the field was largely driven by the fact that Berlyne's formalization permitted researchers in different labs to have more precise understanding of the stimulus and response properties that were being studied in diverse experiments.

2.2.1.2   New tools for studying concepts

A second advantage of formalization comes from recognizing that the language in which a theory is expressed determines the kinds of ways in which the theory can be tested or explored. For instance, after a verbal theory has been formalized mathematically, one can use mathematical operations to investigate its implications (Coombs, Dawes, & Tversky, 1970; Lunneborg, 1994; Wickens, 1982). In other words, formalization not only results in a more precise specification of the concepts in the theory, but also results in a more precise set of tools for studying these concepts.

One example of this can be found in my own research on how the human visual system tracks the identity of moving targets (Dawson, 1991). In one approach, I converted a general theory of this tracking into a particular type of computer simulation. I was then able to use the simulation to generate hypotheses about what human subjects would see when presented with apparent motion displays that had never been studied before (Dawson & Pylyshyn, 1988). In a second approach, I formalized the theory using some of the elementary operations of linear algebra. With this formalization, I was able to prove that the computer simulation would generate unique solutions to tracking problems. I was also able to prove that there was a strong relationship between my model and a more general model that was unrelated to motion processing (Hopfield, 1982). The algebra showed that both models could be described as minimizing identical energy functions. Both of these proofs were examinations of crucial characteristics of my theory, but would have been impossible to conduct had the model not been expressed algebraically.

2.2.1.3   Revelation of hidden assumptions

A third advantage of formalization is that it can reveal hidden assumptions in an informal theory which themselves need to be fleshed out in greater detail in order for the theory to be complete. For example, many theories in cognitive psychology are expressed as flowcharts of black boxes. Ideally, each black box in such a flowchart is supposed to be a primitive operation that needs no further explanation (Cummins, 1983; Dawson, 1998). Bringing the flowchart to life in, for instance, a computer simulation can reveal that some of these alleged primitive operations are themselves very complicated processes that require further analysis and explanation.

As a case in point, consider the study of vision. For most people, visual perception is extremely easy: we just look at something and see it. Because of this, artificial intelligence researchers believed in the 1960s that it would be very straightforward to build computer vision programs. "In the 1960s almost no one realized that machine vision was difficult" (Marr, 1982, p. 16). Indeed, Marvin Minsky has admitted that he assigned computer vision to a student as a summer programming project (Horgan, 1993). However, when serious attempts were directed towards programming a machine to see, astonishing difficulties arose. It became painfully obvious that underlying the process of seeing was a set of enormously complicated information-processing problems that the human visual system was solving effortlessly in real time. Identifying the nature of these problems, let alone solving them, became a staggering challenge for vision researchers – and the core of a new discipline. Vision research has obviously benefited from attempts to formalize our intuitions about perceptual processing.

2.2.2   Problems with formalization

We have seen in the preceding subsection that one general property of the model is that it can result in the conversion of an informal theory into a theory that is stated more rigorously or more precisely. We've also seen that there are several advantages to doing this. However, it is important to realize that the formalization of the theory can also be hazardous. Let's briefly consider some potential disadvantages of formalization.

2.2.2.1   The irrelevant specification problem

One potential problem with formalization is that this process requires a researcher to make design decisions. For instance, in a computer simulation one might have many possible ways for representing information. To build a model, one of these representational formats must be selected. The hope is that the specific choice is *theory-neutral*. If the choice is theory-neutral, this means that the simulation will behave in the same manner whatever representational format is chosen. However, this is often not the case. Many design decisions are *theory-laden*. In other words, the behavior of the model is affected by the design decisions. With one representational code a computer simulation might behave one way, but it will behave differently with another representational code. Lewandowsky (1993) calls this the *irrelevant specification problem*.

To illustrate the irrelevant specification problem, let us consider a model of how human subjects perform in a particular memory task. One of the earliest techniques for studying memory was the paired-associate learning task (Ashcraft, 1989). In this task, subjects were presented pairs of consonant-vowel-consonant nonsense syllables (CVCs), such as XOP-LUD. When presented with the first member of the pair, the subjects' task was to remember the second member of the pair. So, when presented with XOP a subject would respond with LUD. The dependent measure for this task was usually the number of trials that were required before a short list of these pairs was remembered perfectly. The paired-associate learning task was central to the study of interference theories of forgetting.

In 1961, a computer simulation of this type of memory task, called EPAM for Elementary Perceiver and Memorizer, was first described (Feigenbaum, 1995). This model used a discrimination learning process to create a discrimination net to represent remembered CVCs. This discrimination net was very similar to modern decision trees used by computer scientists for pattern recognition (e.g., Quinlan, 1986). Each branch of Feigenbaum's discrimination net was a test that would distinguish one CVC from another. Each terminal leaf of the discrimination net was one of the component letters of a CVC. During learning, EPAM would grow its discrimination net using the minimum amount of information required. As more items were added to the net, the early discrimination tasks might start to fail, which allowed EPAM to model interference effects in paired-associate learning.

One of the key design decisions in EPAM was the assumption that the primitive symbols in the discrimination net were individual letters. Feigenbaum and Feldman (1995) made this design decision for the very plausible reason that "letters are familiar and are well-learned units for the adult subject" (p. 301). However, it turns out that this design decision is theory-laden. In one of my first experiences with computer simulation in a Minds and Machines course taught by Zenon Pylyshyn at the University of Western Ontario, we started with an EPAM model that used Feigenbaum's coding format. We then revised the model by making a different design decision about the internal symbols. In the revised model, we described each letter as a set of visual features. As a result, the discrimination net terminated in featural subcomponents of a CVC's component letters. The revised model had a great deal of difficulty learning any paired associates, indicating that the choice of internal representation strongly affects the model's performance.

2.2.2.2 The relevant formalization problem

Hodges (1983) describes a problem that mathematician Alan Turing encountered when he formalized a method for playing chess. "Alan had all the rules written out on paper, and found himself torn between executing the moves that his algorithm demanded, and doing what was obviously a better move. There were long silences while he totted up the scores and chose the best minimax ploy, hoots and growls when he could see it missing chances" (p. 440). This illustrates a disadvantage that I will call the *relevant formalization problem*. After you formalize a model, like Turing you have to accept its bad properties along with the good. The relevant formalization problem occurs when this is not done, because there is a strong temptation to selectively focus on a formalization's successes, and ignore its failures.

My own experience with the relevant formalization problem came when I taught myself connectionism by programming the equations in a popular account of the generalized delta rule (Rumelhart, Hinton, and Williams, 1986a). After programming the equations, I tested my work by trying to train networks on the problems that Rumelhart, Hinton, and Williams described. To my dismay, I found that in several cases my program didn't converge to a trained connectionist network. Thinking that there must be a bug in my code, I spent a great deal of time poring over it, and was frustrated by failing to find any errors. It turned out that my code was correct, but that in many cases it was failing to converge because the network connection weights were driving the system into a local minimum.

I should have expected this, because the generalized delta rule is, in principle, subject to this kind of problem (Minsky & Papert, 1988). However, I had different expectations because, in my opinion, Rumelhart et al. (1986a) had fallen into the relevant formalization problem. They reported that "we do not know the frequency of such local minima, but our experience with this and other problems is that they are quite rare. We have found only one other situation in which a local minimum has occurred in many hundreds of problems of various sorts" (p. 332). My own experience with this kind of network is that problems like local minima are much more frequent.

Having to take the formalization seriously can be extremely productive. One excellent example of this is found in work that uses production systems to model human search of short-term memory (Newell, 1973), and is described below.

Sternberg (1969) reported one famous study of short-term memory. In the Sternberg memory task, subjects were given a string of digits to hold in short-term memory. After a set delay, subjects were presented with an additional probe digit. Their task was to say whether or not the probe was a member of the memorized list. The dependent measure in this experiment was reaction time. Sternberg found a linear increase in response time as a function of the number of digits in the memorized list. He also found that the slope of the reaction time function for lists that did not contain the probe was twice the slope of the reaction time function for lists that did. Sternberg used these results to propose a self-terminating serial search model of short-term memory; this was one of the first experiments that demonstrated how reaction time data could be used to infer the properties of internal processes.

Newell (1973) described a series of production system models of the Sternberg memory task. Production systems are described in more detail later in Chapter 5. For the time being, a production system is essentially a set of condition–action pairs that scan a memory. When the contents of the memory match a production's condition, then it takes control of the memory and performs its action. Usually this action involves changing the contents of the memory, so that some other production's condition might be met.

Newell (1973) found that it was very easy to create fairly simple production system models of the Sternberg memory task. In fact, he describes seven different production system models written in a language called PSG. Each of these models was capable of making the correct response when given the probe. However, only one of the models generated response latency functions that resembled those of human subjects. Interestingly, this production system was not a model of search. Instead, it was a model of a general encoding and decoding scheme that could be used to perform the Sternberg task, as well as other basic tasks in cognitive psychology.

Given this result, it would have been quite reasonable for Newell (1973) to report only his last production system model. However, had he done so, he would have fallen victim to the relevant formalization problem. This is because one of his basic assumptions was that production systems describe the functional architecture of human cognition. "In this view PSG represents the basic structure of the human information processing system. It follows that any program written in PSG should be a viable program for the human subject" (p. 494). As a result, in addition to coming up with one model that fits the human reaction time data, Newell must come up with a theory about why humans might use that production system, and not any of the other six, some of which are simpler. "Our example makes clear that multiple production systems are possible. Without a theory of which system is selected the total view remains essentially complete."

Newell (1973) went on to explore why an encoding model for performing the Sternberg memory task might be more adaptive than other possible production systems. He proposed that for the Sternberg task, short-term memory is unreliable, and an encoding model of memory processing is better at dealing with this unreliability. He also showed how an encoding strategy works well for a variety of other tasks, which is not the case for the simpler production system models that he was able to devise. However, Newell also identified plausible alternatives to the encoding model that are worthy of further exploration. In short, by avoiding the relevant formalization problem, Newell was able to develop a rich and detailed understanding of the Sternberg memory task that went far beyond what would be possible by only having a single, successful model that fit the data.

2.2.2.3 The communication problem

In formalizing a theory, a typical goal is to convert a set of informal verbal statements into a set of precise expressions that can be manipulated by some formal mechanism – mathematics, logic, or an algorithm. With this goal in mind, it is apparent that a theory will be more technical after formalization than it was before. This leads to another problem that must be faced: communicating the formalization to others, including those who might be interested in the domain, but not as interested in the technical details of the formalization.

Zeigler (1976) points out that the construction and testing phase of modeling can be quite exciting – often more exciting than recasting the model into a form for general distribution. As a result, "once the modeling challenge has been successfully overcome and the modeler's own curiosity satisfied, he may find it difficult to become enthusiastic about the task of clarifying it for himself and communicating to others what he has accomplished" (p. 7). But clarification and communication are both required if the model is to have any impact.

Zeigler (1976) proposes that the effective communication of a model involves the following aspects. First, the researcher must generate an informal description of the model and its underlying goals and assumptions. Second, the researcher must provide a formal description of the model, including a presentation of the program used if the model is a simulation. Third, the researcher should present the tests of the model, including results and analysis. Fourth, the researcher should generate some conclusions about the model's range of application, validity, and cost. Finally, the researcher should relate his or her current model to both past and future models.

Zeigler (1976) notes that when the model is communicated, two different audiences must be kept in mind. One audience is the set of potential users of the model or its variations. The other audience is composed of "people who may not use the program or model directly but may make other uses of it in relation to their own research and development – call them the *colleagues*" (p. 8). With these two different audiences in mind, Zeigler suggests that the "informal description of the model is the most natural and effective way of establishing contact with the reader's intuition and of interfacing your world model with his world model" (p. 9). However, it is important to realize that with the audience of colleagues, this informal account might be the only way that contact is made. They may not be interested in paying the necessary attention to the more formal descriptions of the model, because they are an audience that isn't interested in using it.

2.2.3 Exploration of complex domains

We have already seen that one advantage of modeling is the rigorous specification of theory. A second advantage is that models permit the exploration of complex ideas. "Simulations can be of value in this way either because a seemingly attractive idea might otherwise be too unconstrained to support predictions and tests or because a complex model may resist analytic exploration" (Lewandowsky, 1993, p. 237). Let us briefly explore each of these ideas.

2.2.3.1 The economy of models

In mathematical psychology, as we will see in Chapter 4, one usually attempts to define a relationship between one set of variables and another. Within this framework, it is sometimes the case that there are a great many variables to be explored. Each of these variables can take on one of many different numerical values. The problem for a mathematical psychologist is to explore the set of possible settings for the variables in order to determine the best possible model. Mathematical psychologists have realized that the fastest, most economical approach to exploring the parameter space for a model is to use computer simulations (Estes, 1975; Luce, 1989, 1997, 1999).

The economy of modeling provides advantages for scientists who have little direct interest in mathematical psychology. Many are interested in studying systems that are highly complex, and that are also very difficult and expensive to examine experimentally. For example, neuroscientists who study the nervous systems of animals have to face the combined expenses of maintaining animals, of providing resources for drug or surgical treatments, and of histological examination of manipulated nervous systems – not to mention the ethical expenses of sacrificing animals for the advancement of knowledge. When a neuroscience experiment is performed, it would be very valuable to have a strong sense beforehand that the experiment is going to work, and is also going to provide important information. This kind of research is simply too expensive for "fishing" for interesting results.

One approach for increasing the likelihood that an experiment is going to be successful is to use computer simulation techniques to identify key issues, or predict the likely outcomes of experiments. The simulation is itself much less expensive to run, and can be easily used to simulate a variety of experiments. One can use the simulation to "fish" for interesting results in a fashion that is far faster and cheaper than by actually performing the experiments on animals. Once an interesting set of predictions has been identified using the computer simulation, the result can be verified by actually performing the experiment on animals. The expectation is that the experiment should be successful because of all of the simulation work that was carried out beforehand. The results of the experiment can then be used to refine the computer simulation, so that it reflects an advancing state of knowledge, and so that it can be used to predict more sophisticated results in the future.

One excellent example of exploiting the economy of modeling is found in the research of neuroscientist Gary Lynch and his colleagues (e.g., Lynch, 1986). Lynch is primarily concerned with understanding the neural mechanisms underlying memory, and uses the olfactory system of the rat as his primary research focus. Lynch's research has uncovered many precise details about the neural circuitry that permits rats to remember and process information about different smells. A great deal of this information has been the result of experiments on rat brains. However, computer simulation has also been a central tool in Lynch's research program.

For instance, Granger, Ambros-Ingerson, and Lynch (1989) developed a computer simulation of the olfactory cortex. The simulation consisted of 100 input cells (simulating axons of the lateral olfactory tract) randomly and sparsely connected to up to 500 cells in the olfactory cortex. Processing units in the simulation have a number of mathematical properties that model such characteristics as synaptic conductance, dendritic summation, excitatory and inhibitory signal characteristics, spike generation, and the speed of axon transmission. Depending upon the kinds of pulses transmitted to the network, it can learn by modifying the pattern of connectivity between its processing units. Granger et al. found that after learning a set of distinct groups of odors, the simulation's initial response to a cue odor only indicated the category to which it belonged. Subsequent responses to the same stimulus successively subdivided the category into increasingly specific encodings of the original cue. In other words, the model was demonstrating its ability to organize olfactory memories at a number of different levels of detail.

Importantly, the simulation created by Granger et al. (1989) led to at least five different predictions that were specific, and which were also not intuitively obvious. For example, in the simulation only a small number of cells responded to a specific input; also different cells responded when the simulation was presented different "sniffs," with the patterns of which cells were firing reflecting similarities and differences among odor cues. It is these sorts of specific, surprising predictions made by the model that can be selected as likely candidates for empirical study in animal systems. In the Lynch lab, there is a constant back-and-forth exchange of information between simulations and experiments, with each information exchange resulting in an increasingly detailed understanding of the neural circuitry.

2.2.3.2 Beyond mathematical boundaries

In many disciplines there can be a marked competition between theorists and experimentalists. In physics, Lederman (1993, p. 13) observes, "In the eternal love-hate relation between theory and experiment, there is a kind of scorekeeping. How many important discoveries were predicted by theory? How many were complete surprises?" The tension between theory and experiment is also a frequently observed characteristic of psychology (Kukla, 1989; Paivio, 1986, chs. 1–2).

One reason for this tension is that it is possible for theorists to make predictions about observations that take years for experimentalists to confirm. Many examples of this can be found in physics (e.g., Bodanis, 2000). For example, Einstein's general theory of relativity was first publicized in 1915. One of its major predictions, of the curvature of space, could not be confirmed empirically until observations of star positions during total solar eclipses were made in 1919 and 1922. In the 1930s, Chandrasekhar used special relativity theory to predict that white dwarf stars could only exist up to a certain mass. He proved that if a star were larger than this limit, then it would ultimately collapse into a denser object (a neutron star or a black hole). This theory was extremely controversial when it was originally proposed, and was not supported empirically until observations in the 1960s that discovered pulsars, and which later demonstrated that pulsars were rotating neutron stars.

In these examples from physics, formal theories anticipated experimental results by years or decades. With the advent of computer simulation techniques, however, it is now possible to experimentally study models of systems whose complexity cannot yet be captured by mathematical formalisms.

In a wide variety of fields, researchers are interested in the properties of systems that have a large number of (often simple) components. Frequently, one component can influence the behavior of neighboring components in a manner that can only be captured by nonlinear equations. Furthermore, the behavior of one component's neighbors can influence the behavior of that component via feedback. In spite of the fact that these systems do not have any component that serves as a central controller, they often exhibit interesting, emergent, and systematic regularities. Examples of such systems include slime molds, insect colonies, and biological neural networks, to name a few. A new discipline, called complexity theory, is concerned with studying the properties shared by these diverse systems (Holland, 1998; Johnson, 2001; Waldrop, 1992).

The many nonlinear interactions in a distributed system like an ant colony or a brain make it very difficult to summarize the behavior of the system as a whole mathematically. However, it is possible to program a computer to simulate the interactions between system components. This means that the system can be studied, and understood, by making empirical observations about the behavior of the computer simulation even in the absence of formal theory. The fields of artificial life, genetic algorithms, artificial neural networks, and synthetic psychology all depend crucially upon the fact that one can use computers to explore regularities in domains that are currently too complicated to describe in formal equations.

2.2.4   *Problems with exploring complex domains*

From the preceding subsection, it is clear that models provide a medium that provides many advantages for researchers interested in exploring complicated ideas in an efficient, inexpensive manner. These ideas can even be explored in advance of any mathematical account of the domain. However, while the ability to explore complex domains is a definite advantage of modeling, it can lead to some interesting disadvantages. Two of these are considered in the subsections below.

2.2.4.1   Bonini's paradox

Dutton and Starbuck (1971) used the name *Bonini's paradox* to identify one problem with computer simulations of complex phenomena. Bonini's paradox, named after Stanford business professor Charles Bonini, occurs when a computer simulation is at least as difficult to understand as the phenomenon that it was supposed to illuminate:

> The computer simulation researcher needs to be particularly watchful of the complexity dilemma. If he hopes to understand complex behavior, he must construct complex models, but the more complex the model, the harder it is to understand. . . . As more than one user has realized while sadly contemplating his convoluted handiwork, he can easily construct a computer model that is more complicated than the real thing. Since science is to make things simpler, such results can be demoralizing as well as self-defeating.
>
> *(Dutton & Briggs, 1971, p. 103)*

While any model may fall into this trap, Bonini's paradox is particularly relevant for researchers who use connectionist networks. Connectionist models are introduced in more detail later in this book, and are essentially brainlike networks of simple nonlinear processors that can learn to solve complex pattern recognition problems. Connectionist researchers freely admit that in many cases it is extremely difficult to determine how their networks accomplish the tasks that they have been taught. "If the purpose of simulation modeling is to clarify existing theoretical constructs, connectionism looks like exactly the wrong way to go. Connectionist models do not clarify theoretical ideas, they obscure them" (Seidenberg, 1993, p. 229).

Connectionist networks can fall prey to Bonini's paradox for several reasons. First, because connectionist models are usually taught by example, they do not require a researcher to come up with detailed theory of how to perform a pattern recognition task prior to creating the model. In other words, connectionist networks allow "for the possibility of constructing intelligence without first understanding it" (Hillis, 1988, p. 176). Second, one can train connectionist networks that are extremely large; their sheer size and complexity makes it difficult to understand their internal workings. For example, Seidenberg and McClelland's (1989) network for computing a mapping between graphemic and phonemic word representations uses 400 input units, up to 400 hidden units, and 460 output units. Determining how such a large network works is an intimidating task. This is particularly true because in many parallel distributed processing (PDP) networks, it is very difficult to consider the role that one processing unit plays independent from the role of the other processing units to which it is connected (see also Farah, 1994).

Difficulties in understanding how a particular connectionist network accomplishes the task that it has been trained to perform has raised serious doubts about the ability of connectionists to provide fruitful theories about cognitive processing. McCloskey (1991) warns that "connectionist networks should not be viewed as theories of human cognitive functions, or as simulations of theories, or even as demonstrations of specific theoretical points" (p. 387). In a nutshell, this dismissal was based largely on the view that connectionist networks are generally uninterpretable (see also Dawson & Shamanski, 1994). It is clear that the success of connectionist networks, or of any other type of model, in contributing to psychological theory, depends heavily upon a researcher's ability to avoid Bonini's paradox. Later in this book we will see several examples of how this can be accomplished.

2.2.4.2   The validation problem

In Chapters 3 and 4, we will see that two common modeling approaches in psychology are models of data and mathematical modeling. Both use mathematical equations to describe and predict behavioral regularities. The equations represent a theoretical statement about behavior. The validity of the theoretical statement is usually assessed using "goodness of fit": the equation makes certain predictions about what behavior should be observed in experimental subjects. The validity of the theory depends upon the extent that the predictions are consistent with these empirical observations.

However, the fact that new modeling techniques such as computer simulation permit the study of systems that cannot be formally described has led to a situation in which this traditional notion of theory validation does not work very well. Mathematical psychologists, for example, are deeply disturbed by the fact that it is very difficult to formulate a procedure for measuring the validity of computer simulations (Estes, 1975; Luce, 1999).

This problem is compounded by the bottom-up strategies used in the simulations that are of concern to complexity theorists. In many instances, these simulations involve defining the interactions between neighboring components in the model, without being concerned with the overall outcome of the simulation. In other words, rather than modeling a particular phenomenon (which we will see is the typical top-down strategy used to create models of data and to propose mathematical models), complexity theorists are interested in discovering what surprising properties emerge from the interactions of known components. In many cases, they may have no idea what kinds of regularities will emerge from their simulation.

This makes it particularly difficult to validate a complexity theorist's simulation, because it may not even be known a priori what the model is a model of. This is one of the reasons that many of these simulations are viewed skeptically. For instance, these models have been described as being "fact free science" by evolutionary biologist John Maynard Smith (Mackenzie, 2002). Some have argued that it is impossible to verify or validate these kinds of simulations:

> Like a novel, a model may be convincing – it may ring true if it is consistent with our experience of the natural world. But just as we may wonder how much the characters in a novel are drawn from real life and how much is artifice, we might ask the same of a model: How much is based on observation and measurement of accessible phenomena, how much is based on informed judgment, and how much is convenience?
>
> *(Oreskes, Shrader-Frechette, & Belitz, 1994, p. 644)*

Validating a model is a difficult problem that is a central concern of psychology and cognitive science (Fodor, 1968; Pylyshyn, 1980, 1984). For the time being, let us simply be aware that this problem exists. In several of the later chapters we will have an opportunity to consider how synthetic psychologists approach this problem.

2.2.5   Serendipity

We have already covered two of the main advantages of models: the rigorous specification of theory and the ability to explore complicated domains. There is one further advantage to be considered – the ability of a model to reveal serendipitous discoveries. Lewandowsky (1993) is concerned by the fact that "a widespread opinion among critics is that theories or simulations somehow stand in the way of serendipitous discovery" (p. 238). He goes on to point out the flaws in this view.

In the next three chapters the notion of serendipity will be important in distinguishing different kinds of models. In particular, I will be arguing that some kinds of models (models of data, mathematical models) provide less opportunity to surprise a researcher than do others (computer simulations). However, as a prelude to that more detailed discussion, let us briefly consider some general aspects of how models can lead to surprises.

2.2.5.1   Emergence and surprise

One of the reasons that some researchers believe that models cannot generate surprises is because systems like computer simulations are deterministic. If a computer can only follow its program, then it stands to reason that it should be impossible for the program to surprise the programmer (Haugeland, 1985).

The difficulty with this logic is that it assumes that the purpose of the programmer is to create a program that is responsible for carrying out some overall, holistic behavior. However, sometimes this is not the programmer's goal. Indeed, in many situations the programmer is concerned with programming simple and well-defined local interactions between the components of a system. "Local turns out to be the key term in understanding the power of swarm logic. We see emergent behavior in systems like ant colonies when the individual agents in the system pay attention to their immediate neighbors rather than wait for orders from above. They think locally and act locally, but their collective action produces global behavior" (Johnson, 2001, p. 74).

In many situations, the programmer will have complete understanding of the programmed local interactions, but will be unable to predict the global behavior that the local interactions produce. It is these emergent properties that are surprising, and which are capable of providing new insights.

2.2.5.2   An example: Banding in value units

One example of a serendipitous result from a model comes from my own laboratory's research on connectionist networks. As we will see in more detail later in this book, a connectionist model is a network of simple processors that send numerical signals to one another. One of the basic tasks of any processing unit in this kind of network is to add up the total incoming signal, and to convert it into an internal level of activity. Mathematically, this is done using an equation called an activation function.

By 1989, Don Schopflocher and I had developed a method of training connectionist networks that used a different activation function than is found in typical connectionist networks (Dawson, 1990; Dawson & Schopflocher, 1992a). We called our architecture networks of value units, using terminology borrowed from Ballard (1986), because the activation function tuned the processor so that it had a strong response to a narrow range of incoming signal, and had a very weak response when the incoming signal was too strong or too weak to fall in this narrow range (for more details, see Chapters 10 and 11).

After this architecture had been published, we continued to study it because it had several advantages that we wanted to exploit. However, one problem that we were concerned about was Bonini's paradox: the networks that we trained had an internal structure that was very difficult to understand. We expended a great deal of fruitless effort trying to develop techniques for figuring out the "program" that was encoded in the connection weights of our networks.

In the winter of 1993, we stumbled upon an emergent property of the value unit architecture that aided network interpretation immeasurably. One of my philosophy graduate students, Istvan Berkeley, had trained a network of value units to solve a logic problem developed by Bechtel and Abrahamsen (1991). He had devoted hundreds of hours to examining the structure of this particular network. One kind of data that we collected in this process was analogous to "wiretapping" of neurons by neuroscientists: we simply recorded the activity of each processor within the network to each stimulus that the network was presented.

In an effort to help interpret the network, Don Schopflocher took a copy of the "wiretapping" data, and attempted some multivariate analyses. This didn't provide any breakthroughs. However, Don did notice that in the data a lot of numbers were repeated. He didn't make anything of this, and neither did I. In fact, I pretty much ignored this observation. Importantly, the very next day, Istvan – who had been looking at the very same data – came to me and repeated, almost word for word, Don's observation. Being told the same thing twice finally captured my attention, and I took the data and started to perform some graphical analyses.

In very short order, I had selected a particular type of graph called a jittered density plot. One such graph can be drawn for each one of our processing units. In a jittered density plot, each dot in the graph represents the unit's response to one stimulus pattern. The x-position of the dot indicates the actual level of unit activity. The y-position of the dot is randomly selected, and is used to try to prevent dots from overlapping each other as much as possible.

Now, for a standard processing unit, a jittered density plot is not very informative, because it is not very structured. Usually it is just a smear of dots throughout the whole graph. Our serendipitous finding was that the jittered density plots for value units were much more structured. Rather than being an uninformative smear, as in the example above, we found that the plots for the processors in Istvan's network were organized into tight bands, usually with a great deal of space separating one band from another.

We were tremendously excited and surprised by this result, and our excitement grew and grew as each new jittered density plot came out of the printer. A whole new set of questions jumped to mind. Why did the bands emerge? Was there anything in common among the subset of patterns that fell into one band? In answering these questions, we discovered that the bands provided a method for identifying the kinds of features that were being detected by each unit in the network. We were then able to use these features to determine how the network was solving the logic problem, and to make an argument that connectionist networks might be more symbolic than was traditionally thought (Berkeley, Dawson, Medler, Schopflocher, & Hornsby, 1995; Dawson, Medler, & Berkeley, 1997).

More recently, we have developed a much stronger formal understanding of why banding occurs, and have used it to predict and discover banding for other problems and for other architectures (McCaughan, Medler, & Dawson, 1999). We have also developed more sophisticated interpretation techniques than the purely local ones that we reported in 1995 (Dawson, Boechler, & Valsangkar-Smyth,

2000; Dawson, Medler, McCaughan, Willson, & Carbonaro, 2000; Dawson & Piercey, 2001; Medler, McCaughan, Dawson & Willson, 1999). However, all of these advances have depended upon our original lucky discovery. Don Schopflocher and I had no idea that we were going to produce this result when we developed our learning rule in 1989. Indeed, we were using this algorithm for approximately four years – and encountering numerous dead ends in network interpretation – before we chanced upon this discovery.

2.2.6   Luck: Good and bad

For the other two advantages of modeling, the rigorous specification of theory and the ability to explore complex phenomena, we have outlined accompanying disadvantages. What possible disadvantages might one find with an approach that permits serendipitous discovery? The subsections below briefly consider three different kinds of concerns.

2.2.6.1   Is good luck bad science?

One concern that is often raised when serendipity is a key component of a research program is that the program doesn't seem to be very scientific. The traditional view of science is that it is a careful, gradual, goal-directed advancement of knowledge, in which current information is used to generate and test new hypotheses. Hypotheses "are the first rungs of the ladder of science, becoming theories as the harder factual sides of the ladder are extended, and finally facts when the ladder makes firm contact with structures established by other ladders of hypothesis" (Hocking, 1963, p. 3).

However, "science seldom proceeds in the straightforward logical manner imagined by outsiders. Instead, its steps forward (and sometimes backward) are often very human events in which personalities and cultural traditions play major roles" (Watson, 1968, p. ix). Put another way, "the discoveries of penicillin, X-rays, and America have apparently failed to alert students of memory to the possibility of serendipitous findings within their own field" (Watkins, 1990, p. 333).

Nevertheless, there is still some sense that if the advancement of one's research field depends overtly on serendipity, then this reflects a weakened dependence on theory or on prior knowledge. This simply isn't so. In very general terms, we will see that advances in synthetic psychology come about by taking a set of components, letting them interact, and observing surprising emergent phenomena. However, the role of theory and prior knowledge in this endeavor is still fundamentally important, because it guides decisions about what components to select, and about the possible dynamics of their interaction. In the words of Cervantes, diligence is the mother of good fortune.

2.2.6.2   Good luck, bad control

We will see later that one of the modern arguments in favor of adopting a synthetic approach to modeling, rather than analyzing a system into its components, is the opportunity for generating simpler theories. "Analysis is more difficult than invention in the sense in which, generally, induction takes more time to perform than deduction: in induction one has to search for the way, whereas in deduction one follows a straightforward path. A psychological consequence of this is the following: when we analyze a mechanism, we tend to overestimate its complexity" (Braitenberg, 1984, p. 20).

However, if many of the advances of synthetic psychology are going to depend upon emergent surprises, then this view tells only half the story. There are many solid theoretical and empirical arguments that make the point that analytic approaches are difficult, and lead to overly complicated theories. However, a synthetic approach may be no less difficult. The tacit view of proponents of the synthetic approach, like Braitenberg, is that if one can build a system, then one must be able to understand it. However, we have already seen that this view is not completely correct. The idea that models can lead to serendipitous results comes from the situation in which a modeler has a very precise understanding of a system at one level (i.e., the level of the components), but has little understanding of the system at another level (i.e., a higher level at which emergent surprises can be seen).

In other words, modelers in synthetic psychology are likely going to be in a situation in which they have a high degree of control of their systems at a microlevel, but have much less control of their systems at a macrolevel. Furthermore, they may have little understanding about how microlevel processes result in macrolevel behaviors. We will see later in this book that the only way to deal with this problem is to combine synthetic and analytic approaches. After one discovers an emergent surprise in a synthetic model, a good deal of effort is going to be required to analyze the model in order to account for how the surprise emerged. Finding lucky surprises will not suffice. Synthetic psychology is charged with explaining the surprises too.

2.2.6.3   Going beyond the model

One final concern with the serendipity of modeling is that it requires a researcher to go beyond the direct intent of his or her model. This is a problem because this requires the researcher to move against a tradition that is a strong, tacit component of experimental psychology, as we will see in the next two chapters. When many psychologists think of modeling, their view is that the purpose of a model is to fit or mimic experimental data. The reason for this belief is that it is central to two types of models that have a long history in psychology – models of data and mathematical models. In general, if a model of data or a mathematical model does not fit the data, then the model is abandoned.

The possibility of discovering new and surprising characteristics of a model requires that this very narrow view of what a model is intended to do, or of how a model should be evaluated, must be either abandoned or suspended. This is because the only way that a model can surprise is if one examines how it deals with situations that it was not originally intended to face. Once my students have developed a model of some phenomena, I always ask them to find out what they can "get from the model for free." My request is an attempt to encourage them to determine whether their model has any interesting or surprising emergent properties that they may not have considered. I also tell them that if a model doesn't have any surprises, then it may not be a very good model. My own experience is that this is true – but to be aware of this truth, one must abandon the notion that the only purpose of a model is to fit data that has already been collected from subjects.

Chapter three

Models of Data

Statistics is a field that develops techniques for using observations of small samples to make broad generalizations. Typically, the observations in question are in numerical form, and the methods developed by statisticians are mathematical in nature. At the heart of any statistical method is a *model for data*. "Models for data summarize a set of observations in the behavioral or biological sciences so that we may communicate with our colleagues and the public" (Lunneborg, 1994, p. 1). The purpose of this chapter is to provide a brief overview of models of data, so that later we can contrast this type of model with others more likely to be found in synthetic psychology.

According to Lunneborg (1994), a model of data is both explanatory and statistical. It is explanatory in the sense that it typically describes the influence of one or more variables on another response variable. In other words, if we know the values for the predictor variables then we can predict or explain the value of the response variable. A model of data is statistical in the sense that variability in the predictor variables will be related to variability in the response variable. By determining how strong the relationship is between predictor and response variability, we can determine how well the model fits the data.

3.1 An Example of a Model of Data

To illustrate some of the properties of models of data, we will be using a small set of numbers taken from a published experiment (Dawson & Thibodeau, 1998). In this experiment, the task was to search through for a visual target in a 4×4, an 8×8, or a 12×12 grid of distractor objects. The target was only present in half of the displays, and the type of display that the subject saw from trial to trial was randomly selected. The response variable in this experiment was reaction time – the time that elapsed from when the display was presented to when a subject pressed a response key to indicate whether or not a target was seen.

Table 3.1 Sample data from the Dawson and Thibodeau (1998) study of visual search

Time	Objects	Filter	O × F
766.44	16	0	0
704.62	16	1	16
796.63	16	2	32
1319.71	64	0	0
1230.57	64	1	64
1523.51	64	2	128
2118.9	144	0	0
2086.33	144	1	144
2351.32	144	2	288

Table 3.1 contains data from one subject in this experiment for only those displays in which a target was present. The numbers in the Time column give the average reaction time in milliseconds for detecting the target in a number of different experimental conditions. We would like to come up with a statistical model for these data.

In this particular experiment, there were two conditions that were manipulated in an attempt to affect reaction time. The first was the size of the grid – the number of objects to be searched. Presumably, as more objects were displayed, it would take longer to find the target. The Objects column in Table 3.1 lists the total number of objects that were displayed in each of the three sizes of grid.

One kind of statistical model for the reaction time data would be an equation that used the values in the Objects column to predict the values in the Time column. One mathematical method for creating such a model is called *multiple regression* (Pedhazur, 1982). Multiple regression uses the underlying correlations between variables to come up with a linear equation that uses one or more variables to predict the response variable as accurately as possible. Multiple regression is a standard component of any statistical package. If I take the numbers from the table and provide them to a multiple regression program, then this program will come up with the following equation for predicting reaction time:

$$\text{Time} = (13.55 \times \text{Objects}) + 405.16 \qquad [3.1]$$

What does Lunneborg (1994) mean by describing this kind of model as being both explanatory and statistical? To answer this question, consider Figure 3.1. It is a graph that plots the Time values from the table on the y-axis, and the Objects values on the x-axis. The line on the graph is the line that is defined by the regression equation that predicts Time from Objects.

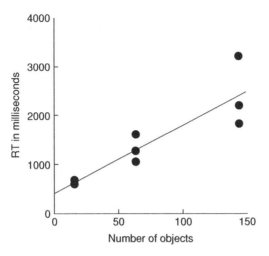

Figure 3.1   Graphing reaction time in milliseconds as a function of the number of objects in a visual search display

The explanatory nature of the regression equation is revealed by the average change in the position of the reaction times when the number of objects changes. As can be seen from the graph, when the number of objects increases, there is a substantial increase in reaction time. The explanatory nature of the model is evident, then, in the slope of the regression line.

The goodness of fit between the model and the data indicates the statistical nature of the model. On the graph, it is clear that the fit is good, because for each Objects value on the x-axis, the corresponding Time values (the dots) are clustered very close together, and the regression line runs through the middle of each cluster. This goodness of fit can be measured quantitatively too, by considering the differences between the actual values in the Time column and the values predicted by the regression equation. The regression software does this automatically by calculating a squared multiple correlation value (R^2) that measures goodness of fit. For the equation above, the value of R^2 was calculated to be 0.79. This indicates very high goodness of fit – it means that 79 percent of the variability in Time was predicted by the variability in Objects.

Other models for these data are feasible, and they show that other "goodness of fit" outcomes are possible. For example, the second manipulation in the Dawson and Thibodeau (1998) experiment was viewing condition. Subjects watched the display through one of three different neutral density filters. A neutral density filter is an optical medium that reduces the amount of light passing through it without changing other properties of the light, such as color. In other words, these filters reduce the brightness of what is seen through them. These filters come in different thicknesses, so that different filters let different amounts of light through. In this experiment, subjects looked through a 0 unit filter which let 100 percent of the light through, a 1 unit filter which let 10 percent of the light through, and a 2 unit filter which let only 1 percent of the light through. The Filter column in Table 3.1 indicates which type of filter was used to obtain the average reaction times that are listed.

If multiple regression is used to predict Time from Filter, then it generates the following equation:

$$\text{Time} = (339.45 \times \text{Filter}) + 1077.73 \qquad [3.2]$$

With respect to goodness of fit, the equation results in an R^2 equal to 0.12. In other words, by itself the Filter variable only accounts for 12 percent of the variance in Time, and is therefore providing a poorer fit to the data than was the case with the Objects variable. If we were to graph this relationship, we would find that it would differ in appearance from Figure 3.1 by having a wider spread within the different sets of dots, and a regression line that was much flatter in slope.

Regression software can also be used to predict a variable using two or more predictors. For instance, we could create a model for Time by using both Objects and Filter as predictors. When this is done, the resulting regression equation is:

$$\text{Time} = (13.55 \times \text{Objects}) + (339.45 \times \text{Filter}) + 65.70 \qquad [3.3]$$

The R^2 for this equation is equal to 0.91, indicating that by using both predictors together, nearly all of the variability in Time can be accounted for. Even though on its own Filter does not provide a very good fit to the data, the relatively small amount of variance that this predictor can explain is important, and is different from the variance explained by Objects. Indeed, Dawson and Thibodeau's (1998) main discovery was that decreasing luminance slowed down visual search.

3.2   Properties of Models of Data

The regression example can be used to illustrate some of the general characteristics of models of data. It will be instructive to keep these characteristics in mind, because we will be interested in determining whether they are true of other types of models to be discussed later in this chapter.

3.2.1   Models of data fit preexisting measurements

First, models of data assume that some phenomenon of interest has already been measured, because these measurements provide the to-be-modeled data. Furthermore, models of data are analytic, because they usually involve decomposing the variability of the measured variable into the separate sources of variability – the variability of the predictors.

Multiple regression provides a good example of the decompositional or analytic nature of this type of model. In the most general sense, the overall variability of the dependent measure is split into two components – the variability that can be accounted for by all the predictors in the equation (called the "sum of squares regression"), and the variability that cannot be accounted for by the predictors (called the "sum of squares error"). In a more particular sense, regression equations can be used to partition the total R^2 into the proportion of variance accounted for by each predictor in the equation, although this is not a practice that is highly recommended by statisticians because it can fail to take into account the correlations among predictor variables (Pedhazur, 1982).

3.2.2 Models of data are usually linear

Second, models of data are usually linear in nature. To say that a model is linear is to accept a principle of superposition: if one knows the effect of predictor A on the dependent measure, and if one knows separately the effect of predictor B on the dependent measure, then the combined effects of A and B on the dependent measure is equal to the sum of the effects of predictors A and B (Luce, 1999). This is particularly evident in the regression equation, because the value for the dependent measure is predicted by summing the (weighted) values of the predictors.

Some might argue that the assumption that a model is linear amounts to the assumption that predictors in a statistical model are not presumed to interact. However, this is not the case. Consider our visual search example. Dawson and Thibodeau (1998) expected an interaction between the Filter and the Objects variables, because they assumed that as the Filter became stronger, the visual search mechanism would slow down considerably, and as a result it would take much longer to move from one object to another. In short, the Objects effect should be influenced by the Filter value.

This expectation can be handled in linear regression in two steps. First, a new predictor variable for the interaction between Objects and Filter is defined. Let us call this predictor $O \times F$, which is an acronym for "Object $\times$ Filter Interaction." $O \times F$ can be calculated by simply taking the value for Objects and multiplying it by the value for Filter, as is also shown in Table 3.1. Second, one takes these three predictor values and uses a regression program to determine the equation for predicting the Time value. When this is done, the following equation is delivered:

$$\text{Time} = (8.49 \times \text{Objects}) + (-38.92 \times \text{Filter}) + (5.07 \times O \times F) + 444.14 \quad [3.4]$$

The R^2 associated with this equation is 0.99, which shows that by including the interaction term as a predictor, we can account for an additional 8 percent of the variance in Time that is not predicted by Objects and Filter alone. Note that this equation is linear, in the sense that the predicted value for Time is a weighted sum of the three predictors in the regression equation.

If a linear model of data can account for interactions, then what kind of model is excluded from traditional statistical analyses? The kind of model that is excluded is some nonlinear transformation of the linear combination of the predictors. For example, one nonlinear transformation that we will frequently encounter in later chapters is defined by the logistic equation. The logistic equation is nonlinear, in the sense that if one were to plot the values obtained by computing $f(x)$ for different values of x (where $f(x)$ is the logistic equation), then the graph of this function would not be a straight line, but would instead be an s-shaped curve (see Figure 10.1c on p. 000).

The kind of statistical model that we would rarely see would be one in which a linear sum of weighted predictors was used to create a value for x that would be passed into an equation like the logistic. Using the visual search data as an example, a very uncommon statistical model would be:

$$\text{Time} = f((a \times \text{Objects}) + (b \times \text{Filter}) + (c \times \text{O} \times \text{F}) + d) \qquad [3.5]$$

In this equation, f is a nonlinear function, and a, b, c, and d are all constants. In later chapters, we will see that many of the models in synthetic psychology are of interest because they explicitly exploit nonlinear relationships.

3.2.3   Models of data are evaluated by goodness of fit

A third property of a model of data is that its utility or value is highly dependent upon the notion of goodness of fit. If only one model of data is being considered, then goodness of fit determines whether it will be used at all. "If the fit is good enough, if enough of the response variability is explained by our model, it is retained. On the other hand, if the fit is not good enough, the model is rejected" (Lunneborg, 1994, p. 15). If more than one model is being considered at one time, then the best-fitting model is retained, and all of the other competing models are rejected. For example, of the four regression equations provided earlier, we would choose Equation 3.4 (using Objects, Filter, and O × F as predictors) over the others, because it led to the highest R^2 value.

The use of goodness of fit as the litmus test for retaining a model of data is a crucial characteristic. First, it indicates that models of data are essentially quantitative in nature, because whether they are adopted depends upon a quantitative evaluation (namely, the value of goodness of fit). Second, it demonstrates that the critical function of a model of data is to fit or predict preexisting data. If one were to think graphically, the best model would be one in which a plot of the actual data and a plot of the data predicted by a model lay directly on top of one another.

Why are these characteristics important to highlight? The main reason is because we can use them to consider alternative forms of models that do not share them. This is the research strategy adopted by roboticist Rodney Brooks (2002, p. 37): "I would look at how everyone else was tackling a certain problem and find the core central thing that they all agreed on so much that they never even talked about it. Then I would negate the central implicit believe and see where it led." Let us take Brooks's perspective for a moment, and imagine the possibility (at least) of a different kind of model, a model whose characteristics are opposite to the ones considered above. Could we create a model that was qualitative in nature, instead of quantitative? Could we design a model that was not intended to fit preexisting data points, but instead was constructed in the absence of such information? We will return to these questions later in this book.

3.2.4 Models of data rarely surprise us

The three properties of models of data that we have considered to this point have been positive in nature. The fourth property is perhaps a bit more negative: models of data leave very little room for surprise. What does it mean to say that a model of data fails to surprise us? Let's explore this issue by using multiple regression as an example.

Usually one starts designing a model of data on the basis of general intuitions about the relationships between variables (Lunneborg, 1994). For example, Dawson and Thibodeau (1998) were aware that a number of theories of how attention is shifted during visual search relied upon inhibitory mechanisms (Fukushima, 1986; Gerrissen, 1991; Koch & Ullman, 1985; LaBerge, Carter, & Brown, 1992; Sandon, 1992). They were also aware of results showing that adapting luminance could be used to affect inhibitory processes (Dawson & Di Lollo, 1990; Matin, 1968; Roufs, 1972; Whitten & Brown, 1973). From this knowledge, Dawson and Thibodeau reasoned that adapting luminance should affect visual search.

The next stage of model development is to convert intuitions into experiments. This requires that concepts be operationalized into variables that can be measured and manipulated. For example, at this stage of modeling Dawson and Thibodeau (1998) made design decisions about how to measure visual search (i.e., in terms of search latency), about the number and type of objects in the different displays, about how to manipulate adapting luminance with neutral density filters, and so on.

The final stage of modeling is to conduct the experiment in order to acquire the data from which the statistical model will be generated. Goodness of fit can then be used to evaluate the regression equation that defines the relationship between the dependent measure and our predictors.

Where in this process can surprises emerge? The model of data that we produce in the final stage can reveal surprises concerning the intuitions that we had at the early stages of development – these intuitions might be shown to be wrong. Indeed, the whole point of conducting an experiment is to test the validity of our intuitions. If we could not be surprised – if our intuitions were guaranteed to be correct – then there would be no point at all to designing and conducting an experiment.

However, a model of data can reveal few other surprises. Consider taking the model and using it to predict new data points. For instance, imagine taking the best regression equation for the visual search data, and using it to predict search latencies for a new number of objects (say, a display size of 50) and for a new filter (say, 1.5 units). The regression equation would predict what the search time should be in this new situation, and we could go out and collect this new data to determine how accurate this prediction was. If the equation was an accurate predictor, then we certainly wouldn't be surprised. But what if the equation did not provide an accurate prediction?

In this latter situation, we might be surprised, but this surprise would only be fleeting. This is because as soon as the model fails to fit the data, it will be abandoned. Instead, we will enter into a new phase of model development, either making slight revisions to the old model (e.g., by adding a new predictor) or by coming up with a completely new model (Lunneborg, 1994). Models of data aren't surprising with respect to future measurements, because they either make accurate, nonsurprising predictions or they are abandoned.

Let us consider surprise from a slightly different perspective. In many instances of computer simulation, surprises emerge because when seemingly simple components are combined, they sometimes generate behavior that is far more interesting than was expected or intended (Lewandowsky, 1993). For example, Dawson (1991) developed a simple model of how the visual system tracks the identities of objects as they move. He then found that this model provided a new theory of how one apparent motion display, called the Ternus configuration, could have more than one appearance depending on how the display was timed (Dawson, Nevin-Meadows, & Wright, 1994; Dawson & Wright, 1994). One way to think about surprises like these is that they are emergent properties of a model (Holland, 1998). We will be talking about emergence in much greater detail in later chapters. For the time being, we can consider it as an example of a principle from Gestalt psychology, in which the whole is more than the sum of its parts (Kohler, 1975).

Unfortunately, most traditional models of data can't surprise us in this way either. This is because of their linear nature. In a linear model of data, the whole is exactly equal to the sum of its parts (Luce, 1999). New and surprising phenomena will not emerge from a linear model of data.

3.2.5   Models of data do not behave

A fifth property of models of data is also related to the issue of surprise. Models of data provide descriptions of behavior, but do not behave.

For example, consider the various regression equations that were given earlier in this chapter. Each of these equations describes a mathematical relationship between one kind of measure (search latency) and one or more predictors (number of objects, filter type, etc.). However, none of these equations actually performs visual search. We can't look at the behavior of these models to find new and surprising properties of visual search.

Contrast this with some possible model that actually performs visual search. If this model actually generated search behavior, then we could examine this behavior from a number of different perspectives. We could, of course, look at how long it took the model to find a target in the display. But we could also look at the kinds of mistakes made by the model, the precise order in which a display of visual objects was examined by the model, how long each individual object was processed, and so on. Because the model behaves, and because we can observe and measure this behavior in many different ways, the model is in a position to suggest new and possibly surprising results. We could then go back to the laboratory, and run new experiments to see if these surprising results were also evident in human search behavior.

Lewandowsky and Hockley (1991) have proposed that one criterion for progress in cognitive psychology is the extent to which data and theory have become interrelated. Progress is being made if theory generates data, and if the data collected in turn constrains the theory that is being developed. This view is an updating of the old empiricist approach to theory evaluation in experimental psychology, which argued that one could measure the quality of a theory in terms of the number of new experiments that it inspired.

Because models of data do not behave, they do not lead directly to new experiments. Instead, models of data are best viewed as a quantitative measure of the validity of the theory that led to a particular experiment being conducted. A regression equation of the type that we saw earlier will only lead to new experiments indirectly, by generating sufficient goodness of fit to data to increase our confidence in the theory or intuitions that directed the design of the experiment in the first place. New experiments will be generated from this theory, not from the model of data that was used to validate it.

Chapter four

Mathematical Models

"It is a familiar historical fact that as science progresses, its theories become more and more mathematical in form. Verbally stated propositions are replaced by exact quantitative logic" (Atkinson, Bower, & Crothers, 1965, p. 2). In the study of behavior, one field that is particularly concerned about converting verbal theories into quantitative theories is called *mathematical psychology*. In the previous chapter, we saw that models of data are quantitative in nature, because they express a mathematical relationship between a variable of interest and a set of predictors. Why do we distinguish the models of mathematical psychology from quantitative models of data?

The primary reason for this distinction can be found in philosophy of science's discussion of the differences between regularities and laws (Bird, 1998, Chapter 1). A regularity is a fact that expresses a true generalization that has been induced from a set of observations. For example, recall one of the regression equations from the previous chapter:

$$\text{Time} = (8.49 \times \text{Objects}) + (-38.92 \times \text{Filter}) + (5.07 \times \text{O} \times \text{F}) + 444.14 \qquad [4.1]$$

Equation 4.1 expresses regularity because it is a generalization that is based upon a set of observations, and because we can make a plausible empirical argument for its truth because this equation accounts for almost 100 percent of the variance of Time.

Some philosophers might argue that laws and regularities are identical. However, there are many objections to this position (Bird, 1998). For instance, one can propose laws in the absence of regularities, and one can identify an indefinite number of regularities that are not laws. As a result, philosophers of science usually require that laws have stronger properties then merely being regularities. One proposal is that a law expresses a causal relation between universal properties.

Equation 4.1 illustrates this latter point. It provides a compact and accurate summary of a set of data, and can easily be seen as expressing regularity. However, we would likely be very uncomfortable about saying that this equation expresses a *law* of visual search. One reason for this is because this equation expresses a regularity that was observed in the search processes of only one subject. We would probably not expect this equation to predict search times perfectly for *every* other subject. It would be much more likely that we would find that the equations generated for other subjects were of the same type of, but had different values for, the constants. In short, we would not expect a model of data to express a universal relationship.

In contrast to this, mathematical psychology really is interested in formulating psychological laws.

> From the first efforts toward psychological measurement, investigators have had in mind the goal of making progress toward generality in psychological theory by developing quantities analogous to mass, charge, and the like in physics and showing that laws and principals formulated in terms of these derived quantities would have greater generality than those formulated in terms of observables.
>
> *(Estes, 1975, p. 273)*

This explains why mathematical psychology has focused upon learning and perception. "In psychology, mathematical theories have developed primarily in the field of experimental psychology, especially in learning, perception, and psychophysics. The data in these areas display the kind of consistent regularities that are necessary for formulating empirical laws" (Atkinson et al., 1965, p. 1).

If we view models of data as being concerned with expressing regularities, and if we view mathematical models as being concerned with formulating laws, then it would be expected that the practice of mathematical psychology is broader than the experimental methods that were briefly discussed in the previous chapter. How does mathematical psychology proceed?

Mathematical models are the product of the cycle of theory formulation, deduction, and verification (Atkinson et al., 1965; Coombs, Dawes & Tversky, 1970). First, an initial theory is inferred from extant data. Second, the theory is stated rigorously as a set of axioms. Third, logical and mathematical operations are used to deduce consequences from this set of axioms. Some of these consequences may be surprising, and some of them may even seem contradictory to expectations. Fourth, new data is collected to see if it agrees with the deduced consequences. If agreement is not observed, then the theory will be rejected and will have to be either revised or replaced. If agreement is observed, then this new data has been explained. In this case, a fifth step can be taken in which the theory is used to predict the outcome of phenomena that have not yet been observed. The mathematical model will evolve by predicting new observations that in turn will result in the model being retained, revised, or replaced.

4.1 An Example of a Mathematical Model

If a puff of air is directed towards one of our eyes, a reflex will be triggered and the eye will blink. Ordinarily, if we hear a tone, this reflex will not be triggered, and the eye will not blink. However, imagine a situation in which we are subject to several trials in which we hear a particular tone, and then shortly afterwards an air puff stimulates our eye. In this situation, learning will occur because it is advantageous (for eye protection) to realize that the tone is a warning that a puff of air is on the way. After this learning has occurred, the tone will produce an eyeblink, even if there is no puff of air.

This eyeblink learning is an example of classical or Pavlovian conditioning (Pavlov, 1927). In Pavlovian conditioning, there are two stimuli: the *unconditioned stimulus* (US) and the *conditioned stimulus* (CS). Prior to learning, the US will produce a definite response in the learner, called the *unconditioned response* (UR). The learner will not generate the UR if only the CS is presented prior to learning. If, however, the US and the CS are paired together in a series of training trials, then eventually the CS will elicit the UR. In this case, it is usually said that the CS elicits the *conditioned response* (CR).

Pavlovian conditioning is generally thought to be the result of a growing association between the learner's representations of the CS and the US. A number of factors have been shown to affect the growth of this association. Informally, effective Pavlovian conditioning depends upon the US being unexpected or surprising, and upon the full attention of the learning being focused upon the CS (Pearce, 1997).

The requirement that the US be surprising for effective Pavlovian conditioning is illustrated in a learning phenomenon called *blocking* (Kamin, 1969). Imagine a two-stage conditioning experiment. In the first stage, CS_1 (a tone) precedes the US (an air puff), so that after a series of trials it will come to elicit the CR (an eyeblink). We then proceed to a second stage, in which two conditioned stimuli are used. CS_1 (a tone) and CS_2 (a tap on the shoulder) are presented at the same time, both preceding the US. In this second stage, it will turn out that our subject will not learn to produce the CR when only CS_2 is presented. It is as if the learning that had already occurred in the first stage blocked any new learning in stage two. One account of this blocking would be to say that the initial learning removed the element of surprise in the US. Because our subject had already learned that CS_1 predicted the puff of air, there was no need to alter that learning when CS_1 was paired with CS_2.

Blocking provided existing data that served as a springboard for the development of a mathematical theory of learning. One important example was the Rescorla–Wagner model of conditioning (Rescorla & Wagner, 1972).

Rescorla and Wagner (1972) assumed that learning affected the strength of the association between the CS and the US. In their model, the strength of this association at trial t can be represented by the symbol V_t. The point of their model was to specify how this associative strength changed from trial to trial. The change in associative strength at trial t can be symbolized as ΔV_t.

In general, Rescorla and Wagner (1972) assumed that if the CS and US were repeatedly paired together then there would be a gradual increase in the association between them. However, this gradual increase was not presumed to be limitless. They proposed that there was a maximum value of this association, and that this maximum value was determined by the magnitude of the US. In their model, this maximum value is represented as λ. The salience of a CS is also known to affect learning; conditioning will occur more rapidly with a strong CS than with a weak CS (Pearce, 1997). Rescorla and Wagner included a parameter in their model that reflected the salience of the CS, and designated this parameter with the symbol α.

Informally, Rescorla and Wagner (1972) proposed that the growth of the association between a CS and the US is determined by the difference between the current strength of the association (V_t) and the maximum strength of the association (λ). Early in conditioning, this difference will be large, and as a result the change in associative strength (ΔV_t) will be large. Later in training, this difference will be smaller, because the current associative strength will have grown to be closer to the maximum. As a result, later in training the change in associative strength (ΔV_t) will be smaller.

Formally, this proposal can be written as the following equation that defines the amount of change in associative strength at trial t, and which also uses α to take into account the salience of the CS:

$$\Delta V_t = \alpha(\lambda - V_t) \qquad [4.2]$$

Given this expression, we can write a second equation that provides the value of the associative strength at trial $t+1$ (V_{t+1}) on the basis of the previous associative strength V_t and the value ΔV_t:

$$V_{t+1} = V_t + \Delta V_t = V_t + \alpha(\lambda - V_t) \qquad [4.3]$$

This kind of recursive equation, in which the new value of a variable depends upon a previous value, will be seen in many of the chapters that follow.

The preceding paragraphs have illustrated some of the preliminary steps in mathematical modeling: the conversion of an informal theory of a phenomenon into a formal statement. The next stage would be to use this formal statement to derive predictions, and to see how well these predictions agree with experimental data.

The Rescorla–Wagner model can easily be used to generate predictions by making some assumptions about the parameters of the model, and then by using the equation to generate predicted values of V_t over a series of learning trials. For example, assume that prior to learning, the initial associative strength (V_0) was equal to 0, and that that the value of α was equal to 0.1. Imagine doing two different learning experiments with these settings. In the first, λ is set to 100, and for the other λ is set to 50. If V_t is plotted on the same graph for both of these studies, it will be seen that the Rescorla–Wagner model predicts that the growth of associative strength is represented by a nonlinear function. This function is exponential in nature, decelerating as it approaches the asymptotic value of λ. In our hypothetical experiment, the first line will climb towards the value of 100, while the other only climbs to the value of 50. Both will reach their maximum value by the time that t takes on the value of 45 or 46. The Rescorla–Wagner model can also be used to predict that the effect of CS salience is to change the rate at which associative strength approaches the asymptote. The larger the salience, the sharper is the bend in the learning curve, and the faster does learning reach the maximum associative strength.

The model can also be used to make predictions about more complicated learning situations. For example, in one paradigm Pavlovian conditioning might proceed for a set number of trials, and then an attempt to extinguish this learning might follow by presenting the CS without the US for some additional trials. This situation can be handled in the Rescorla–Wagner model by changing the value of λ to 0 when the extinction trials begin. Figure 4.1 shows what the model predicts when λ is equal to 100 for the first 50 learning trials, and is then set to 0 for another 50 extinction trials. For the solid line, α was equal to 0.3, and for the dotted line α was equal to 0.1. The graph shows that the model predicts that CS salience also affects the rate of extinction.

The examples of the Rescorla–Wagner model that we have discussed to this point all assume that there is only one conditioned stimulus involved in learning. However, one of the motivations for the model was to come up with a theory that could account for phenomena like blocking. This requires that the equations that we have seen take into account the possibility of there being a compound CS.

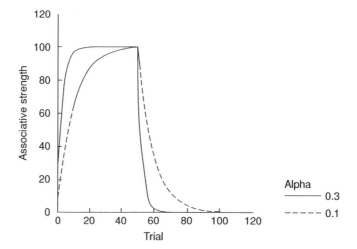

Figure 4.1 Extinction in the Rescorla–Wagner model

To handle multiple conditioned stimuli, Rescorla and Wagner (1972) proposed that the overall associative strength that was being modified was equal to the sum of the individual associative strengths corresponding to each CS. Let us assume that there are three different conditioned stimuli CS_1, CS_2, and CS_3. Each of these, on any given trial, has a strength of association with the US that is represented respectively as V_1, V_2, and V_3. Overall associative strength (V_{total}) for this example would therefore be defined as:

$$V_{total} = V_1 + V_2 + V_3 \qquad [4.4]$$

Once V_{total} has been defined, it can be used to calculate the change in each of the component associative strengths. For example, to determine the change in associative strength for CS_1 at some trial, one would compute the following:

$$\Delta V_1 = \alpha_1(\lambda - V_{total}) \qquad [4.5]$$

Note that this equation requires the use of a value for CS salience that is unique to CS_1 (i.e., α_1). Similar equations would be used to calculate ΔV_2 and ΔV_3. The overall change in associative strength for this example would then be:

$$\Delta V_{total} = \Delta V_1 + \Delta V_2 + \Delta V_3 \qquad [4.6]$$

Rescorla and Wagner's (1972) model was able to make predictions about learning that involved compound stimuli (for an introduction, see Pearce, 1997). For example, it provided an explanation of blocking. It also provided an account of overshadowing, in which learning that involves two stimuli in a compound results in a smaller increase in the associative strength of each than would be observed if each stimulus was used as the only stimulus in Pavlovian conditioning. Miller, Barnet, and Grahame (1995) review 18 different successes of the model.

The ability of the Rescorla–Wagner model to make interesting predictions, and to have these predictions confirmed by later experimentation, has resulted in its continued popularity. However, there are also many results that it does not explain. Miller et al. (1995) also review 23 specific failures of the model. They proceed to argue that such failures are the result of five classes of problematic assumptions that underlie this particular mathematical model.

As we would expect from the fact that mathematical modeling has a cycle of theory formulation, deduction, and verification, the failures of the Rescorla–Wagner model have led to a set of newer models (for an introduction to some, see Pearce, 1997). These newer models typically retain some of the properties of the Rescorla–Wagner formulation, but attempt to address some of its problematic assumptions. None of these models has replaced the Rescorla–Wagner theory, because the newer models tend to be more complicated and also have their own list of failures. "For the time being, researchers would be well advised to continue using aspects of the Rescorla–Wagner model, along with those of other contemporary models, to help them design certain classes of experiments" (Miller et al., 1995, p. 381).

4.2   Mathematical Models vs. Models of Data

Now that we have briefly considered the Rescorla–Wagner model as an example, we are in a better position to consider some general properties of mathematical models, particularly in comparison to models of data.

4.2.1   The need for preexisting measurements

In the previous chapter, we saw that models of data required preexisting measurements to be made in order for the model to be specified. Mathematical models appear to relax this constraint somewhat. On the one hand, the practice of mathematical psychology would suggest that the initial form of a mathematical model is grounded in an existing set of data. Furthermore, the initial tests of a mathematical model will usually examine its ability to be consistent with known phenomena. On the other hand, once a model has shown some promise in dealing with the known, it is then used to generate predictions about phenomena that may not yet have been observed. In this sense, the use of a mathematical model is quite different from the use of a model of data.

4.2.2   Linearity

We have seen that models of data are often constructed using traditional statistical methods, and as a result are usually linear in nature. In contrast, many mathematical models are nonlinear in nature. For instance, the nonlinearity of the Rescorla–Wagner model – evident in Figure 4.1 – emerges from the recursive nature of their equation, in which new association strength is based in part upon a previous value. Mathematical models of judgment and decision are also frequently nonlinear in nature, because they involve modeling discrete decisions (e.g., Bock & Jones, 1968). For example, the notion of a perceptual threshold is a decidedly nonlinear construct.

4.2.3   Goodness of fit

We saw in Chapter 3 that a crucial aspect of models of data was some assessment of the goodness of fit between the model and empirical observations. Mathematical models share this property. "What problems, some will ask, can you see in the matter of testing mathematical theories? Does not one simply construct a model, apply it to data, and accept or reject on the basis of goodness of fit? Well, that is indeed a standard procedure – perhaps the standard procedure" (Estes, 1975, p. 267).

However, the evaluation of a mathematical model using a goodness of fit metric can in some sense be more exciting than is the case for a model of data. This is because a mathematical model can lead to predictions about things that have yet to be observed. In this case, the model is the inspiration for a novel set of experiments, and the issue is assessing goodness of fit to these new data.

4.2.4   Surprise

One of the key differences between models of data and mathematical models concerns the issue of surprise. It was argued earlier that models of data rarely surprise us. In contrast, the goal of a mathematical model is to generate surprise, at least to the extent that it provides us with knowledge that we didn't have prior to creating the model. "The purpose of constructing models is not to describe data, which must be described before models can be applied to them, but rather to generate new classifications or categorizations of data" (Estes, 1975, p. 271). Estes goes on to say:

> What we hope for primarily from models is that they will bring out relationships between experiments or sets of data that we would not otherwise have perceived. The fruit of interaction between models and data should be a new categorization of phenomena in which observations are organized in terms of a rational scheme in contrast to the surface demarcations manifest in data that have only come through routine statistical processing.

Given that both models of data and mathematical models describe quantitative relationships between variables, it is instructive to consider why the former model rarely surprises us, and why the latter model is designed to surprise. One reason that mathematical models are capable of surprise is because they appear to be much closer to a statement of law or theory than are models of data. This means that mathematical models are far more flexible. As we saw in the Rescorla–Wagner example, one can use a single mathematical model to create predictions for a rather diverse set of experimental paradigms. A second reason that mathematical models are capable of surprise is because they are often nonlinear. We will see later in this book that nonlinear interactions between components are a rich source of surprise and complexity.

4.2.5   Model behavior

Finally, let us compare models of data to mathematical models with respect to the issue of whether the model behaves. In this case, it would appear that both types of models are equivalent. As was the case for models of data, mathematical models provide a description of behavior, and do not behave. For example, the Rescorla–Wagner model describes how one parameter, association strength, will change during learning. This model, however, does not itself learn.

The reason for this is that mathematical models attempt to formalize psychological phenomena by translating them into quantitative form. Most models in mathematical psychology are based upon the foundations of measurement theory, which focuses upon procedures for measuring psychological variables. Measurement theory has a central place in textbooks that introduce mathematical psychology (Atkinson et al., 1965; Coombs et al., 1970; Restle, 1971; Restle & Greeno, 1970). However, there is an enormous difference between predicting the value of some measurement related to a psychological process and actually carrying out this process.

Chapter five

Computer Simulations

Mathematical psychologists had high hopes about the potential impact for their discipline on psychology as a whole. Unfortunately, many now believe that the promise of mathematical psychology has not been fulfilled:

> Many of us have hoped that mathematical psychology would prove a major vehicle for developing theoretical interrelationships between psychology and the various social sciences, thus facilitating both theoretical developments and applications. But as things have actually gone, the flourishing of new mathematical models and methods has profited various specific research areas greatly but has contributed less than we would like toward bridging the gaps between disciplines or mediating applications of social science to social problems.
>
> *(Estes, 1975, p. 265)*

Luce (1997, p. 79) shares this view: "On entering the field 45 years ago I anticipated that as mathematical psychology developed, it would increasingly be incorporated into the intellectual life of departments of psychology. In the United States, that has not happened to any great extent."

Why has mathematical psychology had such a limited success? Some mathematical psychologists would argue that this is due to the arrival of computer simulation methods. For Estes (1975, p. 268), one "aspect of the computer revolution which has raised new and, to say the least, challenging problems for us is, of course, the advent of computer simulation models." Luce (1997, p. 80) believes that computers have "made it relatively easy to simulate quite complex interactive systems. For many, it is clearly simpler and more agreeable to program than it is to study processes mathematically."

In what regards does a computer simulation differ from a mathematical model? Luce (1999) has argued that mathematical models are attempts to capture regularities in observable and measurable behavior. In contrast, much of the computer simulation research from cognitive science is concerned with modeling inferred internal processes.

The distinction here is whether the individual (or group) is treated as a "black box" having observable behavioral (phenomenological) properties to formulate the theory, or whether in some sense one attempts to "open" the black box in order to formulate what is going on inside and how these processes give rise to the observed behavior. Of course, behavioral regularities are common to both approaches – they are just dealt with differently.

(Luce, 1999, p. 725)

Why is there this difference in emphasis? The fundamental reason is that mathematical psychology is grounded in measurement. As a result it ultimately attempts to model behavior; that is, it attempts to predict measured values.

Computer simulations, however, are not tied to measurement theory. Instead, the simulations are inspired by the computer metaphor, which is the claim that thinking is identical to the kind of symbol manipulation carried out by a digital computer (e.g., Dawson, 1998). Indeed, some would argue that this view is not a metaphor (e.g., Pylyshyn, 1979a). As a result, computer simulations are not merely models of behavior; they are instead intended to be systems that actually behave.

5.1   A Sample Computer Simulation

To enrich our understanding of the differences between computer simulations and the other types of models that we have already discussed, let us turn to a specific example.

5.1.1   Production system models

Newell and Simon's (1972) *Human Problem Solving* was the culmination of 17 years of research. The goal of the book was to describe a rigorous theory of human problem solving from an information-processing perspective. Rather than focusing on very general characteristics of problem solving, Newell and Simon aimed to generate explicit theories of how individual subjects solved specific problems. Their notion of an explicit theory was a computer simulation. "Such a representation is no metaphor, but a precise symbolic model on the basis of which pertinent specific aspects of human problem solving behavior can be calculated" (p. 5).

At the heart of their computer simulations was a proposal for a specific cognitive architecture or "language of thought" (Fodor, 1975; Pylyshyn, 1984). A cognitive architecture is a theory about the basic programming language that carries out cognitive information processing. Newell and Simon (1972) argued that a plausible form of this architecture is the *production system.*

A production system is a set of operators that manipulate symbols stored in a working memory. Each operator can be thought of as a condition–action pair, or as an "if–then" rule. In general, all of the operators in a production system scan the working memory for the presence of their condition. When a particular operator finds its condition, it seizes control and prevents the other operators from working. It then performs its action, which usually involves rewriting some of the information in the working memory. In other words, control – what to do next – is broadcast by the working memory, and is seized by one of the set of productions. After the production performs its action, control is released, and is again broadcast by the memory.

In the most general sense, Newell and Simon (1972) proceeded by first collecting *verbal protocols* of subjects as they thought aloud when solving a problem. They then took these verbal protocols and used them to create *problem behavior graphs*. A problem behavior graph represents a subject's state of knowledge about the problem being solved, as well as the operators that convert one state of knowledge into the next. It also represents how subjects make progress as they work on the problem. This also includes information about "backtracking," situations in which subjects feel that they have reached a dead end and therefore they return to an earlier state of knowledge about a problem to try a different approach. The problem behavior graph is then used to generate a set of productions that appear to underlie the subject's problem-solving behavior. This set of productions constitutes a theory about problem solving that is instantiated as a working computer program. The computer program is run, and the theory is validated (in part) by comparing the problem behavior graph it generates to the one created from the subject's protocol.

Newell and Simon (1972) successfully used this methodology to create computer simulations of problem-solving behavior for a variety of problems. These included cryptarithmetic, in which subjects must decode a letter expression into numbers; logic, in which a subject is given a starting expression and a set of logical rules, and must use these to convert the starting expression into a goal expression; and chess, in which subjects must choose the best next move when presented with a position from the middle of a chess game. These problems are all well-defined: they have a specific starting state, a solution that can be explicitly defined, and a set of explicit rules that a subject must follow when trying to go from the start of the problem to its solution. The problems that Newell and Simon studied were difficult enough to challenge subjects (i.e., to ensure that they actually engaged in problem-solving behavior), but were not so difficult that they could not be solved in a reasonable amount of time, or that they would produce a verbal protocol that was prohibitively long for later analysis.

5.1.2 A cryptarithmetic example

To provide an example of Newell and Simon's (1972) methodology, let us consider how they modeled the way in which one subject solved the following cryptarithmetic problem: DONALD + GERALD = ROBERT, D = 5. The subject's task is to figure out the digits represented by all of the other letters in the problem, given this starting information. The first step in the analysis was to have a single subject solve the problem, speaking aloud at all times when the problem was being solved. The subject's session was tape recorded, providing the raw data for the analysis. The transcript of the protocol, which contains 2,186 words, is provided in Newell and Simon's book.

When the protocol was transcribed into written form, it was broken up into short phrases that were labeled for later reference. This labeling was the first processing of the raw data, for each phrase was assumed to represent a single task assertion or reference. However, the "phrasing" of the protocol was not presumed to explicitly affect later analysis. Furthermore, there was very little "cleaning up" of the protocol by removing variability and redundancy in what the subject is saying. This was because parts that were easy to code did not require this, and because Newell and Simon (1972) preferred to keep parts of the transcript that were difficult to code in their original form to extract any information that they did happen to contain.

The next step in the analysis was to take the transcribed protocol, and to infer from it the subject's problem space for the cryptarithmetic problem. A problem space defines the representational space in which a system's problem-solving activities take place. A human subject in his or her studies was presumed to "encode these problem components – defining goals, rules, and other aspects of the situation – in some kind of space that represents the initial situation presented to him, the desired goal situation, various intermediate states, imagined or experienced, as well as any concepts he uses to describe these situations to himself" (Newell & Simon, 1972, p. 59).

For instance, by examining the transcribed protocol obtained from one cryptarithmetic subject, Newell and Simon (1972, pp. 166–8) recognized (among other things) that he assigned digits to letters, inferred relations from the columns of the problem, generated digits that satisfied certain relations, used relations like equality, inequality, and parity, and could consider disjunctive sets. Newell and Simon used the protocol to create a problem space that included approximately 25 states of knowledge and rules (see Newell & Simon, 1972, Fig. 6.1).

The reason that Newell and Simon (1972) relied on the notion of a problem space was that they assumed that problem solving was, in essence, a subject's search through this space to find a path (of rules that, when applied, produced intermediate states of knowledge) from the starting state for the problem to the goal state. Because of this assumption that problem solving was a form of search, their next step was to describe the full dynamics of the subject's search using a problem behavior graph. A problem behavior graph consists of a set of nodes connected together by links. Each node represents some state of knowledge about the problem. Each link represents a rule in the problem space that, when applied to the state of knowledge to the left of the link, produces the state of knowledge to the right of the link.

The dynamics of search are represented in two ways in a problem behavior graph. First, time increases from left to right across a single line. Second, sometimes after pursuing a train of thought subjects reach a dead end, and have to backtrack to some earlier point in their search. Newell and Simon (1972) represented this in the problem behavior graph by creating a new line. This line started with the node to which subjects had backtracked, drawn directly beneath its last location in the problem behavior graph. Newell and Simon showed how a detailed problem behavior graph could be constructed by examining the subject's protocol, and by adhering to the components in the problem space that had been derived for that subject (e.g., pp. 173–85).

The next step in Newell and Simon's (1972) approach was to develop a production system to account for the problem behavior graph that had been created from the subject's thinking-aloud protocol. The goal of the program was to make three things explicit: the processes for doing the arithmetic, the processes for deciding what to do next, and the information remembered by the subject as the problem is being solved (e.g., to permit backtracking).

Newell and Simon (1972) were able to use the problem behavior graph to derive a production system that accounted for their subject's behavior. Each link between two nodes in the problem behavior graph represents the input and output for a particular operation. Newell and Simon examined the problem behavior graph to find evidence for the repetition of an operation's occurrence, viewing the operation as being a production. "Repetition of decision situations is the key issue, for if each situation called forth a unique process, then we could never verify that a proposed process was in fact the one used" (p. 191).

For example, the problem behavior graph for one subject solving the DONALD + GERALD = ROBERT problem consisted of 238 nodes. From this graph, Newell and Simon were able to find evidence for 14 different productions. "The total program, then, is the collection of these individual productions, plus the ordering of the productions that resolves conflict if several conditions are satisfied concurrently" (p. 192).

Newell and Simon (1972) demonstrated that this small production system accounted for approximately 80 percent of the structure of the subject's problem behavior graph. Furthermore, "most of the inadequacies of the model appear to be due either to the lack of a detailed account of attention and memory mechanisms or to missing data" (p. 227). In other words, when the production system failed, it seemed to be because the verbal protocol didn't reveal all of the necessary information. Newell and Simon were also able to show that while this approach produced a computer simulation of one subject solving one problem, the discoveries made by this approach generalized quite well to other problems and to other subjects.

5.2 Connectionist Models

The production system simulation that we have just discussed is an example of what cognitive scientists would call a classical model (see also Dawson, 1998,

Chapter 2). A classical model is a distinct set of rules or operations that are designed to manipulate a set of symbols stored in a memory system (Newell, 1980). In recent years, many researchers have become critical of some of the general assumptions that underlie classical models (e.g., Bechtel & Abrahamsen, 1991; Brooks, 1999; Rumelhart & McClelland, 1986a; Smolensky, 1988). These researchers have proposed alternative proposals about the nature of the cognitive architecture.

5.2.1 Properties of connectionism

One example of an alternative type of model is a connectionist or parallel distributed processing (PDP) network. Dawson (1998, Chapter 3) provides a brief introduction to this kind of modeling, particularly in relation to classical cognitive science. Chapters 9 through 12 of the current book present many connectionist ideas in detail. For the time being, let us quickly consider some general properties of connectionism so that we can compare this type of simulation to the other models that have been discussed in this chapter.

A connectionist network is a system of interconnected, simple processing units that can be used to classify patterns presented to it. Such a network is usually made up of three kinds of processing units: *input units* encode the stimulus or activity pattern that the network will eventually classify; *hidden units* detect features or regularities in the input patterns, which can be used to mediate classification; and *output units* represent the network's response to the input pattern (i.e., the category to which the pattern is to be assigned) on the basis of features or regularities that have been detected by the hidden units. Processing units communicate by sending numerical signals through weighted connections.

In most cases, a processing unit carries out three central functions: first, a processor computes the total signal that it receives from other units. A *net input function* is used to carry out this calculation. After the processing unit determines its net input, it transforms it into an internal level of activity, which typically ranges between 0 and 1. The internal activity level is calculated by means of an *activation function*. Finally, the processing unit uses an *output function* to convert its internal activity into a signal to be sent to other units.

The signal sent by one processor to another is transmitted through a weighted connection, which is typically described as being analogous to a synapse. The connection itself is merely a communication channel. The weight associated with the connection defines its nature and strength. For example, inhibitory connections are defined with negative weights, and excitatory connections are defined with positive weights. A strong connection has a weight with a large absolute value, while a weak connection has a weight with a near-zero absolute value. The pattern of connections in a PDP network defines the clausal relations between the processors and is therefore analogous to a program in a conventional computer (Smolensky, 1988).

Unlike a conventional computer, though, a network is not given a step-by-step procedure for performing a desired task. It is instead *trained* to solve the task on its own. For instance, consider a popular supervised learning procedure called the *generalized delta rule* (Rumelhart, Hinton, & Williams, 1986a, 1986b).

To train a network with the generalized delta rule, one begins with a network that has small, randomly assigned, connection weights. The network is then presented with a set of training patterns, each of which is paired with a known desired response. To train a network on one of these patterns, the pattern is presented to the network's input units, and the network generates a response using its existing connection weights. An error value for each output unit is then calculated by comparing the actual output to the desired output. This error value is then used to modify connection weights in such a way that the next time this pattern is presented to the network, the network's output errors will be smaller. If this procedure is repeated a large number of times for each pattern in the training set, the network's response errors for each pattern can be reduced to near zero. At the end of this procedure, the network will have a very specific pattern of connectivity (in comparison to its random start) and will have *learned* to perform the desired stimulus/response pairing.

5.2.2 A connectionist example

The mushroom problem is a benchmark problem to be used in studying machine learning (Schlimmer, 1987). It consists of 8,124 different mushrooms, each defined as a set of 21 different features (odor, color, number of gills, etc.). The task is to use these features to classify a mushroom as being edible or not.

To provide a concrete example of connectionist simulation, let us briefly consider an example of a PDP network trained to solve the mushroom problem. In one study, Dawson, Medler, McCaughan, Willson, and Carbonaro (2000) taught a particular type of PDP network to solve the mushroom problem. The network had one output unit, four hidden units, and 21 input units (one for each input feature). The network was trained using a version of the generalized delta rule (Dawson & Schopflocher, 1992a) that is discussed in depth in Chapters 10 and 11. The network learned to solve the problem (i.e., to correctly classify each of the 8,124 mushrooms) after a training session in which each pattern was presented 1,852 times.

Dawson et al. (2000) were not merely interested in designing a PDP network to solve the mushroom problem. They were also interested in determining how the trained network used the mushroom features to classify the patterns. To do this, they recorded the responses of the hidden units to each of the training patterns. They then used a statistical technique called cluster analysis to identify 13 different network states that were responsible for the network generating a correct response. These internal states are called distributed representations, because each state is defined by a specific pattern of activity across all of the hidden units.

Dawson et al. (2000) then examined the sets of input patterns that caused the network to generate each of these internal states. For example, each of 3,288 different mushrooms caused the hidden units in the network to produce the same internal state. They were interested in determining what all of these patterns had in common to make the network behave in this way. From this type of analysis for each of the internal states, Dawson et al. were able to identify a simple equation that used only seven feature values (cap color = cinnamon, odor = anise, gill color = white, stalk color above ring = white, ring type = evanescent, habitat = meadows, habitat = woods) to correctly classify every pattern in the training set. The hidden units were collectively representing the presence or absence of these specific features. The output unit then used this distributed internal representation to solve the mushroom problem.

5.3   Properties of Computer Simulations

In the preceding sections, we have seen two very different examples of computer simulation models. From these two examples, we are now in a position to compare and contrast computer simulations with models of data and mathematical models.

5.3.1   Requirement for existing data

Earlier, we saw that models of data depend completely upon having preexisting measurements for a model to be formulated. Mathematical models relaxed this need somewhat. They are usually formulated on the basis of existing data, but are then later used to make predictions about phenomena that may not yet have been observed.

Computer simulation models relax the need for preexisting measurements even further. In some instances, computer simulations are similar to mathematical models in that they can be created from preexisting measurements. We saw this earlier when verbal protocols were used as the raw material from which a production system could be created. This model can then be used to make novel predictions.

The example PDP simulation that we saw is even further removed from a model of data and from a mathematical model. While classifying mushrooms as being edible or not is clearly a task that humans are capable of accomplishing, Dawson et al. (2000) were able to build their network without any knowledge of how people solve this classification problem. Indeed, one legitimate question to investigate is whether people and the network classify mushrooms in the same way. PDP networks allow "for the possibility of constructing intelligence without first understanding it" (Hillis, 1988, p. 176).

In short, it would appear that computer simulations do not absolutely require preexisting measurements in order to be created. This is a fairly radical departure from other kinds of models that one would see in psychology (i.e., models of data or mathematical models).

5.3.2 Linearity

Previously we saw that models of data are typically linear. For example, regression uses a linear sum of predictor values to estimate a value for a dependent measure. In contrast, mathematical models frequently incorporate nonlinear relationships between variables. It was argued earlier that this makes them more sophisticated than most models of data.

Although it is not a necessary property, most computer simulations incorporate nonlinear elements or operations. Rather than realizing this as a nonlinear equation relating two variables, computer simulations are often implicitly nonlinear. This is because many computer simulations are designed to model internal information processes, which are tacitly nonlinear, but which also are usually not formulated mathematically (Luce, 1999).

For example, consider the production system for cryptarithmetic. Each production in this model represents a primitive operation to be performed on symbols stored in a memory. As such, productions are not usually considered as being mathematical equations. However, from a mathematical perspective a production could be described as being an object that was in one of two different discrete states (active or not active). This state depends upon the contents of the memory, but not in a way that is linear or even continuous. We would have to say that productions are nonlinear operators.

Our PDP example is also extremely nonlinear. This is because each of its hidden units and its output unit can be described mathematically in terms of the equation that converts net input into internal activity (i.e., the activation function). The activation function for the units in the Dawson et al. (2000) network was a particular form of the Gaussian, which is clearly nonlinear because it is a bell-shaped function, as will be seen in Chapter 10. Most modern PDP networks use nonlinear activation functions.

In principle, the typical nonlinear nature of computer simulations provides them with great power and flexibility. Imagine the set of all possible mathematical functions. Now imagine the subset of these functions that are linear. What is the relative size of this subset compared to the larger set? Luce (1999) points out that the set of possible linear systems is "vanishingly small among the class of all possible systems" (p. 729). What this means is that a linear system is only capable of computing an extremely small subset of the possible mathematical functions.

In contrast to a linear system, a mathematical device called a Turing machine is capable in principle of computing any mathematical function, linear or not (Minsky, 1972). Many of the architectures used to simulate human information processing have this degree of power because of their nonlinear nature. For example, Newell (1980) demonstrated that production systems have this kind of power by showing how a Turing machine could be constructed from a set of productions. Similarly, McCulloch and Pitts (1943) demonstrated how one could construct a Turing machine from units similar to those found in modern PDP networks: "To psychology, however defined, specification of the net would contribute all that could be achieved in the field" (p. 25). Many modern researchers have derived new proofs that demonstrate the tremendous power, in principle, of current PDP networks (Cotter, 1990; Cybenko, 1989; Funahashi, 1989; Hartman, Keeler, & Kowalski, 1989; Hornik, Stinchcombe & White, 1989; Lippmann, 1989; Siegelmann, 1999).

5.3.3   Goodness of fit

Mathematical psychologists have not embraced the arrival of computer simulations with tremendous enthusiasm. "I think that learning to live with computers is perhaps the single most difficult and critical task facing mathematical psychology as a discipline" (Estes, 1975, p. 267). There are three general reasons for this state of affairs, all of which appear to be related to the theme that computer simulations are not easily evaluated in terms of the conventional "goodness of fit" measures used to assess mathematical models and models of data.

First, computer simulations permit the creation of models that outstrip current mathematical methods, and as a result cannot be formally analyzed or specified (Luce, 1999). This is clearly a problem for mathematical psychology, because one cannot evaluate goodness of fit if a mathematical model cannot be formulated.

Second, the general architectures that lie at the heart of both symbolic and connectionist computer simulations are so powerful, in principle, that any stimulus–response function can be approximated to an arbitrary level of accuracy. Indeed, this is exactly the implication of many of the existing proofs concerning the power of connectionist networks (Cotter, 1990; Cybenko, 1989; Funahashi, 1989; Hartman, Keeler, & Kowalski, 1989; Hornik, Stinchcombe & White, 1989; Lippmann, 1989). "If we have the right connections from the input units to a large enough set of hidden units, we can always find a representation that will form any mapping from input to output" (Rumelhart, Hinton, & Williams, 1986a, p. 319). If the goal of a computer simulation were merely to fit data, then there doesn't seem to be much to be gained by this approach with so much power at hand (Massaro, 1988). "The matter of fitting models to data has suddenly become so easy that it no longer constitutes a useful method of tracing theoretical progress" (Estes, 1975, p. 267). Similar arguments have been made against symbolic simulations (Paivio, 1986).

Third, mathematical psychologists are very concerned by the fact that "goodness of fit" seems extremely difficult to define for many computer simulations. "To me the most troubling [trend] is some lack of concern about how complex computer models are to be evaluated empirically" (Luce, 1999, p. 733). Estes (1975, p. 268) states this concern plainly, noting that simulations are models "that can be fitted to data just as readily as the more familiar mathematical models but that have no specifiable mathematical form and for which we are generally unable even to formulate, let alone solve, the problem of testing goodness of fit."

This last point highlights one of the key differences between computer simulations and the other kinds of models that we have encountered. Both models of data and mathematical models are designed to capture precise, quantitative relationships between variables. This is not the case for many computer simulations. For instance, by focusing upon mechanisms that produce behavior, production systems are much more qualitative in nature than the models discussed in previous chapters. This qualitative nature makes goodness of fit very difficult to define – and perhaps a less relevant property.

Goodness of fit becomes even more tenuous to define for connectionist models. Consider the mushroom network that was described above. While this network was given information about which mushrooms were poisonous and which were not, the network was not given any information about how a relationship between input features and mushroom classes was to be computed. Importantly, the network was not designed to model human classification processes – there was no information available to it about how humans classify mushrooms! In other words, there was no behavioral data for the model to fit. In most cases a network will not be of interest just because it solves a particular problem. Rather, the model becomes interesting when we examine the internal representations that it uses to solve the problem (Dawson, 1998; Hanson & Burr, 1990). As far as psychology is concerned, it is interesting to determine whether people use the same kinds of information as that which is found represented inside the network. But to answer this kind of research question, it is the person who is being fit to the model.

5.3.4 Surprise

Many people are reluctant to accept the notion that a computer simulation can lead to surprise. How could a programmer possibly be surprised, when all that a computer does is follow the instructions of a program that the programmer wrote (Haugeland, 1985)?

However, surprise – and in particular surprise to a programmer – is a common outcome of a computer simulation. Consider, for example, artist Harold Cohen's program Aaron, which has been evolving over the last several decades. Aaron comprises hundreds of rules for creating complex drawings, and uses these rules to direct machinery to create drawings on paper. "At first impression the drawings seem a relentless (and, given their source, a surprising) celebration of nature, the earliest drawings an organic world of simple clouds and whimsical creatures that just elude taxonomy; the later, more mature ones settings of frondescent jungles peopled by half-nude innocents" (McCorduck, 1991, p. 113). Aaron's creations have been the subject of numerous successful shows in art galleries.

The drawings that emerge from Aaron are surprising, even to Cohen himself. "The first time the program accumulated closed forms into something it knew to be an approximation of a figure, and I found an array of quasi-people staring eyelessly at me from my old 4014, I recoiled in fright. What was I getting myself into?" (McCorduck, 1988, p. 80). Cohen does not tell Aaron what to draw. Instead, Aaron might be described as having an instinct to draw forms that are governed by the general principles that Cohen has provided. For instance, "Aaron's compositional strategy could be summed up in a little rule that said 'Put it where there's room for it to be seen'" (McCorduck, 1991, p. 69).

During its evolution, Cohen has equipped Aaron with rules about lines, open and closed figures, plants and their growth, and human forms. Cohen views these rules as cognitive primitives, and not as rules of form. "That's one of the reasons the program is able to generate on its own a much richer set of forms than anybody has been able to program by describing only forms" (McCorduck, 1991, p. 68). Cohen eventually realized that only a handful of principles were required, in combination, to provide Aaron with enormous creativity.

This last observation is critical to the issue of surprise in computer simulations. Those who are skeptical of the ability of programs to surprise fail to recognize the fact that programmers do not write the code for the overall behavior of a system, but rather write the code for its specific component functions. The overall behavior that emerges when these component functions are combined can be completely surprising to the programmer who wrote the code. This is particularly true if the component functions are nonlinear in nature. One might have a very precise understanding of how each function behaves, but still be unable to predict the outcome of the nonlinear interactions between different functions.

For example, it is surprising that the complex and detailed structure of a problem behavior graph for a cryptarithmetic problem can emerge from a system comprised of only 14 different productions. However, this property appears to be true of production system models in general. "We need postulate only a very simple information processing system in order to account for human problem solving in such tasks as chess, logic, and cryptarithmetic. The apparently complex behavior of the information processing system in a given environment is produced by the interaction of the demands of that environment with a few basic parameters of a system" (Newell & Simon, 1972, p. 870). Of course, this emerging complexity depends critically upon the fact that the interactions are nonlinear, as we will see later in this book.

The same story is also true for connectionist models. "The study of connectionist machines has led to a number of striking and unanticipated findings; it's surprising how much computing can be done with a uniform network of simple interconnected elements" (Fodor & Pylyshyn, 1988, p. 6). Other more specific surprises emerge from the study of individual networks. For instance, the mushroom network example earlier in the chapter revealed a completely novel decision rule for this categorization task, as well as a completely novel parallel representation of this rule (Dawson et al., 2000). We will see later in Chapter 12 that connectionist networks can reveal surprising regularities in problems that lead directly to questions about whether human problem solvers pay attention to these regularities. However, again the source of such surprises is the fact that connectionist networks rely upon the interactions of nonlinear components to provide mappings from stimuli to responses.

5.3.5 Model behavior

"Modern scientific psychology was started by quantification" (Koffka, 1935, p. 13). The theory and application of behavioral quantification is the primary concern of measurement theory, which supplies the foundations for both models of data and mathematical psychology (Coombs, Dawes, & Tversky, 1970; Lunneborg, 1994; Restle & Greeno, 1970; Zeigler, 1976).

Quantification, or at least calculations involving numerical values, was also a central motivation for the development of modern computers (Williams, 1997). The development of electronic computers was driven primarily by the need to calculate complex ballistic firing tables used to aim artillery. In 1945, John von Neumann wrote a description of the proposed properties for the EDVAC computer, providing the first account of what is now known as the von Neumann computing architecture. In his report, it is quite apparent that the function of the computer was to carry out a variety of numerical calculations – the superiority of EDVAC's design was that it would not be limited to just calculating tables (von Neumann, 1973). There is no suggestion that computers were capable of carrying out computations that were not numerical in nature.

However, computers are not merely number crunchers. Mathematician Alan Turing recognized that a general information processor should properly be viewed as a symbol manipulator, and used this idea to propose the general characteristics of a universal computing device (Turing, 1936). Turing was later involved in using this proposal to aid in the development of one of the first digital computers, the ACE (Hodges, 1983). Shortly after its development, his view of computation as symbol manipulation led Turing to write about the possibility of machine intelligence (Turing, 1950). It is unclear to this day the extent to which von Neumann was aware of some of the deeper implications of Turing's 1936 paper when the EDVAC computer was being designed (Hodges, 1983).

The reason that viewing computers as general symbol manipulators had inevitable implications for psychology was that around the same time that digital computers were being invented, other researchers began to propose that cognitive processes involved symbol manipulation as well. The modern roots of this idea are usually attributed to philosopher Kenneth Craik, who wrote: "My hypothesis then is that thought models, or parallels, reality – that its essential feature is not 'the mind', 'the self', 'sense-data', nor propositions but symbolism, and that this symbolism is largely of the same kind as that which is familiar to us in mechanical devices which aid thought and calculation" (Craik, 1943, p. 57).

Earlier roots for this kind of idea can be found in the seventeenth century proclamation of British empiricist Thomas Hobbes that "by ratiocination, I mean computation" (Haugeland, 1985). By the late 1950s researchers in computer science, linguistics, psychology, philosophy, and neuroscience were all taking Craik's notion of symbolism very seriously, which led to the birth of modern cognitive science. (For an excellent history of these modern developments, see Gardner, 1984.)

Why is this important? A standard argument against machine intelligence argues that computers can't actually duplicate intelligence, that at best they can only simulate intelligent behavior. "No one supposes that a computer simulation of a storm will leave us all wet, or a computer simulation of a fire is likely to burn the house down. Why on earth would anyone in his right mind suppose a computer simulation of mental processes actually had mental processes?" (Searle, 1984, pp. 37–8). The answer to this question is that computers manipulate symbols, and that while no one believes that storms or fires are caused by symbol manipulation, most cognitive scientists believe that intelligence is.

While this view is not universally accepted (Churchland & Churchland, 1990; Dreyfus, 1992; Graubard, 1988; Searle, 1980, 1990, 1992), most cognitive scientists – be they classical or connectionist – endorse it (Dawson, 1998). As a result, one consequence of the assumption that cognition is information processing is that computers are not limited to generating some number related to behavior, but instead are capable of actually behaving. This is a fundamental difference between computer simulations and the two other types of models that we have seen.

The production system for cryptarithmetic *actually solves* these kinds of problems. "We have not treated the task as an unanalyzed 'variable' against which to plot our subject's behavior (as occurs in intelligence testing, or even in many experimental investigations, such as those on functional fixity or the *Einstellung* effect). Rather we have attempted to discern the specific mechanisms whereby each bit of task-oriented behavior is produced" (Newell & Simon, 1972, p. 303). Similarly, the mushroom network actually classifies mushrooms as being edible or poisonous. With these kinds of models, the questions that arise concern whether the behavior of the model is due to the same kind of internal processes that might be found in human subjects. The answer to such questions requires a completely different methodological approach that often seems only remotely related to "goodness of fit" (Pylyshyn, 1984).

Chapter six

First Steps Toward Synthetic Psychology

6.1 Introduction

The preceding three chapters have provided a brief exposure to a variety of different types of models that can be found in psychology. We are now in a position to use this background knowledge to focus our attention on synthetic psychology. The purpose of this chapter is to provide a brief introduction to some of the basic properties that will be found in the synthetic approach. These properties will be introduced by considering how to build a toy robot that walks.

Even within one class of models, computer simulations, we saw that there can be a great deal of variety. Some computer simulations are analytic in nature. For example, one creates a production system by taking a complicated phenomenon, breaking it down into its components, and using these components to construct the simulation. This analytic approach has been highly successful in psychology and in cognitive science. However, this approach is not the primary focus of this book.

We are instead primarily concerned with models that are synthetic in nature. An example of a computer simulation consistent with the synthetic approach is a connectionist network of the sort that was introduced in Chapter 5. When the synthetic approach is adopted, a set of basic building blocks is taken and is assembled into a working system. The question of interest is whether these basic components can be organized into a system that does something complicated, interesting, or surprising.

Why is this book focusing on the synthetic approach? One reason is that in modern cognitive science there is a growing interest in developing models from the synthetic perspective. A number of fairly recent simulation methodologies that are popular in cognitive science are essentially synthetic in nature. These methods include artificial neural networks (e.g., Bechtel & Abrahamsen, 1991;

Dawson, 1998), genetic algorithms (e.g., Holland, 1992; Mitchell, 1996), and artificial life (e.g., Langton, 1995; Levy, 1992).

A second reason for exploring the synthetic approach is that it melds quite nicely with a new tradition in robotics, artificial intelligence, and cognitive science. This new tradition is defining a new field, a field that has been associated with a variety of labels in recent years. These labels include behavior-based robotics (Brooks, 1999), new artificial intelligence, behavior-based artificial intelligence, and embodied cognitive science (Pfeifer & Scheier, 1999). The embodied cognitive science movement is gaining popularity, and is challenging the traditional symbol-based conception of artificial intelligence and cognitive science using many of the same arguments that were put forth by connectionist researchers in the early 1980s.

6.1.1   Synthetic psychology vs. embodied cognitive science

Importantly, embodied cognitive science and synthetic psychology are not identical fields. Embodied cognitive science is a reaction against the traditional view that human beings as information-processing systems "receive input from the environment (perception), process that information (thinking), and act upon the decision reached (behavior). This corresponds to the so-called sense–think–act cycle" (Pfeifer & Scheier, 1999, p. 37). This has also been called the sense–model–plan–act framework (Brooks, 1999). The sense–think–act cycle, which is a fundamental characteristic of conventional cognitive science, is an assumption that the embodied approach considers to be fatally flawed.

One of the aims of embodied cognitive science is to replace the sense–think–act cycle with a principle of sensory-motor coordination (Pfeifer & Scheier, 1999), which might be construed as a sense–act cycle. The purpose of this change is to eliminate, as much as possible, thinking – the use of internal representations to mediate intelligence. What makes this a plausible move to consider is the possibility that if one situates an autonomous agent in the physical world in such a way that the agent can sense the world, then no internal representation of the world is necessary. "The realization was that the so-called central systems of intelligence – or core AI as it has been referred to more recently – was perhaps an unnecessary illusion, and that all the power of intelligence arose from the coupling of perception and actuation systems" (Brooks, 1999, p. viii).

The synthetic approach is an important component of this movement, because it opens the door to discovering behaviors that emerge from the interaction between an agent and the agent's environment. Embodied cognitive scientists seek this kind of emergence because they do not want to explain complex behavior by only appealing to internal mechanisms. Instead, "if we want to achieve wall-following behavior, we should design not a module for wall-following within the agent, but instead basic processes that together, interacting with the environment, engender this desired behavior" (Pfeifer & Scheier, 1999, p. 307). However, the synthetic approach is not equivalent to this embodied movement. For instance, and as we will see throughout this book, connectionist modeling can easily be construed as synthetic simulation (Pfeifer & Scheier, 1999, Chapter 5). Nevertheless, much of what is interesting about connectionist networks are the representational properties that stand between "sensation" and "action" (Dawson, 1998).

6.1.2 Overview: synthesis, emergence, analysis

The purpose of this chapter is to introduce the key characteristics of the synthetic approach as it can be used in psychology. These characteristics can be summarized with the acronym SEA, which stands for synthesis, emergence, and analysis. In my view, these are the three fundamental steps required for the synthetic approach to make contributions to psychology and to cognitive science.

In very general terms, synthetic psychology should proceed by carrying out these three steps in succession. First, a set of basic building blocks is used to synthesize a model. Second, the performance of the model is explored, with particular attention being paid to its emergent properties. Third, the emergent properties are explained in a theory that accounts for them by appealing to internal mechanisms, to the environment, or to an interaction between the two.

For our first exposure to these three steps, this chapter describes a class activity that I have used in one of my graduate courses. This example as it stands is not particularly psychological – a characteristic that is unfortunately true of many of the phenomena modeled by embodied cognitive science. However, it provides a concrete example of the three components of SEA. In later chapters, we will use these foundations to build synthetic models that seem more relevant to higher-order psychological processes.

6.2 Building a Thoughtless Walker

It has been my experience that when you try to teach modeling, students really benefit from hands-on work. So, when I was teaching a course on the synthetic approach in the fall of 2000, I thought that it was important to spend at least some time having students actually construct a working model. This was not merely to expose them to modeling per se. The activity that I had in mind was intended to expose them to the realization that a phenomenon that they took for granted was actually quite complicated.

One of the problems that I faced in doing this was that different students had enormous differences in their backgrounds of computer programming. This meant that the class activity couldn't involve hands-on computer simulation, because

I was not really interested in spending a great deal of time teaching programming as part of this course. My solution was to have students build a walking robot from a particular kind of toy building set, K'NEX.

One week I brought two large containers of K'NEX materials into class, along with an assortment of text aids. The class was asked to build a robot that could walk forward. The text aids were used to provide inspiration, but I didn't give any specific instructions. The class was quite small (eight or nine students), and they spent the first little while organizing themselves into groups, exploring K'NEX, and thinking about how they were going to approach this class problem.

By the end of class a week later, and only working during class time, the students had constructed a set of modular components that could be used to create a two-legged system, a four-legged system, or a six-legged system. Under certain conditions, described in more detail below, the students were successful in creating a robot that could walk the length of the classroom.

In the subsections below, I will describe the next-generation of the robot built in the style that was created by the students. It represents a next-generation system only to the extent that I took the liberty of making some minor improvements to their original model. The original robot, constructed under conditions that weren't necessarily ideal, had a few flaws that needed to be corrected. Some of the flaws involved robot parts that were intended to be identical in each module, but were not. Some of the flaws were structural problems that required solutions involving parts, such as elastics, that were not pure K'NEX. The robot described below is built purely from K'NEX parts in the spirit of the robot that was constructed in class.

The subsections below describe this robot as a project that could be built by the reader. It only mentions the parts and the properties of the final system. However, it is important to remember that when it was designed, students made explicit decisions to build in one way, and not in another. This was because they had many more materials available to them than those that are mentioned below. The reader should keep in mind that other designs are easily possible, and might want to consider alternative approaches to building the robot if they decide to try to replicate the efforts of this class. If the reader is interesting in exploring this robot in more detail, pictorial instructions for how it was built, and videos of the behavior of different versions of this model, are available at the website that provides supplementary material for this book (www.bcp.psych.ualberta.ca/~mike/Book2/).

6.2.1 A class project

The purpose of this project is to build a robot that can walk at least a few steps forward independently. It is not required to be able to turn, or to avoid obstacles. One goal of building the system is to start to have some appreciation for some of the properties that are characteristics of walking systems.

6.2.2 Materials

The entire robot was constructed out of a large set of K'NEX building materials that my daughter and son had accumulated over the years. K'NEX is a toy building system comprised of rods that can be inserted into geometric connectors that hold the rods together to create larger structures. Rods and connectors are made from plastic, and are color-coded to indicate length or shape. While structures built from K'NEX can be quite sturdy, there is a fair amount of "give" in these building materials. This turns out to be advantageous in providing emergent walking behavior in the robot.

In addition to the rods and connectors, the robot-building students also had available to them three identical motors that can be used to provide movement to K'NEX structures. These motors drive plastic gears that can rotate a K'NEX rod inserted as an axle. One of the advantages of using such motors for this project is that they too have a little bit of "give" in them, which was important for getting the robot to work. Having three of these motors was a luxury, as well as an indicator of how many raw materials the students had available. Usually K'NEX kits that use motors of this type only include one.

The only additional material required for building the robot was some literature that described a number of different robot projects, none of which use K'NEX. As we will see below, one important problem the students needed to solve was how to convert the rotating motion of the motors into a stepping action. They found one chapter in McComb (1987) that was particularly useful for providing a solution to this problem.

6.3 Step 1: Synthesis

In adopting the synthetic approach, the first general step is to take a group of basic building blocks and assemble them into a working system. This contrasts with the analytic approach because the researcher does not start with a complete system, and decompose it into component parts or functions.

In the first phase of synthesizing the walking robot, the basic building blocks are the K'NEX parts. In the later phase, a more abstract sense of building block is adopted. This is because you can create larger walking systems by linking together smaller identical walking modules. In order to create these higher-order building blocks, students had to make three important design decisions. These decisions are described below.

6.3.1 From rotation to stepping

In order to create a walking robot, the students decided that the fundamental engineering problem to be solved was converting the rotation of an axle into a stepping motion. In making this decision, the students also made some progress in terms of organizing their work on the whole robot. They had decided to convert each motor into a system that would cause two legs to step. They divided themselves into three small groups of students, each working with one of the motors. When one group had some insight into solving a particular design problem, they communicated it to the other two groups.

The primary inspiration for converting rotation into stepping came from Figure 16.15 in McComb (1987). This figure demonstrated that if one attached a leg to the outside of a rotating wheel, and also permitted the leg to rotate freely at the point of attachment, then the rotation of the wheel would result in the leg being lifted up and pushed down in a stepping motion. The students exploited this design in creating the axle to be rotated by the K'NEX motor (for pictures, please visit the website). The axle was a red rod. On one end of the rod, a white connector was attached sideways. At the other end of the rod, another white connector was attached sideways, but on the opposite side of the rod. These two white connectors represent wheels that would be rotated when the motor rotates the red rod. The white connectors are placed on opposite sides of the rod so that the two legs moved by the motor would do so cooperatively (i.e., one would be stepping in front of the other). A blue rod is placed through the middle of each white rod, and a beige connector is attached to one end to keep it from falling out. When constructed in this way, the blue rod can freely rotate in the white connector. If the leg is attached to the blue rod, then it is possible to make it "step" when the red axle rotates.

6.3.2 Balance

A second design issue to be faced by the students was the nature of the legs that were to be attached to the axles. The problem to be dealt with was this: the legs had to be constructed in such a way that a two-legged module would stand, even if the motor was not turned on. This was a problem because the "body" of the module – which was essentially the motor – was fairly heavy in relation to other components, and the legs were mounted in the middle of this body. The feet at the end of the legs had to be constructed so that the module would balance.

Balance was achieved by attaching a fairly large and wide "foot" to a red rod that served as a leg. The foot was constructed from four white connectors and two yellow connectors held together very solidly with white and green rods. The robot's point of contact with the ground was the two yellow connectors. The leg was attached to the axle by connecting firmly to the axle being moved by the motor. As a result, it was possible for the leg to push upwards with enough force to lift the "body" of the module.

6.3.3 Leg support

In order to create a successful stepping motion, it is not sufficient to connect the foot to the axle. A support must also be provided to the top of the red leg, in order to prevent the entire leg from being rotated around the axle and hitting the ground. In other words, the support must be used to restrain the leg in such a way that it keeps pointing (roughly) up and down during movement.

In order to deal with this problem, the students designed a structure that was used to contain the motor, and was also used to loosely constrain the top of the leg. This structure was essentially a body that had a connector that the leg passed through, but was not directly attached to. This arrangement allows the leg to move fairly freely in an up and down motion, but prevents the top of the leg from being rotated downwards to interfere with any stepping movement. In other words, the legs step; they do not rotate.

6.4 Step 2: Emergence

The first general step in synthetic psychology is to construct a working system. The second general step is to watch it work, paying attention to surprising or emergent properties. As we will see in Chapters 7 and 8, a practitioner of the synthetic approach expects that a system of simple components will generate far more interesting behavior than would be expected, particularly when it is embedded in an interesting environment.

What is an emergent property? One way to think about emergence is in terms of the linear/nonlinear distinction that we explored when discussing models of data, mathematical models, and computer simulations. In a linear system, the behavior of the whole system is exactly equal to the sum of the behaviors of its parts. If one understands the behaviors of all of the parts of a linear system, then this means that there should be no surprises when observing the behavior of the system as a whole. In contrast, in a system in which the components interact nonlinearly, then surprises can emerge. "The hallmark of emergence is this sense of much coming from little" (Holland, 1998, p. 2).

Holland (1998) points out that while emergence is a ubiquitous phenomenon in the natural world, it is exceedingly complicated, and therefore defies definition. However, he argues that the scientific study of emergence is in a position to take advantage of some essential characteristics. First, emergence should be studied in systems that can be described as being governed by rules or laws. Second, an emergent phenomenon should be a pattern that is both recognizable and recurring. Third, theories of emergent phenomena will depend crucially upon modeling. Fourth, emergent phenomena will often be seen in systems that are either adaptive or dynamic over time. Fifth, "emergence usually involves patterns of interaction that persist despite a continual turnover in the constituents of the patterns" (p. 7). These persistent patterns can be used as building blocks for larger systems. In other words, emergent phenomena will often be observed in systems that are organized hierarchically.

The walking robot that was constructed by the class is exceedingly simple. Nevertheless, when its behavior was observed and manipulated, it exhibited many of these fundamental properties of emergence. In the subsections below, we will consider observations made concerning three different versions of the robot: a two-legged robot, a four-legged robot, and a six-legged robot.

6.4.1   Two-legged system

The behavior of a two-legged system was interesting in some respects, but disappointing in others. When the motor was turned on, the robot began to sway back and forth in a surprisingly lifelike fashion. The "body" of the system also rotated back and forth. If one were to call each yellow connector at the base of the leg a "toe," then the stepping behavior of this robot could be described as follows: three "toes" were always in contact with the table. Two were on the leg on one side of the robot; the third was the toe on the back of the other leg. In short, when the robot stepped, it raised the front "toe" of one leg, and then it raised the front "toe" of the other leg.

All of this behavior was interesting, in the sense that it was quite a bit more complicated than the students predicted prior to turning the robot on. However, with all of this swaying, rocking, and toe lifting, one disappointing fact was obvious: the robot did not walk. It carried out all of this movement while staying in one place on the table. A video of this movement can be seen at the website for this book.

6.4.2   Four-legged system

The next stage of exploring the walking behavior of the robot was to take four additional white rods, and to connect two two-legged modules together to create a four-legged robot. When the modules were connected together, care was taken to ensure that both motors were pointed in the same direction. By convention, the rear of a module was the end where the motor switch and the wire connecting the motor to the battery case were found.

K'NEX motors can be run in two different directions, clockwise and counterclockwise, depending upon the setting of the motor's switch. In the first test of the four-legged robot, both motors were turned on in the same direction. The behavior of the robot didn't depend on whether this direction was clockwise or counterclockwise, and also was not affected by whether the motors were started at the same time or not, or by the starting positions of the two legs.

When the students drove the motors in the same direction, the robot as a whole began to sway and to rotate in a very similar fashion to the two-legged system. If one were to watch only one side of the robot, then one would typically see three "toes" in contact with the ground. Occasionally two "toes" would be seen in contact with the ground – one from each foot. Sometimes all four "toes" were in contact with the ground. When these observations were made, the robot was not walking. All of its swaying movement was being done on the spot.

Interestingly, every so often the movement of the two component modules would become uncoordinated. When this happened, the "give" in the K'NEX motor became important. The students would hear a definite clicking sound as the gears of one of the motors jammed, and the rotation of one of the axles would cease for a short period (a second or less). Then the motor that had stopped would start again, and at that moment the robot would lift one entire foot off the ground, and take a definite step forward. The extent of this forward movement was about 1 or 2 cm. Unfortunately, when the next step occurred, it was often in the opposite direction! So, when walking did occur, it was forward, then backward, one labored step at a time.

In short, this first test of the four-legged system led to results that were essentially the same as the results observed in the two-legged system: there was lots of robot movement, but essentially no walking. However, every now and again a definite step would emerge, suggesting that the robot's design was on the right track.

From observing the first test of this robot, it appeared that the coordination between the two leg modules was critical. For the most part, the two modules were in step, and as a result the robot did not walk. Walking only appeared when the stresses on the robot's legs caused a disruption between the coordination of the two legs.

This observation led to a simple manipulation that had dramatic results. If walking in this system required that the two leg modules be out of synch, then perhaps it would walk better if the two motors were run in opposite directions. At face value, this prediction is counterintuitive, because one would expect that if walking were to be achieved then the two sets of legs would have to be moving in the same direction. However, the students could quickly test their hypothesis simply by setting the two motor switches in opposite directions.

When this second test was conducted, the results were much more encouraging. At first, the robot motors protested loudly – angry clicks were heard from both. However, after a few moments, the clicks were heard less frequently, and the robot began to walk forward. When it was walking optimally, it would lift one rear foot completely off of the table's surface, and at the same time lift the front foot on the opposite side. It would then move about 2 cm. In some instances, the motors would lose this nice walking coordination, the stepping behavior would attenuate, and the robot would either slow down or stand still. This only lasted for a moment though – when the robot was in this state, the motors would start clicking back and forth again, and then the robot would begin to step forward. Examples of the movements of this robot are also available on the book website.

6.4.3   Six-legged system

The final exploration of walking by the students involved studying the behavior of a six-legged robot. The students created this robot by connecting a third two-legged module to the four-legged robot. Once again, care was taken to ensure that all three motors pointed in the same direction.

In the first test of the six-legged robot, the behavior of the system was very similar to that of the four-legged robot. The motors would complain when they were first all started in the same direction. The robot would begin to sway back and forth, and rotate a bit towards the left and right. Shortly there-after, the three different motors would be coordinated in a pattern in which all three legs on each side of the robot moved in synch. In this configuration, the robot essentially swayed back and forth in one place, and the closest that it came to stepping would be raising only one "toe" of any of its legs off the table's surface.

On occasion, because the motors were running independently, this relatively stable configuration was disrupted. One or more of the motors would click, the axle would momentarily stop, and suddenly one of the robot's legs would lift completely off the surface. A similar stepping motion would then be initiated in one or both of the other modules, and the robot would take a fairly large step (in the order of 5 cm) in one direction. Shortly afterwards, the system would again stabilize into the configuration in which the legs on each side were in synch, and the machine swayed back and forth on the spot. As was the case with the four-legged robot, when the next stepping action occurred, it was often in the direction opposite to the last step taken.

The second experiment with this robot was conducted by trying to manipulate the coordination of the three leg modules by altering the direction of the motors. In particular, the motor driving the middle pair of legs was set to run in a direction opposite to that being run by the other two motors.

When the motors were set in these directions, the robot walked quite effect-ively, as is illustrated on the book website. After an initial period of competition between the three motors, all three modules coordinated themselves into an arrangement in which each module raised one "foot" entirely off the table surface. In general, the three modules coordinated themselves in such a way that walking was achieved by resting the weight of the robot on one triangle of "feet" while the second triangle of "feet" was stepped forwards. Each triangle was defined by a front and rear leg on the same side of the robot, accompanied by the middle leg on the other side of the robot.

6.4.4 Emergence and surprise

Let us now briefly summarize the main results of this phase of working with the K'NEX robots. One nice aspect of this demonstration project is that it provides an excellent example of emergence. By themselves, none of the two-legged modules built by the students were capable of walking. However, if two or three of these nonwalking modules were coupled together, then walking was possible. It is clear that the walking behavior emerged from an interaction between the modules.

A second point to be made from this demonstration concerns the notion of surprise. In particular, when reliable walking behavior was observed in a robot, this was only achieved when the motors of adjacent two-legged modules were turning in opposite directions. This finding was counterintuitive, because at the outset it was natural to expect that all of the motors needed to turn in the same direction to get the machine stepping forwards. The robot project provides a very nice example of the possibility for surprise in a synthetic project.

Nevertheless, demonstrating that the synthetic approach can generate surprise is a fairly trivial result, and as such does not mark the end of the research program. "It is true that surprise, occasioned by the antics of a rule-based system, is often a useful psychological guide, directing attention to emergent phenomena. However, I do not look upon surprise as an essential element in staking out the territory" (Holland, 1998, p. 5). The lasting value of surprise in the synthetic framework occurs when it directs attention to emergent behaviors that can be explained by appealing to properties of system components. For this reason, after a system has been synthesized, and after emergent phenomena have been observed in its workings, researchers must step back and analyze in an attempt to explain their creation.

6.5 Step 3: Analysis

One of the fundamental characteristics of the synthetic approach is the assembly of components into a working system that exhibits surprising, emergent behavior. The class project that we have been describing has provided a concrete example of this.

A second, less explicit, characteristic of much synthetic research is the assumption that it leads more directly or more easily to explanations than does analytic research. Chapters 7 and 8 will provide more information about this assumption. For the time being, let it suffice to say that it is quite natural to assume that if you build a system, and engineer it out of parts whose workings you understand, then you should be in a position to explain the mechanisms from which surprising regularities emerge.

We will see that this assumption is not correct. In many of the examples that we will consider, building a system, and observing surprises in it, is pretty easy.

The difficult – and interesting – work starts when an attempt is made to generate theories of regularities that emerge from what we synthesize. "Understanding the origin of these regularities, and relating them to one another, offers our best hope of comprehending emergent phenomena in complex systems. The crucial step is to extract the regularities from incidental and irrelevant details" (Holland, 1998, p. 4). A good deal of analysis is required to carry this crucial step out.

The walking robots that we have been describing in this chapter are not particularly sophisticated machines, and were not designed to provide deep insights into the nature of locomotion. Nevertheless, it is instructive to analyze aspects of their behaviors, because even these simple machines reveal some very interesting properties.

6.5.1   Emergence and the thoughtless walker

For a first pass at analyzing the walking robots, it is instructive to consider their behavior in terms of the criteria for emergence that have been proposed by Holland (1998). One reason for doing this is because it helps to support the claim that the walking behavior of the robots really is emergent. A second reason for doing this is because it draws our attention to a number of different properties of these robots. These properties demonstrate that even with these simple toy components, the behavior of the robots is complicated and interesting.

6.5.1.1   Recognizable and recurring patterns

One of the criteria proposed by Holland (1998) as being necessary for emergence is the discovery of recognizable and recurring patterns. Emergent behaviors can't simply be those that are rare and surprising; they have to be results that are replicable. Are the behaviors in our robots of this type? The moment-by-moment behavior of all of the robots is quite complicated, and a detailed classification of the behaviors would likely require a detailed, frame-by-frame analysis of video images of their performance. However, even a casual observation of their movements suggests that there are two general states that the robots "prefer" to be in.

The first state is one in which as many robot "toes" as possible are in contact with the ground. In this state, the motors cause the robot to sway from side to side, and to turn back and forth, but the robot does not step forward. Usually, when a foot moves, it is only a slight movement that causes only one of its two "toes" to be raised off the ground. In multimodule robots, this state is associated with all of the legs on the same side of the robot moving together. The two-legged robot is always in this state.

The second state is one in which a robot is actually walking forward. In this state, more than one leg is lifted completely off the ground, usually at roughly the same time. As the robot steps forward, it still sways and turns, but not to the degree seen in the other state. For the robot to be in this state, there must be definite coordination between different two-leg modules. In particular, modules that are connected to each other are coordinated in a "diagonal" fashion: if one module is lifting the left leg when the robot is in this state, then any attached modules will be lifting the right leg.

The robot is not only seen in these two states. However, other robot states appear to be quite transitory. They occur for fairly brief periods of time as the robot changes from one of the above states to the other. These transitions appear to be more stressful on a robot's structure than either of the two states described above. This claim is supported by the fact that it is during these transitions that the motors stop functioning properly, grinding their gears with a distinctive clicking sound, and failing to rotate the red axle. In order to determine whether any of these transitory behaviors represent recurrent patterns would require detailed analysis (e.g., of slow motion video) of the robot.

When all of the motors are turning in the same direction, the robots are much more likely to be in the swaying state than in the walking state. Every 15 or 20 seconds, there will be a brief transition into the walking state (for one step), followed by a transition back into the swaying state. This situation is reversed when adjacent motors are turning in the opposite direction. In this case, the robots are much more likely to be in the walking state, except that every 15 or 20 seconds there is a brief transition into the swaying state, almost immediately followed by a transition back into the walking state.

6.5.1.2   Rule-governed system

Holland (1998) suggests that a second criterion for the scientific study of emergence is that it occurs in a rule-governed system. "Emergent phenomena also occur in domains for which we presently have few accepted rules; ethical systems, the evolution of nations, and the spread of ideas come to mind" (p. 3). Holland suggests that an understanding of emergence in these domains will have to wait until we have a better understanding of the laws that govern them.

The robots that we have been describing are governed by laws, but not in the usual sense that comes to mind in psychology or cognitive science. Usually, the term "rule-governed" in cognitive science immediately brings to mind a system that is controlled by a computer program. Furthermore, the computer program is usually thought be of a classical or symbolic type, such as the production system that was discussed in Chapter 5. However, it is obvious that no such program is responsible for the behavior of the robots. I call them thoughtless walkers because they have absolutely no capacity to use symbolic representations to control their actions.

Instead, the robots are governed completely by the laws of physics. The motors are supplying kinetic energy that causes robot parts to move, and the movement of these parts generate forces against the surface upon which robot rests. The surface reflects forces back through the robot, which results in other emergent behaviors, such as the side-to-side swaying of the robot body. As we will see below, a great deal of analytic research on the locomotion of multilegged animals proceeds by analyzing the distribution of forces through the walking system.

Describing the robots as being governed by the laws of physics leads to an interesting speculation that would require detailed physical analysis to validate. Each robot represents a physical system that holds kinetic energy, and is subject to a variety of forces. We could imagine measuring a robot in such a way that we could come up with a single number that represents its total stress or energy at any given time. My suspicion is that the two main states of the robot that were described above represent low-energy configurations. When a robot is in either of these two states, it is under the least amount of stress that it can be in when its motors are running. When the physical situation changes – for instance, when forces get redistributed because different motors are out of sequence – a robot moves to a higher energy state. When it is in such a state, it attempts to distribute forces again in such a way that the overall energy is again reduced. This results in the transitory behavior, and the accompanying complaints from one or more of the motors. From this perspective, the swaying state might represent the least energy state for the robot when its motors are running, because this state is the easiest to produce. The walking state might represent a higher energy state (which could explain why walking was unexpectedly hard to produce). However, the energy of the walking state is still lower than any of the transition states. When the motors are running in the opposite directions, the robot is unable to reach the ideal swaying state, and instead has a preference for the next best configuration – walking.

6.5.1.3   Dynamic system

Holland (1998) proposes that emergent phenomena are to be expected when the laws governing a system are invariant, but the system components governed by the laws are changing or dynamic. The thoughtless walkers that we have been discussing are obviously dynamic systems, because they are built from parts that are designed to move.

However, these robots are also dynamic in a subtler and more interesting sense. We have already described the robots in terms of two general lower-energy states, and have pointed out that both of these states depend upon a particular type of coordination between modules controlling different pairs of legs. We have also pointed out that there is no central computer that runs a program that coordinates the different modules. How, then, is coordination between leg modules possible?

The answer to this question is that different modules communicate to one another, but not in the symbolic fashion that is typically thought of in psychology and cognitive science. A different kind of communication is enabled by the dynamic nature of a robot's parts, and of the forces at play through its structure. When two modules become uncoordinated (e.g., because they are rotating at slightly different speeds), a robot's balance is altered in such a way that one module can run easily, but another cannot. In other words, changes in the physical configuration of the robot could be described as one module communicating to another that it is becoming uncoordinated. This message is communicated by changing the forces in the robot in such a way that one of the motors actually stops for a moment, until forces change again in some fashion that permits the motor to resume turning. In other words, even though these robots are thoughtless walkers, they can still be described as information processors.

6.5.1.4 Adaptive system

"The possibilities for emergence are compounded when the elements of the system include some capacity, however elementary, for adaptation or learning" (Holland, 1998, p. 5). The thoughtless nature of the robots that we have been considering precludes most of the possibility for learning. While this is a limitation of these robots (in terms of their generating theories about locomotion), such limitations are not surprising. After all, the robots are simply toys that are being used in a demonstration to reveal some of the general characteristics of the synthetic approach.

Nevertheless, if one were interested in exploring the properties of these robots in more detail, then there is a possibility for adaptation that could be explored with more detailed analyses than those we have reported above. It was mentioned earlier that one of the advantages of K'NEX was the "give" in many of the components. Several of the parts of the robot structure are firm, but flexible. For example, rods can bend, can rotate within the joint of a connector, and can also be rotated a bit in the joint, without the overall structure breaking apart. It would be interesting to determine whether the physical structure of a thoughtless walker changed, because of the forces that the robot is subject to, in such a way that a physical configuration of a rod that was seen early in an experiment was never seen later. This might be evident if there were fewer transition periods between lower-energy states after a robot had been operating for a while. If indeed forces acting upon the robot adjusted its physical structure in this fashion, then this would be an example of elementary learning in a thoughtless system.

6.5.1.5 Persistent patterns, changing components

Holland (1998) points out that emergent phenomena frequently exhibit a dynamic, hierarchical organization. At one level of analysis, parts of a system might be changing very frequently. At a broader level of analysis, though, the system might exhibit stable regularities. "A simple example is the standing wave in front of a rock in a white-water river. The water molecules making up the wave change instant by instant, but the wave persists as long as the rock is there and the water flows" (p. 7).

When the robots are successful in walking, they clearly exhibit this kind of hierarchical organization. For example, walking in the six-legged robot can broadly be described as the successive placing of a triangular configuration of legs onto the ground. However, the legs that make up this stable triangle change from step to step. A more detailed analysis of a robot's behavior would probably provide many more examples of this. For instance, given all of the movement in a robot, and all of the "give" in its components, it would not be surprising that a wide diversity of physical configurations of robot parts could all be classified as a step.

6.5.2   *Comparison to biological walking*

The previous subsection has shown that there are a number of interesting and surprising emergent properties in the walking robots that we have constructed. This illustrates one of the main advantages of the synthetic approach. We could have taken a complicated phenomenon and analyzed it into putative component functions. Instead, we took a very simple set of building materials and a very general construction goal and were able to create a system that delivered several properties that were not explicitly intended.

To my mind, the robot example demonstrates another important advantage of the synthetic approach. By observing the regularities in the behavior of the working system, we started to learn important facts about walking in general. In many cases, the synthetic approach will provide us with insights into the problems that are being solved by the system that we build, and these general insights will often be more important than a specific account of how a particular system works. Synthetic models provide a medium in which to explore phenomena. This medium can be so rich that one can learn a great deal by exploring the properties of models for their own sake.

A complementary approach, though, is to consider the system in the context of other types of knowledge. For instance, when a model is being analyzed one fruitful approach is to relate its observed properties to known properties of other systems. In the case of our current demonstration, we could attempt to do this by relating characteristics of our walking robots to knowledge that other researchers have collected in their study of animal locomotion.

6.5.2.1   **Lifelike motion**

The claim that was made earlier about the appearance of the walking robots was that their movement appears to be "lifelike." What exactly is meant by this claim? What kind of evidence can be cited to support this position? Research on animal locomotion can provide some answers to these questions, and can also provide some guidance about what properties of the walking robots deserve our attention.

At first glance, we might be tempted to think of a leg as being a kind of wheel. If legs functioned exactly like wheels, then movement would be uniform. However, analyses of the locomotion of many different animals have shown quite clearly that movement is not uniform at all. Legs are not wheels; a different metaphor is required to model actions like walking or running.

During a slow motion like walking, a better mechanical metaphor is an inverted pendulum (Dickinson, Farley, Full, Koehl, Kram, & Lehman, 2000). In this metaphor, the pendulum's cable becomes a rigid leg that is attached to a body of mass. When the leg is used for walking, the mass is vaulted over the leg. In the first half of this movement, kinetic energy is transformed into gravitational potential energy. In the second half of this movement, when the body descends, this potential energy is partially recovered as kinetic energy. One consequence of this cycling between kinetic and gravitational energy is that the body of the animal decelerates in the first half of the movement, and accelerates in the second half of the movement. During a faster motion like running, the rigid leg of the inverted pendulum is better viewed as a spring, kinetic and gravitational potential energies are stored as elastic energy, and the system bounces as if it were on a pogo stick cycling between breaking and propulsive phases. Again, the running system does not move uniformly. Instead it accelerates and decelerates with every step. Interestingly, these two metaphors can be applied to describe the locomotion of bipedal, quadrapedal, and polypedal organisms (Blickhan & Full, 1993).

One respect in which the walking robots are lifelike is that their forward movement is not uniform. Even though the motors work by providing a uniform rotation of an axle, when this motion is converted into a step, the legs work like pendulums. When legs are being lifted up, the robot's forward movement is very slow because the feet that are in contact with the ground are in the process of converting kinetic energy into gravitational potential energy. When the legs are being placed down, the robot lunges ahead noticeably faster. This is because the center of mass over each supporting leg is descending and accelerating.

Animal locomotion research points to a second fashion in which the walking robots are lifelike. We saw earlier that getting the robot to walk depended heavily upon leg coordination. For example, the six-legged robot would only walk forward when its motors ran in such a way that the six legs were coordinated to act like two sets of tripods. Walking was accomplished by having one tripod serve the function of the rigid legs of an inverted pendulum, while the other tripod was moved ahead. This kind of leg coordination is commonly seen in the walking of six-legged organisms such as insects (Dickinson et al., 2000).

A third respect in which the walking of our robots was lifelike involves the many movements of their bodies that were not at first glance directly related to walking per se. In particular, the bodies of all of the robots swayed back and forth very noticeably, and the front of the robots rotated between the left and right. Interestingly, these kinds of movements are becoming of more interest to researchers for analyzing animal locomotion. The legs of sprawled-posture animals, such as insects and crabs, generate substantial lateral forces (Dickinson et al., 2000). These forces are orthogonal to the direction of motion. Analyses of these forces suggest that elastic energy storage and recovery may occur within the horizontal plane. "By pushing laterally, legs create a more robust gait that can be passively self-stabilizing as the animal changes speed, moves over uneven ground, or is knocked askew by uneven terrain, a guts of wind, or a would-be predator" (p. 101).

6.5.2.2   Control with no brain

One of the predominant themes in the study of animal locomotion is the integration of many different systems, both neural and mechanical. "An integrative approach to locomotion focuses on the interactions between the muscular, skeletal, nervous, respiratory, and circulatory systems" (Dickinson et al., 2000, p. 100). Researchers are not only interested in determining how each individual component of locomotion system works, but also how all of the components function together as an integrated system.

The integration of motor, sensory, and control systems is also evident in behavior-based robotics. Consider Genghis, a six-legged robot built in 1988 by roboticist Rodney Brooks (Brooks, 1989, reprinted in Brooks, 1999). Two motors drive each leg, one for swinging it back and forth, the other for lifting it up and down. A simple walk is achieved by manipulating the behavior of all of the motors in the robot, on the basis of sensing different positional characteristics of its legs. For example, one reflex notices whenever a leg is not down, and attempts to bring the leg down by turning one motor on in the appropriate fashion. A second reflex notices if any one of the legs happens to move forward for some reason. When this is detected, all of the legs will receive a series of messages that cause them to move backwards slightly. Other reflexes will advance a leg forward when it is noticed that the leg is raised, and will raise legs under appropriate conditions. The combination of these sensory measurements and motor signals lead to a very robust emergent walking behavior in the robot.

We have already pointed out that no sensory control system has been built into our thoughtless walkers. To the extent that there is control or coordination between different two-legged modules, this is mediated completely by the transmission of physical forces through the robot structure.

Recent work by researchers on animal locomotion has explored the capabilities of such thoughtless systems. Kubow and Full (1999) simulated a walking cockroach in which there was no feedback from the equivalent of neural reflexes. The only feedback in the model resulted from the musculoskeletal properties of the cockroach legs that were included in the simulation. When walking was simulated, and the forward movement of the model was perturbed by external forces, the model was self-stabilizing. Depending on the type of perturbation, the model was able to recover in one or more steps. "Essentially, control algorithms can be embedded in the form of the model itself. Control results from information being transmitted through mechanical arrangements. Perturbations change the translation and/or rotation of the body that consequently provide 'mechanical feedback' by altering legged moment arms" (p. 858). This is exactly the kind of coordination that we encountered when examining the conditions under which our robots were able to walk.

6.5.2.3 Limitations and future explorations

Animal walking can be very complicated. Locomotion is required to accomplish many different goals, and each goal might be achieved by a completely different gait in the same animal. A cockroach that walks slowly coordinates six legs in a fashion similar to the six-legged robot described earlier; when fleeing at a speed of 50 body lengths per second the same cockroach runs on only two legs (Full & Tu, 1991). The ecological roles of different types of locomotion are also reflected in the structure and function of different anatomical parts. "Forty percent of the body mass of the shrimp is devoted to the large, tasty abdominal muscles that produce a powerful tail flick during rare, but critical, escape behaviors" (Dickinson et al., 2000, p. 102). Animals who move in the real world are subject to a bewildering variety of different forces. All of these factors contribute to the view that animal locomotion requires the integration of multiple sensory, motor, and control systems.

In comparison to biological systems, the thoughtless walkers described in this chapter are very simple. They are only designed to step forward. They cannot turn, change gait to achieve different goals, or manipulate step size to deal with encountered obstacles. They do not have any neural or sensory control systems. Nevertheless, we have seen that even these exceedingly simple toy robots have many interesting emergent properties that are relevant to the scientific study of animal locomotion. They illustrate one of the main reasons that there is a growing interest in the synthetic approach: very simple components can be used to build systems that generate a far richer set of properties than could have been predicted at the outset.

6.6 Issues Concerning Synthetic Psychology

The simplified nature of the thoughtless walkers can be used to raise a few issues related to the synthetic approach. One issue concerns the sequential nature of applying the steps of synthesis, emergence, and analysis. As portrayed in this chapter, each step is done independently of the other, and there is a definite sequence of steps to be carried out. This portrayal does not do justice to the problem-solving practices of my robot-building students, and does not completely reflect how synthetic psychology is conducted in practice. In building the robots the students moved back and forth between synthesis, emergence, and analysis. They would attempt to solve a problem in one fashion, observe the system to see if the problem was solved, and if the problem remained, then they would analyze the situation to see if they could come up with an alternative solution.

A second issue concerns the advantages of the synthetic approach. While this chapter has attempted to illustrate how one might conduct a synthetic research program, it hasn't made a strong case for *why* this program would be conducted. Chapter 7 addresses this issue with a historical overview of the synthetic reaction against analytic research. It will make the argument that the synthetic approach does have many advantages. But it will also make the argument that synthetic research cannot be performed without also performing analysis.

A third issue concerns the domain of "synthetic psychology" and its relation to embodied cognitive science, including the reaction against the sense–think–act cycle. While the robots described in this chapter have given an example of viewing walking synthetically, they certainly do not qualify as being psychological models. The rejection of the sense–think–act cycle is explicit in their thoughtless nature. But how can such models be psychological? In Chapter 8 it will be argued that the synthetic approach can be conducted without rejecting the sense–think–act cycle. Connectionist networks are synthetic models that have representational properties.

Chapter seven

Uphill Analysis, Downhill Synthesis?

7.1 Introduction

The previous chapter used the construction, observation, and analysis of toy robots to provide a concrete example of the three basic steps that are required in synthetic psychology. The first step is the synthesis of a working system from a set of architectural components. The second step is the study of this system at work, looking in particular for emergent properties. The third step is the analysis of these properties, with the goal of explaining their origin. This general approach was given the acronym SEA, for synthesis, emergence, and analysis.

The demonstration project that was presented in Chapter 6 provides a concrete example of these three basic steps, but is not by its very nature a particularly good example of synthetic psychology. In terms of advancing our introduction of synthetic psychology, the "thoughtless walkers" that we discussed at best raise some important issues that need to be addressed in more detail. These issues were mentioned near the end of Chapter 6.

The purpose of the current chapter is to go beyond our toy robots to consider two related issues in more detail. First, we are going to be concerned with the attraction of the synthetic approach. Why might a researcher choose it instead of adopting the more common analytic approach? Second, we are going to consider claims about the kind of theory that the synthetic approach will produce. Specifically, one putative attraction of the synthetic approach is that theories that emerge from synthetic research are considerably less complex than those that are generated from analytic research. The theme of this chapter will be that the synthetic approach does offer an attractive perspective for explaining complex behaviors. However, it is not an approach that necessarily produces theories that are simpler than those that come from analytic research. Indeed, synthetic research depends heavily upon analysis if its goal is to explain, and not merely produce, emergent phenomena.

This chapter adopts a historical context to explore these issues concerning the relationship between synthetic and analytic traditions. Starting from an example from early research in cybernetics, the chapter will introduce some of the pioneering work on autonomous robots from the early 1950s. Then, the chapter will briefly describe a rebirth – of sorts – of this work in the early 1980s. In reviewing this research, we will see several examples of simple devices that produce behavior that is both intricate and interesting. But we will also become aware that even the researchers who constructed these devices did not have an easy task in explaining their performance.

7.2　From Homeostats to Tortoises

In the early stages of World War II, it was realized that advances in aviation technology needed to be met in kind by advances in antiaircraft artillery. Specifically, the speed and maneuverability of German aircraft were such that classical methods of aiming this artillery were obsolete. New techniques for aiming – techniques that were capable of predicting the future position of a targeted plane, and sending a projectile to this predicted position – had to be developed, and had to be built right into artillery-controlling mechanisms (Wiener, 1948).

One of the scientists who worked on this applied problem was Norbert Wiener (1894–1964), who had received his PhD in mathematical philosophy from Harvard when he was only 18, studied at Cambridge under Russell, and eventually became a professor in the mathematics department at MIT. Wiener realized that feedback was a key factor in designing a mechanism for aiming antiaircraft artillery. For example, "when we desire a motion to follow a given pattern the difference between this pattern and the actually performed motion is used as a new input to cause the part regulated to move in such a way as to bring its motion closer to that given by the pattern" (Wiener, 1948, p. 6). Wiener also realized that processes like feedback were central to a core of problems involving communication, control, and statistical mechanics. He provided a unifying mathematical framework for studying these problems, and this framework defined a new discipline that Wiener called cybernetics, which was derived from the Greek word for "steersman" or "governor." "In choosing this term, we wish to recognize that the first significant paper on feedback mechanisms is an article on governors, which was published by Clerk Maxwell in 1868" (p. 11).

7.2.1　Feedback and machines

A more definite understanding of feedback, and its relationship to synthetic psychology, begins with a very general definition of a machine (Ashby, 1956). William Ross Ashby (1903–72) was one of the pioneering figures for the field of cybernetics, and was director of research at Barnwood House Hospital in

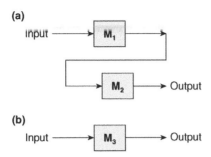

Figure 7.1 Simple coupling of two machines

Gloucester, UK, and later was the director of the Burden Neurological Institute in the Department of Electrical Engineering at the University of Illinois, Urbana. For Ashby, a machine is simply a device which, when given a particular input, generates a corresponding output. In other words, a machine is a device that performs a transformation of an input signal to an output response. Figure 7.1b illustrates this simple and general definition of a machine.

When a machine is defined in this way, then one can easily imagine a situation in which two machines are coupled together. In the simplest case, this is accomplished by having the output of one machine serve as the input to a second machine. With this kind of coupling, the behavior of the second machine is completely determined by the behavior of the first machine. For example, in Figure 7.1a the behavior of machine M_2 is completely determined by the behavior of machine M_1. This means that considering the machines separately does not really provide any additional insight into the function that transforms the input into the output. We could replace the two machines with a single machine (M_3) that maintained the same input/output relationship, as is shown in Figure 7.1b. We saw this kind of relationship earlier in the book when we discussed the linear nature of regression equations, and noted that the behavior of the entire regression equation was exactly equal to the sum of its parts.

A more complicated relationship between machines occurs with a different kind of coupling. The straightforward behavior of the two machines in Figure 7.1 occurred because the inputs of machine M_1 were independent of the outputs of machine M_2. If the output of M_2 is fed backwards to serve as the new input to M_1, then much more complicated behavior will result. At one level of description, the "mechanical feedback" that was described in our analyses of the thoughtless walkers in Chapter 6 is of this type: the forces generated by the robot (machine M_1) are transmitted to the surface (M_2), which in turn transmits forces back to the robot.

Descriptions of feedback need not be limited to pairs of machines. Many more machines may be coupled together to create a more complicated system. Of particular interest to Ashby was a system of four different machines coupled

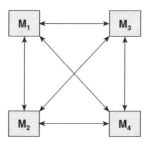

Figure 7.2   Mutual feedback relationships in a system of four different machines

together with feedback, as is shown in Figure 7.2, where the double-headed arrows indicate mutual feedback relationships. To foreshadow observations that we will be making later in this chapter about whether synthetic theories are simple or not, Ashby makes the following observation about a system of this complexity:

> When there are only two parts joined so that each affects the other, the properties of the feedback give important and useful information about the properties of the whole. But when the parts rise to even as few as four, if every one affects the other three, then twenty circuits can be traced through them; and knowing the properties of all the twenty circuits does *not* give complete information about the system.
>
> *(Ashby, 1956, p. 54)*

7.2.2   Ashby's homeostat

Imagine if a researcher was interested in studying a system like the one illustrated in Figure 7.2. If understanding its 20 component circuits cannot provide complete information about the system, then how should the research proceed? Ashby (1960) provided a decidedly synthetic answer to this question by constructing an interesting system that he called the homeostat to study the properties of feedback amongst four mutually coupled machines.

7.2.2.1   Basic design

The homeostat was a system of four identical components. The input to each component was an electrical current, and the output of each component was also an electrical current. The purpose of each component was to transform the input current into the output current. This was accomplished by using the input current to change the position of a pivoted magnet mounted on the top of the component. In essence, each magnet could rotate a needle back and forth. The needle was connected to a wire that was dipped into a trough of water through which another constant electric current was passed. With this physical arrangement, it was possible for the component to output an electrical current that was approximately proportional to the needle's deviation from its central position. All things being equal, a large current that was input to the component would cause a large deflection of the magnet (and needle), which in turn would result in a proportionately large current being output from the component.

The four units were coupled together to create a system of the type that was drawn in Figure 7.2. Specifically, the electrical current that was input to one unit was the sum of the electrical currents that was output by each of the other three units, after each of these three currents was passed through a potentiometer. The purpose of the potentiometer was to determine what fraction of an input current would be passed on to deflect the magnet, and thus each potentiometer was analogous to a connection weight in a parallel distributed processing (PDP) network. The result of this interconnectedness was a dynamic system that was subject to a great deal of feedback. "As soon as the system is switched on, the magnets are moved by the currents from the other units, but these movements change the currents, which modify the movements, and so on" (Ashby, 1960, p. 102).

In order to dictate the influence of one unit upon another in the homeostat, one could set the resistance value of each potentiometer by hand. However, Ashby (1960) used a different approach to allow the homeostat to automatically manipulate its potentiometers. Each unit was equipped with a 25-valued uniselector or stepping switch. Each value that was entered in the uniselector was a potentiometer setting that was assigned randomly. A unit's uniselector was driven by the unit's output via the deflected needle. If the output current was below a predetermined threshold level, the uniselector did not activate, and the potentiometer value was unchanged. However, if the output current exceeded the threshold, the uniselector activated and advanced to change the potentiometer's setting to the next stored random resistance. With four units, and a 25-valued uniselector in each, there were 390,625 different combinations of potentiometer settings that could be explored by the device.

In general, then, the homeostat was a device that monitored its own internal stability (i.e., the amount of current being generated by each of its four component devices). If subjected to external forces, such as an experimenter moving one of its four needles by hand, then this internal stability was disrupted and the homeostat was moved into a higher energy less stable state. When this happened, the homeostat would modify the internal connections between its component units by advancing one or more of its uniselectors to modify its potentiometer settings. The modified potentiometer settings enabled the homeostat to return to a low energy stable state. The homeostat was "like a fireside cat or dog which only stirs when disturbed, and then methodically finds a comfortable position and goes to sleep again" (Grey Walter, 1963, p. 123).

7.2.2.2   Behavior of the homeostat

Ashby (1960) tested the homeostat by placing some of its components under his direct control, manipulating these components, and observing the changes in the system as a whole. For example, in a simple situation only two of the four components might be tested. In this kind of study, the feedback being studied was of the type $M_1 \leftrightarrow M_2$. The relation $M_1 \to M_2$ could be placed under the control of the experimenter by manipulating the potentiometer of M_1 by hand instead of using its uniselector. The reverse relationship $M_2 \to M_1$ was placed under machine control by allowing the uniselector of M_2 to control its potentiometer. After starting up the homeostat and allowing it to stabilize, Ashby manipulated M_1 to produce instability. The result was one or more advances by the uniselector of M_2, which resulted in stability being re-attained.

Even with this fairly simple pattern of feedback amongst four component devices, many surprising emergent behaviors were observed. For example, in one interesting study Ashby (1960) demonstrated that the system was capable of a simple kind of learning. In this experiment, it was decided that one machine (M_3) was to be controlled by the experimenter as a method of "punishing" the homeostat for an incorrect response. In particular, if M_1's needle was forced by hand to move in one direction, and the homeostat did not respond by moving the needle of M_2 to move in the opposite direction, then the experimenter would force the needle of M_3 into an extreme position to introduce instability. On the first trial of this study, when the needle of M_1 was moved, the needle of M_2 moved in the same direction. The homeostat was then punished, and uniselector-driven changes ensued. On the next trial, the same behavior was observed and punished; several more uniselector-driven changes ensued. After these changes had occurred, movement of M_1's needle resulted in the needle of M_2 moving in the desired direction – the homeostat had learned the correct response. "In general, then, we may identify the behavior of the animal in 'training' with that of the ultrastable system adapting to another system of fixed characteristics. Ashby went on to demonstrate that the homeostat was also capable of adapting to two different environments that were alternated.

7.2.2.3   Implications

The homeostat counts, perhaps, as one of the earliest examples of the synthetic approach in action. It was a fairly simple analog device, constructed from well-understood component machines. It was wired up in such a way that complex feedback could be established among these components, and was used to study the dynamic processes that resulted. It had the advantage of permitting these processes to be studied at a time when a mathematical account of the device was not well established, and also at a time when computer simulations of this kind of feedback were not really possible. It demonstrated emergent behaviors, including interesting kinds of learning. Ashby (1960) was quite interested in drawing parallels between the behaviors of the homeostat and behaviors of the nervous system and entire organisms, although he was also aware of many limitations in his machine.

The interesting behavior of the homeostat arises from two general sources. The first is the rich possibilities of interactions between machines, as defined by the feedback relationships that were wired into the device. The second comes from the relatively large number of internal states that could be adopted by the machine when its uniselectors were used to modify potentiometer settings.

As a prelude to one theme that will be developed in more detail later in this chapter, it can be noted that the large number of different internal states that are available to a working homeostat provides the machine with many degrees of freedom with which to produce a low energy state. However, these same degrees of freedom make it difficult for the experimenter to explain the specific mechanisms that the homeostat uses to achieve this state. "A very curious and impressive fact about it, however, is that, although the machine is man-made, the experimenter cannot tell at any moment exactly what the machine's circuit is without 'killing' it and dissecting out the 'nervous system' – that is, switching off the current and tracing out the wires to the relays" (Grey Walter, 1963, p. 124). In other words, it is much easier to produce interesting behavior in the homeostat than it is to explain this behavior.

7.2.3   Grey Walter's tortoises

Ashby's (1960) homeostat could be interpreted as supporting the claim that the complexity of the behavior of whole organisms largely emerges from (1) a large number of internal components, and (2) the interactions between these components. In the late 1940s, William Grey Walter (1910–77) built some of the first autonomous robots to investigate a counterclaim (Grey Walter, 1950, 1951, 1963). His research program "held promise of demonstrating, or at least testing the validity of, the theory that multiplicity of units is not so much responsible for the elaboration of cerebral functions, as the richness of their interconnection" (Grey Walter, 1963, p. 125). His goal was to use a very small number of components to create robots that generated much more lifelike behavior than that exhibited by Ashby's homeostat. Grey Walter was a neurophysiologist who conducted pure and applied research at a variety of London hospitals from 1935 to 1939, and at the Burden Neurological Institute in Bristol from 1939 to 1970. While our interest in his research is with his robotics work, he was also a pioneer in the use of the electroencephalogram, and was the discoverer of theta and delta waves. His EEG research and his robotics work are both described in his 1963 text *The Living Brain*.

7.2.3.1 Basic design

Grey Walter (1963) whimsically gave his autonomous robots the biological classification *Machina speculatrix* because of their propensity to explore the environment. (He gave Ashby's 1960 homeostat the classification *Machina sopora*, pointing
out that if it were to be judged "entirely by its behavior, the naturalist would
classify it as a plant" (p. 124).) Because of their appearance, his robots were more
generally called tortoises. A very small number of components (two miniature
tubes, two relays, two condensers, two motors, and two batteries) were used
to create two sense reflexes. One reflex altered the behavior of the tortoise in
response to light. The other reflex altered the behavior of the tortoise in response
to touch.

At a general level, a tortoise was a small, autonomous motorized tricycle. One
motor was used to rotate the two rear wheels forward. The other motor was used
to steer the front wheel. The behavior of these two motors was under the control
of two different sensing devices. The first was a photoelectric cell that was mounted
on the front of the steering column, and which always pointed in the direction
that the front wheel pointed. The other was an electrical contact that served as a
touch sensor. This contact was closed whenever the transparent shell that surrounded the rest of the robot encountered an obstacle.

Of a tortoise's two reflexes, the light-sensitive one was the more complex.
In conditions of low light or darkness, the machine was wired in such a way
that its rear motor would propel the robot forward while the steering motor
slowly turned the front wheel. As a result, the machine could be described as
exploring its environment. The purpose of this exploration was to detect light
– when moderate light was detected by the photoelectric cell, the steering
motor stopped. As a result, the robot moved forward, approaching the source of
the light. However, if the light source were too bright, then the steering motor
would be turned on again at twice the speed that was used during the robot's
exploration of the environment. As a result, "the creature abruptly sheers away
and seeks a more gentle climate. If there is a single light source, the machine
circles around it in a complex path of advance and withdrawal" (Grey Walter,
1950, p. 44).

The touch reflex that was built into a tortoise was wired up in such a way that
when it was activated, any signal from the photoelectric cell was ignored. When
the tortoise's shell encountered an obstacle, an oscillating signal was generated
that rhythmically caused both motors to run at full power, turn off, and to run at
full power again. As a result, "all stimuli are ignored and its gait is transformed
into a succession of butts, withdrawals and sidesteps until the interference is
either pushed aside or circumvented. The oscillations persist for about a second
after the obstacle has been left behind; during this short memory of frustration
Elmer darts off and gives the danger area a wide berth" (Grey Walter, 1950,
p. 45).

7.2.3.2   Behavior

Grey Walter (1950, 1963) built two tortoises, and named them Elsie and Elmer using the initials of the terms that described them – "Electro Mechanical Robots, Light-Sensitive, with Internal and External stability." The question of interest to him was whether the intricate relationships between the small number of robot components, and the interactions between the robots and their environment, would be sufficient to generate complicated and interesting behaviors. He attempted to answer this question by observing the actions of the robots, together and separately, in a number of different environments. He mounted a light source on the robots, and recorded their behavior using time-lapse photography. As a result, the trajectory of a tortoise was traced out on the photograph by the light. The behavior that he observed was "remarkably unpredictable" (1950, p. 44).

For example, at the start of one experiment, the light was hidden from view by an obstacle. As a result, Elsie began with its exploratory motion. As a result of this exploration, Elsie collided with the obstacle, which produced the avoidance behavior. Because of the movements taken to avoid the obstacle, the robot was able to detect the light. It approached the light, but circled it, because when it came too close to the light it was too bright, and caused the robot to veer away. "Thus the machine can avoid the fate of the moth in the candle" (Grey Walter, 1963, p. 128).

In a second experiment, Elsie was placed in an environment in which there were two lights, and exhibited choice behavior. The robot started by being attracted to one of the two lights, and approached it. However, when it moved too close to that light, it veered away. As a result of veering away, it detected the second, "pleasantly" dimmer light, which it approached. Thus, the robot avoided the problem "of Buridan's ass, which starved to death, as some animals acting trophically in fact do, because two exactly equal piles of hay were precisely the same distance away" (Grey Walter, 1963, p. 128).

In a third experiment, the robot encountered a mirror, and its behavior was driven by the combined effects of its ability to detect its own reflected (and relatively dim) light source, and of its physical contact with the mirror. The result was the so-called "mirror dance." The robot "lingers before a mirror, flickering, twittering and jigging like a clumsy Narcissus. The behavior of a creature thus engaged with its own reflection is quite specific, and on a purely empirical basis, if it were observed in an animal, might be accepted as evidence of some degree of self-awareness" (Grey Walter, 1963, pp. 128–129).

The electric components that were used to create the tortoises themselves led to an interesting emergent behavior. In particular, the sensitivity to light was dependent upon the degree to which the battery of a tortoise was charged. When fully charged, a bright light would repel the robot. However, when its battery was much weaker, the same bright light would attract the robot, because it would be recorded as being of moderate intensity. This enabled Grey Walter to use lights to control the ability of a tortoise to recharge itself. A hutch was built; if the robot entered the hutch its battery would be recharged. Inside the hutch was a light. When a tortoise's battery began to fail, the robot was attracted by the hutch light, entered the hutch, and recharged. However, when the battery was fully recharged, the hutch light repelled the robot, so that it left the hutch and began to explore its environment once again.

Grey Walter (1950, 1951, 1963) reported the results of many different kinds of experiments, including some that involved a particularly complicated environment because it included two tortoises. He also designed a later version of the machine, *Machina docilis*, which was capable of being classically conditioned. It learned to be attracted to a high-pitched whistle. In general, the results of all of his experiments demonstrated quite clearly that the complexity of the behavior of his robots far exceeded the complexity of the components from which they were constructed.

7.2.3.3   Implications

From where does the complexity of behavior arise? Simon (1996) explored this question with his famous parable of the ant. He imagined an ant walking along a beach, and that its trajectory along the beach was traced. This trajectory might be thought of as being a very complicated function; explaining the behavior of the ant was equivalent to explaining how the many twists and turns of this function arose. One might be tempted to attribute the properties of this function to fairly complicated internal navigational processes. Indeed, if one were to adopt an analytic approach, this kind of attribution would be expected. The trajectory would be taken as raw data, analyzed into key components, and the mechanisms that generate these key components would be attributed to the ant. However, Simon pointed out that this would likely lead to an incorrect theory. "Viewed as a geometric figure, the ant's path is irregular, complex, hard to describe. But its complexity is really a complexity in the surface of the beach, not a complexity in the ant" (p. 51). In other words, fairly simple dispositions of the ant – following the scent of a pheromone trail, turning in a particular direction when an obstacle is encountered – could lead to a very complicated trajectory, if the environment being navigated through was complicated enough.

Grey Walter's tortoises provide a robotic analog to the parable of the ant. The trajectories of their movements are very complicated. However, this complexity is not reflected in the internal complexity of the tortoise. The inner workings of Grey Walter's robots were very simple and straightforward by design. The complexity in the observed behavior must be rooted in the complexity of the interaction between a simple robot and its environment. "So a two-element synthetic animal is enough to start with. The strange richness provided by this particular sort of permutation introduces right away one of the aspects of animal behavior – and human psychology – which *M. speculatrix* is designed to illustrate: the uncertainty, randomness, free will or independence so strikingly absent in most well-designed machines" (Grey Walter, 1950, p. 44). Again, feedback is a key – in this case feedback between the world and the machine.

Consider this issue from a different perspective, the analytic one that had to be taken by the "kids in the hallway" who were discussed in Chapter 1. When I introduce synthetic psychology in lectures, I often use Grey Walter's tortoises as an introduction. However, when I do this, I describe the performance of the robots first, presenting images of their movements as behavioral data. Students are asked to infer the internal mechanisms of the machines on the basis of these images. Invariably, after analyzing the data that I have presented to them, they propose a far more complicated theory – one that involves many more internal properties – than is actually required. This is exactly the same situation that was observed in our Chapter 1 examples. It would appear that psychology students – and psychologists – have a strong tendency to ignore the parable of the ant, and prefer to locate the source of complicated behavior within the organism, and not within its environment.

Pfeifer and Scheier (1999) call this the frame-of-reference problem. "We have to distinguish between the perspective of an observer looking at an agent and the perspective of the agent itself. In particular, descriptions of behavior from an observer's perspective must not be taken as the internal mechanisms underlying the described behavior" (p. 112). This is because Pfeifer and Scheier believe that the behavior of a system cannot be explained by only appealing to internal mechanisms; an agent's behavior is always presumed by them to be the result of a system-environment interaction. "The complexity we observe in a particular behavior does not always indicate accurately the complexity of the underlying mechanisms" (p. 112).

Here we see one of the strong appeals of adopting the synthetic approach. By building a system and taking advantage of nonlinear interactions (such as feedback between components, and between a system and its environment), relatively simple systems can surprise us, and generate far more complicated behavior than we might expect. By itself, this demonstrates the reality of the frame-of-reference problem. However, the further appeal of the synthetic approach comes from the belief that if we have constructed the simple system, then we should be in a very good position to propose a simpler explanation of the complicated behavior. In particular, we should be in a better position than would be the case if we started with the behavior, and attempted to analyze it in order to understand the workings of an agent's internal mechanisms. Later in this chapter I will argue that while this perspective is appealing, it is also very deceptive and dangerous.

7.3 Vehicles

Surprisingly and disappointingly, Grey Walter's tortoises appear to have had a very short-lived academic impact, and had essentially disappeared from the scene by the end of the 1950s. To my mind, one of the most striking examples of the disappearance of the tortoises is that Grey Walter's research was not cited in the book that provides the renaissance of his theoretical perspective. In *Vehicles*, Valentino Braitenberg (1984) proposed a series of 14 different thought experiments. Each of these experiments involved conceptualizing a fairly simple machine, and considering how that machine might behave in different environments. Some of these machines are reminiscent of Elmer and Elsie. As Braitenberg's book progresses, the hypothetical machines become more sophisticated, as does their consequent behavior. One of the main themes of the book is one that is familiar from the current chapter: simple machines can generate far more complicated behavior than one might expect. A second theme pursued by Braitenberg is that his synthetic approach will lead to simpler explanations than those that would be attained if vehicle behaviors were approached analytically.

7.3.1 Braitenberg's general approach

Valentino Braitenberg (b.1926) is the emeritus director of the Max Planck Institute of Biological Cybernetics, an emeritus professor at the Institute of Medical Psychology and Behavioral Neurobiology of the Eberhard-Karls-University in Tübingen, Germany, and is the director of the cognitive science laboratory at the University of Trento in Italy. He is a leading researcher in cybernetics and neuroscience, and the thought experiments that he presents in *Vehicles* are an attempt to understand some of the characteristics of the brain by adopting the synthetic approach. The final chapter of the book "sketch a few facts about animal brains that have inspired some of the properties of our vehicles, and their behavior will then seem less gratuitous than it may have seemed up to this point" (Braitenberg, 1984, p. 95). In general, Braitenberg takes an anatomical property of interest, reduces it to a very simple form, and considers the behavior of a simple machine that incorporates it.

In this section, we will briefly explore Braitenberg's (1984) approach by considering a couple of the devices that he proposed. After we have introduced some of these machines, we will be in a better position to seriously consider some of the pros and cons of adopting a synthetic research strategy.

7.3.2 Some example vehicles

7.3.2.1 Vehicle 1: Getting around

Braitenberg (1984) constructed a deliberate evolutionary sequence that is traced from his early vehicles to the later ones. His early machines are very simple, and are easily thought of as organisms that swim around in water. The later, more sophisticated devices are better thought of as "little carts moving on hard surfaces" (p. 2).

His simplest vehicle is a swimming device that is best thought of as a cylinder or torpedo, with a sensor at one end (the front) and a motor at the other. The foundational design principle for this vehicle is the proportional relationship between the response of the sensor and the speed of the motor. As the sensor detects more of whatever quality it is designed to detect, the motor increases its speed. As the sensor detects less of this quality, the motor slows down. Under the assumption that this vehicle is moving in the real world, it will come under asymmetrical frictional influences. As a result, it will not travel in a perfectly straight line, but will instead follow a complicated trajectory that is both difficult to predict and to explain.

From the synthetic perspective used to create this vehicle, its overall behavior is very understandable. However, if faced with analyzing the behavior of the vehicle in the absence of any knowledge about its internal structure, it is likely to be very complicated. On observing this machine, "it is restless, you would say, and does not like warm water. But it is quite stupid, since it is not able to turn back to the nice cold spot it overshot in its restlessness. Anyway, you would say, it is ALIVE, since you have never seen a particle of dead matter move around quite like that" (Braitenberg, 1984, p. 5).

7.3.2.2 More advanced vehicles

The next set of vehicles proposed by Braitenberg (1984) are similar in spirit to Vehicle 1 in that they can be viewed as swimming devices propelled by motors whose speed is determined by the output of sensors. However, for these devices, there are two motors, one on each side at the back of the vehicle. Each sensor drives its own motor. The two sensors are mounted on each side at the front of the vehicle. Of interest is the anatomy of the connections between motors.

For instance, one vehicle might have excitatory connections (i.e., the same kind of sensor–motor relationship described for Vehicle 1) between the sensor and the motor on the same side of the vehicle. If the signal source being detected by the sensors is straight ahead of this vehicle, both motors will run at equal speeds, and the vehicle will run into the source. However, if the source is to one side, then the sensor nearer to the source will detect a stronger signal than will the sensor further from the source. As a result, the two motors will run at different speeds, causing the vehicle to turn away from the source. Braitenberg (1984) describes this vehicle as *disliking* sources; it becomes "restless in their vicinity and tends to avoid them, escaping until it safely reaches a place where the influence of the source is scarcely felt" (p. 9).

One could take the vehicle just described and cross its connections, so that the sensor on the right drives the motor on the left, and the sensor on the left drives the motor on the right. With these crossed connections, the sensor nearest the source drives the motor on the other side faster than the other sensor will drive the motor nearer the source. If the source is directly in front of the source, the vehicle will drive through it, as was the case for the previous vehicle. However, if the source is to one side of it, then the vehicle will turn towards the source instead of away from it. Braitenberg (1984, p. 9) designates this vehicle as being *aggressive*: "it, too, is excited by the presence of sources, but resolutely turns toward them and hits them with high velocity, as if it wanted to destroy them."

One common approach to studying the two types of vehicles that have just been described is to actually construct them, for instance using Lego Mindstorms or Lego Dacta components. The advantage of doing this is that their behavior is removed from the idealized domain of the thought experiment, and becomes subject to real-world influences. These influences include differential forces of friction on different robot parts, and the fact that no two presumably identical robot components will work in exactly the same way. "This means that it is usually more difficult than it seems to get a consistent and reliable automatic response to a stimulus" (Webb, 1996, p. 94). If the goal is to design a robot that will move in a straight line, then this is a serious problem. However, if the goal is to produce complex behavior from a simple system, then these vagaries of the environment become advantages. By adopting the synthetic approach "what seems like complex behavior in a robot can come from a surprisingly uncomplicated control algorithm" (Webb, 1996, p. 95).

The robots that were briefly described as being observed by the "kids in the hallway" in Chapter 1 were versions of the Braitenberg vehicles described in this subsection. These Lego Dacta machines were constructed and programmed by my daughter Michele and myself. Each robot used one motor to drive one rear wheel, and the speed of rotation of the wheel depended upon the output of a light sensor. In one robot, the connections between sensors and motors were crossed, in the other they were not. Videos of the behaviors of these robots are available at the website of supplementary material for this book (www.bcp.psych.ualberta.ca/~mike/Book2/).

Braitenberg (1984) goes on to consider minor advances in the design of this kind of vehicle. For instance, the sensors might be tuned to be maximally sensitive to a particular range of signal from a source. When this is done, with crossed connections, the behavior of the vehicle mimics the phototropism exhibited by Grey Walter's tortoises. The connections between sensors and motors can be made inhibitory, so that a motor slows down when the sensor detects more of the signal. Motors can be driven by more than one sensor, each sensitive to a different kind of signal. In theory, one such vehicle would be straightforward to build, but would exhibit extremely complex behavior: "It dislikes high temperature, turns away from hot places, and at the same time seems to dislike light bulbs with even greater passion, since it turns toward them and destroys them" (p. 12). Again we see that producing emergent properties – where the whole of a system's performance far exceeds the sum of its simple parts – are one of the key goals of the synthetic approach.

7.3.2.3   Vehicle 6: Selection, the impersonal engineer

When Braitenberg's vehicles emerge from the sea to occupy the land, evolutionary ideas take a decidedly different role in his book. Braitenberg (1984) imagines a collection of vehicles, all operating on a table that is surrounded by spare parts. A team of researchers also surrounds the table, and the goal of this team is to build new vehicles. The way that this process works is that a researcher takes one of the vehicles from the table, and uses it as a model for the creation of a copy from spare parts. Then both the original and the copy are placed back on the table.

A further twist to this thought experiment is the notion that the copies are being made in a hurry, and therefore the builders don't have much time to check their work, or to test the adequacy of each copy. As a result, some of the copies that are placed back on the table will not be identical to the original that was used as a model. Many of these copies will be defective, and will therefore fall off the table to be used as parts for later generations of copies. "But it is also possible that we will unwittingly introduce a particularly shrewd variation into the pattern of connections, so that our copy will survive forever while the original may turn out to be unfit for survival after all" (Braitenberg, 1984, p. 27). Braitenberg argues that this is particularly likely if one vehicle is picked up and used as a model for one vehicle component, and a different vehicle is picked up and used as a model for a different vehicle component when the copy is being constructed. Of course, if the lucky mutation results in a longer life span for the copy, then this vehicle will be more likely to be picked up and used as the model for later generation systems.

7.3.2.4 Further sophistications

Braitenberg (1984) proposes several additional modifications, and describes how they can be used to develop more advanced vehicles. Some of these vehicles have spatially organized sensors that permit them to detect the shapes of objects. Others have simple connectionist networks that enable them to learn from experience. Still others have feedback loops that enable them to predict the future.

All of these sophistications have two things in common. First, they are all made possible through the use of fairly straightforward materials and engineering. Second, when they are components of vehicles that are placed in interesting environments, extremely complicated behaviors can emerge. "It is pleasurable and easy to create little machines that do certain tricks. It is also quite easy to observe the full repertoire of behavior of these machines – even if it goes beyond what we had originally planned, as it often does" (Braitenberg, 1984, p. 20).

7.4 Synthesis and Emergence: Some Modern Examples

The historical examples that have been considered thus far in the chapter all point to two underlying themes. First, it is definitely possible to construct informative models by building complete systems from some set of assumed components, without the need of basing the model on extensive analyses of existing data. In other words, if one looks back at the previous examples, then one striking feature that should be noted is that neither the homeostat, the tortoises, nor the vehicles were models that were intended to fit extant behavior. Second, when this synthetic approach is taken, it is almost always the case that interactions between system components, and between these components and a complex environment, can produce surprising and interesting emergent behavior that usually exceeds the expectations of the system designer.

The research that has been reviewed above has inspired a great many modern research programs. In order to reinforce these two themes, let us take a moment to briefly review three more modern examples of complex behavior emerging (often unintentionally) from relatively simple systems that have been created via the synthetic approach.

7.4.1   NETtalk

DECtalk is a program for converting text into audible speech (Hallahan, 1996), and is widely viewed as the best commercially available product for this task. DECtalk consists of eight different processing "threads," each of which is concerned with a major stage of processing, ranging from buffering text in an input memory to generating audio via a computer's sound hardware. It does this by following a two-stage process. Of particular interest in the context of the current chapter is the letter-to-sound (LTS) thread that converts sequences of ASCII text into sequences of phonemes. First, the LTS thread separates the text stream into clauses, and normalizes the text by applying special processing rules to idiosyncratic text entries (numbers, abbreviations, and so on). Second, the remaining unprocessed test items are converted into phonemes in one of two ways. First, a word is looked up to see if it exists in a pronunciation dictionary of common words. (If this first lookup fails, the word will be tested for an English suffix. If the suffix is found, it will be removed, and the remaining word stem will be looked up in the dictionary again.) Second, if the word is not found in that dictionary, then it is converted into speech by applying a set of phonological rules that decompose the text into a sequence of morphemes. The phonological representation of the text that is generated by this two-stage process is then converted into audible speech by applying a set of transition rules to it, and then applying digital speech synthesis. During this stage of processing, the LTS thread will identify syllables in the morpheme sequences, and mark some of them for additional stress to make the ultimate speech output as natural sounding as possible. Also, the LTS thread will identify the context in which a particular phoneme is found (i.e., surrounding phonemes). This is because the pronunciation of some speech sounds will change as a function of context. The LTS thread has a series of rules that instantiate these context-dependent alterations.

While DECtalk exhibits outstanding performance, this is accomplished with considerable cost. Hallahan (1996) notes that the program is the product of over 30 years of development, and consists of around 160,000 lines of code. This large amount of code is required because there is a considerable amount of specific knowledge that is built into the program. For instance, the LTS thread alone has more than 1,500 rules of pronunciation. Even with this large number of rules, it still requires a dictionary of exceptional words that has over 15,000 entries. On older hardware, running DECtalk at settings that produced medium quality output resulted in its using 69 percent of a CPU's processing resources. Producing the highest quality output consumed 89 percent of the CPU's resources. DECtalk has only become more portable recently because of advances in CPU design.

NETtalk is a connectionist network that was intended to replace much of the LTS thread in DECtalk. Rather than handcrafting a large number of rules, and a dictionary of exceptional words, NETtalk was intended to be a fairly small program that learned to convert text into speech (Sejnowski & Rosenberg, 1988). The network had seven groups of 29 input units per group to represent text, 80 hidden units, and 26 output units that represented phonemes for a total of 309 units and 18,629 weighted connections. Text was moved through an input "window," so that the network was trained to pronounce the text in the middle of the "window," while at the same time being aware of the text's context (i.e., the text on either side of the "window," which had either just been pronounced or was to be pronounced next). The network was trained on two different texts. One was phonetic transcription from the informal speech of a child. The other was a set of over 20,000 different words from a dictionary. Training was accomplished using the generalized delta rule that will be discussed in detail in Chapter 11. By the time the network had learned about 5,000 words, its performance was nearly perfect, and its performance generalized quite well to words that it had not seen previously. Interestingly, the network was able to perform at this high level without requiring a large separate lookup table as is used in DECtalk.

NETtalk was explicitly designed to exhibit some of the functionality of DECtalk. It was not intended to have any implications at all for psychology or cognitive science. However, during training, NETtalk's output was channeled into audio hardware. Sejnowski and Rosenberg (1988) noted, "during the early stages of learning in NETtalk, the sounds produced by the network are uncannily similar to early speech sounds in children" (p. 670). They use this surprising finding to hypothesize that NETtalk might have discovered representations that are particularly efficient for use by parallel networks, and that these representations may be similar to those employed by humans. They go on to suggest that the developmental regularities that have been observed in NETtalk and other networks (e.g., Elman, Bates, Johnson, Karmiloff-Smith, Parisi, & Plunkett, 1996; Rumelhart & McClelland, 1986a) "may be a general property of incremental learning in networks with distributed representations" (p. 672). In other words, even though NETtalk was only intended as a particular feat of engineering, its surprising emergent behavior suggested that it might shed light on some topics of psychological interest.

7.4.2   *Cricket phonotaxis*

A second example comes from the study of cricket phonotaxis. This subsection briefly reviews the central points of Webb's synthetic study of this phenomenon (Webb, 1996).

Phonotaxis, the ability to identify a particular sound and move towards it, is fundamental to a female cricket's choosing of a mate. A male cricket will generate a song as a series of syllables produced at a specific frequency and with a specific rhythm. A female cricket can use these properties to isolate the song of a male cricket of her own species from any other sound. After selecting the song, the female cricket will move towards the male producing it, even under conditions in which other males of the same species are chirping at the same time. The mechanisms underlying cricket phonotaxis are not yet completely understood.

Sounds from the world provide external stimulation to a cricket's eardrums, which are mounted on its forelegs. Sound also travels inside the cricket's body to the ears through a tracheal tube that connects the two ears to each other and to openings on the cricket's body called spinnacles. These internal and external sounds travel different distances, and therefore arrive at the same ear at different times, resulting in their being out of phase. The amount of phase shift depends upon the direction of the sound source. In general, the cricket's eardrum that is closer to the sound source will have higher amplitude of vibration.

What mechanisms are responsible for converting differences between eardrum vibration amplitudes into movements in the direction of the detected sound? Each eardrum stimulates a neuron that encodes amplitude. The larger the amplitude, the higher will be the spike train frequency of the neuron, and the sooner will it start to respond.

There are two theories of how the responses of the two neurons are used to direct the cricket's locomotion. One popular theory is that the cricket turns in the direction of the side with the neuron that is firing more frequently. However, this account would work for any sound, and thus requires postulating additional neural mechanisms for picking out the song with the correct rhythm.

A second, simpler theory is that with each sound burst the cricket turns in the direction of the side whose neuron begins to fire first. In other words, this theory ignores spike train frequency. This second theory has the advantage that it does not require additional rhythm-detecting circuitry, because changes in the rhythm of the detected song will naturally alter the onset of neural firing. However, it is not clear that this simple theory is sufficient to account for the regularities of cricket phonotaxis.

Webb (1996) adopted the synthetic approach to evaluate the adequacy of this second theory. She constructed a Lego robot with specialized electronics that mimicked the functionality of the neural circuits in the cricket's auditory system. The robot had two wheels driving it from the rear, each rotated by its own engine. When both motors were running, they pushed the robot forward. The robot was programmed to stop the engine of the side whose "ear circuit" reached threshold first. This resulted in the robot turning in that side's direction – with the aim of having it turn in the direction of the detected song.

The "ear circuitry" of the robot was optimally sensitive to a sound that had a specific frequency and rhythm. Webb (1996) began to test the adequacy of the theory by placing it at one side of an arena, and placing a speaker on the other side. She recorded the trajectory taken by the robot when sounds were broadcast from the speaker. When the sound was of the optimal frequency and rhythm, Webb found that the robot followed a zigzag path towards the speaker that was very similar to the trajectory taken by a female cricket. When the properties of the sound deviated from the optimal, the phonotactic behavior of the robot became far less successful. For example, when the syllable rate of the sound was increased, the robot drove through the arena in predominately straight lines. When the syllable rate was decreased, the robot followed a curved path towards the speaker, but rarely reached the speaker's actual location. These robot behaviors began to establish the adequacy of the second theory. "I discovered afterward that real crickets, too, tend to take curved paths at slower rates while failing more completely for faster rates. So the robot not only succeeds like a cricket but tends to fail like one too" (p. 98).

Female crickets will choose between songs generated by two different males of the same species, usually moving to the louder of the two songs. Webb (1996) realized that she had not explicitly programmed this ability into her robot. Nevertheless, she decided to see what the robot would do in an arena in which two speakers were present, and in which the same sound was being played through both. "To my surprise, the robot seemed to have no problem making up its mind (so to speak) and went almost directly to one speaker or the other" (p. 99). This suggests that the simple theory of phonotaxis may not only explain the general phenomenon of song isolation, but might also account for how a female cricket chooses one mate over another. "Again it appears that it is the interaction of the robot's uncomplicated mechanisms with particular sound fields that produces this interesting – and useful – behavior" (p. 99).

Webb (1996) used this experimental situation to generate a sound scenario that was completely unnatural. She alternated the location of the sound's generation between the two speakers in the arena. Under these conditions, the robot becomes confused, and moves between the two sounds. Experiments with actual crickets presented with this laboratory situation produced very similar results.

These kinds of results provide yet another demonstration of the advantages of the synthetic approach. Webb (1996) explicitly avoided building complicated capacities into her robot, and did not expect that the robot's behavior would be rich and varied. However, when this simple device was situated in the appropriate environment, its performance exceeded her expectations. "It shows that a rather competent and complex performance can come from a simple control mechanism, provided it interacts in the right way with its environment" (p. 99).

7.4.3   Stigmergy and group behavior

If you visit the website for the Collective Robotic Intelligence Project (CRIP) at the University of Alberta (www.cs.ualberta.ca/~kube/research.html), then you will have an opportunity to view some interesting video footage of a small collection of autonomous robots engaged in very complicated group behavior. Six small cylindrically shaped robots move in an arena. In the middle of the arena is a brightly lit box. At the start of the video, four of the robots move directly to the box, while two others wander to one side of the arena. Of the robots that reach the box first, three line up side by side against it, while the fourth pauses behind this group, and then moves away. The three robots attempt to push the box, fail, and then break formation. Two return to a different position on the box, and are then joined by one of the other robots that had originally wandered off. When these three robots come in contact with the box, it begins to slide and turn. The movement of the box causes the three robots to break formation, but soon they return to push again. In a moment, the three other robots join them; the six robots jockey for position near one corner of the box, and push it quite quickly into a corner of the arena that is brightly lit with an overhead spotlight.

This video illustrates performance on a box transport task, which is one of the benchmark tests used to study cooperative behavior in robots. For each robot, the goal of this task is to locate the brightly lit box and to push it into a goal location, which is also brightly lit. Each robot is equipped with light sensors that point forward (for locating the box) and upward (for locating the goal). Once the robot detects a side of the box, it determines if the box is between the robot and the goal location. If it is, the robot pushes against the box. If it is not, the robot attempts to find a different position against the box. In many cases, this will result in the robot losing sight of the box, and having to search for it again. The robot can also lose sight of the box if another robot comes between it and the box.

The box transport task is designed to assess cooperative behavior, because the box is weighted so that at least two robots are required to move it. In order to succeed, the robots must position themselves along the box so that more than one of them push at the same time, and so that they are all pushing in a fairly consistent direction.

The astonishing thing about the behavior that can be seen in the website videos is that while it seems to be highly effective and coordinated, it is accomplished by very simple mechanisms. Furthermore, the robots do not explicitly communicate with each other, and are not centrally controlled. These robots are the culmination of several years of research that began with the study of core abilities in a group of software agents, and evolved into the performance of the physical robots that is illustrated on the website.

Kube and Zhang (1994) used software agents to explore some properties of cooperative behavior that were inspired from the study of social insects. They modeled the sensing and acting of a group of robots totally in a software environment. The simulated robots were provided with three sensors (one for the goal, one for obstacles, and one for other robots), two actuators (left and right wheel motors), and five simple behaviors. The behaviors were constructed using the subsumption architecture of Brooks (e.g., 1999). The default behavior is *find*, which causes the robot to move forward in a large arc. This behavior can be suppressed when the robot detects another; in this case it will change its behavior to *follow* the detected robot. If it gets too close to another robot while following, it will activate its *slow* behavior. If the goal sensor becomes active, then the robot will initiate the goal behavior, which causes it to move towards the goal. This behavior will only be stopped by initiating the *avoid* behavior, which occurs when the robot detects that a collision with another robot is imminent. Note that none of these behaviors involve communicating with other robots to coordinate their attack on a target. The simulation demonstrated the collective box transport behavior of the type that was later produced in real robots that incorporated most of these general behavioral principles (e.g., Kube & Bonabeau, 2000).

How does this cooperative behavior arise in robots that do not communicate directly with one another? The answer to this question again depends upon realizing that the robots (simulated or real) are situated in an environment that they are both sensing and acting upon. By changing the environment (e.g., by pushing the box, or blocking the path of another robot), they change the environment that is sensed by other robots, which in turn alters the behavior of the other robots. This indirect form of communication – accomplished by directly altering the environment, and therefore indirectly altering the behavior of agents in the environment – is called stigmergy. This term comes from combining the terms *stigma* (wound from a pointed object) and *ergon* (work, product of labor) to produce a term whose meaning is "stimulating product of labor" (Holland & Melhuish, 1999).

Stigmergy was a term coined by French zoologist Pierre-Paul Grassé to explain the nest-building behavior of termites (Theraulaz & Bonabeau, 1999). Grassé demonstrated that the termites themselves do not coordinate or regulate their building behavior, but that this is instead controlled by the nest structure itself. The current state of part of the nest stimulates a termite to perform an activity that alters the nest; the alteration in turn triggers a new behavior from either the same termite or from another. Stigmergy also provides an account of the construction of the nests of paper wasps (e.g., Karsai, 1999), and offers an alternative to older theories that attributed a fairly high degree of intelligence or higher-level rules to these insects. Stigmergy is generally viewed as a fairly simple mechanism for producing complex and coordinated performances from a group of agents, but has not been studied extensively. "The potential of stigmergy is still largely untapped in the biology community, in which it originated" (Theraulaz & Bonabeau, 1999, p. 113). Research on collective robotics, such as the box transport research cited above, or studies by Holland and Melhuish (1999) on how robots can exploit stigmergy to sort different objects into clusters, can be viewed as an attempt to increase our understanding of stigmergy, and to identify how it can interact with other principles to organize useful, collective behaviors.

For the purpose of the present chapter, stigmergy is an example of the "law of downhill synthesis," which we will consider in more detail in the next section. From a robot designer's point of view, an individual robot is provided with a very basic set of sensorimotor abilities, and is not required to include any facility for communicating directly with other agents. When placed in a complex environment – made particularly complicated by the presence of more than one agent – the result is complex collective behavior. Importantly, this behavior is completely emergent, because none of the capacities built into the robot are explicitly designed to be social or interactive.

7.5 The Law of Uphill Analysis and Downhill Synthesis

Brooks (2002) describes the behavior of one of his graduate students interacting with Cog, a humanoid robot with a moving head and arm, and with camera eyes that move rapidly to objects of interest. In this interaction, the student first held a whiteboard eraser and shook it. Then Cog would move its eyes toward it, reach for it, and touch it. This sequence of events was then repeated, and it seemed clear that the two were taking turns. However, when this interaction occurred, the capacity for taking turns had not yet been programmed into Cog.

> [The graduate student] had filled in the behavioral details so that the game of turn-taking with the eraser worked out. But she had done it subconsciously. She had picked up on the dynamics of what Cog could do and embedded them in a more elaborate setting, and Cog had been able to perform at a higher level than its design so far called for.
>
> *(Brooks, 2002, p. 92)*

This anecdote illustrates one theme that we have seen in the historical and modern examples of synthetic research that have been presented in this chapter: the generation of behavior that is more complex than expected from a simple system embedded in an interesting environment. It also provides an example that shows, even subconsciously, that humans may have a natural tendency to be overly generous in assigning complexity to the internal systems of agents that we see in the world, or with which we might interact.

These two points are related to two complementary themes that have been argued to be central characteristics of the synthetic approach (Braitenberg, 1984). The first theme is "downhill synthesis," which means that it is fairly straightforward to construct simple devices that, when they interact with the environment, produce surprising and interesting emergent behaviors. This theme is evident in the examples that we have seen in this chapter, as well as when we discussed the "thoughtless walkers" in Chapter 6.

The second theme is "uphill analysis," which Braitenberg (1984) uses as an argument in favor of the synthetic approach, and against an approach in which the behaviors of existing systems are explained via analysis:

> It is much more difficult to start from the outside and try to guess internal structure just from the observation of the data. . . . Analysis is more difficult than invention in the sense in which, generally, induction takes more time to perform than deduction: in induction one has to search for the way, whereas in deduction one follows a straightforward path. A psychological consequence of this is the following: when we analyze a mechanism, we tend to overestimate its complexity.
>
> *(Braitenberg, 1984, p. 20)*

In other words, if the goal of synthetic psychology is to explain how various behaviors arise, then Braitenberg is claiming that the synthetic approach will lead to simpler theories than those arrived at by adopting the analytic perspective. Braitenberg feels strongly enough about this position to proclaim this "the law of uphill analysis and downhill synthesis."

One reason that the law of uphill analysis and downhill synthesis seems to be quite plausible is our sense that if a researcher has constructed a system, then he or she should have an excellent understanding of its inner workings, and therefore should be in an excellent position to offer straightforward mechanistic explanations of complex behavior. Given that the synthetic approach can produce rich and surprising results, this seems to make it an extremely attractive alternative to the more traditional analytic approach. However, it is important to realize that while the law of uphill analysis and downhill synthesis can provide grounds for arguing that the synthetic approach is attractive, it cannot justify abandoning analysis entirely. As a matter of fact, for synthetic psychology to succeed, synthesis and analysis must both be combined in a research program.

7.5.1 From demonstration to explanation

Why is analysis a required component of the synthetic approach? To answer this question, let us consider for a moment what the goals of a synthetic research program might be.

Brooks (1999, pp. 96–7) takes great pains to let us know what, in general, behavior-based robotics and, more specifically, his subsumption architecture, is *not*. It is not connectionism, nor neural networks, nor production rules, nor a blackboard control architecture, nor even German philosophy. What then is it?

It could be that behavior-based robotics merely demonstrates that complex behaviors frequently emerge from simple systems. To this point, this chapter could be considered to be a short catalogue of such demonstrations. However, of biologically inspired robots like the one used to study cricket phonotaxis, Webb (2000, p. 545) asks, "such examples of engineering can be attention grabbing, but what is their value for biological science? In particular, beyond the 'gimmick' of resemblance to natural systems, is any deeper understanding of how animals behave brought about by the building of such robot systems?"

The answer to questions like these depends first on determining whether the synthetic approach to robotics is intended to be anything more than attention-grabbing demonstrations. Even a cursory glance at the literature would indicate that roboticists are interested in going beyond demonstrations, and coming up with theories of intelligence. For example, Adams, Breazeal, Brooks, and Scasselati (2000, p. 28) note, "just as computer simulations of neural nets have been used to explore and refine models from neuroscience, we can use humanoid robots to investigate and validate models from cognitive science and behavioral science." Webb (2000) argues that biologically inspired robots can be used to test existing hypotheses, to alter assumptions about stimuli and responses when confronted with a real environment, to enforce complete theories (and identify incomplete ones), and to produce novel hypotheses. Pfeifer and Scheier (1999) propose that the goal of embodied cognitive science is to achieve a better understanding of intelligence. "The methodology of embodied cognitive science is synthetic, its goal is understanding by building" (p. 631). With these goals in mind, merely generating complicated behavior is not a sufficient research program. The synthetic approach is in the business of explaining, and not just demonstrating.

If the synthetic approach is to generate new explanations of intelligent behavior, then analysis is going to be required. To see why this is so, imagine that a researcher is constructing autonomous systems according to a scheme similar to that described in Section 7.3.2.3, in which more successful systems are being selected for copying, and in which the copying process can introduce random mutations. (This hypothetical example is not so far fetched, as it captures the spirit of how problems are solved by genetic algorithms, e.g., Holland, 1992; Mitchell, 1996.) Imagine that after this process had been carried out for a certain period of time, one of the constructed systems exhibited a surprising and complicated behavior that was of considerable interest to psychologists. How would this system be used to contribute to psychological theory?

Simply demonstrating the interesting behavior would be important, but would not be satisfactory on its own. After all, a psychologists would already know of some other system that generates the behavior (i.e., a person or an animal), and would only be interested in this new system if it shed some light on how these other agents of interest worked. If the new system that demonstrated the behavior did not do this, it would be actually be complicating the situation, because instead of having one unexplained system (the person or animal), we would have two (the person/animal and the new autonomous system). As a result, in order to contribute to psychological theory, there would be a very strong demand for the researcher to explain the behavior of this new system – to say exactly how its inner mechanisms interacted with each other and with the environment to produce the behavior, and how the absence of such interactions resulted in the behavior not appearing in less successful systems

In this particular hypothetical example, though, synthesis does not imply an easy route to understanding and explanation. The fact that the researcher constructed the system using selection implies that explanation must depend upon a later stage of analysis. This is because the success of this particular system (and the failure of other similar systems) was due to some random mutation that affected its internal mechanisms. This mutation was caused by the researcher, but not intentionally. To explain its behavior, the researcher would have to take the system apart, examine its inner workings, and probably take other systems apart as well to identify the differences between successful and unsuccessful systems. This later stage of analysis, while necessary, is likely to be difficult and intensive. Of vehicles created by natural selection, as is the case in this hypothetical example, Braitenberg (1984) writes "we can imagine that in most cases our analysis of brains in type 6 vehicles would fail altogether: the wiring that produces their behavior may be so complicated and involved that we will never be able to isolate a simple scheme" (p. 28).

Of course, synthetic researchers recognize that the analysis of their creations will be challenging. Nevertheless, they also realize that such analysis is required to generate explanations. For example, Pfeifer and Scheier (1999, p. 131) outline a 10-step research program for conducting experiments with agents. The last three steps of this program are purely analytic. They involve collecting data about the agent's behavior, as well as its internal states; the behavior is then described and analyzed statistically. The ultimate goal of this research program is to "formulate explanations of the agent's behavior."

Webb (2000) provides an additional argument for the need for analysis in her assessment of how biorobotics can contribute to biology. She notes that just because a robot generates the same behavior as an animal, it is not appropriate to conclude that they two systems exploit the same control mechanisms. This is because a standard realization in modeling is that the same behavior can be generated by, in principle, an infinite number of different algorithms (see also Dawson, 1998, chs. 5 and 6). As a result, a great deal of analysis is required to determine whether the synthetic system and the modeled animal are strongly equivalent. "Proper experimental evaluation is needed to determine fully the real strengths or limitations of the implemented hypothesis. Behavior qualitatively similar to the animal in a few trials, while encouraging, cannot be taken as confirmation, yet too few studies do more" (Webb, 2000, p. 553).

7.5.2 Implications of Braitenberg's law

According to Braitenberg's (1984) law of uphill analysis and downhill synthesis, the synthetic approach should produce simpler theories than those that would be generated by the analytic approach. However, we have just seen that synthetic researchers have the goal of generating explanations of intelligence and behavior, and because of this goal must include analysis as a crucial component of their research program. What then is really implied by the law of uphill analysis and downhill synthesis? This law is not a claim that analysis should be abandoned, but is instead a claim that the route to understanding and explanation should first involve performing synthesis, and then later conducting analysis. It is this combined approach – with an emphasis on early synthesis – that holds the promise of generating simpler theories than an approach that exclusively involves analyzing the behavior of existing agents.

One reason for this promise is the fact that, as we have seen repeatedly, the synthetic approach is an explicit attempt to make the most by using the least. Synthetic modelers usually attempt to design fairly simple systems, in the hope that complex behaviors will emerge when they are situated in an environment. A second reason for this promise is that even in cases when researchers may not know precisely how to explain emergent behavior, the fact that they have constructed the model should make analysis easier, because they already have an accurate understanding of its main functional components, and should therefore be in a position to target their analyses efficiently and appropriately.

7.5.3   Towards synthetic psychology

Almost all of the examples of synthetic research that we have considered to this point have involved sensorimotor systems. Do such systems exclusively define the domain of the synthetic approach? A second question is whether systems of the type that we have been considering, which are predominately antire-presentational, are of any interest to psychologists. Is synthetic psychology going to be reduced to studying nonrepresentational systems that act on the world, or can the synthetic approach be applied to systems that use representations and are of more interest to cognitive science? These questions are addressed in the next chapter.

Chapter eight

Connectionism as Synthetic Psychology

8.1 Introduction

In Chapter 6, we introduced the synthetic approach with the "thoughtless walker" examples. In Chapter 7, we turned to a historical review of more serious research to examine why researchers might be attracted to the synthetic approach. We saw that one of the main attractions was the possibility of generating interesting and surprising behaviors from the interaction between a fairly simple system of components and the environment in which this system was embedded.

One concern raised at the end of Chapter 6, and not addressed in Chapter 7, involved the relevance of the synthetic approach to the study of psychological processes. In particular, the modern renaissance of the synthetic approach that was pioneered by such researchers as Ashby and Grey Walter is strongly associated with the movements of behavior-based robotics (Brooks, 1999) and embodied cognitive science (Pfeifer & Scheier, 1999). These research traditions are strongly antirepresentational, and are largely dedicated to removing the "think" component from the sense–think–act cycle. This is strongly reminiscent of a failed tradition in experimental psychology, called behaviorism, that attempted to limit psychological theory to observables (namely, stimuli and responses), and which viewed as unscientific any theories that attempted to describe internal processes that mediated relationships between sensations and actions.

> I believe we can write a psychology, . . . and never go back upon our definition: never use the terms consciousness, mental states, mind, content, introspectively verifiable, imagery, and the like. I believe that we can do it in a few years without running into the absurd terminology of Beer, Bethe, Von Uexküll, Nuel, and that of the so-called objective schools generally. It can be done in terms of stimulus and response, in terms of habit formation, habit integrations and the like.
>
> *(Watson, 1913, p. 166)*

Modern cognitive psychology emerged from a strong reaction against behaviorism's antirepresentational stance (Leahey, 1987). In psychology, there is a long history of powerful theoretical and empirical arguments against behaviorism, and as a result behaviorism is no longer an accepted position (but see Leahey, 1987, pp. 461–3). The standard view in psychology is that many phenomena cannot be adequately explained without appealing to mental representations. Given this situation, and given that we have only considered the synthetic approach in the context of antirepresentational research, this leads to an obvious question: is there anything in the synthetic approach that can be applied to the study of representational processes?

The purpose of this chapter is to consider one version of the synthetic approach that can be applied representationally, and which as a result can truly be considered to be synthetic psychology. This position will be supported in this chapter as follows: first, we will consider the properties of connectionist simulations in the context of the synthetic approach. This will be done to argue that connectionism offers one – though not the only – medium in which representational synthetic research can be conducted. Second, we will discuss one case study that has recently appeared in the literature (Dawson, Boechler, & Valsangkar-Smyth, 2000). This case study examines how connectionist simulations can be used to investigate issues related to one "higher-order processing" topic: spatial cognition. We will then use this case study as a motivator to step back and consider a variety of techniques for performing synthetic psychology using connectionism.

8.2   Beyond Sensory Reflexes

The complexity of the behaviors of all of the machines that were surveyed in Chapter 7 was rooted in a set of simple sensorimotor reflexes that were embedded in a complicated environment. For example, the behavior of all robots that were discussed in the chapter was based upon simple routines in which a particular sensation (e.g., a value detected by a light sensor, or a switch depressed on a touch sensor) was immediately converted into a particular response (e.g., a particular motor speed, or a change in motor direction). The extent to which the behavior of these robots was complex, surprising, or interesting was due to the interaction of these simple reflexes with the environments in which the robots were placed.

The purpose of this section is to briefly consider the extent to which sensorimotor reflexes can be relied upon to form the basis of synthetic psychology. First, some evidence supporting the existence of visuomotor modules in humans will be described. This evidence indicates that sensorimotor reflexes should be plausibly considered as a component of synthetic psychology. Second, the limitations of such reflexes will also be considered. The claim that will be made is that synthetic psychology cannot rely exclusively on such reflexes, and should therefore explore other foundations – some of which might be representational.

8.2.1 Visuomotor modules

One of the most influential ideas that has been proposed in cognitive science is that of the modularity of perceptual processing (Fodor, 1983). While "perception is smart like cognition in that it is typically inferential, it is nevertheless dumb like reflexes in that it is typically encapsulated" (p. 2). A module is a domain-specific perceptual system that solves a very particular problem, and is incapable of solving other information-processing problems. The operations performed by a module are rapid, mandatory, and run to completion once they are initiated. Fodor argues that all of these characteristics are achieved by associating each module with fixed neural architecture – modularity is physically built into the brain. The corollary of this position is that general inferential processing, which by definition is not modular, is *not* going to be associated with a fixed neural architecture. It is because of this that Fodor (p. 119) is not surprised that we have a neuroscience of sensory systems, but that we do not have a neuroscience of thought.

The modularity proposal is usually portrayed as being part of the "sense–think–act" cycle that defines much of the status quo in cognitive science (Dawson, 1998, ch. 7). Specifically, modules solve many problems in early vision (sense). The output of these modules is then passed on to visual cognition or higher-order cognition for inferential or semantic processing (think). The results of this higher-order processing are then used to generate actions. However, this is not the only way in which modularity has been incorporated into cognitive science.

In some of the earliest work on the neuroscience of vision, Lettvin, Maturana, McCulloch, and Pitts (1959) identified neurons in the visual system of the frog that only responded to specific visual stimuli, and which in some sense were modular feature detectors. For instance, one type of cell appeared to be a "bug detector," because it only responded to a stimulus that could be described as a small, moving black spot. However, such feature detectors in the frog do not appear to feed into a higher-order thinking mechanism. Instead, the frog's visual system appears to be organized into a system of "sense–act" or visuomotor modules. Not only do these modules detect a specific visual stimulus, but they also generate a specific motor response.

The existence of visuomotor modules in the frog was first demonstrated by Ingle (1973). In a seminal experiment, Ingle surgically removed one hemisphere of the optic tectum of a frog. This lesion produced a particular form of blindness in which the frog pursued prey presented to the eye that was connected to the remaining tectum, but did not respond to prey presented to the eye that would have been connected to the ablated tectum. The lesion did not affect the frog's ability to avoid a stationary barrier placed between it and its prey. Importantly, the amphibian brain is very plastic, and Ingle found that six to eight months after surgery, the nerve fibers from the "bad eye" regenerated, and became connected to the remaining optic tectum on the "wrong" side of the animal's head. In this case, when a prey target was presented to the "bad eye," the frog was no longer blind to it, and attempted to catch it. However, because of the tectal rewiring, the animal's responses were in the wrong direction. The frog always moved toward a location that was mirror-symmetrical to the actual location of the target, and this incorrect response was shown to be due to the topography of the regenerated nerve fibers. In other words, one role of the optic tectum in the frog is to mediate a visuomotor module that converts a visual sensation directly into a motor response.

Perhaps surprisingly, studies of brain-injured patients have demonstrated that the human visual system may also be organized into visuomotor modules (Goodale, 1988, 1995; Goodale & Humphrey, 1998). For instance, Goodale and his colleagues have studied one patient, DF, who suffered irreversible brain damage as a result of carbon monoxide poisoning. One result of this brain damage was that DF's ability to recognize visual shapes or patterns was severely impaired. She "was unable to describe the orientation and form of any visual contour, no matter how that contour was defined" (Goodale, 1995, p. 167). However, DF's visuomotor abilities were not impaired at all. "Even though she cannot recognize a familiar object on the basis of its visual form, she can grasp that object under visual control as accurately and as proficiently as people with normal vision" (p. 169). Another patient, VK, had the exact opposite pattern of dysfunction after a series of strokes. VK had normal form perception, but her visuomotor control – in particular, her ability to form her hand to grasp objects of different shapes – was severely impaired.

8.2.2   Reflexes vs. representations

The evidence that there exists, even in humans, modular systems that involve direct linkages between sensation and action is consistent with behavior-based robotics and embodied cognitive science. Specifically, research in these fields is based upon the assumption that intelligence emerges situating a system in the world, and is not a result of representational processing. The existence of visuomotor modules is strongly suggestive of a human information-processing architecture that is similar in many ways to Brooks's (1989, 1999) subsumption architecture. However, even researchers of visuomotor modules in humans would agree that such reflexes are not the sole foundations of psychological processing.

For example, Goodale and Humphrey (1998) point out that "while there is certainly plenty of evidence to suggest that visuomotor modularity of the kind found in the frog also exists in the mammalian brain, the very complexity of day-to-day living in many mammals, particularly in higher primates, demands much more flexible organization of the circuitry" (p. 184). They propose a reformulation of Ungerleider and Mishkin's (1982) proposal of two separate anatomical streams of visual processing. Ungerleider and Mishkin proposed a ventral stream from primary visual cortex to inferotemporal cortex for the processing of visual appearances, and a dorsal stream from primary visual cortex to posterior parietal cortex for the processing of visual locations – the so-called what–where distinc-tion. Goodale and Humphrey distinguish these two streams in terms of the kinds of representations that they construct, and their purpose. The dorsal stream computes representations of object locations and shapes in an egocentric frame of reference. These representations are components of visuomotor modules, and are used to control a variety of movements (e.g., saccades, grasps, etc.). The ventral stream computes representations of object features in an allocentric frame of reference. These representations become part of later semantic processing.

Furthermore, the dorsal and ventral streams as described by Goodale and Humphrey (1998) are not independent, but are required to interact with one another. For instance, "certain objects such as tools demand that we grasp the object in a particular way so that we can use it properly. In such a case both streams would have to interact fairly intimately in mediating the final output" (p. 203). The fact that the two systems can interact is supported by theoretical arguments and anatomical evidence (DeYoe & van Essen, 1988) that shows that they are far more interconnected than was originally proposed by Ungerleider and Mishkin (1982). These interactions are, of course, the source of the flexibility and control that Goodale and Humphrey note is required by higher-order visual systems to deal with complicated environmental demands.

That stimulus–response reflexes are not sufficient to account for many higher-order psychological phenomena is a theme that has dominated cognitivism's replacement of behaviorism as the dominant theoretical trend in experimental psychology. In the study of language, this theme was central to Chomsky's (1959) critical review of Skinner (1957). Many of the modern advances in linguistics were the direct result of Chomsky's proposal that generative grammars provided the representational machinery that mediated regularities in language (Chomsky, 1965, 1995; Chomsky & Halle, 1991). Similar arguments were made against purely associationist models of memory and thought (Anderson & Bower, 1973). For example, Bever, Fodor, and Garrett (1968) formalized associationism as a finite state automaton, and demonstrated that such a system was unable to deal with the clausal structure that typifies much of human thought and language. Paivio (1969, 1971) used the experimental methodologies of verbal learners to demon-strate that a representational construct – the imageability of concepts – was an enormously powerful predictor of human memory. The famous critique of "old connectionism" by Minsky and Papert (1988) could be considered proof about the limitations of visual systems that do not include mediating representations. These examples, and many more, have led to the status quo view that represen-tations are fundamental to cognition and perception (Dawson, 1998; Fodor, 1975; Jackendoff, 1992; Marr, 1982; Pylyshyn, 1984).

Some robotics researchers also share this sentiment, although it must be remembered that behavior-based robotics was a reaction against their representa-tional work (Brooks, 1999). Moravec (1999) suggests that the type of situatedness that characterizes behavior-based robotics (for example, the simple reflexes that guided Grey Walter's tortoises) probably provides an accurate account of insect intelligence. However, at some point systems built from such components will have at best limited abilities. "It had to be admitted that behavior-based robots did not accomplish complex goals any more reliably than machines with more integrated controllers. Real insects illustrate the problem. The vast majority fails to complete their life cycles, often doomed, like moths trapped by a streetlight, by severe cognitive limitations. Only astronomical egg production ensures that enough offspring survive, by chance" (p. 46). Internal representations are one obvious medium for surpassing such limitations.

Interestingly, arguments that representations provide an adaptive advantage for an organism, as well as flexibility and control of processing, are both central to the philosophical views of Karl Popper. Popper proposed an evolutionary theory in which organisms are constantly engaged in a process of problem solving, a process that Popper viewed as always being resolved through trial and error. "Error-elimination may proceed either by the complete elimination of unsuccessful forms (the killing-off of unsuccessful forms by natural selection) or by the (tentative) evolution of controls which modify or suppress unsuccessful organs, or forms of behavior, or hypotheses" (Popper, 1979, p. 242). Popper viewed consciousness as an evolved system of "plastic control," a system that could be used to control behavior, but which was also subject to changes via feedback. He argued that the purpose of representations was to supply "controls which can eliminate errors without killing the organism; and it makes it possible, ultimately, for our hypotheses to die in our stead" (p. 244).

In summary, the synthetic models developed in behavior-based robotics and embodied cognitive science can be described as systems of sensorimotor reflexes or visuomotor modules which, when embedded in a complicated environment, can generate surprising or interesting behavior. These models are consistent with the antirepresentational motivation of this research trend, namely, the elimination of the "think" component of the "sense–think–act" cycle. These models are also consistent with evidence of the existence of visuomotor modules in highly complex organisms, including humans. However, theoretical and empirical arguments would suggest that not all psychological phenomena are equivalent to sensorimotor reflexes. Some representational processes must exist as well, and it is these processes that are of keen interest to psychologists. The question that this leads to is this: can the synthetic approach be conducted in a way that provides the advantages that have been raised in previous chapters, but that also provides insight into representational processing?

8.2.3 Synthesis and representation

Of course, the answer to the question that was just raised is a resounding yes. There is nothing in the synthetic approach per se that prevents one from constructing systems that use representations. Describing a model as being synthetic or analytic is using a dimension that it is completely orthogonal to the one used

Table 8.1 Classification of some example research programs according to two separate dimensions, analytic vs. synthetic and representational vs. nonrepresentational

	Analytic	Synthetic
Representational	Production system generated from analysis of verbal protocols (e.g., Newell & Simon, 1972)	Multilayer connectionist network for classifying patterns using abstract features (e.g., Dawson, Boechler, & Valsangkar-Smyth, 2000)
Nonrepresentational	Mathematical model of associative learning based upon analysis of learning behavior of simple organisms (e.g., Rescorla & Wagner, 1972)	Behavior-based robotics system constructed from a core of visuomotor reflexes (e.g., Brooks, 1989)

when describing a model as being representational or not. This is illustrated in Table 8.1, which categorizes some examples of research programs in terms of these two different dimensions.

The placing of most of the research examples in Table 8.1 should be clear from discussions that we have had in preceding chapters. For example, production system research is designated as being both analytic and representational. It is analytic because production systems are almost always derived from an intensive analysis of the verbal protocols of human problem solvers (Ericsson & Simon, 1984; Newell & Simon, 1972). It is representational in the sense that production systems define a set of definite rules that detect, and modify, data structures that are stored in a working memory. Indeed, production systems are one of the prototypical examples of the power of symbolic representations in classical cognitive science (Newell, 1980, 1990).

Behavior-based robotics is designated as being both synthetic and non-representational. As we have seen in Chapter 7, it is explicitly synthetic in the sense that researchers build robots from fairly simple subsystems, and then examine the interesting kinds of behaviors that emerge when the robots are situated in an environment (Pfeifer & Scheier, 1999). It is also an attempt to be as antirepresentational as possible. "In particular I have advocated situatedness, embodiment, and highly reactive architectures with no reasoning systems, no manipulable representations, no symbols, and totally decentralized computation" (Brooks, 1999, p. 170). One of the foundational assumptions of behavior-based robotics is that if a system can sense its environment, then it should be unnecessary for the system to build an internal model of the world.

Mathematical models of associative learning, such as the Rescorla–Wagner model (Rescorla & Wagner, 1972), are designated as being both analytic and nonrepresentational. Such models are described as being analytic because they are usually based upon an analysis of behavioral regularities (see Chapters 3 and 4). They are described as being nonrepresentational because such models do not appeal to representational content to explain behavior, and frequently model direct relationships between stimuli and responses.

8.3 Connectionism, Synthesis, and Representation

Connectionism was placed in the final cell of Table 8.1. In my view, modern multilayer parallel distributed processing (PDP) networks permit research that is both synthetic and representational, and therefore offers one plausible avenue for conducting synthetic psychology. The following subsections will elaborate on why connectionism can be viewed in this way. Specifically, we will briefly discuss connectionism in the context of the three hallmarks of the synthetic approach: synthesis, emergence, and analysis.

8.3.1 Connectionism and synthesis

In adopting the synthetic approach, a researcher is committed to identifying a basic set of building blocks. Each of these building blocks defines a primitive element. The set of all of the available primitives defines an entire architecture. For a cognitive scientist, an architecture dictates "what operations are primitive, how memory is organized and accessed, what sequences are allowed, what limitations exist on the passing of arguments and on the capacities of various buffers, and so on. Specifying the functional architecture of a system is like providing a manual that defines some particular programming language" (Pylyshyn, 1984, p. 92). The goal of synthetic research is to see what variety of systems can be constructed from a particular architecture.

In cognitive science, an architecture is usually a kind of programming language. However, this is not a necessary property. In some cases, there may not be any programming environment at all. For example, in building our "thoughtless walkers" in Chapter 6, the architecture that we restricted ourselves to was a set of K'NEX rods, connectors, and motors. In other cases, an architecture might involve a combination of hardware and software elements. This kind of combined architecture is typical of research in embodied cognitive science (Pfeifer & Scheier, 1999).

The architecture is a foundational idea in cognitive science, and therefore it is not surprising that many different research programs revolve around proposals for the architecture of cognition. In some cases, researchers present a particular architecture as a candidate proposal for the "language of thought." For instance, Newell and Simon (1972) made very strong claims that production systems defined the functional architecture of the mind. Dawson (1998, p. 170) provides a table (incomplete) of proposed cognitive architectures that lists 24 different examples. In other cases, theoretical and empirical debates in cognitive science revolve around whether particular properties are part of the architecture or not. For example, in the 1970s and 1980s the imagery debate was about whether the visual properties of mental images were built directly into the architecture (Block, 1981). A more recent debate concerns whether the architecture of mind is analogous to the architecture of a digital computer (Bechtel & Abrahamsen, 1991; Churchland, Koch, & Sejnowski, 1990; Clark, 1989, 1993; Fodor & Pylyshyn, 1988; Pylyshyn, 1991; Smolensky, 1988), and has spawned a new architectural proposal, connectionism (McClelland & Rumelhart, 1986; Rumelhart & McClelland, 1986b).

PDP models, or connectionism, are based on general assumptions about the kind of information processing carried out by the brain. First, it is assumed that the primitives for this type of information processing are individual neurons. Second, it is assumed that the pattern of connections between neurons is analogous to the program in a conventional computer, because these connections define the causal interactions between neurons (Smolensky, 1988). Third, it is assumed that because the brain is composed of a set of primitive units that operate in parallel, and because representations are distributed across a wide array of neurons and synapses, the kind of information processing carried out by the brain must be quite different from that found in a digital computer. "The analogy between the brain and a serial digital computer is an exceedingly poor one in most salient respects, and the failures of similarity between digital computers and nervous systems are striking" (Churchland et al., 1990, p. 47).

PDP models represent the embodiment of these general assumptions in a computer simulation environment that permits the construction of networks that can solve problems in an incredibly diverse set of domains (Dawson, 1998). Essentially, the building blocks of PDP models represent abstract mathematical descriptions of the kind of information processing that neurons do. This functional approach ignores many of the biological properties of neurons, and attempts to simplify information processing as much as possible. We will consider the building blocks of connectionism in more detail in the remaining chapters of this book.

With respect to synthesis, connectionist research typically proceeds as follows: first, a researcher identifies a problem of interest, and then translates this problem into some form that can be presented to a connectionist network. Second, the researcher selects a general connectionist architecture, which involves choosing the kind of processing unit, the possible pattern of connectivity, and the learning rule. Third, a network is taught the problem. This usually involves making some additional choices specific to the learning algorithm – choices about how many hidden units to use, how to present the patterns, how often to update the weights, and about the values of a number of parameters that determine how learning proceeds (e.g., the learning rate, the criterion for stopping learning). If all goes according to plan, at the end of the third step the research will have constructed a network that is capable of solving a particular problem. The next subsection illustrates this aspect of connectionist research by describing an example network that was trained to make judgments about the distances between cities on a map of Alberta (Dawson, Boechler, & Valsangkar-Smyth, 2000).

8.3.2   Connectionism and synthesis: An example

8.3.2.1   **Metric representations of space**

Our everyday interactions with the visual and spatial world are grounded in the essential experience that space is metric. Mathematically speaking, a space is metric if relationships between locations or points in the space conform to three different principles (Blumenthal, 1953). The first is the *minimality principle*. According to this principle, the shortest distance in the space is between a point *x* and itself. The second is the *symmetry principle*. According to this principle, the distance in the space between two points *x* and *y* is equal to the distance between points *y* and *x*. The third is the *triangle inequality principle*. According to this principle, the shortest distance in the space between two points *y* and *x* is a straight line.

One recurring theme in the study of cognition, perception, and action is that intelligent agents have internalized the metric properties of the space in which they find themselves situated. As a result, the mental representations used by these agents are thought by some researchers to have metric properties in their own right. The paragraphs below briefly introduce three different examples of such proposals: similarity spaces, mental images, and cognitive maps.

Similarity is one of the most important theoretical constructs in cognitive psychology (Medin, Goldstone, & Gentner, 1993). The notion of similarity is central to theories of learning, perception, reasoning, and metaphor comprehension. One of the goals of cognitive psychology has been to determine the mental representations that enable similarity relationships to affect this wide range of psychological phenomena. One proposal that received a great deal of attention in the 1970s was that concepts were represented as points in a multidimensional space, where the dimensions of the space stood for either simple or complicated featural properties (Romney, Shepard, & Nerlove, 1972; Shepard, Romney, & Nerlove, 1972). In this kind of representation, the similarity between two different concepts was reflected in the distance between their locations in the multidimensional space. Researchers conducted a number of different studies in which ratings of concepts were used to position a set of concepts in the metric space. This empirically derived space was then used to predict behavior on a variety of different tasks, including analogical reasoning (Rumelhart & Abrahamsen, 1973) and judgments of the aptness of metaphor (Tourangeau & Sternberg, 1981; Tourangeau & Sternberg, 1982). Importantly, one of the main assumptions underlying the similarity space proposal was that this space was metric.

On the basis of this assumption, one would expect that the metric properties of the space would be reflected in the behaviors that were governed by the space.

For example, if a subject used the similarity space to rate the similarity between two concepts A and B, then one would expect these ratings to be symmetric: the similarity between A and B should be the same as the similarity between B and A, because the distance between A and B in the similarity space is presumed to be symmetric.

A second example of a proposed representation that preserves the metric properties of space is mental imagery. Mental imagery is a visual experience that is usually elicited when people solve visuospatial problems. Not only does mental imagery provide a visual or pictorial experience, but mental images give the sense of being manipulated in a spatial manner – for instance, by being scanned, rotated, or zoomed in to (Kosslyn, 1980). Early behavioral studies of the manipulation of mental images have provided data that suggest that they are indeed spatial in nature. For example, many studies recorded the reaction times of subjects as they used mental images to perform some task, and found, for instance, that latencies increased linearly as a function of increases in the distance that an image had to be scanned or of increases in the amount that an image had to be rotated (Kosslyn, 1980; Shepard & Cooper, 1982).

More recent research has turned to cognitive neuroscience in an attempt to explore the representations responsible for mental imagery. Kosslyn and others have used a variety of modern brain-imaging techniques to show that when people generate mental images, they use many of the same brain areas that are also used to mediate visual perception (Farah, Weisberg, Monheit, & Peronnet, 1989; Kosslyn, 1994; Kosslyn et al., 1999; Kosslyn, Thompson, & Alpert, 1997; Kosslyn, Thompson, Kim, & Alpert, 1995; Thompson, Kosslyn, Sukel, & Alpert, 2001). In particular, mental imagery elicits activity in the primary visual cortex, a brain area that is organized topographically. Kosslyn has used this kind of evidence to propose an information-processing system that is responsible for the generation and manipulation of images. He argues that mental images are patterns of activity in a visual buffer that is a spatially organized structure in the occipital lobe.

A third example of a proposed representation that preserves the metric properties of space is the cognitive map. Beginning with Tolman's (1932, 1948) proposal that the spatial abilities of the rat were mediated by cognitive maps, representations that preserve the metric properties of space have been fundamentally important to the study of how humans and animals navigate (Kitchin, 1994). Behavioral studies have demonstrated that animal representations of space do indeed appear to preserve a good deal of its metric nature (for introductions, see Cheng & Spetch, 1998; Gallistel, 1990, ch. 6). Many researchers are now concerned with identifying the biological substrates that encode metric space. Single-cell recordings of neurons in the hippocampus of a freely moving animal have provided compelling biological evidence that one function of the hippocampus is to instantiate a metric cognitive map (O'Keefe & Nadel, 1978). In particular, neuroscientists have discovered *place cells* in the hippocampus that respond only when a rat's head is in a particular location in the environment (O'Keefe & Nadel, 1978). These place cells can be driven by visual information (e.g., by the presence of objects or landmarks in the environment), and appear to be sensitive to some of the metric attributes of space. For example, O'Keefe and Burgess (1996) found evidence that the receptive field of a place cell can be described as the sum of two or more Gaussian tuning curves sensitive to the distance between an animal and a wall in the environment.

8.3.2.2   Are spatial representations metric?

While research on each of these three proposals for spatial representations has provided evidence that the metric properties of space can be internalized, this evidence is not univocal. With respect to similarity spaces, Tversky and his colleagues conducted a number of experiments that demonstrated that similarity judgments were not metric, because in different situations it could be shown that these judgments were not always symmetric, did not always conform to the minimality principle, and did not always conform to the triangle inequality (Tversky, 1977; Tversky & Gati, 1982).

With respect to mental imagery, it has been shown that by manipulating the tacit beliefs of subjects (Bannon, 1980), or by altering the complexity of the image being used (Pylyshyn, 1979b), the linear relationship between reaction time and image properties could be eradicated. These findings were used to argue that our experience of mental images is based upon more primitive and nonspatial representational components (Pylyshyn, 1980, 1981, 1984). Even the evidence from neuroscience is not without controversy. In a detailed review of the literature, Mellet, Petit, Mazoyer, Denis, and Tzourio (1998) cite several studies that have found that some mental imagery tasks do not produce activity in primary visual cortex.

With respect to cognitive maps, it has been argued that place cell circuitry by itself does not provide a cognitive map that can be considered to be metric in the mathematical sense. First, place cells are not organized topographically; the arrangement of place cells in the hippocampus is not isomorphic to the arrangements of locations in an external space (Burgess, Recce, & O'Keefe, 1995; McNaughton et al., 1996). Second, it has been argued that place cell receptive fields are at best *locally* metric (Touretzky, Wan, & Redish, 1994), and that as a result a good deal of spatial information (e.g., information about bearing) cannot be derived from place cell activity. Some researchers have argued that place cells make up only a part of the cognitive map, and that the neural representation of metric space requires the coordination of a number of different subsystems (McNaughton et al., 1996; Redish & Touretzky, 1999; Touretzky et al., 1994).

8.3.2.3   A synthetic approach to spatial representation

The three examples that were briefly reviewed above all involve proposals for metric spatial representations that mediate spatial behavior. However, in each example it was shown that such proposals are not without controversy. In some instances, behavior that is presumably guided by the representation can violate the metric properties of space. In other instances, inspections of the representational or neural structures that mediate spatial behavior or experience reveal regularities that are inconsistent with the notion that the underlying structure is metric in nature.

One reason that such inconsistencies emerge may be because these representational proposals were the product of an analytic research strategy. Cognitive psychologists typically develop theories about underlying representations by decomposing complex behavior into more basic functions (Cummins, 1983; Dawson, 1998). While this approach, called functional analysis, has been extremely successful, it can be dangerous to use. One problem with it that we saw in Chapter 7 is that it can lead to theories that are more complicated than necessary, because the decomposition can fail to partition behavior appropriately into three different categories (behavior caused by the organism, behavior elicited by a complex environment, and behavior that emerges at the interface between an agent and its environment) (Braitenberg, 1984; Simon, 1996). A second problem is that the decomposition is theory-driven, and as a result can miss regularities that are real, but not intuitively obvious. "The tendency will be to break different capacities down into different constituent processes. As a result, explanations that are given of the capabilities in question will rest on a false and artificial theory, one that is, in effect, *engineered* to account for data but that is not a realistic model of human neuropsychology" (Rollins, 2001, p. 271).

The synthetic approach is one alternative to functional analysis. Dawson, Boechler, and Valsangkar-Smyth (2000) decided to explore the notion of spatial representations synthetically by building a PDP network that could make judgments that preserved the metric properties of space. Could a simple network learn to make such judgments? If so, then what kind of internal representation would it use? Would the representation be metric or nonmetric?

8.3.2.4   Defining the problem

As was noted earlier, the first step in synthesizing a connectionist network is to choose a problem of interest, and to translate this problem into a form that could be dealt with by a PDP model. Dawson, Boechler, and Valsangkar-Smyth (2000) wanted to create a network that could perform a behavior that was complicated enough to be of psychological interest, and which also preserved the metric properties of space. The task that they selected was a ratings task, in which a network was presented a pair of cities, and had to rate the distance between the two cities on a scale from 0 to 10. This kind of task is of psychological interest, because it is often used to collect distance-like data from human subjects (Shepard, 1972). By basing the ratings on distances measured between cities on a map, one can also ensure that a system that can make such judgments is preserving the metric properties of space as well.

Dawson, Boechler, and Valsangkar-Smyth (2000) chose 13 different locations in the province of Alberta. They took all possible pairs from this set to create a set of 169 different stimuli, each of which could be described as the question "On a scale from 0 to 10, how far is City 1 from City 2?" The desired ratings for each stimulus were created as follows. First, from a map of Alberta they determined the shortest distance in kilometers between each pair of locations. Second, they then converted these distances into ratings. If a stimulus involved rating the distance from one place to itself, the rating was assigned a value of 0. Otherwise, if the distance was less than 100 kilometers, then it was assigned a value of 1; if the distance was between 100 and 199 kilometers, then it was assigned a value of 2; if the distance was between 200 and 299 kilometers, then it was assigned a value of 3; and so on up to a maximum value of 10 which was assigned to distances of 900 kilometers or more.

These ratings were designed to preserve the metric properties of the map of Alberta. To confirm that a system that could generate the ratings must have, in some sense, internalized the map, Dawson, Boechler, and Valsangkar-Smyth (2000) analyzed the ratings with a statistical technique called multidimensional scaling (MDS). MDS is designed to take proximity information as input, and to then convert this information into a geometric configuration of points from which the proximities can be derived (Kruskal & Wish, 1978). For example, if one were to give MDS a table of distances between cities (e.g., a table commonly found on a roadmap), MDS would produce a map with each city situated in the correct location. When the ratings data is analyzed using MDS, it generates a plot in which each of the 13 cities are located very near the position in which they would be found if one examined a road map of Alberta.

8.3.2.5   Choosing the network architecture

The second step in synthesizing a connectionist network is to choose a particular architecture, and to train this architecture to solve the problem of interest. Part of this step involves making fairly general architectural choices. Dawson, Boechler, and Valsangkar-Smyth (2000) decided to train a feedforward network to solve this spatial judgment task. The first layer of this network was a set of 13 different input units. The input units used a very simple unary notation to represent pairs of places to be compared. Each input unit represented one of the 13 place names. Pairs of places were presented as stimuli by turning two of the input units on (that is, by activating them with a value of 1). For example, to ask the network to rate the distance between Banff and Calgary, the first input unit would be turned on (representing Banff), as would the second input unit (representing Calgary). All of the other input units would be turned off (that is, were activated with a value of 0). This unary representational scheme was chosen because it contains absolutely no information about the location of the different places on a map of Alberta. In other words, the input units themselves did not provide any metric information that the network could use to perform the ratings task.

Ten output units were used to represent the network's rating of the distance between the two place names presented as input. To represent a rating of 0, the network was trained to turn all of its output units off. To represent any other rating, the network was trained to turn on one, and only one, of its output units. Each of these output units represented one of the ratings from 1 to 10. For example, if the network turned output unit 5 on, this indicated that it was making a distance rating of 5.

The middle layer of the spatial judgment network was a set of six hidden units. Dawson, Boechler, and Valsangkar-Smyth (2000) selected this number of hidden units because pilot simulations had shown that this was the smallest number of hidden units that could be used by the network to discover a mapping from input to output. When fewer than six hidden units were used, the network was never able to completely learn the task.

In addition to making decisions about the input representation, the output representation, and the number of hidden units, Dawson, Boechler, and Valsangkar-Smyth (2000) had to make specific decisions about the properties of the hidden and output units, and about how the network was to be trained. They decided that the hidden and output units should all be value units, which are described in more detail in Chapters 10 and 11. A value unit uses a particular type of Gaussian activation function to convert net input into internal activity that ranges between 0 and 1. Such units are tuned to respond to only a narrow range of net inputs. Value units were used because one of the primary goals of the research was to interpret the internal representations discovered by the network. As will be discussed in Chapter 12, a number of different studies have demonstrated that networks of value units permit their internal structure to be interpreted in great detail.

8.3.2.6   Training the network

The final step in synthesizing a connectionist network is to actually carry out the training, and create a network that is capable of generating the correct response for every pattern in the training set. Dawson, Boechler, and Valsangkar-Smyth (2000) were able to train their network to make the correct spatial judgment for every pattern in the training set. With this successful training, the issues of emergence and analysis became central to their study.

8.3.3   *Connectionism and emergence: A prelude*

In the robot examples of Chapters 6 and 7, after a robot was synthesized, the next step was to place it in an environment and observe its behavior. The point of this observation was to identify interesting and surprising actions that emerged from the interaction between the robot and its world. Connectionist networks can surprise us, but not exactly in this way.

According to Hanson and Olson (1991, p. 332), "the neural network revolution has happened. We are living in the aftermath." At the time when the neural network revolution was in full swing, it was important to demonstrate that PDP models were capable of dealing with domains that were prototypically symbolic. I tell my students that this practice can be called "Gee Whiz connectionism," because its main goal was to allow researchers to exclaim "Gee whiz – PDP networks can do x, so x can be done without explicit rules." Classical researchers did take note of such results, acknowledging that it was surprising that models built from such simple components were capable of providing accounts of complex phenomena (Fodor & Pylyshyn, 1988).

However, in the aftermath of the neural network revolution, there really is no role for Gee Whiz connectionism. As is discussed in slightly more detail below, modern analyses have demonstrated conclusively that a broad variety of PDP architectures have the same computational power as the architectures that have been incorporated into symbolic accounts of cognition (Dawson, 1998). What this means is that a connectionist network can learn to perform any task that can be accomplished by a classical model. In the heyday of Gee Whiz connectionism, the mere demonstration that a network could do something of interest to classical cognitive science was by itself an emergent phenomenon of considerable interest. Now, with a better understanding of connectionist power, it is expected that networks can perform these tasks. As a result, the fact that a network can learn a task is no longer an emergent phenomenon of any interest to researchers.

Where, then, does emergence enter a synthetic psychology that uses PDP models? The answer to this question is that it is neither interesting nor surprising to demonstrate that a network can learn a task of interest. However, it can be extremely interesting, surprising, and informative to determine what regularities the network exploits. What kinds of regularities in the input patterns has the network discovered? How does it represent these regularities? How are these regularities combined to govern the response of the network? In many instances, the answers to these questions can reveal properties of problems, and schemes for representing these properties, that were completely unexpected. In short, this means that before connectionist modelers can take advantage of the emergent properties of a PDP network that is being used as paradigm for synthetic psychology, the modelers must analyze the internal structure of the networks that they train. In Chapter 12, we consider in detail several different approaches to interpreting connectionist networks.

8.3.4 Connectionism and analysis

In most cases, the identification of interesting emergent properties in a modern PDP network requires a detailed analysis of the internal structure of a trained network. In particular, after a network has learned to solve some problem of interest, a researcher will take the network apart and examine the properties of the internal representations that it has developed. In many cases, it is expected that this kind of analysis will reveal that the network has discovered interesting and surprising regularities in the problem. These surprises are one of the main ways in which connectionist simulations can push research in new directions.

However, if the analysis of connectionist representations is to provide a vehicle for synthetic psychology, then there are two general criticisms that have to be faced first. The first criticism is the general view that the kinds of representations that one will find in PDP networks are not the kinds of representations that will provide accounts of psychological phenomena. The second criticism is that even if these representations were of potential interest, they are nearly impossible to uncover in a trained network. We will consider each of these points below.

8.3.4.1   Connectionism and representation

One major debate in cognitive science concerns potential differences (and similarities) between symbolic models and connectionist networks (Dawson, 1998). For example, it has been argued that, in contrast to symbolic theories, PDP networks are *subsymbolic* (Smolensky, 1988). To say that a network is subsymbolic is to say that the activation values of its individual hidden units do not represent interpretable features that could be represented as individual symbols. Instead, each hidden unit is viewed as indicating the presence of a *microfeature*. Individually, a microfeature is unintelligible, because its "interpretation" depends crucially upon its context (i.e., the set of other microfeatures which are simultaneously present, Clark, 1993). However, a collection of microfeatures represented by a number of different hidden units can represent a concept that could be represented by a symbol in a classical model.

One consequence of the proposal that PDP networks use subsymbolic representations is the further proposal that they process information in a completely different way than one would find in a symbolic model such as a production system. "Subsymbols are not operated upon by symbol manipulation: they participate in numerical – not symbolic – computation" (Smolensky, 1988, p. 3). The kinds of numerical operations that are carried out are formal descriptions of the kind of energy minimization that we used to characterize the "thoughtless walkers" in Chapter 6. For example, Smolensky puts forth a "connectionist dynamical system hypothesis" as a proposed account of connectionist information processing. According to this hypothesis, at any state in time a connectionist network can be described as a vector of numbers, with each number representing the state of activity of a processing unit. In some instances, such as an account of learning, the vector might also include the values of a network's weights. The system is dynamic, in the sense that this vector changes over time. Differential equations precisely describe such changes, which in most cases can be thought of as defining a trajectory in some multidimensional space through which the system travels to minimize some energy or cost value.

The claims that PDP networks represent and process information in completely different ways than symbolic models has led to strong criticisms about their role in cognitive science and psychology. Specifically, some researchers have made strong arguments that the kinds of (nonsymbolic) representations that are found in connectionist models are not adequate to account for many of the regularities of human cognition (Fodor & McLaughlin, 1990; Fodor & Pylyshyn, 1988). In particular, Fodor and Pylyshyn argue that connectionist information processing does not involve a combinatorial syntax and semantics, and does not involve processes that are sensitive to constituent structure. They go on to argue that connectionist information processing shares many of the properties (and limitations) of the associationist theories that cognitivism reacted against in the 1950s (see also Bechtel, 1985). In short, their position is that connectionism doesn't provide the kind of representational account that psychology needs. "The problem with connectionist models is that all the reasons for thinking that they might be true are reasons for thinking that they couldn't be *psychology*" (Fodor & Pylyshyn, 1988, p. 66).

There are both theoretical and empirical reasons to believe that this dismissal of connectionism is premature. The symbolic paradigm in cognitive science is based upon the assumption that whatever the architecture of cognition is, it must have the computational power of a universal Turing machine (UTM) (Dawson, 1998). It would appear that connectionist networks also have this level of computational power. In some of the earliest work on neural networks, McCulloch and Pitts (1943) examined finite networks whose components could perform simple logical operations like AND, OR, and NOT. They were able to prove that such systems could compute any function that required a finite number of these operations. From this perspective, the network was only a finite state automaton (see also Hopcroft & Ullman, 1979; Minsky, 1972). However, McCulloch and Pitts went on to show that a UTM could be constructed from such a network, by providing the network the means to move along, sense, and rewrite an external "tape" or memory. "To psychology, however defined, specification of the net would contribute all that could be achieved in that field" (McCulloch & Pitts, 1988, p. 25). It has already been noted that more recent results have validated and extended this pioneering research.

Empirical evidence also supports the view that the distinction between connectionist and classical models is fairly blurred. For example, in one study (Dawson, Medler, and Berkeley, 1997) my students trained a network of value units on a logic problem developed by Bechtel and Abrahamsen (1991). When they analyzed the internal structure of the network, they found evidence for network states that represented standard rules of logic. A second study provided even stronger evidence of the representational equivalence of the two types of models. Dawson, Medler, McCaughan, Willson, and Carbonaro (2000) were able to translate a symbolic theory directly into a connectionist network using a technique called extra-output learning.

8.3.4.2   Connectionism and Bonini's paradox

It would appear, then, that examining the internal representations of PDP networks is an appropriate activity for synthetic psychology. Unfortunately, connectionist researchers freely admit that it is extremely difficult to determine how their networks accomplish the tasks that they have been taught. There are a number of reasons that PDP networks are difficult to understand as algorithms, and are thus plagued by what we called Bonini's paradox in Chapter 2.

First, general learning procedures can train networks that are extremely large; their sheer size and complexity makes them difficult to interpret. For example, Seidenberg and McClelland's (1989) network for computing a mapping between graphemic and phonemic word representations uses 400 input units, up to 400 hidden units, and 460 output units. Determining how such a large network computes a particular function is an intimidating task. This is particularly true because in many PDP networks, it is very difficult to consider the role that one processing unit plays independent from the role of the other processing units to which it is connected (see also Farah, 1994).

Second, most PDP networks incorporate nonlinear activation functions. This nonlinearity makes these models more powerful than those that only incorporate linear activation functions (e.g. Jordan, 1986), but it also requires particularly complex descriptions of their behavior. Indeed, some researchers choose to ignore the nonlinearities in a network, substituting a simplified (and often highly inaccurate) qualitative account of how it works (e.g., Moorhead, Haig, & Clement, 1989).

Third, connectionist architectures offer (too) many degrees of freedom. One learning rule can create many different networks – for instance, containing different numbers of hidden units – that can each compute the same function. Each of these systems can therefore be described as a different algorithm for computing that function. One does not have any a priori knowledge of which of these possible algorithms might be the most plausible as a psychological theory of the phenomenon being studied.

8.3.4.3   Interpreting connectionist networks

Difficulties in understanding how a particular connectionist network accomplishes the task that it has been trained to perform has raised serious doubts about the ability of connectionists to provide fruitful theories about cognitive processing (e.g., McCloskey, 1991). Because of the problems of network interpretation, McCloskey (1991) suggested "connectionist networks should not be viewed as theories of human cognitive functions, or as simulations of theories, or even as demonstrations of specific theoretical points" (p. 387). Fortunately, connectionist researchers are up to this kind of challenge. Several different approaches to interpreting the algorithmic structure of PDP networks have been described in the literature. They are discussed in more detail in Chapter 12. In short, network interpretation is both necessary and possible.

8.3.5 Connectionism and analysis: An example

To provide an example of connectionism and analysis, let us return to the spatial judgment network of Dawson, Boechler, and Valsangkar-Smyth (2000). After they were able to successfully construct the network, their interest turned to the kinds of internal representations used by the network to generate its metric behavior. In what way do the hidden units of this network represent the metric structure of a two-dimensional map of Alberta? Have the hidden units developed a metric representation of space? Or have the hidden units instead developed some complex nonmetric representation from which metric behavior can be derived?

8.3.5.1 Relating the map of Alberta to hidden unit connection weights

Dawson, Boechler, and Valsangkar-Smyth (2000) began by exploring the possibility that the network might have developed internal representations similar in nature to those that have been attributed to cells in the hippocampus. For example, consider the possibility that each hidden unit occupies a position in the map of Alberta, and uses its connection weights to represent the distances from the hidden unit to each of the Albertan cities. If this hypothesis is correct, then one should be able to find a position for each hidden unit on the map of Alberta such that there is a substantial correlation between the unit's connection weights and the distances from each city to the hidden unit location.

Dawson, Boechler, and Valsangkar-Smyth (2000) used the Solver tool in Microsoft Excel to move each hidden unit to a latitude and longitude on the map of Alberta. The spreadsheet that they designed computed the distance between the (current) position of the hidden unit and each of the 13 Albertan cities. The spreadsheet then computed the correlation between these 13 distances and the 13 connection weights feeding into the hidden unit. The Solver tool in the spreadsheet then changed the position of the hidden unit, finally stopping when it identified the position on the map that produced the highest correlation between map distances and connection weights. There was a very strong relationship between distances and connection weights, with the absolute values of the correlations ranging from 0.48 to 0.88. In other words, after this analysis was performed, Dawson, Boechler, and Valsangkar-Smyth were able to create a map that not only contained the 13 cities, but which also contained the hidden units from their network.

8.3.5.2 Relating connection weights to hidden unit MDS spaces

Dawson, Boechler, and Valsangkar-Smyth's (2000) first analysis indicated that each hidden unit could be viewed as occupying a position on the map of Alberta, and that its connection weights were related to distances between the hidden unit and the 13 cities on the map. However, while the correlation between map distances and connection weights were substantial, they were not as strong as might be expected. They noted that one problem with the first analysis was that it imposes our notion of the space in question (i.e., the map of Alberta) onto the behavior of the hidden units. It does not permit the possibility that the hidden units are spatial, but the space to which they are sensitive is quite different from the space used to create the map. There are at least two reasons to expect that the hidden units have a distorted representation of the map.

The first reason is theoretical. If connection weights leading into a hidden unit represent distance, then these distances are dramatically transformed by the Gaussian activation function of the hidden unit when connection weight signals are converted into hidden unit activity. This kind of transformation would be equivalent to a distortion of the map of Alberta.

The second reason is empirical. For any input pattern, a hidden unit's activity can be viewed as being analogous to that hidden unit's rating of the distance between cities. If we examine hidden unit activity to various pairs of cities, then we can see that the hidden unit's "ratings" do not seem particularly accurate. Consider, for example, hidden unit 2. When the network is asked to rate the distance between Red Deer and Jasper, this unit generates an activation value of 0.69. On the map of Alberta, the distance between Jasper and Red Deer is 413 km. However, nearly identical behavior is produced in the unit by two other cities, Edmonton and Lloydminster, which are much closer together on the map (251 km). When these two cities are presented to the network an activation of 0.71 is produced in hidden unit 2.

If the hidden units are spatial in nature, but are dealing with a space that is quite different from the one that we might expect, then how should their behavior be analyzed? One approach would be to consider each hidden unit as being a subject in a distance-rating experiment. For each stimulus, the rating generated by the hidden unit is the hidden unit's activity. If all of these ratings are taken and organized into tables, then MDS can be applied to this data. This analysis determines the structure of the space that underlies the hidden units behavior, which can then be related to the connection weights that feed into each unit.

Dawson, Boechler, and Valsangkar-Smyth (2000) performed this analysis on the 13×13 "activity matrix" for each hidden unit, in which each row and each column corresponded to an Albertan city, and each matrix entry a_{ij} was the hidden unit's activation value when the network was asked to rate the distance between city i and city j. They found that a two-dimensional plot provided a nearly perfect account of the activity matrix of each hidden unit. They then repeated the Solver analysis that was reported above. However, instead of using the map of Alberta, for each hidden unit they used the coordinates of the cities obtained from the MDS analysis of the unit's activity matrix. With these analyses, for each hidden unit they found a location in the MDS space that produced a near perfect correlation between distances and connection weights.

8.3.5.3   Coarse coding from hidden unit activations to distance ratings

Up to this point, we have seen evidence that the spatial judgment network developed a spatial representation of map locations, in which the weights that fed into a hidden unit encoded information about the distance between the hidden unit's position in a two-dimensional space and city locations in the same space. However, we have not yet discussed how the network exploits the features detected by the hidden units to produce the desired ratings as output.

We saw earlier that an individual unit's responses to different stimuli were not necessarily accurate. For instance, when presented with two cities that were relatively close together, a unit might generate internal activity very similar in value to that generated when presented with two other cities that were much further apart. To verify this claim quantitatively, Dawson, Boechler, and Valsangkar-Smyth (2000) took the activity of each hidden unit and correlated it with the desired rating for the input patterns. For units H0 through H5, these correlations were −0.32, 0.04, 0.04, −0.10, 0.04, and 0.16. It would appear that the activities of individual hidden units were at best weakly related to the desired distance ratings. How is it possible for such inaccurate responses to result in accurate outputs from the network?

The answer to this question is that the hidden unit activations in the network are a form of representation called *coarse coding*. In general, coarse coding means that an individual processor is sensitive to a broad range of features, or at least to a broad range of values of an individual feature (e.g., Churchland & Sejnowski, 1992). As a result, individual processors are not particularly useful or accurate feature detectors. However, if different processors have overlapping sensitivities, then their outputs can be pooled, which can result in a highly useful and accurate representation of a specific feature. Indeed, the pooling of activities of coarse-coded neurons is the generally accepted account of hyperacuity, in which the accuracy of a perceptual system is substantially greater than the accuracy of any of its individual components (e.g., Churchland & Sejnowski, 1992).

The coarse coding that is used in the spatial judgment network can be thought of as follows: each hidden unit occupies a different position on the map of Alberta. When presented with a pair of cities, each unit generates an activation value that reflects a rough estimate of the combined distance from the two cities to the hidden unit. While each hidden unit by itself generates only a rough estimate, when all six hidden units are considered at the same time, a much more accurate estimate of the distance between the two cities is possible. To demonstrate this, Dawson, Boechler, and Valsangkar-Smyth (2000) used regression to predict the distance rating (an integer ranging from 0 to 10) from the activations generated in six of the hidden units by each of the 169 stimuli that were presented to the network during training. The regression equation produced an R^2 of 0.71. In other words, a linear combination of the hidden unit activities can by itself account for over 70 percent of the variance of the distance ratings. After being trained to solve the problem, the network, in virtue of the nonlinear transformations performed by the Gaussian activation functions of its output units, can combine the hidden unit activities to account for 100 percent of the distance ratings.

8.3.6 Connectionism and emergence: An example

Several different analyses of the internal structure of the spatial judgment network were reported above, and all of these analyses converged on one general finding: the hidden units of the network developed metric representations of space. First, two-dimensional MDS analyses accounted for almost all of the variance in the activation matrix that was created for each hidden unit. Second, if one assumed that each hidden unit occupied a location on the map of Alberta, one could find a location for each hidden unit that produced a high correlation between the connection weights feeding into the hidden unit and the distances on the map between cities and the position of the hidden unit. Third, if one replaced the map of Alberta with a customized two-dimensional space for each hidden unit (a space revealed by the MDS analyses), near perfect correlations between connection weights and distances in the space were revealed.

With these analyses completed, we can now return to the issue of connectionism, analysis, and emergence. Specifically, now that a spatial judgment network has been synthesized, and now that its internal structure has been thoroughly analyzed, what are the implications of this simulation? Dawson, Boechler, and Valsangkar-Smyth (2000) discussed two general insights that were provided by their research. The first had to do with a controversy about how the hippocampus represents space. The second had to do with the relationship between metric representations and nonmetric behaviors. These two issues are discussed in the subsections that follow.

8.3.6.1 Implications for the hippocampal cognitive map

The strong interest that neuroscientists have taken in the study of spatial behavior and cognitive maps can largely be traced back to the discovery of place cells in the hippocampus (O'Keefe & Dostrovsky, 1971). The properties of place cells have been used as evidence for the neural basis of a cognitive map in the hippocampus (O'Keefe & Nadel, 1978). This map was argued to be a Euclidean description of the environment based on an allocentric frame of reference. In other words, locations in this map were defined in terms of the world, and not in terms of a coordinate system based upon (and moving with) the animal. Additional support for this proposal came from the fact that lesions to the hippocampus produce deficits in a variety of spatial tasks (for an introduction, see Sherry & Healy, 1998). Furthermore, robots that use a representational scheme based upon the properties of place cells can navigate successfully in their environment, indicating that the place cell architecture is a plausible proposal for a cognitive map (Burgess, Donnett, Jeffery, & O'Keefe, 1999).

One common analogy used by researchers is that a cognitive map is like a graphical map (Kitchin, 1994). "This does not mean that there must be a region in the brain onto which the environment is physically mapped, but rather that there will be a correspondence between input–output behaviors of the storage and retrieval functions of the two representations" (p. 4). The aforementioned properties of place cells would appear to support this analogy. One might plausibly expect that the cognitive map is a two-dimensional array in which each location in the map (i.e., each place in the external world) is associated with the firing of a particular place cell.

However, anatomical evidence does not support this analogy. First, there does not appear to be any regular topographic organization of place cells relative to either their positions within the hippocampus or to the positions of their receptive fields with respect to the environment (Burgess et al., 1995; McNaughton et al., 1996). Second, place cell receptive fields are at best *locally* metric (Touretzky et al., 1994). This is because one cannot recover information about bearing from place cell representations, and one cannot measure the distance between points that are more than about a dozen body lengths apart because of a lack of place cell receptive field overlap. Some researchers now propose that the metric properties of the cognitive map emerge from the coordination of place cells with cells that deliver other kinds of spatial information, such as head direction cells which fire when an animal's head is pointed in a particular direction, regardless of the animal's location in space (McNaughton et al., 1996; Redish & Touretzky, 1999; Touretzky et al., 1994).

Dawson, Boechler, and Valsangkar-Smyth (2000) observed that the hidden units in the spatial judgment network also appear to be subject to the same limitations that have brought into question the ability of place cells to provide a metric representation of space. First, because the hidden units were all connected to all of the input units, the network had no definite topographic organization. Second, each hidden unit appeared to be at best locally metric. While the input connections were correlated with distances on the map, the responses of individual hidden units did not provide an accurate spatial account of the map. Nevertheless, the fact that the network could be trained to accurately generate the ratings indicated that the responses of these locally metric inaccurate processors represented accurate spatial information about the entire map of Alberta. This was possible because the network did not base its output on the behavior of a single hidden unit. Instead, it relied on coarse coding, and generated its response on the basis of the activities of all six hidden units considered simultaneously.

Dawson, Boechler, and Valsangkar-Smyth (2000) noted that one implication of this coarse coding is that spatial relationships among locations in Alberta can be captured by a representational scheme that is not isomorphic to a graphical map. In particular, if one views the hidden units as being analogous to place cells, then the network demonstrates that spatial relationships among 13 different landmarks can be represented by a system which assigns place cells to only six different map locations.

The reason that this is possible is because the representational scheme discovered by the network is allocentric, but in a fashion that might not be immediately expected. Taken literally, the term *allocentric* means "centered on another," but there are at least four distinct kinds of representations for which this would be true (Grush, 2000). In two of these, the locations of objects are either specified with respect to one object in the environment (an object-centered reference frame) or with respect to a position in the environment at which no object is located (a virtual or neutral point of view). The representation used in the PDP network is allocentric in this latter sense, because the positions of cities are represented relative to the positions of hidden units, and the hidden units are not positioned at city locations. However, the network representation extends this notion of allocentric, because city locations are not encoded with respect to a single virtual location, but instead with respect to a set of six different virtual positions, all of which have to be considered at the same time to accurately retrieve spatial information from the network (i.e., to judge the distance between cities). Dawson, Boechler, and Valsangkar-Smyth (2000) called this a *coarse allocentric code*.

The major hypothesis about the hippocampus that was suggested by the spatial judgment network is that place cells also implement a coarse allocentric code. As a result, the place cells need not be organized topographically, because they don't represent the environment in the same way as a graphical map. Instead, locations of landmarks in the environment could be represented as a pattern of activity distributed over a number of different place cells. If this were the case, then in spite of their individual limitations, coarse coding of place cell activities could be used to represent a detailed cognitive map without necessarily being coordinated with other neural subsystems. In other words, Dawson, Boechler, and Valsangkar-Smyth's (2000) discovery of coarse allocentric coding in their network provides one plausible manner in which the spatial abilities of the hippocampus can be reconciled with its nonmaplike organization.

8.3.6.2 Coarse allocentric coding and nonmetric judgments

The spatial nature of the network's internal representations is perhaps not surprising, given that the network was trained to internalize a metric space.

However, as was noted earlier in this chapter, there does exist a tension between the metric properties of a representation and the properties of the behavior that the representation mediates. Specifically, is it possible for a metric representation to mediate nonmetric behavior?

This issue is important, because the discovery that human similarity judgments were nonmetric had a severe impact on proposals about the representations that mediated this behavior. Tversky and his colleagues conducted a number of experiments that demonstrated that similarity judgments were not metric, because in different situations it could be shown that these judgments were not always symmetric, did not always conform to the minimality principle, and did not always conform to the triangle inequality (Tversky, 1977; Tversky & Gati, 1982). As a result, many researchers completely abandoned the notion of the similarity space, and instead moved to feature based comparison models that could easily handle nonmetric regularities. This was in spite of the fact that it is possible to elaborate a perfectly metric representational space in such a way that it can be used to mediate nonmetric judgments. For example, Krumhansl (1978, 1982) demonstrated that if one took a metric space and augmented the kind of operations that were applied to it one could easily account for asymmetric similarity judgments.

Dawson, Boechler, and Valsangkar-Smyth's (2000) discovery of the coarse allocentric code was exciting because it raised the possibility of a metric representation that might be flexible enough to mediate spatial judgments that were not completely metric. In other words, they were interested in the possibility that coarse allocentric coding could support nonmetric judgments without the need for additional rules or processes.

One of the reasons for the rise in the popularity of connectionist networks over symbol-based models is that network models degrade gracefully and are damage-resistant (McClelland, Rumelhart, & Hinton, 1986). To say that a network degrades gracefully is to say that as noise is added to its inputs, its output responses become poorer, but it does not stop responding (Dawson, 1998). The model deals as best it can with less than perfect signals. To say that a network is damage-resistant is to say that as noise is added to its internal structure (e.g., by damaging connections or by ablating hidden units), its output responses become poorer, but it still functions as well as it can. Traditional symbol-based models do not degrade gracefully, and are not damage-resistant.

The damage resistance and graceful degradation of PDP networks is due to the redundancy of their internal representations when they employ coarse coding. One further advantage that this kind of representation can provide, which is related to graceful degradation, is generalization. When presented with a new stimulus – one that the network was never trained on – a network often can generate a plausible response, taking advantage of the similarity between the new stimulus and old stimuli, and the fact that such similarity can be easily exploited in redundant representations. In fact, if too many hidden units are used, and if these units start to pay attention to specific stimuli, then generalization will be poorer. This is one aspect of what is called "the three bears" problem (Seidenberg & McClelland, 1989)

In a second simulation, Dawson, Boechler, and Valsangkar-Smyth (2000) were concerned with a different type of generalization – the generalization of representation type from one problem to another. Specifically, imagine if the spatial judgment network's task was changed in such a way that the distance ratings violated one of the metric properties of space. Could allocentric coarse coding still be used to represent a solution to the problem? Or would a change in task result in a completely different representational approach?

The problem that Dawson, Boechler, and Valsangkar-Smyth (2000) trained a network to solve in the second simulation was a distance estimation task that was identical to the one that we have described above, with the exception that the network was trained to make different judgments when asked to judge the distance between a city and itself. In the first simulation, such judgments obeyed the minimality principle of metric space, and the network was trained to make a judgment of 0 when presented with such stimuli. In the second simulation, the minimality principle was violated. Instead of making a judgment of 0 when rating the distance of a city to itself, the network was trained to make a rating of 0, 1, or 2 depending upon the city.

When the minimality constraint was violated in this way, Dawson, Boechler, and Valsangkar-Smyth (2000) found that the ratings task became more difficult. In particular, the problem could not be solved when the network had six hidden units. An additional hidden unit was required. In spite of the task being more difficult, though, there was no evidence that the network created a qualitatively different representation to solve the problem. Dawson, Boechler, and Valsangkar analyzed this second network in the same fashion that they used to analyze the first network, and which was described above. They found that the second network used allocentric coarse coding to make distance judgments. Each hidden unit could be considered as occupying a position on the map of Alberta, and the weights feeding into each unit were correlated with the distances between the hidden units and the Albertan cities. The responses of individual hidden units provided relatively inaccurate sensitivity to distance information. However, when the responses of all seven hidden units were pooled, very accurate distance judgments were possible. Finally, and most importantly, there was no evidence that any one of the hidden units had a special role in making the subset of judgments that defined the violation of the minimality principle.

In particular, one possibility that Dawson, Boechler, and Valsangkar-Smyth (2000) considered was that six of the hidden units in the new network were performing the same function as were the six in the first network, and that the seventh hidden unit was a special purpose unit designed to deal with the nonmetric judgments taken from the diagonal of the new ratings matrix. This was not the case – all seven hidden units could be described in the same general way, all seven could be positioned on a map of Alberta, and all seven were involved in coarse allocentric coding.

8.3.6.3 Implications

Earlier in this chapter, we briefly considered three different research areas related to spatial cognition: similarity spaces, mental imagery, and cognitive maps. For each of these areas, it was argued that there existed a tension between behavioral regularities and representational properties. For example, consider the relationship between similarity judgments (which are strongly related to the distance judgments used in the current study) and representational proposals. In the beginning, similarity judgments were assumed to obey the metric properties of space, and as a result researchers proposed that these judgments were mediated by a metric spatial representation (Romney et al., 1972; Shepard et al., 1972). However, later research revealed that the judgments that subjects made were not always metric. What were the representational implications due to these behavioral observations?

One alternative was to completely abandon metric spatial representations, and to adopt representations that were less structured. For example, some researchers replaced the similarity space with a proposal in which concepts were represented as sets of features, and nonmetric behavioral regularities emerged from the procedures used to compare feature sets (Malgady & Johnson, 1976; Ortony, 1979; Tversky, 1977; Tversky & Gati, 1982). This approach has the advantage of being able to account for nonmetric behavioral regularities. However, it has disadvantages as well. The ability to fit nonmetric behavior emerges from manipulating constants in feature comparison equations. These constants provide additional degrees of freedom that must be fit from study to study to predict human judgments. Because of these additional degrees of freedom, this kind of theory is less powerful – less constrained – than the similarity space that it replaced (Pylyshyn, 1984).

A second alternative was to modify the similarity space proposal in such a way that this metric space could mediate nonmetric behaviors. For instance, Krumhansl (1978, 1982) modified the similarity space by including new rules that measured the density of points in the space, where density reflected the number of neighbors that were close to a point in the space. Krumhansl included density calculations in addition to distance in the rules that were used to compare different points in the space. The inclusion of density permitted nonmetric judgments to emerge from the space. This approach has the advantage of maintaining some of the attractive properties of the similarity space. However, the density calculations also introduce new degrees of freedom that reduce the explanatory power of theory.

A third example is provided by the synthetic approach taken by Dawson, Boechler, and Valsangkar-Smyth (2000). A model based on relatively simple building blocks, with few underlying representational hypotheses, was trained to generate metric spatial judgments. Once the model had been synthesized, they took great pains to analyze its internal structure. The result was the discovery of a particular kind of representation – allocentric coarse coding – that would not have been an obvious proposal had our starting point been the analysis of behavior. A second study demonstrated that this kind of representation was also capable of mediating spatial judgments that violated the minimality principle of metric space. In other words, the synthetic approach utilized by Dawson, Boechler, and Valsangkar-Smyth (2000) has shown how a connectionist representation can account for both metric and nonmetric regularities.

8.4 Summary and Conclusions

In Chapters 6 and 7, the synthetic approach was illustrated with examples that used robots, toy and otherwise. Much of this research, which is now known as behavior-based robotics and embodied cognitive science, is aimed at challenging the assumption that cognition and intelligence is based upon mental representations. While it is of considerable interest that many complicated behaviors can be produced by systems that only exploit visuomotor reflexes, many domains of cognitive science and psychology are still likely to need to appeal to representations. One question addressed in this chapter was whether the synthetic approach could be employed in a fashion that still permitted representations to be explored.

It was argued in this chapter that PDP models offered one plausible method for conducting psychological research that was both synthetic and representational. The synthetic component of this kind of research involves using components defined by a connectionist architecture to construct a network capable of solving some problem of interest. Once the network has been constructed, its internal structure is analyzed in detail. The purpose of this analysis is to discover the regularities in the training patterns that are used by the network to solve the problem, as well as the manner in which these regularities are represented in the network's connections. Once this analysis is complete, it is expected that the discovered regularities and representations will lead to unexpected insights into the problem. In other words, in a connectionist synthetic psychology emergence will follow analysis.

This chapter also presented one case study in synthetic psychology, the spatial judgment network of Dawson, Boechler, and Valsangkar-Smyth (2000). One reason for choosing this example was to show that fairly simple components could be used to construct a system capable of performing a task of psychological interest. A second reason was to illustrate an instance of "representational emergence." When the spatial judgment network was originally created, the only general issue in mind was building a PDP system that could respond as if it had internalized a spatial map. We were interested in identifying how such a map was internalized, but had no pet theory about its structure. At the end of the analysis, when we had identified the coarse allocentric coding in the hidden units, we found that we had something to say about spatial representation in the hippocampus and about the ability to generate judgments that were nonmetric.

These insights were surprising to us, and demonstrate some of the power that can emerge from adopting a synthetic paradigm.

We have now come to the end of the first phase of this book. We have discussed different types of models, and have contrasted analytic and synthetic approaches. We have ended with a case study that shows how connectionism can contribute to synthetic psychology. In the remaining chapters, we will step back a bit and consider some of the basic properties of connectionism as an example medium in which synthetic psychology can be conducted. In Chapters 9, 10, and 11 we consider three different "building blocks" for this enterprise, and show how these building blocks can be used to create networks of interest to psychologists. In Chapter 12, we consider in detail three different approaches that can be used to analyze the representations that can be discovered in networks built from these general components.

Chapter nine

Building Associations

The first part of this book developed an argument that synthetic psychology was one approach that could be fruitfully explored in the study of mind. In very general terms, the aim of synthetic psychology is to build mental phenomena from the bottom up. A synthetic psychologist could proceed by proposing some basic "building blocks" to be used, and then by seeing what kinds of interesting and surprising phenomena could be created when these basic components are combined. Some researchers have argued that the synthetic approach promises to provide theories of mental phenomena that are simpler than those that can be produced by applying more traditional analytic methodologies.

The purpose of the current chapter is to begin our exploration of synthetic psychology by examining a proposal for a set of "building blocks." In this chapter, we will describe one key building block for connectionist models: the storing of an association between two patterns by modifying a set of connection weights. We will see that a memory system that is created from this key component has some interesting properties. But we will also see that there are many stimulus–response pairings that cannot be encoded in this kind of system. As a result, additional building blocks must be proposed. These additional building blocks will be introduced in Chapters 10 and 11.

This chapter proceeds as follows. First, it presents a brief historical overview of associationism. This culminates in an account of William James's theory of association, which is used to motivate a more modern account of associative mechanisms. Second, it introduces this modern account by describing the properties of a particular connectionist network, called a distributed associative memory. This account defines the properties of processing units, modifiable connections, and the general operations used to train the network and to retrieve associations that have been stored in it. Third, the chapter describes a particular learning rule for this type of connectionist network, the Hebb rule. Mathematical analyses and the results of computer simulations are used to show the advantages and disadvantages of this learning rule. Fourth, a second training procedure, the delta rule, is defined in an attempt to overcome some of the problems that were uncovered with Hebb-style learning. The chapter ends with some brief reflections about how one might use a computer simulation of a distributed associative memory to explore some issues that have arisen in the modern study of association and learning.

9.1   From Associationism to Connectionism

In 1921, Howard Warren published *A History of the Association Psychology*, which traced associationism from Aristotle's (384–322 BC) reflections on memory to the psychological theories proposed by Herbert Spencer and George Henry Lewes in the 1870s. As far as Warren was concerned, association psychology in its most focused form ended at this time: "The association psychology culminated with Bain, Spencer, and Lewes. The evolution doctrine of the two last writers affords a wider scope to the play of association; but at the same time it opens the door to other factors, which have tended to lessen the importance of association in the eyes of the empirical investigator" (Warren, 1921, p. 16). Accordingly, Warren organized his history by considering four different periods of thought that ended with the work of a select group of nineteenth-century thinkers.

In this section of the chapter, I will provide a highly selective history of associationism, and I will organize this history by adopting Warren's (1921) method of considering different periods of thought. However, we will be parting company with Warren in two important ways. First, we will consider some aspects of associationism that persisted beyond the era of Bain. In particular, we will examine the associationism of William James, a psychologist whose contributions are only briefly considered by Warren. Second, we will use James's thoughts about associationism as a springboard to very modern associationist models in cognitive science. In particular, we will see that James laid the foundation for a particular type of connectionist model, called a *distributed associative memory*. Contrary to what Warren's history implies, associationism has survived, and even flourished, into the new millennium.

9.1.1   Philosophical considerations

A very long line of philosophers and psychologists are responsible for the development of associationism. They studied associations empirically, through introspection. One of the main observations that introspection revealed was that there existed sequences of thought that were experienced during thinking. Associationism grew out of the attempt to provide lawful accounts of these sequences of thought.

9.1.1.1 Aristotelian contributions

The earliest detailed introspective account of such sequences of thought can be found in the writings of Aristotle. In his short essay *De memoria et reminiscentia*, Aristotle provided an account of memory that "is fuller than that to be found in the best-known British empiricists" (Sorabji, 1972, p. 1). In the early part of this essay, Aristotle argued that the contents of memory are essentially visual images that resemble the things being memorized.

> For it is clear that one must think of the affection, which is produced by means of perception in the soul and in that part of the body which contains the soul, as being like a sort of picture, the having of which we say is memory. For the change that occurs marks in a sort of imprint, as it were, of the sense-image, as people do who seal things with signet rings.
>
> *(Sorabji, 1972, p. 50)*

Later in the essay, Aristotle turned to the process of recollecting thoughts that have been remembered. His account of recollection has all of the elements of associationism from the nineteenth century. He focused upon the sequence of thought: "Acts of recollection happen because one change is of a nature to occur after another" (Sorabji, 1972, p. 54). A particular sequence of images occurs because either this sequence is a natural consequence of the images, or because (through repetition) the sequence has been learned by habit. Recall of a particular memory, then, is achieved by cuing that memory with the appropriate prior images. "Whenever we recollect, then, we undergo one of the earlier changes, until we undergo the one after which the change in question habitually occurs" (p. 54).

For Aristotle, recollection by initiating a sequence of mental images was not a haphazard process. The first image in the sequence could be selected in such a way that the desired image would be recollected fairly easily, by taking advantage of possible relationships between the starting image and the image to be recalled. Aristotle considered three different kinds of relationships between the starting image and its successor: similarity, opposition, and (temporal) contiguity: "And this is exactly why we hunt for the successor, starting in our thoughts from the present or from something else, and from something similar, or opposite, or neighboring. By this means recollection occurs" (Sorabji, 1972, p. 54).

In Aristotle's account of recollection, we see three characteristics that recur in all the later theories that defined association psychology. First, there is the (introspective) observation that thought occurs in sequences. Second, there is a claim about the nature of the mental entities that make up this sequence (e.g., mental images). Third, there is a claim about lawful relationships between these entities, such that when one comes to mind, this relationship will lead to the recollection of the next component of the sequence. These relationships are generally considered to be laws of association, and Aristotle's proposal of three such laws (which in later theories would be called the law of similarity, the law of contrast, and the law of contiguity or the law of habit) is completely consistent with proposals made centuries later.

Later researchers accepted the main points of Aristotle's associationism with only minor qualifications. For instance James (1890, p. 594) wrote, "Aristotle seems to have caught both the facts and the principle of explanation; but he did not expand his views." However, Aristotle's observations on memory were essentially ignored (perhaps because they were not understood – see (Warren, 1921, p. 28) – for many centuries. Advances in associationism did not occur until the seventeenth century.

9.1.1.2   Seventeenth-century associationism in philosophy

One prominent feature of Aristotle's treatment of associationism was that he only applied the laws of association to one domain of experience, that of memory. This feature was preserved through the middle ages. "The many commentators on Aristotle during the middle ages took up the passage on recollection which has been quoted. They discussed and amplified it, as they did every saying of the master, but without throwing any new light on association" (Warren, 1921, p. 30). One reason for this very long period of dormancy was the fact that departures from Aristotle were akin to heresy: "Any freshness or originality was frowned upon; the only advances came from new interpretations – and these too often were misinterpretations" (p. 30).

This situation began to change in the seventeenth century with the philosophical writings of Thomas Hobbes (1588–1679). Hobbes was particularly important for setting the stage to broaden the import of association, by applying it to thought processes in general, and not just to memory. He presented three separate themes that permeated the writings of those that followed him. First, he distinguished sense (or sensations) from memory; memory was viewed as mental images of what was sensed. Second, he noted that images are experienced in succession, and argued for the need to explain this succession. Third, he attempted to use principles of association to explain sequences of thought.

Hobbes's work on this third issue was not particularly successful, but his work inspired later philosophers who had greater success than he did. "The British thinkers who followed him developed their systems of psychology along the lines that he marked out; the notion of association, which he did little more than outline, became more and more prominent as the analysis was perfected" (Warren, 1921, p. 33).

The most important philosopher who followed Hobbes in this era was John Locke (1632–1704). Locke coined the phrase "association of ideas," which first appeared as a chapter title in the fourth edition (1700) of *An Essay Concerning Human Understanding*. Locke's fame as a philosopher came late in his life; the first edition of this book was published in 1690 when he was 57 years old. However, his fame and influence was long lasting, and his chapter on association launched British empiricism.

Locke's work was a reaction against the nativism espoused in the philosophy of Descartes, and was primarily concerned with establishing experience as the foundation of all thought. Following Hobbes, Locke distinguished between ideas of sensation and ideas of reflection. He was particularly interested in the composition of simple ideas into more complex ideas, as well as the sequence of appearance of ideas. One reason for this interest was because these connections (from simple to complex, or from one idea to the next in a sequence) did not seem necessarily to reflect a natural order. Instead, Locke realized that these connections were due to experience.

> There is another connexion of ideas wholly owing to chance or custom: ideas that in themselves are not at all of kin, come to be so united in some men's minds that it is very hard to separate them, they always keep in company, and the one no sooner at any time comes into the understanding but its associate appears with it; and if they are more than two that are thus united, the whole gang, always inseparable, show themselves together.
>
> *(Locke, 1977, p. 219)*

Interestingly, while Locke anticipated the law of frequency that was later endorsed by J. S. Mill, and alluded to association by contiguity and by similarity, he did not explore specific associative laws. One reason for this may be that his primary goal was to argue for the existence of ideas formed by association; this was more important to him than an analysis of associative mechanisms. A second reason may be because Locke was not in a position to offer any strong arguments in favor of any particular causal process underlying association. After describing association as being responsible for a keyboard player retrieving a long sequence of finger movements during a performance, Locke noted "whether the natural cause of these ideas, as well as that regular dancing of his fingers, be the motion of his animal spirits, I will not determine, how probable soever, by this instance, it appears to be so" (Locke, 1977, p. 220).

It is clear that the primary result of seventeenth-century philosophy's analysis of association was to renew scholarly interest in this topic, and to set the stage for more technical advances that would come later. Issues that were pioneered by Aristotle once again became central concerns to philosophers, and did so in a context that permitted Aristotle's views to be criticized and modified.

9.1.1.3   Eighteenth-century philosophy and associationism

Locke's immediate philosophical successor was the Bishop of Cloyne, George Berkeley (1685–1753). Berkeley was primarily important for transforming the problem of knowledge from one that was essentially philosophical to one that was more consistent with the strong psychological overtones that marked theories of association that developed later. Like Hobbes and Locke, Berkeley divided mental content into ideas of sensation and into ideas of imagination, and was primarily interested in accounting for the natural succession of ideas. He reiterated Aristotle's law of contiguity, and extended it to account for associations involving different modes of sensation. "From a frequently perceived connection, the immediate perception of ideas by one sense suggests to the mind others, perhaps belonging to another sense, which are wont to be connected with them" (Warren, 1921, p. 41). In other words, Berkeley – unlike Locke – was one of the first philosophers after Aristotle to develop an account of "modes of association," which described the laws that determined how associations came to be.

A more detailed and elaborate theory of modes of association was to be found in the work of philosopher David Hume (1711–76). Hume, like his predecessors, began by dividing experience into impressions and ideas, and viewed the latter as being weaker or less vivid copies of the former. He then turned to consider principles that explained the connection between successive ideas.

In his original treatment, Hume, who was likely unaware of similar ideas put forth by Aristotle, proposed three different laws of association: resemblance, contiguity in time or place, and cause or effect. "That these principles serve to connect ideas will not, I believe, be much doubted. A picture naturally leads our thoughts to the original; the mention of one apartment in a building naturally introduces an enquiry or discourse concerning the others; and if we think of a wound, we can scarcely forbear reflecting on the pain which follows it" (Hume, 1952, p. 23). Later, Hume argued that association by cause or effect could not be distinguished from association by contiguity, and thus settled on two associative laws: contiguity and resemblance (or similarity).

Hume's work on association was monumentally influential, but did have one shortcoming, in that Hume did not attempt to use his laws of association to account for all mental phenomena. This was not attempted until the treatment of association offered by David Hartley (1705–57). Hartley was not only able to show the broader implications of Hume's theory, but also provided one of the earliest examples of an attempt to root association in terms of brain function. Hartley constructed a theory of vibrations that attempted to draw a close correspondence between mental associations and neural activity. He saw contiguity as the primary source of associations, and ignored Hume's law of resemblance. He also anticipated the associationism of J. S. Mill by recognizing repetition as a source of association, or at least as a factor that could affect the strength of an association.

9.1.1.4   Nineteenth-century philosophy and associationism

The nineteenth century marked a period in which associationism evolved from a topic that was primarily philosophical into one that was predominately psychological. In 1829, James Mill (1773–1836) published his *Analysis of the Phenomena of the Human Mind*. The third chapter of this psychological text was on associationism. Many of the ideas put forth in this chapter were familiar: Mill divided mentality into sensations and ideas, where ideas were once again proposed as being copies or traces of sensations. Mill observed that sensations occur either simultaneously or in successive order, and that ideas presented themselves in the same sequence as did the sensations that they copied. His associationism, like those of the philosophers that we have already discussed, attempted to account for the succession of ideas.

The nineteenth century was also an era in which writers assumed the fundamental notions of associationism as a given, and turned to fleshing out the details. For Mill, the only law of association was contiguity. He explicitly denied Hume's laws of cause or effect and resemblance. Mill also emphasized the importance of individual associations varying in strength. For Mill, association was essentially a mechanical process by which complex ideas were created by associating simpler ideas together. Because of his mechanical metaphor, emergence played no role in Mill's associationism. For Mill, a complex idea was no more than the sum of its components, and if one understood these, then one should be able to completely understand the larger idea that they comprised.

Mill's ideas were challenged and modified by his son, John Stuart Mill (1806–73). John Stuart Mill argued that ideas were indistinguishable from sensations, and were not just less vivid copies. He then posited a completely different set of associative laws, which included a reintroduction of Hume's law of similarity:

> The first is that similar ideas tend to excite one another. The second is that when two impressions have been frequently experienced (or even though of) either simultaneously or in immediate succession, then whenever one of these impressions or the idea of it recurs, it tends to excite the idea of the other. The third law is that greater intensity in either or both of the impressions is equivalent, in rendering them excitable by one another, to a greater frequency of conjunction.
>
> *(Warren, 1921, p. 96)*

One of John Stuart Mill's most interesting departures from his father's associationism was replacing a mechanistic account of complex ideas with an account that was described as a "mental chemistry." In this mental chemistry, when complex ideas were created via association, the resulting whole was more than just the sum of its parts. As a result, the laws governing the whole (e.g., successions to other ideas) could not be predicted by knowing the laws governing the simpler ideas that served as parts. In other words, John Stuart Mill proposed an associationism that endorsed an early form of emergence.

The associationism of Alexander Bain (1818–1903) is, in many respects, a refinement of John Stuart Mill's. Bain invoked four different laws of association, and attempted to reduce all intellectual processes to these laws. One of these laws was the law of contiguity, which has been present in every theory of association that we have reviewed. A second was the law of similarity, which was revived from Hume by both Bain and J. S. Mill after being banished by James

Mill. The third was the law of compound association: "Past actions, sensations, thoughts, or emotions are recalled more easily, either through contiguity or similarity, with *more than one* present object or impression" (Warren, 1921, pp. 107–8). This law was an important precursor to William James's treatment of associations between patterns, which we will consider in more detail shortly. The fourth was the law of constructive imagination: "By means of association the mind has the power to form new combinations or aggregates, different from any that have been presented to it in the course of experience" (p. 109). This law represents an important psychological contribution of Bain, in that he was attempting to explain creative thought in terms of associative principles.

9.1.2   Psychology, associationism, and connectionism

Bain represents a bridge between philosophical and psychological treatments of association. He stood "exactly at a corner in the development of psychology, with philosophical psychology stretching out behind, and experimental physiological psychology lying ahead in a new direction. The psychologists of the twentieth century can read much of Bain with hearty approval; perhaps John Locke could have done the same" (Boring, 1950, p. 240). In this section, we will consider some of the key developments of the psychological associationism that was inspired by Bain's work. However, this review will be extremely selective, because we will use it to motivate a discussion of a very particular kind of connectionist network.

9.1.2.1   Nineteenth-century contributions of William James

The pioneer of the "New Psychology" in North America was William James (1842–1910). James created the first demonstrational psychology laboratory in North America, and in 1890 published a profoundly influential psychology text in two volumes, *The Principles of Psychology*. "The key to his influence lies . . . in his personality, his clarity of vision, and his remarkable felicity in literary style" (Boring, 1950, p. 509).

James's treatment of association is found in Chapter 14 of *The Principles Of Psychology*. He was in particular concerned about the fact that philosophical associationism had not made any serious proposals concerning the causal mechanisms that instantiated modes of association. For example, he offers the following assessment of Bain: "His pages are painstaking and instructive from a descriptive point of view; though, after my own attempt to deal with the subject causally, I can hardly award to them any profound *explanatory* value" (James, 1890, p. 601).

James was of the opinion that explanatory accounts had eluded previous associationists because of a fatal flaw in their approach. This flaw was the assumption that associations were made between mental contents (e.g., the images, reflections, or ideas that had been proposed by most of James's predecessors as being copies or traces of sensations). James argued that if association was a mechanical process, then it must apply to objects and not ideas; he then proposed a particularly psychological theory by arguing that the objects being associated were brain states:

> *Association*, so far as the word stands for an *effect, is between* THINGS THOUGHT OF – *it is* THINGS, *not ideas, which are associated in the mind.* We ought to talk of the association of *objects*, not of the association of *ideas.* And so far as association stands for a *cause*, it is between *processes in the brain* – it is these which, by being associated in certain ways, determine what successive objects shall be thought.
>
> *(James, 1890, p. 554)*

In terms of viewing association as an effect, James's theory was not a radical departure from others that we have considered in this chapter. First, he was primarily concerned with providing an account of the succession of thoughts. Second, his theory attempted to explain this succession via associative law. For James, the only explanatory mode of association was contiguity, which he called the law of habit. While he admitted that other factors could be described as affecting association (similarity, vividness, recency, emotional congruity), he attempted to show how all of these could be explained in terms of contiguity.

James was able to reduce other laws of association to the law of contiguity when he departed from the traditional view of association as an effect, and replaced it with the view of association as a cause. There are several central elements to his physiological account of association. First, James recognized that one idea or event could be represented in the brain as a pattern of activity across a set of more than one neuron. Second, he expressed his law of habit in terms of a process that affected the ease of transit of a nerve-current through a tract: "The psychological law of objects thought of through their previous contiguity in thought or experience would thus be an effect, within the mind, of the physical fact that nerve-currents propagate themselves easiest through those tracts of conduction which have been already most in use" (James, 1890, p. 563). Third, he viewed the succession of thoughts that one experiences as due to the fact that activity in one brain state (i.e., some set of neurons) leads to activity in some different brain state that had previously been associated with the first. "When two elementary brain-processes have been active together or in immediate succession, one of them, on reoccurring, tends to propagate its excitement into the other" (p. 566). Finally, James was predominately concerned with predicting which subsequent brain state would be activated by a prior brain state, given that one idea might be associated with a number of different ideas, other at different times or in different ways. James attempted to explain this kind of variation by realizing that any given neuron would be receiving signals from a number of other neurons, and that its degree of activation would depend on an entire pattern of input, and not upon an association with a single incoming signal.

The amount of activity at any given point in the brain-cortex is the sum of the tendencies of all other points to discharge into it, such tendencies being proportionate (1) to the number of times the excitement of each other point may have accompanied that of the point in question; (2) to the intensity of such excitements; and (3) to the absence of any rival point functionally disconnected with the first point, into which the discharges might be diverted.

(James, 1890, p. 567)

The main physiological points of James's theory of association are summarized in Figure 9.1, which is analogous to his own Figure 40 in his chapter on association (James, 1890, p. 570). The figure represents two ideas, one (A) being the last act of a dinner party, the other (B) being walking home through the frosty night. Each of these ideas is represented in the brain as a pattern of activity in a set of neurons. A is represented by activity in neurons a, b, c, d, and e; B is represented by neurons l, m, n, o, and p. The association is made between A and B because A preceded B in the course of an evening. As a result, the neurons representing A were active immediately prior to the activity of the neurons representing B, and the tracts connecting the neurons (represented as the lines in Figure 9.1) were modified according to the law of habit. The ability of A's later activity to lead to the thought of B, is due to these modified connections between the two sets of neurons.

The thought of A must awaken that of B, because a, b, c, d, e, will each and all discharge into l through the paths by which their original discharge took place. Similarly they will discharge into m, n, o, and p; and these latter tracts will also each reinforce the other's action because, in the experience B, they have already vibrated in unison.

(James, 1890, p. 569)

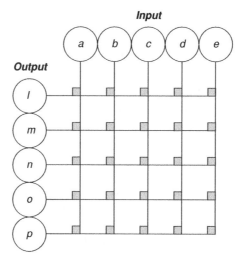

Figure 9.1   An associative memory in the spirit of James

9.1.2.2 The paired associate task

The type of association envisioned by James, and illustrated in Figure 9.1, leads to one methodological topic that will be central to the simulations that will be introduced later in the chapter. In James's example, associative memory is viewed as having two different functional stages. The first is learning, in which an association between two ideas is stored. As we saw in the previous subsection, this occurs when two ideas (an input pattern and an output pattern) occur either simultaneously or in close succession to one another. As a result of this co-occurrence, the connections between the neurons representing both patterns are modified to permit easier transmission of "nerve-currents." The second stage is recall. During this stage, only one of the two previous ideas is presented as input. When its underlying neural processes become active, they serve to activate those associated with the other idea (output), bringing it to mind.

This two-stage account of association was used to develop a particular paradigm used to study human memory, called the paired associate task. This method of examining memory presents stimuli in a fashion similar to what would be the case if someone were learning the vocabulary of a foreign language (Kintsch, 1970). Subjects learn a list of stimulus–response pairs. Sometimes this was learned via the "study–test method." With this method, subjects are presented with both members of the pair at the same time, and attempt to remember the association between the two. In the test phase of this method, subjects are only presented the stimulus, and must attempt to recall the associated response on their own. The paired-associate learning task was used with great success to study the issue of whether learning was all-or-none or was instead due to an increment in continuously varying response strength.

Mary Whiton Calkins (1863–1930) was among the first generation of women to enter psychology (Furumoto, 1980). In 1896, she published a paper in *Psychological Review* that provided the first description of the paired associate task. There is no doubt that she was inspired to invent this technique by considering ways in which James's theory of association could be put to the test in an experimental laboratory.

9.1.2.3 Twentieth-century models of distributed memory

After the cognitive revolution in the second half of the twentieth century, many researchers turned to using computer simulations to study human memory processes. In this subsection of the chapter, we will be interested in simulations that share two general characteristics. First, they are designed to perform the paired associate task, and are generally trained using some variation of the study–test method. Second, they are closely related to the kind of associative memory envisaged by James, and which was illustrated in Figure 9.1.

Some of the earliest research on parallel systems was concerned with the development of distributed memories capable of learning associations between pairs of input patterns (e.g., Steinbuch, 1961; Taylor, 1956), or of learning to associate an input pattern with a categorizing response (e.g., Rosenblatt, 1962; Selfridge, 1956; Widrow & Hoff, 1960). The basic structure of this kind of connectionist network, which has come to be called the *standard pattern associator* (McClelland, 1986), is essentially identical to James's memory that was illustrated in Figure 9.1.

As will be detailed below, the standard pattern associator is constructed from the processing units and modifiable connections defined in the PDP architecture. It consists of two sets of processing units; one is typically called the input set, the other the output set (see Figure 9.1). During a learning stage, the activation states of the input processing units are used to represent a cue pattern and the activation states of the output processing units are used to represent a to-be-recalled pattern. The connection weights are then modified to store the association between the two patterns. The standard pattern associator is called a distributed memory because this association is stored throughout all the connections in the network, and because one set of connections can store several different associations. During the recall stage, a cue pattern is presented to the network by activating the input units. This causes signals to be sent through the connections in the network. These signals, in accord with James's theory, activate the output processors. If the memory is functioning properly, then the pattern of activation in the output units will be the pattern that was originally associated with the cue pattern.

9.2   Building an Associative Memory

Up to this point in the chapter, we have reviewed a history of associationism that has culminated in the standard pattern associator. The remainder of this chapter is intended to provide a technical account of this kind of memory system.

9.2.1   Defining the problem

The purpose of the computer simulation is to build a memory system that is capable of storing associations between pairs of items. During a learning phase, the system will be presented with pairs of stimuli. For each pair, it will determine how they are to be associated together, and store this association in memory. During a recall phase, the system will be presented with only one member of a pair. Using this member as a cue, it will use its memory to attempt to recall the other member of the pair to the best of its ability. In order to create a system that will behave in this fashion, we will construct a very simple connectionist network. The network will consist of an input "bank" of processing units, an output bank of processing units, and a set of modifiable connections between these two banks. The basic design of the network was illustrated in Figure 9.1. As we will see, several independent associations can be stored in the same set of connection weights.

9.2.2 The network architecture

9.2.2.1 Processing units

Ultimately, both the input units and the output units can be considered as sets of numbers, with each number representing a property of an individual unit (e.g., its internal level of activity), and with the entire set of numbers representing a pattern across a whole bank of units (e.g., the pattern of activity of the bank of input units). It will be useful to represent these sets of numbers as vectors, because linear algebra provides an extremely compact and useful notation for exploring the properties of distributed associative memories and of other connectionist networks.

For example, we might represent the activity of input unit 1 with the numerical value a_1, the activity of input unit 2 with the numerical value a_2, and so on. The set of activities for all of the input units could be represented as the vector a, whose first entry would be the value a_1, whose second entry would be the value a_2, and so on. By convention, when we talk about the vector a we will assume that it is a column vector. This means that when all of the values of the vector are listed out, they are strung out vertically in a column, as is shown in Figure 9.2. In some cases, the operations of linear algebra assume that a vector is a row vector, which means that when its values are listed out, they are strung out horizontally in a row, as is also shown in Figure 9.3. The operation that converts a column vector into a row vector is called transposition. Because of this, if we were to indicate that a vector was a row vector, then we would do so with a notation that included a superscript "T" to explicitly indicate that the vector had been transposed. For instance, if vector a is a column vector of unit activities, then vector a^T would be a row vector of the same numerical activities.

In order to represent the properties of banks of units as vectors, we need to define some equations that dictate what numerical values should be inserted into the vectors. Any processing unit in a connectionist network can be described using three different mathematical equations. The first equation is the net input function, which describes how a processing unit computes the total signal coming into it from other processors in the network. The second equation is the

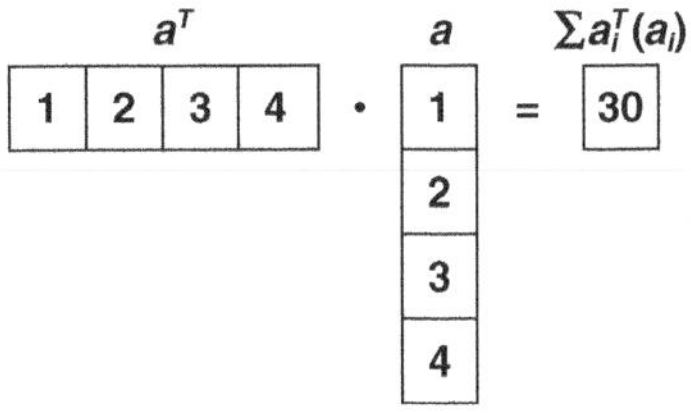

Figure 9.2 The inner product (see Equation 9.5) of the row vector a^T and the column vector a is a single number, which is the sum of the products of the entries of the two vectors

(a)

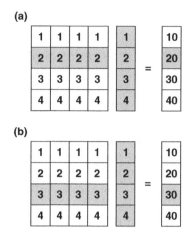

(b)

Figure 9.3 Recall as the premultiplication of a column vector by a matrix. (a) The second entry of the recall vector is the inner product of the second row of the matrix with the vector (see grey); (b) Similar logic defines the third entry of the recall vector

activation function, which determines how a processing unit converts this input signal into a number that represents its internal level of activity. The third equation is the output function, which defines how a processor's internal level of activity is converted into a numerical signal that can be sent through connections to other processors in the network. When these three equations are used to describe the processors used in our memory network, it will become apparent that they are particularly simple.

In the distributed associative memory network that we are constructing, the activity values of the input units are always set by the programmer, who simply turns each input unit on to the desired level of activity (i.e., the level of activity that represents information about one member of the to-be-associated pairs of patterns). For the sake of consistency with later chapters, we will describe this in terms of a net input function. Specifically, the net input for input unit i (net_i) is equal to the environmental stimulation for that input unit (e_i):

$$net_i = e_i \qquad [9.1]$$

The input processors in the distributed associative memory are particularly simple because after their net input is computed, its value is used as the value of the processor's internal activity and as the value that the processor outputs to the output units. Mathematically speaking, the activation function and the output function for the input units are both identity functions. That is, the internal activity of input unit i (a_i) is defined as:

$$a_i = net_i \qquad [9.2]$$

Similarly, the activity that input unit i sends to other units (o_i) is defined as:

$$o_i = a_i \qquad [9.3]$$

During the learning phase, the output units are treated exactly as are the input units. That is, the programmer sets their activity values to represent the other member of the to-be-associated pair. Because of this, during learning, the output units can be described using exactly the same equations that were used to describe the input units (i.e., Equations 9.1, 9.2, and 9.3). During the recall phase, the output units have their net input determined by signals that are sent from the input units, and therefore require a slightly more elaborate net input equation.

Imagine a very simple network in which there are eight different input units, and only one output unit. Each of the input units is linked to the output unit by a connection. Each connection is weighted, where a connection weight is simply some numerical value. When a numerical signal is sent through a connection, the connection scales the signal by multiplying it by the value of its connection weight. Let us represent the weight of the connection between input unit 1 and the output unit as w_1, between input unit 2 and the output unit as w_2, and so on. During recall in this simple network, each of the input units will be sending a signal to the output unit. Input unit 1 will be sending the signal o_1, input unit 2 will be sending the signal o_2, and so on. The signal o_1 will be multiplied by the weight value w_1 before it reaches the output unit. So part of the signal that reaches the output unit will be the value $o_1 w_1$. Following the same logic for the other input units, the output unit will also be receiving the signal $o_2 w_2$, $o_3 w_3$, and so on. In other words, the total signal for the output unit – its net input – will be:

$$net_1 = o_1 w_1 + o_2 w_2 + o_3 w_3 + \ldots + o_8 w_8 = \Sigma o_i w_i \qquad [9.4]$$

Linear algebra can be used to make this equation more compact. (For an excellent introduction to linear algebra that is framed in the context of connectionist networks, the reader is referred to Jordan, 1986.) Let us take the signals being output by the input units and represent them as the row vector o, and let us take the set of connection weights between the input units and the output units and represent them as the column vector w. These two vectors can be combined using an operation called the inner product or the dot product (see Figure 9.2). The result of this operation is a single number (net_1, representing the net input for output unit 1) whose value is defined in Equation 9.4 – in fact, Equation 9.4 shows how an inner product is to be computed. In the notation of linear algebra, the inner product that defines the net input for the output unit is:

$$net_1 = o^T \bullet w \qquad [9.5]$$

One way to remember that the result of an inner product like Equation 9.5 is a single number is to note the number of rows in the first component (o^T is a row vector, and therefore has only one row) and to note the number of columns in the second component (w is a column vector, and therefore has only one column). The result of the operation will have the same number of rows as the first component, and the same number of columns as the second component. In other words, the result of an inner product will be a single number – a vector with only one row and only one column.

The inner product described in Equation 9.5 defines the net input for a single output unit. We will see in later chapters that the inner product is a standard net input function for all of the processors in more sophisticated connectionist networks.

9.2.2.2 Modifiable connections

In the previous subsection, when we defined the net input function for a single output unit during recall, we represented the set of connection weights from a bank of input units to the output unit as a vector. Our goal in designing the distributive associative memory is to have a system that uses more than one output unit, so that it can recall a complete pattern of activity. It stands to reason that we would need to represent the connection weights for this more complicated memory with a set of weight vectors, with each vector in the set holding the connection weights associated with one of the output units.

In linear algebra, this set of vectors would be represented as a single entity called a matrix. If our memory had n input units, and m output units, then all of the connection weights between the input and output processors would be represented by one weight matrix, W, which would have n rows and m columns. Each entry in this matrix, w_{ij}, would contain a number representing the weight of the connection from input unit i to output unit j.

By representing all of the connection weights with the matrix W, we can take advantage of linear algebra to create a very compact mathematical description of how weights are modified, and we can also define very simple equations that describe how information stored in this matrix can be retrieved when the memory system is presented with a cue. When the distributed associative memory stores associations between patterns, it does so by modifying the strengths of its connection weights. This is done in two steps.

First, the memory computes changes in weights that are required to represent the association between the pair of patterns presented to it during a learning trial. Later in this chapter we will discuss two different equations that could be used to compute the desired weight changes. In this first step, all of the desired weight changes are stored in the matrix Δ_{t+1}, where the subscript $t+1$ indicates the learning trial during which the changes have been computed. This matrix has the same number of rows and columns as does matrix W, and each entry δ_{ij} in this matrix represents the value by which the connection weight between input unit i and output unit j should be changed.

Table 9.1 Associative learning described as a series of matrix additions

Trial ($t + 1$)	Equation describing weight values
0	$W_0 = 0$
1	$W_1 = W_0 + \Delta_1 = 0 + \Delta_1 = \Delta_1$
2	$W_2 = W_1 + \Delta_2 = (\Delta_1) + \Delta_2$
3	$W_3 = W_2 + \Delta_3 = (\Delta_1 + \Delta_2) + \Delta_3$
4	$W_4 = W_3 + \Delta_4 = (\Delta_1 + \Delta_2 + \Delta_3) + \Delta_4$

Second, the memory uses the matrix Δ_{t+1} to change the existing connection weights. Let us use the subscript t to represent the network's connection weights at a particular trial of learning. Using the current weights, represented in the matrix W_t, and the desired weight changes, stored in the matrix Δ_{t+1}, the goal is to compute the new values of weights, which will be stored in the matrix W_{t+1}. This is done by computing the sum of the matrices that represent the current weights and the desired weight changes: $W_{t+1} = W_t + \Delta_{t+1}$. Every value w_{ij} at row i and column j of the new weight matrix is simply equal to the sum of the value w_{ij} in matrix W_t and of the value δ_{ij} in matrix Δ_{t+1}.

With this notation, learning can be described as a series of matrix additions. Imagine that prior to learning, our memory system is truly a "blank slate," because all of its connection weights are equal to zero. The null matrix, **0**, is the special matrix that has every value in it equal to zero. So at time 0, before learning as started, we could declare that $W_0 = \mathbf{0}$. At learning trial 1, the new weights (W_1) are equal to the old weights (the null matrix) plus the desired weight changes (Δ_1). At learning trial 2, the new weights (W_2) are equal to the old weights (W_1) plus the desired weight changes (Δ_2). As can be seen from Table 9.1, this kind of learning can continue for as many trials as is desired. Furthermore, Table 9.1 demonstrates that at any point in time after learning has begun, the memory's connection weights are essentially the sum of a series of matrices each of which contains the weight changes that are desired to store an association between a pair of stimuli.

9.2.2.3 The retrieval operation

Before introducing a specific equation for calculating the association between pairs of stimuli, let us assume that we have a distributed memory that has already undergone some training, and therefore has a pre-existing set of connection weights that are represented in the matrix W. What we would like to do is to present a vector of activity to the input units of this memory that will be used as a cue to retrieve some information, which will also be represented as a vector of activity in the memory's output units. To define this kind of retrieval mathematically, let the column vector c represent the cue pattern, and let the column vector

r represent the recalled pattern. In linear algebra, the equation for recall from the distributed associative memory is:

$$r = Wc \qquad [9.6]$$

In other words, if one takes the matrix of weights that have been produced by learning, and uses this matrix to premultiply the cue pattern's vector, the result will be a column vector that holds the recalled pattern.

For those unfamiliar with linear algebra, let us briefly examine the logic of Equation 9.6. When retrieving information from the distributed associative memory, the input units are activated, and send signals through weighted connections to the output units. The output units use these signals to compute their net input, which is also equal to their activation and to their output, as indicated in Equations 9.2 and 9.3. We saw earlier that the net input for a single output unit was the inner product between a vector of weights and a vector of activities. It stands to reason, then, that in order to compute the net input for several different output units, we will have to compute a series of different inner products.

The notation in Equation 9.6 represents performing a series of inner products. Each entry in the recall vector r is the inner product between the cue vector and one of the rows of the weight matrix. For example, the second entry in r is equal to the inner product between the second row of W and the column vector c (see Figure 9.3a). Similarly, the third entry in r is the inner product between the third row of W and the vector c (see Figure 9.3b). This operation is consistent with the rule of thumb that we introduced earlier when discussing the inner product. The matrix W will have m rows, and the vector c has one column. So, we expect the result of Equation 9.6 to be a vector with m rows and one column – in other words, a column vector of the same size as c.

9.2.2.4   Hebb-style learning

Up to this point, we have described how vectors are used to represent properties of processing units, how matrices are used to represent connection weights, how linear algebra provides a mathematical operation that uses a cue vector to retrieve a recall vector from a matrix of existing weights, and how associative learning can be described in generic terms as a series of sums of matrices. The only remaining piece of information required for a complete description of a distributed associative memory is a specific equation that defines how the desired weight changes are to be computed and stored in the matrix Δ_{t+1}. In this subsection, we will introduce one simple and historically important learning rule, called the Hebb rule. Later in this chapter, we will explore the Hebb rule's advantages and disadvantages, and use its disadvantages to motivate a second learning rule.

Donald Hebb (1904–85) was one of the most influential figures in psychology (Klein, 1999). Hebb's seminal contribution to psychology was his book *The Organization of Behavior: A Neuropsychological Theory* (Hebb, 1949). At the time that this book was published, physiological psychology was in decline because of the popularity of behaviorism. Hebb's book reversed this trend by attempting to explain behavior by appealing to properties of the nervous system. The book "wielded a kind of magic in the years after its appearance. It attracted many brilliant scientists into psychology, made McGill University a North American Mecca for scientists interested in brain mechanisms of behavior, led to many important discoveries, and steered contemporary psychology onto a more fruitful path" (Klein, 1999, p. 2).

One of the central ideas that made Hebb's (1949) work so influential was the notion of a cell assembly. "The general idea is an old one, that any two cells or systems of cells that are repeatedly active at the same time will tend to become 'associated,' so that activity in one facilitates activity in the other" (p. 70). The result of this kind of process is the creation of coordinated systems, or assemblies, of cells that act in sympathy with one another. Activity in one of the cells would lead to activity in the other cells that were part of the assembly. Hebb emphasized the utility of this kind of biological construct for explaining a variety of perceptual and motivational phenomena.

A crucial component of cell assembly theory was an account of how assemblies came into existence. Hebb (1949) is perhaps most famous for his statement of a principle of synaptic change for the creation of cell assemblies: "When an axon of cell A is near enough to excite a cell B and repeatedly or persistently takes part in firing it, some growth process or metabolic change takes place in one or both cells such that A's efficiency, as one of the cells firing B, is increased" (p. 62). Hebb believed that the mechanism underlying the change in the strength of the synapse between the two neurons was an increase in the area of contact between the two, but such hypotheses could not be tested at the time his work was published. Advances in neuroscience have led to a discovery of a phenomenon, called long-term potentiation, that is often cited as a biologically plausible instantiation of Hebb's theory (e.g., Brown, 1990; Martinez & Derrick, 1996).

In the late 1950s, the advent of digital computers enabled researchers to use simulations to explore the advantages and disadvantages of Hebb's (1949) theory of synaptic change. In one famous study, Rochester, Holland, Haibt, and Duda (1956) simulated a network of 69 simple neurons, with each neuron connected to 10 others. Rochester et al. updated connection weights using a modified version of Hebb's proposal. While the general spirit of the proposal was maintained, when weights were updated, they were normalized to prevent them from growing out of bounds. What this meant was that if the strength of one connection were increased, then the strength of other connections would be decreased at the same time. As well, Rochester et al. introduced the notion of "neural fatigue," which meant that one of their simulated neurons was less likely to fire if it had recently been active. After running this simulation, Rochester et al. examined the connection weights that emerged in an attempt to identify whatever cell assemblies had emerged. They found no evidence for the existence of cell assemblies in their simulation, and concluded that Hebb's theory as stated was not sufficient for their production.

Rochester et al. (1956) developed a second simulation using an unpublished modification of Hebb's theory that was proposed by Milner, and which later appeared in *Psychological Review* (Milner, 1957). In Hebb's original theory, and in Rochester et al.'s first simulation, there were no inhibitory connections. All of the connection weights (and all of the neural signals) in the simulation were positive and excitatory. Milner's proposal was to include inhibitory connections in the theory, under the assumption that there would be excitatory connections within a cell assembly, but activity in one cell assembly would tend to decrease activity in other cell assemblies via inhibitory signals. This proposal – endorsed by Hebb in a revision of his original theory (Hebb, 1959) – led to a simulation that did produce evidence of the emergence of cell assemblies.

In modern connectionist simulations, the goal of Hebb-style learning is not specifically to create cell assemblies, but is instead to create associations between patterns of activity, so that later when one pattern of activity is presented, the other pattern will be recalled. In other words, modern Hebb-style learning is one approach to defining "association by contiguity" or "the law of habit." Nevertheless, inhibition is an important component of this type of learning, and is included in a distributed associative memory in two different ways.

First, and consistent with proposals described above, connections between processing units can either be excitatory (i.e., have a positive connection weight) or be inhibitory (i.e., have a negative connection weight). Second, and deviating from research in the 1950s, processing units can themselves be sending a signal that is excitatory (i.e., positive processing unit activity) or inhibitory (i.e., negative processing unit activity). In many respects, these assumptions violate Hebb's attempt to develop a biologically plausible account of behavior. For instance, in the version of the distributed associative memory that we will develop below, at one moment a processing unit (or connection) can be excitatory, but at another moment the same unit (or connection) can be inhibitory. This kind of proposal is biologically implausible (Crick & Asanuma, 1986). However, it leads to a very simple mathematical description of Hebb-style learning, as we will see shortly.

As was noted above, Hebb's (1949) basic idea about learning was that if an input neuron and an output neuron were both active at the same time, then the synapse between them should be strengthened. "The assumption, in brief, is that a growth process accompanying synaptic activity makes the synapse more readily traversed" (p. 60). The logic of this proposal was that with the strengthening of the synapse, in situations in which the input neuron became active, there would be an increased likelihood of the output neuron becoming active as well. This is because the output neuron would receive increased stimulation (via the reinforced synapse) from the input neuron.

In modern variations of Hebb-style learning, particularly those based upon the assumption that processor activity can be either inhibitory or excitatory, the goal of connection weight changes is not to increase the likelihood of activity in an output unit. Rather, the goal is to change the weight in such a way that the relationship between input and output unit activities is enhanced. In other words, if at some learning trial an input unit is in one state x, and the output unit is in some other state y, then the connection weight should be changed so that later if the input unit returns to state x, then its signal through the connection should increase the likelihood of recreating state y in the output unit.

Hebb's (1949) view of learning is an example of enhancing one aspect of this relationship. To place his original proposal in the more modern context of a connectionist network, it was assumed that if an input unit and an output unit were both excited (positive activity), then the weight of the connection between them should be made more excitatory (i.e., more positive). Later, if the input unit exhibits positive activity, this would lead to a more positive signal (the positive activity multiplied by the more excitatory connection weight) being sent to the output unit, which would increase the net input to the output unit, and which would in turn increase the likelihood that the output unit would also exhibit positive activity.

Importantly, connection weights can be changed to enhance other relationships between input and output unit activities. For example, consider the situation where both an input unit and an output unit were inhibited (negative activity). To increase the probability that this pattern would occur later, one would again make the weight of the connection between them more excitatory. Later, if the input unit exhibits negative activity, this would lead to a more negative signal (the negative activity multiplied by the more excitatory connection weight) being sent to the output unit, which would decrease the net input to the output unit. As a result, the output unit would be more likely to assume negative activity. Similarly, imagine the situation in which the input unit was inhibited, but the output unit was excited. To increase the probability that this pattern would occur later, one would make the weight of the connection between the two units more *inhibitory*. Later, if the input unit exhibits negative activity, this would lead to a more *positive* signal (the negative activity multiplied by the more inhibitory connection weight) being sent to the output unit, which would increase the net input to the output unit. As a result, the output unit would be more likely to assume positive activity. Similar logic would dictate that if the input unit was excited and the output unit was inhibited at the same time, then the connection between them should again be made more inhibitory. Table 9.2 summarizes the desired direction of weight changes given the possible states of connected input and output units.

What remains is to convert the qualitative account of desired weight changes that is given in Table 9.2 into a quantitative equation that will generate numbers that can be used to fill in the values of the matrix Δ_{t+1} during learning. An examination of the table provides a clear indication of the kind of mathematical

Table 9.2   The direction of weight changes that will enhance the relationship between patterns of input and output unit activities

Activity of input unit	Activity of output unit	Direction of desired weight change
Positive	Positive	Positive
Negative	Negative	Positive
Negative	Positive	Negative
Positive	Negative	Negative

operation to use. Note that if one were to take the value (i.e., the mathematical sign) of each of the first two columns and multiply them together, then the result would be the value in the third column of the table. In modern Hebb-style learning, the basic assumption is that the desired weight change for the connection between input unit i and output unit j is equal to the product of the activities of the two units:

$$\delta_{ij} = a_i \bullet a_i \qquad [9.7]$$

Equation 9.7 has two main advantages. First, under the assumption that unit activities can have negative or positive values, this equation creates weight changes of the desired sign according to Table 9.2. Second, this equation generates weight changes that reflect the relative amount of activity in both units. Imagine that the two processing units were both exhibiting positive activities, but that the two activities were very weak (e.g., values of, say, 0.05). It would seem plausible in this situation not to make a very large change to the connection weight. Equation 9.7 accomplishes this. For example, when two fractional positive values are multiplied together, as would be the case in our imagined situation, the resulting connection weight change is positive, but is also very small. Conversely, if both processing units were exhibiting very large activities, then it stands to reason that the connection between them should be changed a great deal. Again, Equation 9.7 automatically accomplishes this.

One minor modification to Equation 9.7 permits the exploration or manipulation of a richer notion of learning. One can imagine some situations in which a system is capable of learning a great deal, and other situations in which a system is less capable of learning. For instance, kids are more likely to learn things in school when they are rested than when they are tired. In Hebb-style learning, such general effects can be modeled by using a learning rate, which is a constant used to scale the result of Equation 9.7 up. Traditionally, the Greek letter η represents the learning rate. When η is small or fractional, the desired weight changes will be small, which is analogous to the situation in which a tired child is trying to learn. When η is large, the desired weight changes will be amplified, which is analogous to the situation in which a rested child is trying to learn. This is all accomplished by multiplying the desired weight changes by the learning rate, as is indicated in Equation 9.8.

$$\delta_{ij} = \eta(a_i \bullet a) \qquad [9.8]$$

To bring this discussion to a close, Equation 9.8 defines how Hebb-style learning can be used to compute the desired change for a single weight in the distributed associative memory. Linear algebra provides a very compact notation for defining every entry in the matrix Δ_{t+1}. Remember the rule of thumb that claimed that the result of combining two vectors together had as many rows as the first vector in the combination, and had as many columns as the second vector. We used this rule of thumb to predict that when the inner product was computed (e.g., Equation 9.5) the result would be a number (i.e., a vector with one row and one column). Imagine we had two vectors, c and d, and combined them in the reverse order than that used in Equation 9.5. In other words, what if they were multiplied together in an expression in which the transposed vector was the second component, instead of being the first: $d \bullet c^T$? Using our rule of thumb, we would not predict that we would get a single number. Instead, we would predict that the result of this equation would be a full matrix with as many rows as were in vector d, and as many columns as were in c^T. This matrix-producing operation is called the outer product (Figure 9.4).

The outer product is used to define how all of the desired weight changes for the distributed associative memory are to be calculated. Imagine that vector d represents some pattern of activity that has been presented to the output units of the memory, and that vector c represents some pattern of activity that has been presented to the input units of the memory. The desired weight changes are defined as:

$$\Delta_{t+1} = \eta(d \bullet c^T) \qquad [9.9]$$

The calculation of the outer product is illustrated in Figure 9.4. Every entry δ_{ij} in the matrix Δ_{t+1} is equal to the value c_i multiplied by the value d_j. This is the outer product. The result of this operation is then scaled by the learning rate, by multiplying it by the learning rate constant η.

η	$\cdot$	c	$\cdot$	d^T				$=$	Δ_{t+1}			
0.1	$\cdot$	1	$\cdot$	1	2	3	4	$=$	0.1	0.2	0.3	0.4
		2							0.2	0.4	0.6	0.8
		3							0.3	0.6	0.9	1.2
		4							0.4	0.8	1.2	1.6

Figure 9.4 Using the outer product to define the desired weight changes in accordance with Hebb-style learning

9.2.3 Behavior of the distributed associative memory

9.2.3.1 Computational account of the model

Dawson (1998) has argued that one of the key approaches taken by cognitive scientists to explain an information-processing system is computational. In adopting the computational approach, one formally defines some characteristics of interest in a system (i.e., in some mathematical or logical notation). Then one uses formal operations to explore the properties of the system, typically by constructing mathematical or logical proofs.

One of the reasons that linear algebra was used to define the properties of the distributed associative memory in the previous subsections was because it permits us to examine the system computationally. In particular, we can quickly manipulate the memory system's equations to generate proofs about its ability to function. We can also use the equations to determine whether there are some general situations in which it will fail to operate as intended.

As the first step in the computational analysis of a distributed associative memory governed by Hebb-style learning, let us make some simplifying assumptions. First, let us assume during learning that η has a value of 1. Because of this, it will be omitted from the learning equations. This is only being done to simplify the equations.

The second assumption involves the properties of the to-be-learned vectors that will be used in the equations below. Let us imagine that there are four of these vectors: a, b, c, and d. We will assume that this set of vectors is orthonormal. At a general level, what this assumption means is that each of these vectors has a length of 1.00, and is completely uncorrelated with the other three vectors in the set. Mathematically, this assumption involves assuming certain properties are true of the inner products of the vectors in this set. In particular, it is assumed that if one takes the inner product of a vector with itself, the result will be equal to 1. However, if the inner product is taken between a vector and a different member of the set, the result will be equal to 0. For example, this assumption means that $a^T \bullet a = 1$, but that $a^T \bullet b = 0$, $a^T \bullet c = 0$, and $a^T \bullet d = 0$. The importance of this second assumption will be apparent shortly.

Now let us define a simple learning sequence in which the distributed associative memory first learns the association between a and b by computing the outer product $b \bullet a^T$ and then learns the association between c and d by computing the outer product $d \bullet c^T$. This process of learning is detailed in Table 9.3, which is essentially the same as Table 9.1 with a few more specific details added because of our knowledge of which vectors are being learned at each trial.

Now that the distributed memory has learned two different associations, we can use linear algebra to predict its ability to recall remembered information. In this example, information is retrieved from the memory system by presenting either vector a or vector c as a cue and using the retrieval operation that was

Table 9.3 Learning two pairs of vectors

Trial $(t+1)$	Operation	Equation describing weight values
0	Start with the 0 matrix	$W_0 = 0$
1	Associate a with b	$W_1 = W_0 + \Delta_1$
		$= 0 + (b \bullet a^T)$
		$= (b \bullet a^T)$
2	Associate c with d	$W_2 = W_1 + \Delta_2$
		$= (b \bullet a^T) + \Delta_2$
		$= (b \bullet a^T) + (d \bullet c^T)$

Table 9.4 Correct recall of different associations from the same memory

Cue	Recall equation	Comments
a	$r = W_2 a$	Equation 9.6
	$= ((b \bullet a^T) + (d \bullet c^T))a$	Expand W_2 from Table 9.2
	$= b \bullet a^T \bullet a + d \bullet c^T \bullet a$	Move vector a into the parentheses
	$= b \bullet (a^T \bullet a) + d \bullet (c^T \bullet a)$	Identify the inner products with parentheses
	$= b(1) + d(0)$	Compute inner products (orthonormal assumption)
	$= b$	b is correctly recalled
c	$r = W_2 c$	Equation 9.6
	$= ((b \bullet a^T) + (d \bullet c^T))c$	Expand W_2 from Table 9.2
	$= b \bullet a^T \bullet c + d \bullet c^T \bullet c$	Move vector c into the parentheses
	$= b \bullet (a^T \bullet c) + d \bullet (c^T \bullet c)$	Identify the inner products with parentheses
	$= b(0) + d(1)$	Compute inner products (orthonormal assumption)
	$= d$	d is correctly recalled

defined in Equation 9.6. If recall is correct, then when the vector a is presented as a cue, the vector b should be retrieved; when c is the cue, d should be retrieved. Table 9.4 provides the mathematical details about recall from the memory. It takes Equation 9.6, and replaces the weight matrix with the more detailed expression for the weights that was provided in Table 9.2. It then works the cue vector into the parentheses. When this is done, two inner products are revealed. Because of our assumption that the set of vectors is orthonormal, one of the inner products works out to 0, canceling out a vector. The other inner product works out to 1. As a result, correct recall is achieved.

The equations that we have just been manipulating in Tables 9.3 and 9.4 make two important points. First, they have shown that when we make a particular assumption about the relationships between the patterns being associated, Hebb-style learning works. Furthermore, they show that this is accomplished with a single set of connections between processing units. The weight matrix W_2 is a single entity, but from Table 9.4 it is clear that it holds information about the associations between a and b and between c and d. Second, these equations demonstrate a computational analysis (Dawson, 1998) of this kind of memory system. We have been able to use mathematics to demonstrate correct learning and recall; we did not need to program a simulation of this system to investigate these properties.

Computational analyses can also be used to demonstrate some of the problems with Hebb-style learning. The assumption that the set of to-be-associated vectors is orthonormal is extremely strong. What it amounts to is the claim that there can be absolutely no correlation between different patterns at all. If we were to be learning associations between entities in the world, then this assumption would be very limiting. For instance, in many cases we would expect there to be similarities or correlations between these objects. Indeed, one would expect – as did many of the associationists – that such correlations would be an important aid to memory.

To examine the effect of correlation on Hebb-style learning, let us make a slight modification to our orthonormality assumption. We will again be interested in learning associations between four different vectors, a, b, c, and d. We will assume once again that the inner product of any of these vectors with itself will result in a value of 1. We will also assume that a, b, and d are uncorrelated, so that the inner product of one of these vectors with one of the other two in this group of three will result in a value of 0. All of these assumptions were used in our previous analyses. Our change in assumptions will involve vector c. We will assume that this vector is still not correlated with vectors b or d, but that it does have a strong correlation with vector a. In particular, we will assume that the inner product of c with a is equal to $\frac{1}{2}$.

Table 9.5 provides the equations for recall with our change in assumption about the relationship between c and a. In this case, because these two vectors are correlated, their inner product does not equal 0, and as a result does not completely cancel out part of the recall equation. As a result, there is noise or error added to the recall. Instead of recalling b when presented with a as a cue, the memory recalls b plus some added noise: $b + \frac{1}{2}d$. Instead of recalling d when presented with c as a cue, the memory recalls d plus some added noise: $d + \frac{1}{2}b$. The amount of noise that is evident in the recall is exactly equal to the correlation between c and a. If this correlation were to increase, then the amount of noise in the recalled vectors would also increase. If this correlation were to decrease, then the amount of noise in the recalled vectors would also decrease. It is only when this correlation is equal to 0 that there is no noise and recall is perfect.

The linear algebra that we have just reviewed has shown that Hebb-style learning of associations has problems when the to-be-associated patterns are correlated with one another. This provides one strong suggestion that a different

Table 9.5 Incorrect recall due to correlation between c and a

Cue	Recall equation	Comments
a	$r = W_2 a$	Equation 9.6
	$= ((b \bullet a^T) + (d \bullet c^T))a$	Expand W_2 from Table 9.2
	$= b \bullet a^T \bullet a + d \bullet c^T \bullet a$	Move vector a into the parentheses
	$= b \bullet (a^T \bullet a) + d \bullet (c^T \bullet a)$	Identify the inner products with
	$= b(1) + d(\frac{1}{2})$	parentheses
	$\neq b$	Compute inner products
		b is *not* correctly recalled!
c	$r = W_2 c$	Equation 9.6
	$= ((b \bullet a^T) + (d \bullet c^T))c$	Expand W_2 from Table 9.2
	$= b \bullet a^T \bullet c + d \bullet c^T \bullet c$	Move vector c into the parentheses
	$= b \bullet (a^T \bullet c) + d \bullet (c^T \bullet c)$	Identify the inner products with
	$= b(\frac{1}{2}) + d(1)$	parentheses
	$\neq d$	Compute inner products
		d is *not* correctly recalled!

approach to learning associations should be considered if one is interested in training a distributed associative memory. In the next subsection, we will explore Hebb-style learning with a computer simulation in an attempt to identify some further problems. Later, these problems will lead to a reformulation of the rule that we use to modify connections in the memory system.

9.2.3.2 Observing the behavior

The preceding subsections have provided a mathematical description of a distributed associative memory, a formal definition of one method for storing associations in this memory, and mathematical proofs that show situations in which this memory works perfectly, as well as circumstances in which this memory does not function as well as desired. In this subsection, we will examine this same memory and learning rule, but instead of working with the system computationally, we will work with it algorithmically by observing the performance of a computer simulation.

Given the mathematical understanding of the memory that we have already achieved, one might wonder about the need for creating a computer simulation. However, a working computer simulation can quickly shed some light on practical issues that are not explicitly addressed in mathematical proofs. How fast is this type of learning when the memory is simulated on a digital computer? How is performance affected when the size of the memory grows? How does the learning rate affect performance?

Behavior is sometimes explainable in retrospect, but it is necessary to do the numerical experiments to see if ideas are actually workable, or if unforeseen problems appear. They often do. As only one example, there are a number of learning rules that can be proved to work mathematically. Unfortunately, when simulations are done, learning times are found to be enormous, totally outside the boundaries of practicality. Or the results are immensely sensitive to noise, or error, or to values of particular parameters.

(Anderson & Rosenfeld, 1988, p. 65)

We have developed a simulation tool that was programmed in Visual Basic 6.0 as an instructional tool to be used to explore a distributed associative memory. This software is available, free of charge, from the website that provides supplementary material for this book: http://www.bcp.psych.ualberta/~mike/Book2/. This software comes with a number of example files that can be used to examine the advantages and disadvantages of distributed associative memories, and will save the results in a variety of formats (text files, Microsoft Excel spreadsheets) for later exploration and analysis. Readers can also use the instructions to create their own training sets in a format that can be read by the network.

One can use this software to empirically verify the computational claims that were made earlier. For instance, in two of the example training sets that are provided with the software, eight different paired associates are created from an orthonormal set of vectors. If these stimuli are presented 10 times to a distributed associative memory, associated using the Hebb rule, with a learning rate of 0.1, the network will be able to perform perfect recall for each stimulus. However, if correlations exist between two or more of the vectors used to create the stimuli, then the total network error will never reach zero no matter what the learning rate is, or how many stimulus presentations are made.

An examination of the weight matrix that is produced when the memory learns associations between vectors that are variable (e.g., whose values are a complex mix of negative and positive fractional values) indicates that the system is creating representations that are indeed distributed. We know from the recall performance of the network that these weights are storing information about eight different associations. However, in looking at these weights, we do not see any evidence that these associations are stored locally. For instance, it does not appear that one row of the weight matrix stores information about one association, and that another row stores information about a different association. All of the weights have been affected by training, and information about all eight associations is distributed throughout the entire weight matrix. If the structure of this network was to be interpreted, mere inspection would not do the job.

The software can also be used to reveal a different problem with Hebb learning. Imagine training the memory with a set of orthonormal patterns, with a learning rate of 0.1. Learning is evident early in training, because the network sum of squared error (SSE) – computed over all outputs and all patterns – steadily decreases, reaching a value of 0 by the 10th epoch. However, additional training beyond this point actually causes error to increase with each epoch. Our general sense about learning is that this shouldn't be happening. We would normally expect that more learning should result in better performance. So, if learning is operating the way that we would expect, then SSE should not increase. This unfortunate finding is due to the fact that Hebb learning modifies weights after each stimulus presentation, even when the weights should not be changed. In other words, Hebb learning does not use any feedback about the errors that the network is making. If it did, then this would prevent it from making unnecessary changes to its weights, and from undoing the learning that it has already accomplished.

9.3 Beyond the Limitations of Hebb Learning

9.3.1 The limitations of Hebb learning

There are three general reasons that the Hebb learning rule has enjoyed a great deal of popularity among researchers who are interested in developing theories of associative memory. First, we saw in the historical review of associationism that one of the constants from one theory to the next was the inclusion of the law of contiguity. The Hebb rule is an elegant statement of this fundamental mode of association. Second, in modern cognitive science there is an increasing desire to relate properties of functional theories to neural mechanisms (Dawson, 1998). The Hebb rule is one of the few biologically plausible learning rules. Many researchers have taken pains to point out the similarities between Hebb's account of learning and the biological mechanisms that govern long-term potentiation in the brain (Brown, 1990; Cotman, Monaghan, & Ganong, 1988; Martinez & Derrick, 1996). Third, even when memory systems trained by Hebb-style learning rules make mistakes, these mistakes are interesting, because in many cases they are analogous to the kinds of errors that one finds in human experiments on associative learning (Eich, 1982; Murdock, 1982, 1997).

In spite of these attractions, the theoretical and empirical evidence that we have collected earlier in this chapter points to some severe limitations of a distributed associative memory that is trained by the Hebb rule. First, the memory only works well when the stimuli being associated are completely uncorrelated. As soon as the orthonormality assumption is violated, one cannot guarantee that the memory will recall the correct response when given a cue. Second, the Hebb rule is not sensitive to the performance of the memory system. This means that the Hebb rule will modify network connections even in situations where these modifications are not required because perfect recall has been achieved.

9.3.2 Overcoming the limitations

The combination of these problems with Hebb learning and the general attractiveness of this learning rule suggests that we should attempt to explore some ways in which the rule can be improved without throwing away many of its attractive properties. The purpose of this subsection is to describe such a refinement, and to define a new rule called the *delta rule*. We will see that the delta rule ultimately relies on association by contiguity, and therefore maintains many of the essential properties of the Hebb rule. However, the delta rule is explicitly designed to teach a network by providing it feedback about the kinds of errors that it makes. As a result, the delta rule provides one approach to overcoming some of the limitations of Hebb learning that we have already encountered.

9.3.2.1   Supervised learning

In connectionist research, a common distinction is made between unsupervised learning and supervised learning. In unsupervised learning, a network modifies its connection weights in an attempt to remember regularities that it has discovered in its environment. However, it never receives any information about what some programmer might think are desirable regularities. It therefore also never receives any feedback about whether its responses are correct or incorrect. In this regard, Hebb learning is an example of unsupervised learning. The fact that Hebb learning does not take into account errors that are being made by a network accounts for problems like the increase in network SSE that was discussed above.

In supervised learning, the goal of learning is for a network to generate a set of responses that are desired by a programmer (or a teacher). When the network generates a response to a stimulus, this observed response is compared to a desired response, which is often called the target response. Typically, one compares these two responses by subtracting the observed response (0) from the target response (T) for each output unit in the network. That is, the error for output unit i (ε_i) is:

$$\varepsilon_I = T_i - O_i \qquad\qquad [9.10]$$

One of the advantages of supervised learning is that learning is only driven by mistakes. This implies two different things. First, if no mistake is made, then no learning will occur, because no learning is required. Second, the degree of learning should be proportional to the degree of error. If a system makes a very large error, then there should be very large changes to its connection weights. However, if a system makes a very small error, then there should be a correspondingly small change to its connection weights. If we could replace the Hebb rule with a supervised learning rule that operated in this fashion, then we would definitely be in a position to solve one of the problems with Hebb learning that we have already identified. To be more specific, if our distributed associative memory was supervised when it learned, then once total SSE had dropped to 0, no more connection weight changes would occur.

Table 9.6 The logic of weight changes during supervised learning. T represents the target value for an output unit, and O represents the observed value for the output unit.

Activity of input unit	T − O	Implication	Operation to reduce error	Direction of desired weight change
Positive	Positive	T > O	↑ O	Positive
Positive	Negative	T < O	↓ O	Negative
Positive	Zero	T = O	None	Zero
Negative	Positive	T > O	↑ O	Negative
Negative	Negative	T < O	↓ O	Positive
Negative	Zero	T = O	None	Zero

The question is how to reformulate the Hebb rule in such a way that it can be converted from an unsupervised learning rule to a supervised learning rule. As a first pass at the logic of this reformulation, consider Table 9.6, which is a variation of Table 9.2. The purpose of Table 9.6 is to consider the activity in a single input unit, treating it for the sake of simplicity as being merely positive or negative. This input unit is connected to a single output unit, and the error for this unit has been calculated according to Equation 9.10 after some pattern has been presented to the network. Again, for simplicity's sake, we consider the result of this calculation to be a value that is positive, negative, or equal to zero. The table lays out the possible combinations of input values and error values in order to make clear what would need to happen to the weight of the connection between the two units in order to reduce the error that was produced the next time that the pattern was presented to the network.

For example, consider the first three rows of the table, for which the input unit has been activated with some positive value. In the first case, the error value is positive. This means that the target activity is greater than the observed activity. In order to reduce error, this means that the observed activity must be increased. For this pattern, this could be accomplished by making the connection weight more positive, because this would amplify the positive signal being sent by the input unit. In the second case, the target activity is smaller than the observed activity, which means that the observed activity has to be made smaller to reduce error. This would be accomplished by making the connection weight more negative, because this would attenuate the positive signal being sent by the input unit. In the third case, the target activity is equal to the observed activity, which indicates that no change should be made at all to the connection weight.

Similar logic can be followed for the remaining three rows in the table. However, because in these instances the input unit activity is negative, the change to the connection weight will be opposite in direction to the changes that were just described. In the first case, the connection weight must be made more negative in order to amplify (i.e., make more positive) the negative signal being sent by the input unit. In the second case, the connection weight must be made more positive in order to attenuate (i.e., make more negative) the negative signal coming from the input unit. Of course, in the third case there again would be no change made to the connection weight because there is zero error being generated by the output unit.

Earlier in this chapter, we motivated the rule for Hebb-style learning by observing that if we multiplied the first two columns of Table 9.2 together, the result would be the third column. A similar situation now arises in our discussion of supervised learning. If one were to take the first two columns of Table 9.6 and multiply them together, the result would be the last column of the table, which indicates the direction of weight change to make in order to reduce error. This inspires the following learning rule for a single connection between input unit i and output unit j:

$$\delta_{ij} = a_i(T_j - a_j) \qquad\qquad [9.11]$$

where δ_{ij} is the desired weight change, a_i is the activity of the input unit, T_j is the target activity for the output unit, and a_j is the observed activity in the output unit.

Equation 9.11 has two very nice properties that suggest that it is an excellent choice for a supervised learning rule for connections in a distributed associative memory. First, the equation changes the weight in the direction that is required to reduce error, because the equation is consistent with the logic that we worked through when discussing Table 9.6. Second, it is sensitive to amount of error. If the value of $T_j - a_i$ is large, then the change in the weight will be large. If the value is small, then the change in the weight will be small. If the value is zero, then – crucially – there will be no change in weight. This equation places a natural brake on the learning process, solving one of the problems that we identified with the Hebb rule.

9.3.2.2   The delta rule

The final step in defining a supervised learning rule for the distributed associative memory is to take Equation 9.11 and modify it by including a learning rate, and by expressing it in terms of linear algebra so that we can use one equation to define the changes for all the weights in a network that consists of multiple input and output units. When we defined the Hebb rule, we used the outer product of two vectors – scaled by a learning rate – to define the matrix of weight changes Δ_{t+1}. We can also follow this procedure for defining our supervised learning rule, which is called the delta rule. Let us assume that vector c^T represents some pattern of activity that has been presented to the input units of the memory. Let us also assume that the vector t (for target) defines the vector that *should* be correctly recalled from the memory when c is used as the cue in Equation 9.6. Let vector *o* (for observed) be the actual activity that is generated in the output units when *o* is the cue. The desired weight changes, scaled by the learning rate η, are defined as:

$$\Delta_{t+1} = \eta((t - o) \bullet c^T)$$ [9.12]

The expression *t* – *o* in Equation 9.12 is the difference between two vectors. The result of this operation will be another vector, with the same number of entries that would be found in either vector *t* or vector *o*. Let us name this third vector ε, to represent the fact that it is a vector of error values. Consistent with our definition of error in Equation 9.10, each entry ε_i in this vector is equal to the value $(t_i - o_i)$. With this definition of the error vector, we can rewrite Equation 9.12 as:

$$\Delta_{t+1} = \eta(\varepsilon \bullet c^T)$$ [9.13]

Equation 9.13 is important in that it makes very explicit the relationship between the delta rule and the Hebb rule. If you compare it to Equation 9.9, you will see that the two learning rules are very similar. The delta rule essentially involves Hebb learning, but this learning is not carried out until after a couple of preliminary steps have been taken. First, a cue vector is presented to the existing memory to see what vector would be recalled from the memory if no weight changes were made at all. Second, an error vector is computed by subtracting this observed recall vector from the target vector. Third, Hebb learning is performed, but the association that is learned is between the cue vector and the error vector. The point of doing this – as was explained in our discussion of Table 9.6 – is to only make changes in weights that are necessary to reduce error. If the error vector is full of zeroes, then no weight changes will be made when Equation 9.13 (or 9.12) is applied.

9.3.2.3 The power of the delta rule

In this subsection, we are going to briefly examine the performance of the delta rule, and compare it to the performance of Hebb learning, by repeating the four simulation experiments that were described earlier. It is also possible to compare the two rules by doing a computational analysis of the delta rule, and comparing the conclusions drawn from that analysis to those that we drew after working through the proofs about the abilities of Hebb learning. While this isn't done in the current chapter, mathematical examinations of the delta rule are available in the literature. Stone (1986) provides a particularly good treatment.

When the delta rule is used to train the distributed memory on the associations between patterns constructed from an orthonormal set of patterns, using the same learning rate as was used with the Hebb rule, the network will converge to a solution. It usually takes longer than is observed with the Hebb rule, though if training is continued, the delta rule continues to improve performance. In other words, this particular memory system is performing in a fashion that is more in accordance with our intuitions: when the memory has more repetitions on the paired associates, its performance improves. Furthermore, performance does not get worse with additional training.

If one plots network SSE as a function of epochs when the delta rule is used, then one sees an important emergent property. Network SSE decreases exponentially, with a great deal of learning occurring early in training, but with learning slowing down as training proceeds. This is to be expected because the amount of learning depends upon the amount of error that the network is making (see Equation 9.12). As the network learns more, its error is reduced, and as a result learning slows down. We saw this pattern earlier in Chapter 4 when we discussed mathematical models of learning in general, and the Rescorla–Wagner learning rule (Rescorla & Wagner, 1972) in particular. One of the important findings that demonstrated a strong relationship between connectionism and mathematical models in psychology was a proof that showed that learning rules like the delta rule are indeed equivalent to the Rescorla–Wagner rule (Sutton & Barto, 1981).

One of the interesting and important properties of the delta rule is that it is more powerful than Hebb learning. Because the rule works explicitly to reduce output unit error, it turns out that there are some associations that can be stored in a network using the delta rule, but which cannot be stored if the network is trained using the Hebb rule. For instance, we created a set of linear independent vectors to define patterns to be associated. Linearly independent vectors are correlated with one another, but you cannot express one of these vectors as a weighted sum of any of the other vectors in a set. When the Hebb rule is used to train a network to associate vectors of this type, perfect learning never occurs. However, when this set of associations is trained using the delta rule, the network is able to learn the problem. In one simulation, after 775 iterations network SSE dropped below 0.01, and the training was stopped. With this small level of total error, network performance is near perfect for all eight stimulus–response pairs.

How is it possible for the delta rule to come up with a set of connection weights that can store these eight associates, while this was not possible when the Hebb rule was used to train the network? One empirical clue to this additional power comes from examining the connection weights in the network at the end of training. For simpler problems (i.e., learning associations involving orthonormal vectors), the matrices of connection weights that resulted were symmetric, and the same set of weights is produced by either learning rule. In a symmetric matrix the value in cell w_{ij} is the same as the value found in cell w_{ji}. For linearly independent vectors, though, the delta rule produces a weight matrix that is not symmetric at all. The ability of the delta rule to create a set of connection weights that are not symmetric means that it can store a wider range of associations than can be learned via the Hebb rule. This is because the Hebb rule is constrained to always produce a symmetric set of connection weights.

This is not to say that the delta rule is all-powerful, however. Computational analyses of this rule have demonstrated that it permits associations to be learned when some correlations exist between vectors, but it is unable to learn associations when other correlations exist. In particular, the delta rule is not capable of correctly recalling associations when the training set is linearly dependent. We ran one simulation of this for 20,000 epochs. However, after all of this training, the network had not converged upon a solution. By the end of the first 1,000 sweeps of training, total error had dropped to about 0.544. Further training did not lead to any noticeable improvement. (However, further training also did not lead to the network performing any poorer, which demonstrates again one advantage of the delta rule over the Hebb rule.)

9.4 Associative Memory and Synthetic Psychology

The primary goal of describing the distributed associative memory in this chapter was to introduce some basic notions about connectionist models. We will see in the chapters that follow that many advances in connectionist architectures can be described as elaborations of some of the concepts that were introduced in this chapter. However, it is important to realize that distributed associative memories are interesting in their own light, and can be used to synthetically explore some issues in the psychology of learning and memory.

One key area of research is the study of associative learning in animals. Throughout the history of this topic, the underlying assumption has been that the discovery of elementary associative laws that govern animal learning can be used to aid in the understanding of more complex types of learning and cognition observed in humans. However, the current state of this field would suggest that these associative laws are complex, and a surprising variety of theories have been proposed in recent years. For example, it is frequently argued that there are a number of regularities in learning that cannot be explained by the Rescorla–Wagner model (Miller, Barnet, & Grahame, 1995). Because of this, many different models have been proposed in an attempt to either broaden the scope of the Rescorla–Wagner model, or to replace it with a theory that has been derived from an alternative framework (for reviews see Pearce & Bouton, 2001; Wasserman & Miller, 1997). "Other cognitive processes such as attention, memory, and information processing are now being invoked to help explain the facts of associative learning. The next several years of research will be exciting ones, as neuroscientists and cognitive scientists join experimental psychologists in an interdisciplinary attack on the challenging problems of associative learning and behavior change" (Wasserman & Miller, 1997, p. 598).

With respect to this interdisciplinary research program, distributed associative memories may provide an interesting environment in which new ideas about associative learning can be explored. For instance, we noted earlier that the delta rule has been proven to be formally equivalent to the Rescorla–Wagner rule

(Sutton & Barto, 1981). Presumably, this implies that it too suffers from the same limitations that have been motivating new theories about associative learning in animals. Can these new theories be implemented in the contiguity-based scheme that we have been developing in this framework? Can attentional modulations be added to a distributed associative memory by manipulating stimulus encodings, and then applying something like the delta rule?

There has also been a considerable amount of interest in using models like the one that has been introduced in this chapter to account for a number of different regularities in human memory (Anderson, Silverstein, Ritz, & Jones, 1977; Eich, 1982; Hinton & Anderson, 1981; Murdock, 1982, 1985; Pike, 1984). One reason for this interest has been the fact that when distributed memories make errors, these errors are systematic, and can be related back to the kinds of errors that are made by human subjects in associative memory experiments. For example, we saw earlier that under certain conditions a distributed associative memory will generate responses that represent "blends" of different memories. Memory models of this type also exhibit emergent behaviors that suggest that they provide an excellent environment in which human associative memory can be explored. "Current connectionist models have been successful in accounting for a range of basic phenomena such as the effect of contingency on associative learning, as well as more complex effects such as enhanced responding to an unseen prototype pattern and partial memory for the training items" (Shanks, 1995, p. 151).

Interestingly, one of the primary attractions of distributed associative memories has been the fact that they offer theories that appear to be more biologically plausible than their competitors (Hinton & Anderson, 1981; Shanks, 1997). Indeed, many researchers have recently been interested in taking networks like the ones that have been described in this chapter, or more sophisticated networks, and using these simulations to study neural mechanisms of learning and memory (Brown, 1990; Cotman et al., 1988; Foster, Ainsworth, Faratin, & Shapiro, 1997; Gluck & Myers, 1997; Lynch, 1986; Martinez & Derrick, 1996).

The reason for this interest has been the discovery of a particular neural phenomenon, called long-term potentiation. Long-term potentiation is the long-lasting increase of synaptic efficiency that occurs when two connected neurons are active (or nearing activity) at roughly the same time. This increase in efficiency appears to be related to the properties of a particular receptor mechanism, the NMDA receptor. It also appears to be related behaviorally to memory and spatial learning mediated by the hippocampus, because chemicals that block NMDA receptors disrupt these behaviors. In short, the biochemical study of long-term potentiation appears to be revealing the mechanisms that underlie the kind of neural changes that motivated theories of association by both James (1890) and Hebb (1949).

However, with this increased understanding of long-term potentiation, and with an emerging and detailed understanding of neural mechanisms, there has also been an increased need to propose more sophisticated models of synaptic change. Brown (1990) notes that there have been anywhere from 50 to 100 theories of this type, and proceeds to review only a subset of these. Brown classifies them as being Hebbian algorithms, generalized Hebbian algorithms, and global control algorithms. Again, one question to ask is how might these more sophisticated rules be incorporated into the models that have been described in the current chapter. Do these rules result in solving some problems that were not solved by the delta rule? If implemented, do these rules lead to behavioral results that are more or less consistent with the performance of human subjects in memory experiments?

One theme that seems to be emerging in even this cursory glance at the current state of research related to distributed associative memories is that, while interesting, the versions of the networks that were described in this chapter are not as powerful as would seem to be required to keep up with advances in the field. What general approach could be used to increase the power of these networks? In the next two chapters, we will consider two very basic – but critical – modifications. In Chapter 10, we will look at some of the implications of changing the activation function from being linear (as is the case in Equation 9.2) to being nonlinear. In Chapter 11, we will discuss how the use of a nonlinear activation function permits even more power through the use of additional layers of processing units separating network input from network output.

Chapter ten

Making Decisions

In the most general sense, a psychological theory attempts to explain the relation-ship between stimuli and responses. One psychological theory differs from another in terms of the "machinery" that it proposes for converting inputs into outputs. For example, behaviorism argued that environmental stimuli alone could dictate behavioral responses, and did not propose any additional intervening causal variables. In contrast, cognitivism argued that environmental stimuli were transformed into numerous intervening representational states, and that behavioral responses were dictated by these intermediate representations. As a result, for a cognitivist, behavior did not directly depend upon the environment.

As we will see in more detail below, the main source of the weakness in a distributed associative memory is analogous to the difference between behaviorist theory and cognitivist theory. In particular, a simple distributed associative memory attempts to represent association as a direct link between stimulus and response. While some interesting relationships can be modeled in this way, these relationships are still quite simple. More complicated relationships cannot be captured unless intervening processing units, used to transform input patterns into intermediate representational states, are added to the associative memory.

10.1 The Limits of Linearity

10.1.1 A chain of distributed memories

Connectionist models are often described as being neuronally inspired. What this means is that connectionist theorists often look to properties of the brain in order to discover new methods for processing information.

One brain property that is critical for the search for additional power in an associative memory is that cortical tissue is organized into different layers of interconnected neurons. Human neocortex, which is the neural basis for most of our complex cognitive and perceptual processing, can be viewed as a thin sheet of tissue that is arranged into six different layers (labeled with the Roman numeral I through VI). The fourth layer in this arrangement is itself characterized as being organized into three different sublayers (IVa, IVb, and IVc) (Kuffler, Nicholls, & Martin, 1984). For the most part, neural processes run up and down through these layers at right angles to the cortical surface. Each layer can be characterized as having neurons that have different functional properties. For instance, in visual cortex, neurons whose receptive fields lead them to be classified as simple cells are found in Layer IV, and project to complex cells in Layers II and III. These complex cells in turn provide the major output to other cortical areas, as well as into Layer V of visual cortex. The projections of one layer into another are consistent with a functional account of how a complicated receptive field for a neuron can be constructed by combining simpler receptive fields from neurons that are located in a more peripheral layer. This kind of hierarchical construction of the ability to detect complexity provides one rationale for incorporating multiple layers of processors into a distributed associative memory.

The layering of the neocortex provides one obvious approach to improving a distributed associative memory. Instead of having direct connections between input units and output units, we could include one or more layers of intermediate processing units. The functional role of these intermediate layers of "hidden" units would be to transform the pattern of activity in the input units. For instance, hidden units might detect complex features that characterize important properties of input patterns, just as complex cells have complicated receptive fields in virtue of their ability to combine the inputs of cells that have simpler receptive fields. Perhaps the identification of more complex features would in turn permit the distributed associative memory to store more complicated associations, and possibly enable the memory to store arbitrary associations between inputs and outputs.

A first pass at adding layers of processors to a distributed associative memory can be based on the linear algebra that we already have seen in Chapter 9. Imagine a distributed associative memory that consists of three different layers of processing units: a layer of input units (whose activity can be represented by the vector i), an intermediate layer of "hidden" units (represented by the vector h), and a layer of output units (represented by the vector o). Let us assume that some learning has already occurred in this memory, so that associations between at least one input pattern and one output pattern have been stored in this memory. This information would be stored in a matrix X of weights representing connection strengths between the input units and the hidden units, and in a second matrix Y of weights representing connection strengths between the hidden units and the output units.

Recall from this memory would proceed as follows. First, a cue pattern would be used to set the values of the input units. This in turn would cause a signal to be sent through the first layer of connection weights to produce a vector of activities in the hidden units. This second vector of hidden unit activity, h, would serve as an intermediate cue pattern that would serve as an input signal to the second set of connection weights. This signal would produce activity in the output units (the vector **o**), which would represent the networks response to the original cue pattern. Mathematically, this sequence of recall operations would be written as follows:

$$\mathbf{o} = \mathbf{Y}(\mathbf{Xi}) = \mathbf{Yh} \qquad [10.1]$$

This equation is equal to a chain consisting of two applications of the recall equation that was defined in the previous chapter.

10.1.2   Removing the links of the chain

However, a closer look at Equation 10.1 will show that the sequence of recall operations that it represents does not increase the power of this two-layer memory system beyond that which would be found in a single-layer distributed associative memory. One important operation in linear algebra is multiplying two matrices together. For example, one could multiply some matrix **Y** and some matrix **X** together to produce a third matrix, which we can represent as matrix **P** (for "product"). Each entry in row i and column j of matrix **P** is equal to the inner product between row i of matrix **Y** and column j of matrix **X** (for details see Jordan, 1986).

In Equation 10.1, the parentheses represent our emphasis on an initial operation, which is to send an input vector through matrix **X** to create a cue vector **c**. However, we could rearrange the parentheses in this equation to emphasize a different initial operation, which is the matrix multiplication of the two sets of connection weights, as is shown in Equation 10.2:

$$\mathbf{o} = (\mathbf{YX})\mathbf{i} = \mathbf{Pi} = \mathbf{Yh} = \mathbf{Y}(\mathbf{Xi}) \qquad [10.2]$$

What this second equation shows is that we could take the two sets of connection weights, **X** and **Y**, and multiply them together to create a new matrix **P**. The recall operation defined earlier in Equation 10.1 is mathematically identical to sending input vector **i** as a signal through matrix **P**. In other words, linear algebra is showing us that we can replace our two-layer distributed associative memory with a different memory that uses *only* one set of connection weights – just as we saw in Chapter 9 – and which would generate *exactly* the same responses as our two-layer system. This proves that we are not adding any power to the distributed associative memory with our second set of connection weights. Our two-layer distributed associative memory is mathematically equivalent to a single-layer memory, and is therefore subject to exactly the same limitations. "For linear systems at least, the distinction between two-layer systems and one-layer systems is more apparent than real. The two systems are identical in the sense that they compute the same function. Of course, they may have different internal dynamics and therefore take different amounts of time to compute their outputs" (Jordan, 1986, p. 397).

10.2 A Fundamental Nonlinearity

10.2.1 The need for nonlinearity

Equation 10.2 proved that a two-layer distributed associative memory could be collapsed into a single-layer network with identical computational power. Why is this collapse possible? In Chapter 3 of this book, we encountered some of the properties of linear systems, and argued that linearity is responsible for the fact that some psychological models fail to surprise us. We saw that in a linear system the behavior of the whole system is equal exactly to the combined behaviors of the systems components. It is exactly this notion of linearity that is responsible for the collapse of the two-layer system into a single-layer memory. The linear nature of the distributed associative memory is reflected in the operations – written in linear algebra – described in Equation 10.2. In order to prevent the collapse of a linear chain of operations into a single operation that reflects the total effects of all the links in the chain, some sort of nonlinearity has to be introduced. In the next subsection we consider one neuronally inspired candidate for this nonlinearity.

10.2.2 The all-or-none law

How do neurons process information? Very generally, neurons begin to process information by detecting inputs that stimulate, and travel through, their dendrites. These inputs are weak electrical signals, called graded potentials, whose quality deteriorates as they travel toward the body or soma of the neuron. However, if enough of these weak graded potentials arrive at the soma at the same time, then their cumulative effect disrupts the resting electrical state of the neuron. This results in a massive depolarization of the membrane of the neuron's axon, called an action potential, which travels along the axon to eventually stimulate some other neuron.

A crucial property of the action potential is that it is an all-or-none phenomenon. While the graded potentials that travel through dendrites gradually decrease in intensity over time and distance, the depolarization that defines an action potential does not. An action potential is an electrical signal of constant intensity. The fact that neurons generate action potentials of fixed intensity is one of the fundamental discoveries of neuroscience, and has been called the all-or-none law. "The all-or-none law guarantees that once an action potential is generated it is always full size, minimizing the possibility that information will be lost along the way" (Levitan & Kaczmarek, 1991, p. 43).

In Chapter 9, the activity in an output unit was exactly equal to its net input. When net input was small, output activity was small. When net input was medium, output activity was medium. When net input was large, output activity was large. This was because the relationship between net input and output unit activity was linear. In contrast, if we had a neuron as an output unit, then there would not be a linear relationship between net input and activity. When net input was small, activity would be small in the sense that no action potential would be generated. However, as net input gradually changed from being small to medium, activity would not change – the output unit would still fail to generate an action potential. It is only in the case that the net input became sufficiently large that action potential would be generated.

Figure 10.1 illustrates the difference between the relationship between net input and activity for the standard output unit of a distributed associative memory (Figure 10.1a) and for a neuron of the type that was described above (Figure 10.1b). In the former case, the linear relationship between net input and activity is evident as a straight line drawn on the graph. In the latter case, the relationship is nonlinear and discontinuous. For a wide range of small net inputs, activity is equal to zero.

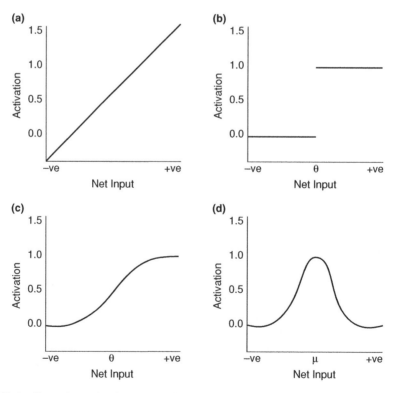

Figure 10.1 Illustrations of activation functions: (a) a linear function; (b) threshold function; (c) logistic function; (d) Gaussian function.

When net input becomes sufficiently large, activity suddenly jumps to a value of 1. However, activity remains at 1 for a wide range of large net inputs. This represents the nonlinearity that is consistent with the all-or-none law.

In 1943, McCulloch and Pitts published a pioneering article in the *Bulletin of Mathematical Biophysics*. The purpose of this article was to provide a mathematical account of the basic information processing carried out by neurons. McCulloch and Pitts ignored the detailed biology of neural function, and instead described neurons very abstractly as devices that made true or false logical assertions about input information. The logical description of neurons was made possible by recognizing the binary nature of the action potential.

> The all-or-none law of nervous activity is sufficient to ensure that the activity of any neuron may be represented as a proposition. Physiological relations existing among nervous activities correspond, of course, to relations among the propositions; and the utility of the representation depends upon the identity of these relations with those of the logical propositions. To each reaction of any neuron there is a corresponding assertion of a simple proposition.
>
> *(McCulloch & Pitts, 1988, p. 21)*

McCulloch and Pitts fleshed out this insight by designing 16 different kinds of logical neurons, each one asserting the truth or falsehood of a logical operation performed on two input variables. They were able to show that a network comprised of many of these neurons arranged in a systematic fashion had enormous computational power. For instance, they were able to prove that they could construct a network that was equivalent in power to a universal Turing machine. "Thus in psychology, introspective, behavioristic or physiological, the fundamental relations are those of two-valued logic" (1988, p. 38).

While the architecture designed by McCulloch and Pitts was enormously powerful, it did suffer from one major drawback. A McCulloch–Pitts network was *not* adaptive: in order to create a working network, one had to program it by choosing and "wiring" together all of the processors by hand. A McCulloch–Pitts network was built; it was not taught. Later, other researchers developed networks that included a nonlinear activation function to instantiate the all-or-none law, and to ensure that network outputs could be assigned a logical interpretation. However, these networks differed from those designed by McCulloch and Pitts in that their connection weights were modified by a learning rule. One such architecture was the perceptron proposed by Rosenblatt (1962).

10.3 Building a Perceptron: A Nonlinear Associative Memory

Rosenblatt's (1962) perceptron was designed to be a model of brain function. "By brain model we shall mean any theoretical system which attempts to explain the psychological functioning of a brain in terms of known laws of physics and mathematics, and known facts of neuroanatomy and physiology" (p. 3). Rosenblatt realized that there were two different kinds of brain model that could be developed.

The first kind of model was called *monotypic*. In developing a monotypic model, a researcher is primarily interested in creating a device capable of carrying out an input/output mapping. As a result, the researcher's first step is to define the desired mapping as accurately as possible. Then a system is constructed to compute this mapping, usually under the constraint that the components of the system should be analogous to biological components. For Rosenblatt, a McCulloch–Pitts network was the prototypical example of a monotypic model.

The second kind of model was called *genotypic*. In a monotypic model, the properties of all of the components and the properties of their interconnections are all specified in advance in order to compute a single prespecified function as accurately as possible. This is not the case for the genotypic model. In the genotypic model, the properties of the components might be specified in advance, but the organization of these components into a system was not. Instead, general principles were applied to the model in order to evolve its organization. As a result, instead of producing a single model capable of computing a single function, the genotypic approach was capable of generating a number of different models, each with their own unique organization, but all capable of solving the same problem. "The genotypic approach, then, is concerned with the properties of systems which conform to designated laws of organization, rather than with the logical function realized by a particular system" (Rosenblatt, 1962, p. 20). The perceptron was Rosenblatt's example of the genotypic model.

It is interesting to note that Rosenblatt's (1962) distinction between monotypic and genotypic models bears some resemblance to the distinction between analytic and synthetic models that has been a theme of the current book. "In the monotypic approach, the functional properties are generally postulated as a starting point. In the genotypic approach, they are the end-objective of analysis, and the physical system itself (or the statistical properties of the class of systems) constitutes the starting point" (p. 20). Because of this difference, and because of the fact that the perceptron is viewed as being genotypic, the perceptron was thought of as a medium in which one could explore issues concerning types of organization, hypothetical memory mechanisms, and biological models. "The model is not a terminal result, but a starting point for exploratory analysis of its behavior" (p. 28). The subsections that follow describe the components of a perceptron, and some general principles that can be used to organize these components into a system capable of performing some task of interest.

10.3.1 *From distributed associative memory to the perceptron*

The perceptron is very similar to the distributed associated memory. It too consists of a bank of input units, a bank of one or more output units, and a set of modifiable connections that link every input unit to every output unit. A learning rule is used to modify the connection weights in order to train the perceptron to create an association between an input pattern and an output pattern. The only crucial difference between the two architectures is the fact that the output units in a perceptron use a nonlinear activation function. As was discussed earlier, the purpose of the nonlinear activation function is to model the all-or-none law governing the generation of action potentials.

The nonlinear activation function in the output units of a perceptron leads to a slight difference in interpreting the kind of task that a perceptron should be trained to perform. The output units of a perceptron are trained to generate a response that will be interpreted as being either on or off. This means that the output units can be assigned a logical interpretation, in the sense of McCulloch and Pitts. As a result, while a perceptron can be viewed as a kind of associative memory, the kinds of associations that it learns to make will usually be interpreted in a different fashion than were the associations that were described in the previous chapter. The logical nature of an output unit's activity means that a perceptron is usually described as a device that makes decisions – it classifies input patterns. The nonlinear activation function in a perceptron is used to assign input patterns to a particular category, where this assignment is all or none.

For example, consider a simple kind of problem called the majority problem. In a majority problem, a perceptron would have N input units, and a single output unit. If the majority of the input units were turned on, then the output unit of the perceptron would be trained to turn on to those patterns. If less than the majority of the input units were turned on, then the output unit of the perceptron would be trained to turn off. Imagine that N was equal to 5. In this case, whenever three, four, or five of the input units were activated, then the perceptron would be trained to turn on. If zero, one, or two of the input units were activated, then the perceptron would be trained to turn off. Thus while it is perfectly legitimate to view the perceptron as learning to associate one kind of response with some inputs, and a different kind of response with others, more specifically we can say that the perceptron has learned to decide that some patterns have the majority of their input units turned on, while others do not. Our account of the perceptron as a pattern classifier is almost completely due to the fact that it uses a nonlinear activation function that is binary in nature.

10.3.2   The perceptron's architecture

10.3.2.1   Processing units

The input units in a perceptron are identical in nature to the input units for the distributed associative memory that was described in Chapter 9. The input units are used to represent patterns that are to be presented as stimuli to the perceptron. The activities of the input units can either be binary or continuous, depending on the desired interpretation of what each input unit represents. Input unit activities can be used to represent features that are either very simple or very complicated, depending on the problem to be presented to the network. As an example of a simple input, an input unit could be turned on or off to represent whether some simple stimulus was present or absent in the environment. This is the kind of representation that is used below when perceptrons are related to studies of animal learning.

The output units in a perceptron represent an elaboration of the output units in a distributed associative memory. The two are identical with respect to their net input function. The output units in a perceptron calculate their net input by summing the signal being sent by each input unit after the signal has been scaled by a connection weight. Mathematically, this can be described as computing the inner product of a vector that represents the input pattern and a vector that represents the weights of the connections between each input unit and the output unit. The difference between the output units in the two different kinds of networks is with respect to the activation function that is used to convert net input into internal activity. In the distributed associative memory, output activity was made equal to net input, which established a linear relationship between the two. In the perceptron, net input is "squashed" into the range between 0 and 1 by passing it into a nonlinear activation function. In the current chapter, we will consider three different kinds of nonlinear activation functions to be used in the output units of a perceptron.

The first nonlinear activation function to consider was used by Rosenblatt (1962), and is called the *step function*. The step function represents a nonlinear and discontinuous description of the all-or-none law governing the action potential. Let some output unit j have some threshold value θ_j. If the net input is less than this value, then the unit's activity will be equal to 0. If the net input is equal to or greater than θ_j, then the unit's activity will be equal to 1. A graph of the step function was presented earlier in Figure 10.1b.

The second nonlinear activation function to consider is one that is quite commonly used in modern connectionist networks. It represents a continuous approximation of the step function. A continuous approximation of the step function is an important tool in connectionism because it permits calculus to be used to derive more powerful learning rules, as we will see below.

The approximation of the step function that we will be using is the *logistic equation*. When graphed, the logistic equation is a sigmoid-shaped line that reaches an asymptote of 0 as net input approaches negative infinity, and reaches an asymptote of 1 as net input approaches positive infinity. A graph of this function was presented earlier in Figure 10.1c. The logistic equation that we will be using is written as follows:

$$f(net_i) = 1/(1 + \exp(-net_i + \theta_j)) \qquad\qquad [10.3]$$

In this equation, $f(net_i)$ is the activation being calculated for output unit i, net_i is the net input for that output unit, and θ_j is called the bias of the output unit.

When the net input to the logistic equation is equal to the bias (i.e., equal to θ_j), the activity that is generated is equal to 0.5. Because of this, it is typical to consider the bias of the logistic activation function as being analogous to the threshold of the step function.

Both the step function and the logistic equation are attempts to model the all-or-none law governing the generation of action potentials. Ballard (1986) has used the term *integration device* to describe neurons whose activation as a function of net input is sigmoid in nature. He points out that cells that behave in this fashion are commonly found in the oculomotor system of the mammalian brain. However, Ballard has also observed that not all neurons respond in a sigmoid fashion to net input. For instance, cone cells in the retina are tuned to particular ranges of light wavelength. Such a neuron will generate a strong response to a wavelength that has a value that falls in a narrow intermediate range. If the wavelength is too short to fall in this range, then the cone cell will not respond. Such behavior would also be expected of an integration device. However, unlike an integration device, if the wavelength is too long to fall in this range, then the cone cell will also not respond. Ballard calls neurons that behave like this *value units*. The activation function for a value unit, when plotted against net input, is bell shaped, as is illustrated in Figure 10.1d.

The third nonlinear activation function that we will be considering for a perceptron is the bell-shaped function that is characteristic of a value unit. Don Schopflocher and myself first described networks of value units in 1992, and networks of value units have been central to my research since that time. The particular equation that we use to describe the activation of a value unit is the *Gaussian equation*:

$$G(net_i) = \exp(-\pi(net_i - \mu_j)^2) \qquad [10.4]$$

In this equation, $G(net_i)$ is the activation being calculated for output unit i, net_i is the net input for that output unit, and μ is the mean of the Gaussian. When the net input to the Gaussian equation is equal to the mean (i.e., equal to μ_j), the activity that is generated is equal to 1.0. As a result, μ_j can be thought of as being similar to the bias of the logistic function or the threshold of the step function.

10.3.2.2 Modifiable connections

In a perceptron, input units are connected to output units by connections that have modifiable weights. These modifiable connections are identical in nature to those that were described for the distributed associative memory in Chapter 9. An input unit sends a numerical signal through a connection. The connection takes the signal and multiplies it by the connection weight before the signal reaches the output unit at the other end of the connection. If the connection is weak, then the absolute value of the connection weight will be near zero. As the connection grows stronger, the absolute value of the connection weight will grow larger. If the connection weight is positive, then the connection is excitatory. If the connection weight is negative, then the connection is inhibitory. Associations between input patterns and output unit responses are stored as a set of connection weights. A learning rule, which will be described in more detail below, is used to modify connection weights in order to create these associations.

10.3.2.3 Decision: The retrieval operation

Once associations have been stored in the connection weights of a perceptron, one can present a cue stimulus to the perceptron in order to retrieve information from it. As was discussed above, the nonlinear – or decisive – nature of the perceptron's output means that information retrieval is usually not viewed as a memory operation, but is instead interpreted as a classification operation. Regardless of the interpretation, the response of the perceptron is computed as follows. First, the cue pattern is used to activate the input units. Second, the activity from the input units is sent through the connections of the perceptron, and is modified by the connection weights at the same time. Third, each output unit in the perceptron calculates its net input. Fourth, each output unit in the perceptron passes its net input into a nonlinear activation function to calculate unit activity. The activity that is computed for each output unit represents the perceptron's response to the stimulus that was presented.

10.3.3   Learning with nonlinearity

How are connection weights modified in a memory system that uses nonlinear activation functions? In the sections that follow, we will consider three different learning rules. Each of these learning rules is associated with one of the three activation functions that were described above. While there are important technical differences between each of these learning rules, it will be apparent that they all share a general format. Each learning rule defines a change in a connection weight as being the product of three different numbers: a learning rate, the activity of the unit at the input end of the connection, and the error of the unit at the output end of the connection.

10.3.3.1 Rosenblatt's learning rule

The first learning rule that we will consider is a rule that Rosenblatt used to train perceptrons that used the step function to activate the output units. The logic of this learning rule is that connection weight modifications are contingent upon network performance. Let us define the error of some output unit j as the value $(t_j - a_j)$, where t_j is the desired or target value of the output, and a_j is the actual activity that the output unit generates. In calculating $(t_j - a_j)$ there are three possible outcomes. First, the value of $(t_j - a_j)$ could be equal to 0. In this case, the output unit has generated the correct response to an input pattern and no connection weight changes are required. Second, the value of $(t_j - a_j)$ could be equal to 1. In this case, the output unit has generated an error by turning off when it was desired that the unit actually turn on. In order to deal with this situation, it is necessary to increase the net input to the output unit. This could be accomplished by increasing the size of the connection weights. Third, the value of $(t_j - a_j)$ could be equal to –1. In this case, the output unit has made an error by turning on when it should have turned off. The remedy for this problem would be to decrease the unit's net input by subtracting from the values of the connection weights.

An examination of the three possible values for error, and of the resulting change that these values imply for connection weights, indicates that the delta rule that was described in Chapter 9 could be used as a learning rule for a perceptron based upon the step function. The value of the error term $(t_j - a_j)$ provides the direction of change required in the connection weights in order to reduce error if error occurs. In other words, Rosenblatt's learning rule for a perceptron is identical to the delta rule that we have already seen. Mathematically, the desired change to the weight connecting input unit i to output unit j can be expressed as:

$$\Delta w_{ij} = \eta (t_j - a_j) a_i \qquad [10.5]$$

In Equation 10.5, η is a learning rate that will ordinarily range between 0 and 1, $(t_j - a_j)$ is the error calculated for output unit j, under the assumption that a_j is calculated using the step function, and a_i is the activity of input unit i.

An output unit that uses the step function can be described as a classifier that makes a single straight cut through a pattern space. Each input pattern is represented as a point in that pattern space, with the position of each point being defined by the activity of each input unit. The input unit activities are used to define coordinates in the pattern space. Patterns that fall on one side of the cut the output unit makes will result in the output unit turning off. Patterns that fall on the other side of the cut will result in the output unit turning on. When a perceptron's weights are trained using Equation 10.5, the result is that the cut through pattern space made by the output unit is rotated. However, to solve some problems we also need to be able to translate this cut through space instead of just rotating it. In order to translate the cut, we need to be able to modify the threshold θ_j of the output unit. This can easily be done by assuming that the threshold is the value of the connection weight that comes from an additional input unit that is always on. With this interpretation, the desired change in the threshold θ_j of some output unit j can be defined as:

$$\Delta \theta_j = \eta (t_j - a_j) 1 \qquad [10.6]$$

The delta rule, when applied to a perceptron, is very powerful. Rosenblatt used it to derive his famous perceptron convergence theorem. This theorem proved that if a solution to a pattern classification problem could be represented in the connection weights of a perceptron, then the delta rule was guaranteed to find a set of connection weights that solved the problem. For our purposes, the fact that the delta rule can be used to train a perceptron also provides additional evidence about the similarity between perceptrons and distributed associative memories.

10.3.3.2   The gradient descent rule

Imagine being at the southwest corner of Sir Winston Churchill Square in Edmonton, Alberta. This square is a small downtown park that is a city block wide and long. If I wanted to meet someone at the northeast corner of the square, the shortest route to the meeting place would be for me to walk in a straight line diagonally through the park, from the southwest to the northeast. However, this isn't the only route that could be taken. Perhaps, for some unknown reason, I feel compelled to remain on the city sidewalks. Because of this compulsion, I could reach the meeting place by walking one block north, and then one block east. I could also go to my destination by walking one block east, and then one block north. However, by restricting myself to moving in only certain directions, both of these routes are longer than the one that I would have taken had I permitted myself to walk through the park. A slave to my compulsion, I arrive at my desired destination, but I take longer than was necessary.

Rosenblatt (1962) proved that the delta rule is guaranteed to find a solution to a pattern classification problem, provided that it is possible for the solution to be represented in a perceptron's weights. However, this does not mean that this rule is the most efficient one to use. In fact, the delta rule is restricted in a manner that is very similar to my example of walking around the park instead of through it.

The potential inefficiency of the delta rule becomes evident when we think about what weight changes it permits during learning. Imagine that the input units of some perceptron are only activated with values of 0 or 1 for some problem of interest, and that the output units of this perceptron employ the step function. If this perceptron is trained with the delta rule, then this means that when a weight is changed, it will only be changed in one of two ways. One change would be to add the value of the learning rate η to the weight, while the other change would be to subtract η from the weight. No other changes are possible, given the equations that were provided in Section 10.3.3.1.

The problem with this is that in some cases, the shortest route to a desired destination – that is, the fastest way to learn to perfectly classify the input patterns – might be if the weights were changed in a "diagonal" direction, by a value of $\frac{1}{2}\eta$, or $\frac{1}{4}\eta$, or some other value. However, speeding up learning in this way is not possible because the delta rule restricts us to moving in a "city block" direction of $\pm\eta$.

In order to have greater flexibility in the way in which weights are to be changed, the first thing that we need is to have greater flexibility in assigning activation values to our output units. The step function is the primary source of restriction on the delta rule, because when an output unit can only take on one of two possible activation values, this in turn restricts the possible values for unit error. To remove this source of restriction, we can approximate the step function with a continuous function, such as the logistic equation that was described earlier. Because of its continuous nature, an output unit that uses the logistic equation can generate an activity value that can be any real number in the range between 0 and 1. In turn, this means that when output unit error is measured by the expression $(t_j - a_j)$, it will not be restricted to returning values of –1, 0, or 1. Instead, output unit error will be any real number in the range between –1 and 1. The fact that our error values fall in a continuous range is what provides us with the opportunity to optimize the rate of learning by moving weights in a "diagonal" direction.

However, the flexibility to change weights in a continuous range, instead of in just two directions, presents a different problem. With all of the possible values that are now available to modify a weight at any given time, which value is the best one to use? Which weight change will reduce output error by the largest amount? The continuous nature of the logistic activation function provides us with an opportunity to use calculus to answer this question.

Rumelhart, Hinton, and Williams (1986a) defined the total error for a network with logistic output units as the sum of squared error, E, where the squared error is totaled over every output unit and every pattern in the training set:

$$E = \frac{1}{2}\Sigma\Sigma(t_{jp} - a_{jp})^2 \qquad [10.7]$$

In this equation, t_{jp} represents the target activity for output unit j when it is presented pattern p, and a_{jp} represents the observed activity for output unit j when it is presented pattern p. The first summation sign is performed over the total number of patterns in the training set, and the second summation sign is performed over the total number of output units in the perceptron.

With network error defined as above, and with a continuous activation function, Rumelhart, Hinton, and Williams (1986a) were in a position to use calculus to determine how a weight should be altered in order to decrease error. They derived equations that determined how a change in a weight changed the net input to an output unit, how the resulting change in net input affected the output unit's activity, and how altering the output unit's activity affected error as defined in Equation 10.7. They then used these equations to define how to change a weight, when a given pattern has been presented, in order to have the maximum effect of learning. This definition was a new statement of the error for an output unit j, which we will represent as δ_j. They found that the fastest way to decrease network error was to take the error that was used in the delta rule, and to multiply this error by the first derivative of the logistic equation, $f(net_j)$. The first derivative of the logistic equation is equal to the value $a_j(1 - a_j)$. So the new equation for output unit error was:

$$\delta_j = (t_j - a_j)f(net_j) = (t_j - a_j)a_j(1 - a_j) \qquad [10.8]$$

A new learning rule for a perceptron that uses the logistic activation function can be defined by inserting the error term from Equation 10.8 into the delta rule equation. This results in what we will call the gradient descent rule for training a perceptron:

$$\Delta w_{ij} = \eta\delta_j a_i = \eta(t_j - a_j)a_j(1 - a_j)a_i \qquad [10.9]$$

As was the case with the delta rule, the bias of the logistic function can also be modified by the learning rule. To do this, the bias is treated as if it were equal to the weight of a connection between the output unit and an additional input unit that is always activated with a value of 1 for every training pattern in the training set. With this assumption, the gradient descent rule for modifying bias can be stated as:

$$\Delta\theta_j = \eta\delta_j 1 = \eta(t_j - a_j)a_j(1 - a_j)1 \qquad [10.10]$$

What is the purpose of multiplying the output unit's error value by the derivative of the activation function before modifying the weight? At any point in time during learning, a perceptron can be represented as a single point or location on a surface. The coordinates of the location are given by the current values of all of the perceptron's weights (and of its bias). Each point on this surface has a height, which is equal to the value of total network error. One can think about learning as a process that moves the perceptron along this error surface, always seeking a minimum error value. Every time that the perceptron changes its connection weights, it takes a step "downhill" on the error surface, moving to a location that has lower height (i.e., a lower error value). The size of the step that is taken is determined by the size of the learning rate. The direction in which the step is taken is dictated by the error calculated for an output unit. In order to minimize total network error as quickly as possible, it is desirable that at each step the perceptron move in the direction that is the steepest "downhill." The first derivative of the activation function is the part of the equation that determines the direction from the current location on the space that has the steepest downhill slope. By multiplying output unit error by the derivative, the network is permitted to take the shortest "diagonal" path along the error surface. This is why Equation 10.9 is called a gradient descent rule – it results in the perceptron navigating a gradient surface by moving, step by step, in the steepest downhill direction. This is also why the gradient descent rule is more flexible than the delta rule.

10.3.3.3 Perceptrons and linear nonseparability

We saw earlier that Rosenblatt's (1962) perceptron convergence theorem was a proof that the delta rule was guaranteed to find the set of weights required for a perceptron to solve a problem, provided that the problem was one that could be represented in a perceptron's weights. What this implies is that there must be some problems that a perceptron cannot solve, no matter how much training it receives. What sorts of problems are these? What are the formal limitations of a perceptron?

In Section 10.3.3.1, the delta rule was described as a technique for changing the position of a cut through a pattern space that separated different groups of input patterns. In this pattern space, each pattern is represented as a point whose coordinates are determined by the activity of each input unit. The perceptron can be described as a system that makes a single straight cut through this space to separate the patterns that turn the output unit off from the patterns that turn the output unit on. When an input pattern falls on one side of the cut, its net input to the output unit is below threshold. When an input pattern falls on the other side of the cut, its net input to the output unit is above threshold. When a perceptron's weights are changed, the position of the cut is rotated around in the space, and when its threshold is changed, the position of the cut is translated through the space. Learning, then, is a process by which the perceptron finds where it should make a cut through the pattern space to solve a desired problem.

When the output unit of a perceptron employs the logistic equation, a similar story can be told. Because the logistic function is a continuous approximation of the step function, it too can be described as an equation that is used to make a single straight cut through the pattern space to separate one class of patterns from another. Weight changes rotate the cut, and changes in bias translate the cut.

As a result of this description, it can be said that a perceptron that uses either the step function or the logistic function can only represent solutions to problems for which all of the "off" patterns can be separated from all of the "on" patterns by a single straight cut through a pattern space. If a problem can be solved in this fashion, then it is called *linearly separable*. Perceptrons are formally limited to solving linearly separable problems.

This is not to say that the set of linearly separable problems is either small or uninteresting. For instance, consider the domain of two-valued logic that McCulloch and Pitts (1988) argued provided the core of any psychological theory. Imagine having a perceptron for dealing with this logical domain. It will have one output unit, used to represent whether some logical relationship is either true or false. It will also have two input units, used to represent the truth or falsehood of two different input variables (x and y). In this situation, there are four possible input patterns (x and y both false, x true and y false, x false and y true, x and y both true) that are represented in the four columns on the right of

Table 10.1 Logical operations on two input variables

Inputs	Pattern 1	Pattern 2	Pattern 3	Pattern 4
x	0	0	1	1
y	0	1	0	1
	Output 1	Output 2	Output 3	Output 4
Contradiction	0	0	0	0
~x ∧ ~y	1	0	0	0
~x ∧ y	0	1	0	0
~x	1	1	0	0
x ∧ ~y	0	0	1	0
~y	1	0	1	0
x ⊗ y	0	1	1	0
~(x ∧ y)	1	1	1	0
x ∧ y	0	0	0	1
~(x ⊗ y)	1	0	0	1
y	0	1	0	1
x ⊃ y	1	1	0	1
x	0	0	1	1
y ⊃ x	1	0	1	1
x ∨ y	0	1	1	1
Tautology	1	1	1	1

Table 10.1. In this situation, there are also 16 possible patterns of response made by the output unit to the four input patterns, ranging from turning off to all four to turning on to all four. These possibilities are represented in the bottom 16 rows of Table 10.1. The pattern of responses in each of these rows defines a truth table for a particular logical relationship between two variables. Of all of these possible logical relationships, 14 are linearly separable, and as a result can be learned by a perceptron (Quinlan, 1991, p. 17). This indicates that perceptrons have a high degree of logical power.

However, this logical power is not complete. There are two logical relations in this table that are not linearly separable, and as a result cannot be realized as primitive operations by a perceptron. The first is the exclusive-or (XOR) relationship $x \otimes y$, which amounts to the statement in English "*x or else y*." For XOR, the output unit must turn on when only one input unit is activated, and must turn off when either both input units are off, or when both input units are on. The second is the identity function that is the negation of XOR, and is represented as $\sim(x \otimes y)$. In English it can be stated as "*both or else neither*." It is the opposite of XOR, in the sense that the output unit must turn on when either both input units are off, or when both input units are on, but must turn off when only one input unit has been activated.

Why is a relationship like XOR not linearly separable? One way to answer this question is to try to design a perceptron to compute XOR, and see why it fails. When computing XOR, if both input units are off, the output unit must turn off. To accomplish this, we need to set the threshold of the output unit high enough above zero to ensure that the output unit will not turn on to the net input of zero. This is because net input of zero will be produced when both input units are off, regardless of what the connection weights are. So, for a first step, let us set the output units threshold equal to 0.5.

For two of the input patterns of the XOR problem, only one of the two input units is on, and the output unit is required to turn on to each of these patterns. This can be accomplished in our second design step by keeping the output unit's threshold at 0.5, and by setting both of the connection weights equal to +1. Under these conditions, when only one of the input units is activated, the net input to the output unit will be equal to 1. Because this is greater than the threshold of 0.5, the output unit will generate an activity of 1 when only one input unit is turned on.

With a threshold of 0.5, and two weights of +1, the output unit will generate the correct response for three of XOR's possible input patterns. However, this configuration will not permit a correct response to the fourth. For the fourth pattern, in which both input units are turned on, the net input will be even stronger – equal to 2 – and as a result will be even further above threshold than was the case for the two patterns that involve activating only one input unit. As a result, the output unit will turn on. However, this is an incorrect response, because the output unit is required to turn off to this pattern.

This last scenario provides one sense about why XOR is not a linearly separable problem. It shows that a single cut – represented in this case by a single threshold – is not sufficient to separate the "off" patterns from the "on" patterns. The threshold of 0.5 separates the two patterns in which only one input unit is on from the one pattern in which both inputs are off. However, it does not separate them from the one pattern in which both inputs are on. In order to do this, a second cut would be required, which is why the problem is not linearly separable. For instance, if we could define a unit that had two thresholds, and that would only turn on to net inputs that were between the two thresholds, then the XOR problem could be solved. A second threshold equal to 1.5 would suffice to deal with XOR. However, a second threshold is not a possibility when the output units of a perceptron use either the step function or the logistic function.

The inability of perceptrons to represent solutions to linearly nonseparable problems was a severe blow to research on artificial neural networks. Minsky and Papert (1988) provided a detailed mathematical analysis of what perceptrons could and could not do in the late 1960s. They were able to prove that a number of discriminations that could easily be made by humans, such as detecting whether a figure was connected or not, were linearly nonseparable, and were therefore beyond the ken of perceptron simulations. This led to a dramatic decrease in interest in this type of modeling. Artificial neural networks did not regain widespread popularity until the mid-1980s, when learning rules for training more complex architectures were discovered.

10.3.3.4   The Dawson–Schopflocher learning rule

The standard approach to dealing with linearly nonseparable problems such as XOR is to adopt a more complicated architecture that includes layers of processors. The idea in using this architecture is that intermediate processing units can detect patterns in the input that can be used to modify or "gate" the direct effects of the inputs on the output unit.

> Of the 16 possible logical functions of neurons with two inputs, two functions cannot be calculated by any one neuron. They are the exclusion or, A or else B, and both or else neither – the if and only if of logic. Both limitations point to a third possibility in the interaction of neurons, and both are easily explained if impulses from one source can gate those from another so as to prevent their reaching the output neuron.
>
> *(McCulloch, 1988, p. 12)*

The basic properties of so-called multilayer perceptrons are dealt with in detail in the next chapter.

A less standard approach is to modify the activation function of the perceptron, and to replace the step function or the logistic function with a function that can be described in qualitative terms as having two different thresholds, and which leads to an "on" response when the net input falls between the two thresholds. This was the architectural move made by Dawson and Schopflocher (1992a) when they developed a rule for the training of networks of value units. In a perceptron that uses value units, the output units will employ an activation function like the Gaussian function that was defined in Equation 10.4. Because this function is "tuned" or "bell shaped," as was illustrated in Figure 10.1d, it can be thought of as providing an output unit with two functions, and as a result should be capable of solving a problem like XOR.

How would one train a perceptron whose output units are value units? The first plausible approach would be to adopt the gradient descent rule. To do this, one would define a new error term by taking Equation 10.8 and replacing the first derivative of the logistic function ($f(net_j)$) with the first derivative of the Gaussian function ($G(net_j)$), which is equal to $-2\pi(net_j)G(net_j) = -2\pi(net_j)(\exp(-\pi(net_i - \mu_j)^2))$. However, Dawson and Schopflocher found that when they did this, learning was very inconsistent. In some cases, training proceeded very quickly. However, in the majority of cases, the network did not learn to solve the problem. Instead, its connection weights were changed in such a way that the network learned to turn off to all of the training patterns by moving all of the net inputs into one of the tails of the Gaussian function.

To correct this problem, Dawson and Schopflocher (1992a) elaborated the equation for total network error by adding a heuristic component to Equation 10.7.

This heuristic component was designed to keep some of the net inputs in the middle of the Gaussian function. It was a statement that asserted that when the desired activation value for output unit *j* was 1, the error term should include an attempt to minimize the difference between the net input to the unit net_j and the unit's mean μ_j. Their elaborated expression for total network error was:

$$E = \tfrac{1}{2}\Sigma\Sigma(t_{pj} - a_{pj})^2 + \tfrac{1}{2}\Sigma\Sigma t_{pj}(net_{pj} - \mu_j)^2 \qquad [10.11]$$

After defining this elaborated error term, Dawson and Schopflocher (1992a) used calculus to determine what kind of weight change was required to decrease total network error. As was the case for the derivation of the gradient descent rule, this resulted in a new expression for output unit error to be included in an expression that was similar to the delta rule. However, because their elaborated error expression had two components, Dawson and Schopflocher found that the error for an output value unit also had two components.

The first component was identical to the expression in the gradient descent rule that defined the term δ_{pj}, with the exception that it used the first derivative of the Gaussian function instead of the logistic function:

$$\delta_{pj} = (t_{pj} - a_{pj})G(net_{pj}) = (t_{pj} - a_{pj})(-2\pi\,(net_{pj})(\exp(-\pi(net_{pj} - \mu_{pj})^2))) \qquad [10.12]$$

The second component was represented with the term ε_j, and was the part of output unit error that was related to the heuristic information that Dawson and Schopflocher (1992a) added to the equation for total network error. The equation for this error term was:

$$\varepsilon_{pj} = t_{pj}(net_{pj} - \mu_j) \qquad [10.13]$$

The complete expression for an output unit's error was found to be the difference between these two expressions of error, and Dawson and Schopflocher discovered that a learning rule for a network of value units was defined by a gradient descent rule that used this more complex measure of output unit error:

$$\Delta w_{ij} = \eta(\delta_j - \varepsilon_j)a_i \qquad [10.14]$$

Similarly, Dawson and Schopflocher (1992a) found that the mean of an output unit's Gaussian function could also be trained. This was done by assuming that the value j was the weight from an additional input unit that was always turned on. This assumption results in a learning expression very similar to the ones that were provided earlier for training the threshold of a step function or the bias of a logistic function:

$$\Delta\mu = \eta(\delta_j - \varepsilon_j) \qquad [10.15]$$

In summary, Dawson and Schopflocher (1992a) demonstrated that a perceptron with output units that used the Gaussian activation function could be trained with a variant of the gradient descent rule that was derived for integration devices. The learning rule that they developed differed from the more traditional gradient descent rule in only two ways. First, it used the first derivative of the Gaussian equation. Second, it used an elaborated expression for output unit error, which included a heuristic component that is not found in the traditional gradient descent rule.

There are both advantages and disadvantages associated with using value units as the outputs in a perceptron. On the one hand, this kind of perceptron is capable of solving some linearly nonseparable problems. For instance, it can solve XOR, and can also detect connectedness in the figures that Minsky and Papert (1988, p. 13) used to examine the limitations of more traditional perceptrons. Dawson and Schopflocher (1992a) also found that their learning rule led to very fast learning for a number of benchmark problems.

On the other hand, a perceptron constructed from value units is also subject to limitations. When the activation function is the Gaussian function defined in Equation 10.4, there is a very narrow gap between the two thresholds that can be assigned. In other words, while this Gaussian function makes two parallel cuts through a pattern space, these two cuts are very close together. Because of this, it cannot solve all of the logic problems in Table 10.1 (at least when the inputs to the problems are encoded with 0 and 1). For example, it cannot solve $x \vee y$ because it cannot arrange its two cuts so that all three "on" patterns for this problem fall between them. As a result, there is still a need for the multilayer architectures that will be described in the next chapter.

10.3.3.5   Exploring the three learning rules

The website of supplementary material (www.bcp.psych.ualberta.ca/~mike/Book2/) for this book provides a program called "Rosenblatt." This program can be used to train perceptrons using any of the three learning rules that were described above. The program also comes with a number of example training files, including ones for all of the logic problems from Table 10.1. The reader is invited to use this program to explore the relative merits and limitations of these three different kinds of perceptrons. Some suggestions for exploring the properties of perceptrons are included in the manual that describes how to use the program, which is also available at that website.

10.4   The Psychology of Perceptrons

Modern cognitive science has very little interest in the perceptron. Primarily, this is because perceptrons are generally restricted to solving linearly separable problems, although we saw above that this could be circumvented to a certain degree by adopting a Gaussian activation function. This restriction means that perceptrons are inappropriate models for a wide range of cognitive phenomena, because perceptrons are not powerful enough to capture them. Nevertheless, there is some mileage to be gained by considering the kinds of contributions perceptrons could make to some areas of cognitive science or psychology. This is consistent with the general perspective on synthetic psychology that I like to communicate to my students. When you have a set of building blocks, no matter how small that set is, it can still be fruitful to ask what can be done with it. At this point in the chapter, we are armed with two basic connectionist building blocks. The first is the storing of associations in modifiable connection weights. The second is the use of nonlinear activation functions in output units. In the sub-sections that follow, we will see that the perceptron can use these two building blocks to make some interesting contributions to a modern debate in the study of discrimination learning.

10.4.1 Supervised learning and classical conditioning

In Chapter 4, we were introduced to the notion of classical conditioning. At the start of a classical conditioning experiment, a conditioned stimulus (CS) will not elicit a desired response. However, if when it is repeatedly paired with an unconditioned stimulus (US) it does elicit the desired response without the need of training, then eventually the conditioned stimulus will become capable of eliciting the response as well. One account of classical conditioning considers the product of learning to be a stronger association between the conditioned stimulus and the response.

With a little imagination, one can see how classical conditioning could be represented in a perceptron. Each input unit of the perceptron can be used to represent the presence or absence of a particular conditioned stimulus. If the stimulus is present, then its input unit will be turned on. Otherwise, the input unit will be turned off. The response that is being conditioned must be the activity of the output unit of the perceptron; this response will either be present or absent. (All of the networks that we will consider below will have only one output unit.) The pairing of a conditioned stimulus with an unconditioned stimulus is represented by using target values to train the perceptron to make desired responses. The results of learning are the changes of weights in the perceptron, which represent changes in association between conditioned stimuli and the response.

By thinking about a perceptron in this way, and placing it in the context of classical conditioning, we can begin to see that there may be important relation-ships between the learning rules used to train perceptrons and the regularities that govern associative learning in humans and animals. As a matter of fact, by drawing the parallel between perceptrons and classical conditioning, Sutton and

Barto (1981) were able to prove that there is a formal equivalence between the delta rule and the Rescorla–Wagner learning rule that was discussed earlier in Chapter 4. In short, a rule that can be used to train a perceptron must be viewed as a plausible theory of classical conditioning. Furthermore, one can use a perceptron as a simulation in order to explore potential empirical relationships between perceptron learning and animal learning.

10.4.2   The patterning problem

10.4.2.1   Patterning problems in classical conditioning

One example of the kind of learning that could be accomplished by a perceptron is called discrimination learning. In discrimination learning, an animal is trained to make a response to one stimulus, and to not make the response to a different stimulus. This learning requires that the animal discriminate between the two different stimuli. For example, an animal might be presented with two different sounds, such as a pure tone (stimulus A) and white noise (stimulus B), and then trained to press a bar when stimulus A is heard, but not when stimulus B is heard. For learning theorists, this kind of training would be represented as [A+, B−]. This kind of training could be accomplished in a perceptron as follows: first, the perceptron would have two input units, one to represent the presence or absence of stimulus A, the other to represent the presence or absence of stimulus B. Second, a learning rule would be used to train the perceptron to turn on to stimulus A, and to turn off to stimulus B.

Discrimination learning is of interest to modern researchers because it can be used to study how animals learn to respond to combinations of stimuli. One learning paradigm that focuses upon stimulus combinations is the patterning experiment. In a patterning experiment, an animal learns to respond in one fashion to a single stimulus, and to respond in the opposite fashion when stimuli are combined. In positive patterning, the animal is trained not to respond to single stimuli and to respond to their conjunction [A−, B−, AB+]. In negative patterning, the animal is trained to respond to single stimuli, and not to respond to their conjunction [A+, B+, AB−].

The basic perceptron model of classical conditioning that is illustrated in Figure 10.2a represents one possible theory of patterning, called the configural approach. "According to this view, subjects represent compound stimuli holistically and as being different from but similar to their components" (Delamater, Sosa, & Katz, 1999, p. 98). The basic perceptron model is configural in the sense that the net input to the output unit is a holistic representation that would have to distinguish compound stimuli from their components. However, the fact that this particular type of theory can be expressed in the form of a perceptron is not advantageous. Modern learning theorists usually begin by pointing out that a theory that can be expressed in this way, such as the Rescorla–Wagner

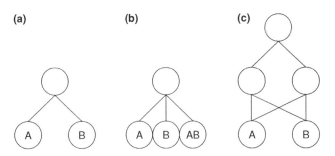

Figure 10.2 Three examples of network models of conditioning paradigms: (a) a configural model; (b) an elemental model; (c) A multilayered model

model, is not powerful enough to account for negative patterning. The reason for making this claim is that learning theorists equate negative patterning with the XOR problem, which we have already seen cannot be solved by a perceptron that uses a step function or a logistic function in its output unit. "This is not a problem that is unique to this particular theory. There have been other attempts to develop a single layer learning networks, and it has long been appreciated that they are unable to solve negative patterning discriminations, or, as it is more generally known, the *exclusive-or* problem" (Pearce, 1997, p. 131).

Because of this limitation, learning theorists who are interested in connectionism adopt two different approaches to elaborating the configural model that is illustrated in Figure 10.2a. The first is the elemental approach, in which an additional input unit is used to represent the presence of conjoined stimuli. This is shown in Figure 10.2b. The logic of this approach is that there is something unique in the conjunction of stimuli, and this uniqueness can serve by itself as an additional conditioned stimulus or cue. The second is what I will call the multilayer approach. "According to this approach, it is assumed that conditioned stimulus representations change during conditioning, and that configural and/or elemental solutions develop according to the nature of the task" (Delamater et al., 1999, p. 98). One example of a multilayer approach would be to add hidden units to the perceptron, as is shown in Figure 10.2c. Such a system "assumes that these unique cues or configural stimuli are not present from the outset of training but rather are themselves the product of learning" (p. 98).

Unfortunately, there is a serious flaw in the argument that a perceptron is incapable of handling negative patterning, and that as a result a model of the form of Figure 10.2a is not appropriate for studying this kind of learning. If negative patterning is defined as responding in particular ways to three different stimulus conditions, as is represented in the expression [A+, B+, AB−], then negative patterning is *not* identical to XOR. As a matter of fact, learning to respond [A+, B+, AB−] turns out to be a linearly separable problem whose solution *can* be represented by any of the perceptron types that we have described in this chapter.

The reason for this is that the expression [A+, B+, AB−] does not include a fourth stimulus condition, in which the animal learns not to respond when neither stimulus is present. When learning theorists say that a perceptron cannot learn negative patterning, they really intend to define negative patterning as [~A~B−, A~B+, ~AB+, AB−], where ~A represents the absence of A, and ~B represent the absence of B. Importantly, this is not a minor semantic point. This is because when connectionist models are used to explore negative patterning, the network is not trained to not respond in a null condition in which no conditioned stimuli are presented. The connectionist models are instead trained on patterns that correspond to the traditional definition of negative patterning, that is [A+, B+, AB−]. Because of this, learning theorists are exploring negative patterning with connectionist networks that are more powerful than necessary. To demonstrate this, let us consider a recent experiment that adopted the multilayer approach, and then let us demonstrate that a variety of simpler perceptrons could have also been exploited quite usefully.

10.4.2.2   A multilayer account of negative patterning

Delamater, Sosa, and Katz (1999) reported an interesting study in which an attempt was made to relate the learning of a PDP network to the kind of learning observed in an experiment involving animals. The general focus of this study was learning to respond to combinations of stimuli. In particular, the study was interested in determining how pretraining to discriminate between stimuli affected later learning in positive and negative patterning paradigms.

Delamater et al. (1999) were in particular interested in exploring the properties of a configural model of patterning in which configural representations emerged because of learning. As a result, they explored patterning using a multilayer PDP network of a type similar in design but with more units than the network illustrated in Figure 10.2c. Their particular network had six different input units. Four of these were used to encode the presence of four different stimuli (A, B, C, or D). The other two were used to represent stimulus type. Both stimuli A and B were of type X. So, whenever either of these two stimuli was presented to the network, the input unit representing type X was also turned on. Similarly, stimuli C and D were of type Y; this was represented by also activating the sixth input unit whenever C or D was presented to the network. The network also had one output unit and four intermediate or hidden units; all of these units employed the logistic activation function.

Delamater et al. (1999) used this type of network because they wanted to explore the effect on patterning of representations that emerged in the intermediate layers of processors during a pretraining period. In the first phase of their experiment, the network was trained, using four different input patterns, to make discriminations between the four different individual stimuli (AX+, BX−, CY+, DY−). In other words, it was reinforced (i.e., trained to activate) to stimuli A and

C, and not reinforced (i.e., trained to turn off) to stimuli B and D. With this pattern of responding, the network was discriminating, because it was generating different responses to the two X-type stimuli, as well as to the two Y-type stimuli. Once a network had learned to make these discriminations, it was placed in one of four different post-training conditions, each of which involved training the network with three different input patterns.

Two of these conditions required the network to undergo a period of positive patterning. In one, this positive patterning involved the stimuli that had been previously reinforced in the pretraining (AX–, CY–, AXCY+). In the other, positive patterning was based on the stimuli that had not been previously reinforced (BX–, DY–, BXDY+). Delamater et al. (1999) found that learning in the first condition was much faster than learning in the second condition, which indicated that previous reinforcement created internal representations that aided later positive patterning.

The other two post-training conditions in their study involved negative patterning. In one, the negative patterning was based on the previously reinforced stimuli (AX+, CY+, AXCY–). In the other, it was based on the stimuli that had not been previously reinforced (BX+, DY+, BXDY–). Delamater et al. (1999) found that learning in the first condition was slower than learning in the second, which demonstrated that previous reinforcement created internal representations that hindered later negative patterning.

What was particularly interesting about the Delamater et al. (1999) study was that after examining the performance of their networks, they proceeded to conduct a parallel animal learning study to determine whether pretraining affected animal patterning in the same way that it affected network patterning. In a pretraining phase, Sprague-Dawley rats learned to discriminate between two different sounds (tone vs. white noise) and between two different visual stimuli (steady light vs. flashing light). The rats then underwent a post-training patterning phase, in which they were placed in either a negative or a positive patterning paradigm, which involved either the stimuli that had been reinforced in the pretraining phase or the stimuli that had not been reinforced.

Interestingly, the results of the Delamater et al. (1999) animal study were quite different from the predictions made on the basis of the performance of their PDP network. First, for the rats there was strong evidence that previous reinforcement of stimuli aided negative patterning – a result that was completely opposite to the prediction made by the network. Second, there was at best weak evidence that previous reinforcement aided positive patterning. "The present data suggest that if changes in the internal representations of stimuli occur throughout training, they do not do so in the manner anticipated by the standard multi-layered network" (p. 108).

10.4.2.3 Perceptrons and patterning

Why are the results of Delamater et al. (1999) network markedly different from the results of their animal study? One possible answer to this question is that the multilayer network that they used was far too powerful for the patterning problems that they studied. As was noted earlier, learning theorists assume that perceptron-like systems are incapable of learning patterning problems because these problems are assumed to be linearly nonseparable. However, the patterning problems used by Delamater et al. (e.g., AX+, CY+, AXCY–) are linearly separable, and can in fact be learned by a perceptron. As a result, any one of the hidden units in their network was capable of learning the pretraining patterns, as well as any of the four post-training patterning problems. Is it possible that a simpler network – a perceptron – could generate results that were more similar to those observed in the animal learning experiment? To explore this question, and to demonstrate the adequacy of perceptrons' patterning (as defined by learning theorists), we replicated the network portion of the Delamater et al. study. However, instead of using a multilayer approach, we used a number of different perceptrons. These networks were used to study predictions from both the configural type of model illustrated in Figure 10.2a, and the elemental type of model illustrated in Figure 10.2b.

For the configural models, we presented stimuli to the perceptrons using the same coding scheme that was employed by Delamater et al. (1999). There were six input units, four for representing the presence or absence of four different stimuli (A, B, C, D), and two for representing stimulus type (X, Y).

For the elemental models, we adopted an encoding scheme of the type described by Pearce (1997, p. 131). This scheme used the same six input units that were used in the configural representation, plus an additional two units that were used to represent the two possible "unique cues" provided by combinations of stimuli in the patterning experiment. One of these units represented the cue AXCY, while the other represented the cue BXDY. When combined stimuli were presented to the networks during patterning, five of the eight input units were turned on – four representing the individual stimuli and their type, and the fifth representing the unique configural cue. For instance, when AXCY was the stimulus being presented, the units for A, X, C, Y, and AXCY were all turned on; the units for B, D, and BXDY were turned off. When individual stimuli were presented, only two units were turned on – the one representing the stimulus, and the other representing the stimulus type.

We conducted our experiment as follows: First, we trained a network until it converged on the pretraining task that was used by Delamater et al. (1999). The training was conducted using the default options that are available with the Rosenblatt perceptron program, and usually was completed after 140 to 150 training epochs. Second, the network was then trained without resetting its weights on one of Delamater et al.'s post-training patterning experiments. We trained 10 different networks in each of the four post-training conditions that were described earlier, and computed the average number of sweeps for a perceptron to converge on this second task as our dependent measure.

In our first study, we used the gradient descent rule to train a perceptron whose output unit was defined by the logistic activation function. For the

Table 10.2 Average number of epochs for pretrained perceptrons to converge to solutions of patterning problems. Each cell represents an average of 10 different simulations

	Elemental encoding		Configural encoding	
	Positive patterning	Negative patterning	Positive patterning	Negative patterning
Previously reinforced	226.1	287.8	656.3	837.1
Not previously reinforced	292.7	226.1	829.8	656.8

configural encoding, such a perceptron is equivalent to one of the hidden units in the Delamater et al. (1999) network. Table 10.2 presents the average results of this experiment for both types of stimulus encoding. There are a number of conclusions that can be drawn from this table. First, the patterning problems used by Delamater et al. to train their multilayered network were obviously not linearly separable, because they can all be learned by a perceptron. Second, the elemental encoding leads to much faster learning, in general, than does the configural encoding. This is not surprising, because when configural encoding is used, the network has to develop an internal representation that distinguishes single stimuli from combined stimuli, while a unique cue for this is already available to the networks in the elemental encoding conditions. Third, regardless of the type of encoding that was used, previous reinforcement helped positive patterning, and hindered negative patterning. This pattern is identical to what Delamater et al. (1999) observed in their multilayered network, but is quite different from the pattern that they observed in their animal studies.

Why does previous reinforcement aid positive patterning, and hinder negative patterning? One way to answer this question is to examine the total sum of squared error (SSE) of the network on a patterning task, before any training on the second task has begun. This will provide an indication about what state the network is in after the pretraining has been completed. Table 10.3 presents

Table 10.3 Average sum of squared error for pretrained perceptrons on patterning problems before training on the patterning problems has begun. Each cell represents an average of 10 different simulations.

Gradient descent error	Elemental encoding		Configural encoding	
	Positive patterning	Negative patterning	Positive patterning	Negative patterning
Previously reinforced	1.62	0.99	1.62	1.00
Not previously reinforced	0.99	1.62	1.00	1.62

network SSE on the patterning task for all of the conditions in the first simulation study. This table shows, for both versions of problem encoding, that previous reinforcement leads to higher initial error for the positive patterning task, but not for the negative patterning task. Similarly, negative patterning begins with higher error in the condition that uses stimuli that were not previously reinforced in comparison with positive patterning. That the conditions that begin with higher degrees of error lead to faster training on the patterning problem might seem counterintuitive, but is perfectly consistent with the gradient descent learning rule. Equation 10.9 indicates that one of the elements that drive weight changes is network error, and when error is higher, more learning will occur. Thus it is perfectly reasonable to find that the patterning training that begins with a higher degree of error will also be associated with faster learning.

What produces the pattern of errors provided in Table 10.3? Let us take one perceptron trained with the configural encoding as a test case. After 140 sweeps of pretraining (i.e., after each of the four training patterns was presented 140 times), the network had learned to generate a response of 0.9 to two of the stimuli (AX, CY) and to produce a response of 0.1 to the other two (BX, DY) to be consistent with the desired pattern of responses (i.e., AX+, BX−, CY+, D−). The network structure that resulted from this training was quite straightforward. First, the bias of the output unit was near zero (−0.06). Second, the weights from the input units representing stimuli were fairly large, with absolute values over 2. For the two stimuli to which the network was to respond to (A, C), the weights were 2.22 and 2.23 respectively. For the two stimuli to which the network was not to respond to (B, D), the weights were both equal to −2.18. Third, the two input units used to code stimulus type (X, Y) both had near zero weights equal to 0.04. This indicates that these two units provided redundant information that was not required by the perceptron to learn the pretraining discrimination.

This pattern of connectivity leads directly to the errors that were presented in Table 10.3. For example, consider positive patterning. After the pretraining, when the network is then given the positive patterning stimuli that involve stimuli that were not reinforced (BX−, DY−, BXDY+), the network already responds correctly to the first two patterns (responses to both were equal to 0.1). For the third pattern, which involves turning on both input units B and D, a much stronger negative signal is sent to the output unit, which leads to an even smaller response (0.01). Thus almost all of the error for this condition in Table 10.3 is due to turning off BXDY, which is a response opposite to that which was desired. In contrast, when the network is given the positive patterning task involving stimuli that were previously reinforced (AX−, CY−, AXCY+), more errors will be made. Because of the pretraining, the network has learned to turn on to AX and CY, which is the incorrect response to both of these patterns. However, for the third pattern both A and C are turned on. This produces a larger net input because of the perceptron's positive connection weights, and the network generates its strongest response to this pattern (0.99), which is correct. Therefore for this cell in Table 10.3, almost all of the squared error reflects incorrect responses to the individual stimuli.

Now consider the errors produced by this perceptron for the two negative patterning conditions. When given the patterns involving stimuli that have already been reinforced (AX+, CY+, AXCY−), the network has already learned to respond correctly to the first two patterns. It generates an even stronger "on" response (0.99) to the third pattern, because it uses two input units that have very positive connection weights. This is incorrect, and is responsible for almost all of the squared error seen in the corresponding cell in Table 10.3. When presented with patterns involving stimuli that have not been previously reinforced (BX+, DY+, BXDY−), the network has learned to make incorrect responses (equal to 0.1) to the first two stimuli. However, because the third is a compound stimulus that involves sending signals through two strongly negative weights, the output unit generates a very weak response of 0.01, which is correct. Thus almost all of the error in the corresponding cell of Table 10.3 is due to incorrect responding to the individual stimuli.

Interestingly, exactly the same story could be told to explain the pattern of errors found for the perceptron that used elemental encoding to represent the input patterns. This is because when one of these perceptrons is given the pretraining task, the six connection weights that it shares with a configural-encoding perceptron are nearly identical in weight. Furthermore, the two additional connection weights associated with the two units that represent unique compound stimuli (AXBY and BXDY) have nearly zero weights. For instance, in one network, the weights for these two additional input units were −0.091 and 0.062 respectively. In other words, the information provided by the elemental encoding of the pretraining patterns is redundant with other information in the training set, and is not used by the network.

In accounting for the errors in Table 10.3, we saw that in some instances a network's response was more extreme (a stronger "on" or "off") to a compound stimulus than to either of the individual stimuli that make up the compound. This is analogous to an effect called summation that is found in animal learning experiments. For example, Delamater et al. (1999) found that after pretraining, animals placed in a negative patterning condition started off by generating stronger responses to compound stimuli than to individual stimuli. Finding evidence of summation in perceptrons using either type of stimulus encoding is interesting, because it is generally assumed that summation can easily be explained by elemental theories, but not by configural theories. One of our contributions to this topic in animal learning that comes from using perceptron models of patterning is that configural encoding can elicit summation.

Summation can also be used to motivate the use of other perceptrons to model patterning. One account of summation due to pretraining that was also explored experimentally by Delamater et al. (1999) was that "reinforced stimuli are processed more effectively than non-reinforced stimuli" (p. 109). Differential processing of "on" and "off" stimuli can be explored in a perceptron by using the Gaussian activation function. This is because when this activation function is employed, "on" patterns carry more information than "off" patterns, where information is measured using standard mathematical models of information. This difference in the amount of information is because only a very narrow range of net inputs can be used to turn a value unit "on," while a very large range of net inputs can be used to turn it "off." This is different than the sigmoid, because for an integration device, the range of net inputs that can be used to turn the unit "off" is equal to the range that can be used to turn it "on."

With this reasoning in mind, the second simulation experiment that was conducted was identical to the first, with the exception that the perceptrons used a value unit as their output processor, and were trained using the Dawson–Schopflocher learning rule. The training parameters that were used were the default values that are set by the Rosenblatt program when this learning rule is selected. For positive patterning, previously reinforced stimuli led to convergence in an average of 50.3 epochs, while not previously reinforced stimuli led to convergence in an average of 28.1 epochs. For negative patterning, the reinforcement conditions led to near identical results (55.4 and 54.7 epochs respectively). As was the case in the previous simulation study, the connection weights revealed that there was no essential difference between the networks trained with configural encoding and those trained with elemental encoding. As a result, only the configural encoding results are reported. However, to keep these results as comparable as possible to those found by Delamater et al. (1999), input units representing stimulus types X and Y were still included.

These results provide some interesting findings relative to those that were presented in Table 10.2. First, learning in all four patterning conditions was much faster. This is not surprising, given that Dawson and Schopflocher (1992a) reported that their learning rule led to faster learning for a wide range of problems in comparison to standard gradient descent methods. Second, the pattern of results is quite different. For this perceptron, pretraining had very little effect on negative patterning. However, the pretraining produced much faster learning in positive conditioning when the stimuli were not previously reinforced, in comparison to the condition in which stimuli had been previously reinforced. Third, while this pattern of results is quite different than those found in Table 10.2, it is still markedly at odds with the results obtained by Delamater et al. (1999) in their animal experiments. The same can be said for this type of perceptron when elemental coding is used, for it produces results that are nearly identical to those in Table 10.2.

The simulation studies reported to this point in the chapter have shown that patterning problems defined by learning theorists such as Delamater et al. (1999), are linearly separable, and can be handled by a perceptron. However, they have also shown that the kind of learning demonstrated by these perceptrons does not resemble the kind of learning demonstrated by animals placed in patterning paradigms. Why is this the case?

The logic of the simulation studies was to take the training sets that Delamater et al. (1999) used, and to show that perceptrons could handle them. An equally plausible approach would be to take training sets that they didn't actually use, but intended to use. We saw earlier that learning theorists assume that patterning problems are not linearly separable, because they are equivalent to logical problems like XOR. One further simulation study that could be conducted would be to add a null training pattern to the pretraining and to each of the post-training problem sets. This null pattern would be defined by turning all of the input units off (indicating that no stimuli were present at all). The networks would then be trained to turn off to this null pattern. The addition of this null stimulus to each of the four patterning conditions would convert them from being linearly separable problems to being linearly nonseparable, which is already assumed by learning theorists to be the case. The addition of the null stimulus to all five training sets would ensure that the network behaves the way that animals behave – that is, the network will learn not to respond in the absence of any stimuli at all.

Typically, the addition of a training pattern to make a problem logically equivalent to XOR takes it beyond the ability of the perceptron, and into the realm of the multilayered networks that will be described in the next chapter. However, we saw earlier that a perceptron that uses a value unit to generate responses is capable of representing a solution to XOR. So, in the final simulation study, such a perceptron was run in a version of the Delamater et al. (1999) study that included a null pattern in each of the five training sets. As was the case in the previous simulation, this network was trained using the default settings that the Rosenblatt program provides for the Dawson–Schopflocher training rule. The results of this final simulation are as follows. For positive patterning, previously reinforced stimuli converged after an average of 51.3 epochs, while stimuli that were not previously reinforced converged after an average of 50.7 epochs. For negative patterning, previously reinforced stimuli converged after an average of only 2.3 epochs, while stimuli that were not previously reinforced converged after an average of 22.5 epochs.

The results of the final simulation are qualitatively very similar to results obtained by Delamater et al. (1999) in their animal experiments. They found a very weak effect of previous reinforcement on positive patterning; for some blocks of training, they found no statistically significant effects of previous reinforcement. There is no statistical difference between the two positive patterning conditions in the final simulation. Delamater et al. also found that previous reinforcement strongly facilitated negative patterning, in comparison to negative patterning that involved stimuli that were not previously reinforced. This effect too is evident in this final set of results.

10.4.2.4 Summary and implications

We have seen in the previous sections that while learning theorists assume that patterning is logically equivalent to XOR, their operationalization of patterning is not. Because the "null pattern" is usually excluded from the definition of patterning, it is not linearly separable, and can be modeled using perceptrons.

This was demonstrated above by showing that the six hidden unit network used by Delamater et al. (1999) in one simulation study could be replaced by a number of different perceptron architectures. These perceptron simulations demonstrated that summation could also be found in a configural theory of patterning, and suggest that perceptrons offer an interesting medium in which to make contributions to theories about patterning.

Of course, for the linearly separable version of the patterning problem, none of the perceptrons that were described above generated results that were similar to those observed by Delamater et al. (1999) in their animal experiments. However, neither did the multilayered network that they used. In a final simulation, the patterning problems were operationalized in a format that ensured that they were logically equivalent to XOR. When this experiment was conducted on a network that used a Gaussian activation function in its output unit, the results looked much closer to those found in the animal experiments.

What are the implications of the simulations that are described above? On the one hand, if animal learning theorists wish to operationalize patterning by excluding the "null pattern" then they should acknowledge that patterning can be performed by perceptrons, and they should avoid trying to model patterning using networks that are far more complicated than necessary. On the other hand, if the linear nonseparability of patterning is a critical feature, then learning theorists should make sure that they operationalize patterning in a nonseparable format when they conduct their simulations and generate their theories. Perhaps the Delamater et al. (1999) network would have generated results more similar to the animal data had it been also been trained with a "null pattern" in its training sets.

10.5   The Need for Layers

In spite of these interesting results, it must be acknowledged that perceptrons are indeed limited in power. As a result, if we want to use connectionism as a technique in which to explore complex phenomena in synthetic psychology, then we must move to more powerful architectures. Our final building block to consider is the one that we failed to realize earlier – the creation of networks that have multiple layers of connections. However, now that we are armed with the nonlinear activation functions that have been introduced in the current chapter, we are in a position to successfully create multilayer networks.

Chapter eleven

Sequences of Decisions

The previous two chapters have introduced two of the major building blocks of a connectionist synthetic psychology. The first was storing associations in the weights of connections between processing units. The second was using nonlinear activation functions in processing units, which provided them with the ability to make the kinds of decisions that could be described in two-valued logic. The purpose of the current chapter is to introduce a third major building block – the use of multiple layers of processing units to create a chain of decisions that link input patterns to output responses.

11.1 The Logic of Layers

In many respects, perceptrons and multilayered perceptrons share a number of properties. Both have a layer of input units that are used to receive stimulus patterns from the environment. Both have a layer of output units that employ nonlinear activation functions, and which are usually used to generate a response that can be interpreted as a classification of a presented pattern. Both use learning rules to store associations between input and output patterns by modifying connection weights. The one crucial difference between the two kinds of networks involves what happens to the signals from the input units before they reach the layer of output units. In a perceptron, the signal is not modified at all, because there are direct connections between input and output units. In contrast, in a multilayered perceptron the signal from the input units is modified by at least one layer of intermediate or "hidden" units before reaching the output units.

The addition of hidden units provides connectionist networks with incredible power, at least in principle. In Chapter 10, we saw that perceptrons were subject to definite computational limitations. For instance, none of the perceptrons that we described were able to represent the correct responses to all of the logic problems that were presented in Table 10.1. In contrast, multilayered networks have been proven to be capable of representing any computable mapping between inputs and outputs. Lippmann (1987) was able to show that a network with two layers of hidden units could carve arbitrarily shaped decision regions in a pattern space, and therefore could be considered an arbitrary pattern classifier. Several researchers have proven that networks with a single layer of hidden units can approximate any continuous function, over a finite range, to an arbitrary degree of precision (e.g., Cybenko, 1989; Hornik, Stinchcombe & White, 1989). Finally, there exist both old (McCulloch & Pitts, 1943) and modern (e.g., Siegelmann, 1999) proofs that multilayered networks have the same computational power as a universal Turing machine. It is clear that the addition of intermediate processing units provides networks with a formidable increase in computational power. Why is this the case? What is it that hidden units do?

11.1.1 Hidden units detect higher-order features

To consider one fashion in which hidden units can extend the computational power of a network, let us return to one logic problem that provides difficulty for a traditional perceptron. In the Exclusive Or (XOR) problem, a network that has one output unit and two input units is presented with one of four different problems. It must learn to turn its output unit off to two of these patterns ([0,0] and [1,1]) and to turn its output unit on to the other two ([0,1] and [1,0]). We saw in Chapter 10 that a traditional perceptron could not represent a solution to this problem, because the problem is not linearly separable. To solve XOR, two cuts must be made in the pattern space that contains the four different patterns. One of these cuts separates [0,0] from the two patterns that cause the network to turn on. The other separates [1,1] from these same two patterns. Because in a traditional perceptron the output unit can make only a single cut in the pattern space, it cannot learn to respond correctly to all four of these patterns.

How might we make this problem linearly separable? One approach would be to elaborate the input patterns by adding a third input (Rumelhart, Hinton, & Williams, 1986a). This third input would pull the four patterns apart in a three-dimensional pattern space, and would make them linearly separable. One sensible approach to creating a third input would base it on a feature computed from the two "true" inputs. For example, we could make the third feature the logical AND of the two input units, which would only be true of the fourth pattern, because AND is only true when both of its inputs are also true. This would mean that our four input patterns would become [0,0,0], [0,1,0], [1,0,0], and [1,1,1], where the first two values are the original inputs, and the third is the AND of these inputs. A perceptron could learn to respond to these four patterns correctly, because they are linearly separable.

Of course, it would be much easier if we could design a network architecture that could figure out on its own what kind of additional features are necessary to convert a linearly nonseparable problem into one that is linearly separable. One

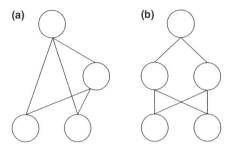

Figure 11.1 Two multilayer perceptrons for XOR. There are direct connections between input and output units in a, but not in b

reason for this is that it may be difficult, in advance, to determine what additional features are needed. A second reason for this is because if we are interested in using networks to provide us with insights about complex phenomena, then it is better to let the network discover regularities entirely on its own, instead of depending upon our guidance.

For the XOR problem, one kind of architecture that could learn to elaborate the inputs on its own is illustrated in Figure 11.1a. It has two input units that are directly connected to a single output unit, which is equivalent to the traditional perceptron architecture. It differs from a perceptron by having an additional hidden unit. This hidden unit receives input from the two input units, activates to their combined signal, and then passes this activation on to the output unit. Imagine that when this architecture was trained, this hidden unit learned to compute AND. Because of this, it would not turn on to the first three patterns of XOR ([0,0], [0,1], and [1,0]). So, for these first three patterns, the network would in essence be behaving like a traditional perceptron, and could use the direct connections between inputs and output to learn to turn off to the first pattern, and on to the second two. For the pattern [1,1], the AND-detecting hidden unit would activate. If this hidden unit had a strong inhibitory connection to the output unit, then it could use its activity to send a signal that would turn the output unit off, regardless of the other (excitatory) signals that the output unit would be receiving from the two input units. In other words, the network in Figure 11.1a is capable of representing a solution to XOR.

The Figure 11.1a network provides us with one example of the role of a hidden unit in a multilayered network. One function that such units can serve is to detect more complex features that depend on some or all of the input units. These features can in turn be used to modify the response of the output units. One way in which these additional features increase the overall power of the network is by expanding the pattern space. In the XOR example, detecting the AND property would add a third dimension to the pattern space, and would arrange the four patterns in this space in such a way that they were linearly separable.

11.1.2 Hidden units transform pattern spaces

The network illustrated in Figure 11.1a is not the only multilayered network that is capable of representing a solution to XOR. A second architecture that can solve this problem is illustrated in Figure 11.1b. This kind of network is more removed from the traditional perceptron than was the network in Figure 11.1a, and typifies the kind of multilayered network that is almost always employed in modern connectionist simulations. One of its key features is that it does not have direct connections between the input and output units. Instead, the signals from the input units are only sent to the hidden units. The hidden units process these signals, activate in a particular fashion, and are the only units responsible for sending signals on to the output unit.

How could these two hidden units solve XOR? If both of the units use the logistic activation function, then each of these hidden units is by itself equivalent to a traditional perceptron, and cannot solve XOR alone. However, the two hidden units could solve different parts of the XOR problem. The output unit could then combine the two partial solutions to solve the whole XOR problem.

Consider the first hidden unit. Imagine that it learned to turn off to three of the patterns: [0,0], [1,1], and [0,1], and that it only turned on to the pattern [1,0]. This would mean that it had learned to perform the logical operation $x \wedge \sim y$. Now imagine that the other hidden unit had learned to perform the complementary operation $\sim x \wedge y$, by turning on to the pattern [0,1], and turning off to the other three patterns.

By having these two hidden units perform these two logical operations on the input patterns, they transform or "morph" the pattern space. When the input units deliver [0,0] to the hidden units, they in turn deliver the pattern [0,0] to the output unit, because both hidden units will turn off. When the input units deliver [0,1] or [1,0] to the hidden units, the hidden units will also deliver [0,1] or [1,0] to the output unit. However, when the input units deliver [1,1], the hidden units transform this into a different pattern that is passed on to the output unit [0,0]. In other words, the hidden units have essentially folded the pattern space, so that the input pattern [1,1] becomes the pattern [0,0]. The output unit only has to learn to deal with three patterns (off to [0,0], on to [0,1] or [1,0]), and so the hidden units have reshaped the pattern space to convert XOR into a linearly separable problem.

This example demonstrates another interpretation of how hidden units increase the power of an artificial neural network. Hidden units can transform the pattern space, moving input patterns to different positions in the transformed space. This transformation can be performed in such a way that a problem that is linearly nonseparable in the pattern space defined by the input units becomes linearly separable in the new space defined by the output units.

It is important to note that both of the interpretations of the role of hidden units are essentially the same. For instance, while it is perfectly appropriate to describe the two hidden units in Figure 11.1b as transforming the input pattern space, it is also appropriate to describe them as computing more complex features from the input values (i.e., as computing $x \wedge \sim y$ and $\sim x \wedge y$). Depending on the particular network of interest, one approach to explaining what hidden units do might be easier to formulate than the other.

11.2 Training Multilayered Networks

Since 1943, it has been known that multilayered networks are far more powerful than perceptrons; McCulloch and Pitts proved that a multilayered network could be equivalent in power to a universal Turing machine. Why, then, were far simpler networks of such interest to researchers in the late 1950s and early 1960s? Why did Rosenblatt (1962) bother to investigate perceptrons, given that more powerful networks had been developed decades earlier?

The reason that simpler networks were explored is that there is a difference between *building* a powerful network and *training* a powerful network. Multilayered McCulloch–Pitts networks had been developed, but had to be hand wired. Researchers were unable to train such networks. Learning rules, like those developed by Rosenblatt (1962), emerged as researchers explored ways in which associations could be stored in the connection weights of networks that used nonlinear activation functions. However, while these rules could be used to train perceptrons, they were unable to train the connection weights in a multilayered network. Indeed, after Minsky and Papert (1988) published the first edition of their critique of perceptron research in 1969, interest in artificial neural networks waned dramatically (e.g., Medler, 1998). It was not until the mid-1980s that there was a resurgence of interest in connectionist research. This was almost completely due to the discovery of new, more powerful, learning rules that were capable of training all of the weights in a multilayered network.

11.2.1 The credit assignment problem

What is so difficult about training a multilayered network? To demonstrate the difficulty, let us take the network illustrated in Figure 11.1b, and let us imagine training it to solve XOR using the gradient descent rule that was discussed in the previous chapter.

To begin this training, we initialize the weights and biases of the networks to random values. We then select one of the XOR patterns, and present it to the input units. This results in a net input being computed by both hidden units, which each use the logistic activation function to compute their activity. These activation values are then sent through the next layer of connections to create the net input for the output unit, which then uses the logistic activation function to compute a level of activity. The activity produced by the output unit is the network's response to this first pattern, which can be compared to the desired response. This comparison allows us to compute the error for the output unit. After we have selected some value for the learning rate η, we can compute the desired weight change for the two connections leading into the output unit. Using the gradient descent rule from Equation 10.9, the weight changes become the learning rate multiplied by the output unit's error (scaled by the first derivative) multiplied by the activation value of a hidden unit. Equation 10.10 can be used to modify the bias of the output unit. Up to this point, everything seems to be going quite smoothly, and there does not appear to be any reason that the learning rules from Chapter 10 cannot be used to train this network.

Unfortunately, this optimistic outlook changes when we consider the next necessary step in training our network: modifying the connection weights between the hidden units and the input units. According to the learning rules that were described in the last chapter, these weights will be changed by using the triple product of a learning rate, a hidden unit error, and an input unit activity. However, we only have two of these values – the learning rate and the input unit activity. We are missing a necessary ingredient, hidden unit error.

Why are we missing this value? For the output unit, we know how to define error, because it is equal to the difference between the actual response of the output unit and the desired response. We do not have a similar error term for a hidden unit, because we do not know what the desired responses for each hidden unit should be. Indeed, the whole idea of training a multilayered network on a problem of interest is because we are looking for emergent properties in the hidden layers. We would like the network to surprise by finding a novel or interesting representation that can be used to solve the problem. Because we are looking for surprises here, we have no *a priori* method of defining hidden unit error.

The absence of hidden unit error is related to the *credit assignment problem* (Minsky, 1963).

> In playing a complex game such as chess or checkers, or in writing a computer program, one has a definite success criterion – the game is won or lost. But in the course of play, each ultimate success (or failure) is associated with a vast number of internal decisions. If the run is successful, how can we assign credit for the success among the multitude of decisions?
>
> *(Minsky, 1963, p. 432)*

The version of this problem that faced neural network researchers prior to the 1980s was that they could not assign the appropriate "credit" to each hidden unit for its contribution to output unit error. In connectionist networks, the inability to assign such credit translated into an inability to train any of the weights that feed into a layer of hidden units.

11.2.2 *Error backpropagation*

Connectionism was reborn in the mid-1980s for two reasons. First, many researchers were dissatisfied with the state of classical research in cognitive science. These researchers believed that classical research had failed to deliver its promised advances, because discrete rules and representations were not thought to be appropriate for modeling many cognitive phenomena. Second, accompanying their dissatisfaction were significant advances in connectionist learning algorithms. In particular, a solution to the credit assignment problem was discovered, giving researchers the ability to train multilayered networks.

Rumelhart, Hinton, and Williams (1986a) were able to solve the credit assignment problem after they decided to use the logistic equation to approximate the step function that was used in older connectionist architectures such as McCulloch–Pitts networks and perceptrons. We saw in Chapter 10 that this allowed them to use calculus to determine how to change the weights that fed into a network's output units. Their learning rule was similar to the delta rule, in that any weight change was defined as the triple product of a learning rate, the error of the unit at the output end of the connection, and the activity of the unit at the input end of the connection. Their advance over the delta rule was a refined definition of output unit error, which could be used to accelerate learning. The error for any output unit i, represented by the term δ_j, was defined in Equation 10.8 as the desired activity of the output unit minus the actual activity of the output unit, scaled by the derivative of the logistic fuction:

$$\delta_j = (t_j - a_j)f'(net_j) = (t_j - a_j)a_j(1 - a_j) \qquad [11.1]$$

Rumelhart et al. (1986a) also used calculus to determine how network error could be altered by changes in a hidden unit's weight. In essence, their equations defined hidden unit error. They discovered that the error for any hidden unit was the sum of the error for each output unit (i.e., error as defined in Equation 11.1) scaled by the connection weight between each output unit and the hidden unit. This summed error was then scaled by the derivative computed for the hidden unit's activation function. To be more precise, let us define the error for hidden unit x, which we will represent as δ_x. Let the weight between this hidden unit and output unit i be represented as w_{xi}. The total error for the hidden unit is defined in Equation 11.2, where the sum is taken over the total number of output units connected to the hidden unit:

$$\delta_x = (\Sigma w_{xi}\delta_i)f'(net_j) = (\Sigma w_{xi}\delta_i)a_j(1 - a_j) \qquad [11.2]$$

What this equation indicated was that the error for any hidden unit in a multiple-layer network could be considered as a signal that was sent to the hidden unit from the output units. The raw signal from each output unit was its error. This raw signal was then scaled by the weight between the output unit and the hidden unit, and the hidden unit's error was the "net input" of this error signal – the inner product of the vector of output unit errors and the vector of weights from the output units to the hidden unit. Because this error term could easily be viewed as a signal being sent backwards from the output units to the hidden units, the learning rule that was developed by Rumelhart et al. (1986a) became known as the "error backpropagation" rule.

11.2.3   The generalized delta rule

With hidden unit error defined as in Equation 11.2, Rumelhart et al. (1986a) were in a position to modify all of the weights in a multilayered network. In their algorithm, every weight was changed by adding to it a value that was the product of a learning rate, an error term, and an activation value, as was the case in the delta rule that we first saw in Chapter 9. Because of this, the error backpropagation rule is also known as the generalized delta rule.

For any pattern, the generalized delta rule involves two phases of processing. The first phase is the forward propagation of the signal. The input units are activated with some stimulus pattern, which causes activation to arise first in the network's hidden units, and then in the network's output units. This observed activation is compared to the desired activation, and an error value is computed for every output unit (i.e., the difference between the desired and the observed activations).

The second phase of processing in the generalized delta rule is the backward propagation of error. This involves a number of different steps. First, the output unit error terms are multiplied by the derivative of the logistic equation. Second, the weights of the connection weights are modified according to Equation 11.3, where w_{ij} is the weight of the connection between output unit i and hidden unit j, δ_j is the error for output unit i, and a_i is the activation of hidden unit j to the pattern that was presented:

$$\Delta w_{ij} = \eta \delta_j a_i \qquad\qquad [11.3]$$

Note that this equation is identical to Equation 10.9, and only differs from it in the assumption that the connection weight is between an output unit and a hidden unit. In other words, the connection weights feeding into the output units in a multilayered network are trained in exactly the same fashion as was described in Chapter 10.

Once the output unit weights have been modified, the third step in error backpropagation can be performed. In this step, hidden unit errors are calculated using Equation 11.2. In other words, each output unit sends its error term through the modified connection weights, whose weights are used to scale these error signals. Each hidden unit adds up these incoming weighted error signals to determine what its own error should be.

The fourth step in this phase of the generalized delta rule is to modify the weights that feed into the hidden units. This is also accomplished via Equation 11.3, using the appropriate activation value, and using hidden unit error instead of output unit error. In most typical networks, this means that the input unit activities will be used. However, in some networks, there is more than one layer of hidden units. One of the advantages of the generalized delta rule is that the equations that have been described above can be iterated through more than one hidden unit layer. In this case, the errors that have been calculated for one layer of hidden units can be propagated backwards to the next, after the connection weights between them have been modified. This process continues until all of the connection weights in the network have been modified. Then the next pattern is presented to the network, and the two phases of the generalized delta rule are repeated.

The paragraphs above have described how the generalized delta rule is applied to the connection weights in a network. Of course, once a unit's error term has been calculated, the bias of that unit can be modified as well. This is done in exactly the same fashion as was described in the previous chapter, by applying Equation 10.10. This is the case whether the unit is an output unit or a hidden unit.

11.2.4 The Dawson–Schopflocher rule

Dawson and Schopflocher (1992) modified the generalized delta rule to train networks of value units. In Chapter 10, we saw that the training of perceptrons that used value units required two main changes to the gradient descent rule. First, an elaborated definition of overall network error is required. Second, the derivative of the Gaussian equation had to be substituted into any equation that ordinarily used the derivative of the logistic equation, because value units use the Gaussian activation function.

Provided that these changes are also used for multilayered networks, Dawson and Schopflocher's (1992) method for training networks of value units is exactly the same as the generalized delta rule. In their learning rule, output unit errors are calculated (using their elaborated definition of error), and weights and biases are changed, in exactly the same fashion that was described in Chapter 10. Hidden unit errors can then be calculated in exactly the same fashion that was used in the generalized delta rule (i.e., Equation 11.2), with the exception that the error term is scaled by the derivative of the Gaussian equation. Hidden unit weights can then be modified using Equation 11.3. In other words, the only difference between the two learning rules is the definition of output unit error. This permits training hybrid multilayer perceptrons that contain both integration devices and value units.

Dawson and Schopflocher (1992) demonstrated that networks of value units had many advantages over networks of integration devices by studying a set of benchmark pattern recognition problems. In general, networks of value units learned to solve these problems significantly faster, and required fewer hidden units to classify patterns. These two advantages are due to the use of the elaborated error term and to the fact that value units carve two "cuts" through a pattern space, instead of just one. In the next chapter, we will also see that networks of value units also have emergent properties that enhance the process of network analysis.

However, networks of value units do not have universal advantages over networks of integration devices. As a result, all the different kinds of networks that can be trained with variations of the generalized delta rule should be viewed as available tools in a toolbox, and a researcher should explore the architecture of a multilayer network to determine what kind of network is best for the problem at hand.

11.2.5 *Exploring learning in multilayered networks*

The website of supplementary material (www.bcp.psych.ualberta.ca/~mike/ Book2) for this book provides a program called "Rumelhart." This program can be used to train multilayer perceptrons using either of the learning rules that were described above. The program also permits the training of hybrid networks, in which one layer of processing units are integration devices, and another layer of processors are value units. Furthermore, the program permits the user to decide whether or not to include direction connections between input and output units. The program also comes with a number of example training files, including ones for all of the case studies that are introduced below. The reader is invited to use this program to explore the relative merits and limitations of the different kinds of multilayer perceptrons.

11.3   A Simple Case Study: Exclusive Or

There are many different learning rules available for training multilayer networks. Furthermore, there is a vast array of different activation functions that are also in use (e.g., Duch & Jankowski, 1999). The purpose of this chapter is not to provide an exhaustive introduction to training multilayer perceptrons; the reader interested in more extensive treatments of this type has other resources to explore (e.g., De Wilde, 1997; Hagan, Demuth, & Beale, 1996; Kasabov, 1996; Ripley, 1996; Rojas, 1996; Shepherd, 1997). Instead, this chapter introduces multilayer perceptrons as a plausible medium for exploring synthetic psychology. The remainder of the chapter attempts to accomplish this goal by describing some example simulations. To begin, let us return to XOR.

11.3.1 *Using hidden units to detect additional features*

In our first XOR simulation using multilayer perceptrons, we decided to use a network of integration devices that had only one hidden unit, as well as direct connections between its two input units and its one output unit. In other words, this network had the appearance of the one illustrated in Figure 11.1a, and both its output unit and its hidden unit used the logistic activation function.

When we trained this network, all of the connection weights were initialized by randomly selecting numbers from the range −0.1 to +0.1. Unit biases were initialized at 0.0. The network was then trained using the generalized delta rule, with a learning rate of 0.9. The order of pattern presentation was randomized every epoch. This means that prior to training the network, the order of the four stimulus patterns was randomized. Then each pattern was presented once in this random order, and connection weights and biases were updated with each presentation. Once each of the patterns had been presented, the order of the patterns was randomized again prior to the next epoch of training.

The network converged to a solution to the XOR problem after 1,197 epochs – that is, after each of the four training patterns had been trained 1,197 times. At this time, the network generated a "hit" to each pattern when it was presented. At the start of training, the minimum squared error for defining a "hit" was set at the value of 0.01. This means that when the network converged, the output unit generated an activation value of 0.9 or higher for the two patterns whose desired response was 1, and it generated an activation value of 0.1 or lower for the two patterns whose desired response was 0. The total squared error for the network (summing over all of the training patterns) after it converged was 0.031.

After this training, the network had the following structure: the bias of the output unit was −3.13, and the bias of the hidden unit was −2.68. The connection weight from the hidden unit to the output unit was 10.45. The connection weights from each of the input units to the output unit were both equal to −4.76, and the weights from each of the input units to the hidden unit were both equal to 6.57.

How does a network with this structure solve XOR? Let us start by considering the hidden unit. It generates an activation of 0.98 to all of the patterns except the one in which both input units are off. To this latter pattern, it generates a response of 0.06. Thus, it would appear that this unit is detecting the $x \vee y$ relationship that was defined earlier in Table 10.1. How does the network convert the ability to compute OR into the more sophisticated ability to compute XOR? It does so via the combination of the input unit signals and the hidden unit signal when the output unit computes its net input.

To be more precise, consider the first pattern [0, 0]. This pattern fails to generate a response in the hidden unit, and sends no signal to the output unit. As a result, the output unit's net input is zero, and it (correctly) fails to respond. Now consider either pattern in which one input unit is on, and the other is off. Either of these patterns will activate the hidden unit, which in turn will send a signal with a value over 10 to the output unit. The one input unit that is on, however, will also send an inhibitory signal of nearly −5 to the output unit. So, the net input of the output unit to either of these patterns will be about equal to 5, which is high enough to (correctly) turn the output unit on to either of these two patterns. Finally, consider the pattern [1, 1]. This pattern causes the hidden unit to send a signal of 10 to the output unit. However, because both of the input units are sending inhibitory signals of nearly −5 to the output unit at the same time, the signal from the hidden unit is essentially canceled, and the output unit (correctly) fails to turn on. In short, negative signals from the two input units, combined with a hidden unit that detects an additional feature, permits this multilayer perceptron to compute XOR.

One reason that this network is interesting is because it is completely different from the hypothetical network that was described in section 11.1.1 that solved XOR by detecting the AND feature with its single hidden unit. Clearly, there is more than one way for a network of this general type to detect additional features to solve this problem. Training a number of different networks, with different random starts, would lead to the discovery of a number of different solutions to the problem. Networks are capable of discovering solutions to problems that can be unanticipated by researchers. These surprises will provide the core discoveries for synthetic psychologists who use connectionist networks.

11.3.2 Using hidden units to transform the pattern space

In our second simulation, we used a network with the architecture illustrated in Figure 11.1b. The network used two hidden units and one output unit, all of which were integration devices. There were no direct connections between the input and output units in this study. The network was trained using exactly the same settings that were used in Section 11.3.1. It converged to a solution after 1,218 epochs, with a total squared error of 0.032.

At the end of training, the network had the following structure: the bias of the output unit was equal to −3.01, the bias of hidden unit 1 was −2.19, and the bias of hidden unit 2 was −4.78. The connection weight from hidden unit 1 to the output unit was 6.70, and the connection weight from hidden unit 2 to the output unit was −7.11. The connection weights from the input units to hidden unit 1 were 5.95 and 5.91; the weights from the input units to hidden unit 2 were 3.18 and 3.17.

How does this network structure solve XOR? First, let us consider an interpretation of the role of each hidden unit. Hidden unit 1 was an $x \vee y$ detector, responding in the same fashion as the hidden unit in the previous network: generating a near 0 response to [0, 0] and a near 1 response to the other three patterns. In contrast, hidden unit 2 was an $x \wedge y$ detector, only generating a high degree of activity to the pattern [1, 1], and generating very weak activity to the other three patterns.

These two detectors can be used to solve XOR by folding the pattern space. For the pattern [0, 0], both hidden units are off, resulting in a near zero net input for the output unit, which results in it correctly turning off. For the pattern [0, 1] and the pattern [1, 0], hidden unit 1 responds, but hidden unit 2 does not. As a result, the output unit receives a strong excitatory signal from the hidden unit that is on, and correctly activates. For the final pattern [1, 1], both of the hidden units are activated. The excitatory signal sent by hidden unit 1 to the output unit is nullified by a stronger inhibitory signal that is sent to the output unit by hidden unit 2. As a result, the output unit does not turn on. The competition between the two activated hidden units has caused the stimulus [1, 1] to generate a similar output unit signal to that which is generated by the pattern [0, 0], which is equivalent to folding the pattern space so that both of these points occupy the same position.

Again, as we saw in section 11.3.1, the features that the network has used to fold the pattern space are quite different from the features that were discussed for the hypothetical network that was discussed earlier in this chapter. There is obviously more than one way in which the XOR pattern space can be transformed to become linearly separable, which highlights the need for network analysis and interpretation.

11.4   A Second Case Study: Classifying Musical Chords

We saw earlier that, in principle, multilayer perceptrons have the computational power of universal Turing machines. Because of this, they certainly have the capability of dealing with problems that are far more complicated – and psychologically relevant – than XOR. Indeed, we have already seen one example of this in Chapter 8 when a multilayer perceptron was trained to internalize a spatial map of the province of Alberta. Connectionist models are attractive because you can train a network to solve any pattern recognition problem of interest, provided that you can formulate some coding scheme that can be presented to a network. This section provides one example of this.

11.4.1   Defining the problem

Imagine a small piano keyboard consisting of only 24 keys, black and white. The first 12 keys of this minipiano represent the following notes: A, A#, B, C, C#, D, D#, E, F, F#, G, and G#. In this pattern, every note paired with the # symbol corresponds to a black key on the keyboard, and all of the other notes correspond to white keys. (For the sake of simplicity, we only use the # symbol in this example, and pretend that we cannot represent black keys with the ♭ symbol, such as representing the note A# as B♭.) Moving from the left to right in this pattern, each note is a semitone higher than the note on its left. The 13th key on this keyboard plays another A that is an octave higher than the A that started the keyboard. From this 13th key to the last (24th) key on the piano, the pattern of notes is repeated. So, while there are 24 different keys on this keyboard, they are only associated with 12 different note names, and each note is repeated an octave higher than its first instance. Each of these 12 different notes can serve as the starting note, or *root*, of a major scale. For instance, we could have a scale in the key of A major that starts on the root A, a scale in the key of A# major that starts on the root A#, and so on, up to the key of G# major.

For any scale that we choose, there exists a basic harmonic structure. Harmony is the combination of two or more notes into a compound in which all of the notes are played at the same time. To our ears, some of these combinations are dissonant – they simply don't sound right. Others, however, are consonant, and are the basis of Western music (Jourdain, 1997).

For example, let us consider the C major scale. One important, consonant, harmonic combination for this scale is the *major chord* that can be built upon its root, which is C. The most common version of this chord is the C major triad. This is the set of notes C, E, and G that are the first, third and fifth notes in the C major scale. We could convert this into a four-note chord (a tetrachord) by adding the C that is an octave higher than the root note of this triad (i.e., by using the notes C, E, G, and C). On our keyboard, we could play this chord by finding the lowest C on it, and then playing it along with the other three notes that make up this chord. We will call this the *root position* of the chord. However, we could play this chord in other ways too. For instance, we could start with the lowest E on the keyboard, and play the notes E, G, C, and E, where the last E is an octave higher than the first. In this version of the chord, the same notes are being played, but they are arranged in a different order. This order is called the *first inversion* of C major. We could also start with the lowest G that we can find on the keyboard, and play the notes G, C, E, and G. This is called the *second inversion* of the chord.

All of the chords that could be created from the above description are major. With a slight change, any major chord can be converted into a different kind of chord, called a *minor chord*, that is associated with a minor scale. To convert a major chord into a minor chord, first take the major chord in root position. Then, take the second note in the chord, and lower it by a semitone. For instance, the C major chord (C, E, G, and C) can be converted into the C minor chord (C, D#, G, and C) by lowering the E by a semitone to the note D#. As was the case for the major chords, we can write minor chords in first and second inversions as well. The first inversion of C minor is D#, G, C, and D#, and the second inversion of C minor is G, C, D#, and G.

Other harmonic patterns are available as well. For example, every major scale is associated with a *dominant chord*. A dominant chord is created as follows. First, take a major scale of interest. Let us choose C major as our example. Second, find the fifth note in this major scale, which is known as the *dominant*. The dominant of C major is the note G. Third, build a major triad that has this dominant note as its root. The major triad for G is G, B, and D. Finally, add a fourth note that is three semitones (i.e., three piano keys on our keyboard) higher than the highest note in this triad. In our example, the note F is three semitones higher than D. So the dominant chord for the key of C major is the four-note pattern G, B, D, and F.

As was the case with the major and minor chords, you can arrange the same notes into different orders to produce various inversions of dominant sevenths. To do this, you take the lowest note of one pattern, and move it an octave higher to become the highest note of the inverted pattern. Following this rule, for the dominant chord of C major the first inversion is B, D, F, and G; the second inversion is D, F, G, and B; the third inversion is F, G, B, and D. On our keyboard, we are able to take one of these patterns (i.e., the root, and first, second, or third inversion) and repeat it, so that one version is a full octave higher than the other. In other words, we are able to play five different versions of any dominant chord on our 24-key piano.

Each major scale has its own dominant chord. Similarly, each minor scale has its own tetrachord that is called *diminished*. The diminished chord for a minor scale is created as follows: First, take a minor scale of interest. Let us choose C# minor as our example. Second, take the note that is a semitone lower than the root of this scale. The note C is a semitone lower than C#, which is the root of C# minor. From this selected note, add a second note that is three semitones (three piano keys) higher; then add a third that is six semitones higher; finally add a fourth note that is nine semitones higher. For C# minor, the four notes selected according to this procedure are C, D#, F#, and A.

This pattern is the diminished chord of this minor scale. As was the case for dominant chords, we can create different inversions of a diminished chord. For the diminished chord of C# minor, the first inversion is D#, F#, A, and C; the second inversion is F#, A, C, and D#; the third inversion is A, C, D#, and F#. When we "fit" the diminished chords onto our minipiano, we will be able to find room to repeat one of these patterns a full octave higher. So, for any minor key, we can play five different versions of its diminished chord on our imaginary keyboard.

All of the harmonic structures that have been described above are crucial elements to musical understanding and performance. For instance, I am currently learning to play the piano. As part of my training in musical theory, I have to learn how to classify any of these chord structures when they are presented in written form – identifying the type of chord (e.g., dominant seventh), the key that the chord is associated with (e.g., C major), and the pattern of the chord (e.g., second inversion). As part of my technical training, I have to learn how to play all of these chords for a wide variety of keys with both hands. As part of my ear training, I have to learn to recognize the difference in sound between a major chord, a minor chord, a dominant seventh, and a diminished seventh. All of these are fairly complicated and challenging tasks – as my piano teacher, Marg Tompkins, is painfully aware from hearing me perform! From the perspective of cognitive science, any challenging task that can be accomplished by humans is a task worthy of further exploration. This leads to the following question: would it be possible to train a network to identify the different kinds of chords that could be "played" on our imaginary keyboard?

All that stands in the way of answering these questions is translating the information that was provided above into a training set that can be presented to a network. There are a number of different ways of doing this. The following paragraphs describe one straightforward encoding that we used to develop a network capable of recognizing the four different types of tetrachords, and also suggest some possible alternatives.

First, consider the encoding of the network's responses. Ultimately, we want a trained network to be capable of distinguishing between four different kinds of chords – major, minor, dominant, and diminished. We built a network with four output units, each of which was associated with one of the four chord types. The network is trained to turn the correct output unit on when presented with a representation of the chord. Other approaches would also be interesting to explore. For example, because we want the network to make four different responses, we really only require two output units, which are capable of representing four different states ([0, 0] for major, [0, 1] for dominant, [1, 0] for minor, and [1, 1] for diminished). It would be interesting to see whether changing the representation of the network's responses affected its internal representations of chord structures. For instance, in the two-output unit encoding that was just suggested, the desired value of the first output unit reflects the fact that dominant chords are related to major scales, and that diminished chords are related to minor scales.

Second, consider how to encode the stimuli that are to be presented to the network. We adopted a very simple local encoding by providing the network with 24 different input units, each one representing a different key on our minipiano. A "note" was presented to the network by turning the unit associated with its key on, indicating that the key was pressed down. For any of the stimuli that were presented to the network, four input units were turned on, and all of the others were turned off. Again, there are alternative encodings that are more sophisticated, and it would be very interesting to explore how these might affect network performance and structure. For instance, any sound that would be generated by a single key of our minipiano would be a sine wave of a particular amplitude and frequency, and would also produce resonant vibrations in other piano components. This would result in other sine waves, of higher frequencies and diminishing amplitudes, being added to our primary sine wave (Jourdain, 1997). We could represent a stimulus by having different input units correspond to different sine wave frequencies, and by using input values to represent the amplitude.

Once an encoding for network inputs and outputs has been chosen, all that remains is to create a training set. We created a training set based on the 12 different notes that formed the basis for the first octave of our minipiano. For each of these 12 notes, we began by treating it as the root of a major scale. We then created three different major chords for this scale (root position, first inversion, second inversion). We also created five different dominants for this scale (root position, first inversion, second inversion, third inversion, and one of these four chords repeated an octave higher, depending on how the chords could be fit onto the minipiano). In other words, for each of the 12 possible major key signatures, we created three different major chords and five different dominants, resulting in 96 different patterns.

We then took each of the 12 notes again, but treated them as the root of a minor scale. For each of these, we created three different minor chords (root position, first inversion, second inversion). We also created five different diminished chords (root position, first inversion, second inversion, third inversion, and one of these four chords repeated an octave higher, depending on how the chords could be fit onto the minipiano). This resulted in another 96 different training patterns, for a total of 192 training patterns in the training set. All of the stimuli that we defined were tetrachords (instead of triads), so that the network could not use the number of activated input units as a cue to distinguish a major or minor triad from a dominant or a diminished, which are always defined with four notes. The network was then trained to recognize what type of chord was being presented, regardless of the key that the chord was based on, or of how the chord was inverted.

11.4.2   Classifying chords with a network

In our use of the Rumelhart program to train a network to classify musical chords, we decided to make all of the output and hidden processors value units. The network was trained with a learning rate of 0.01. The connection weight values were randomly selected from between −0.1 and +0.1, and the biases of all the units were initialized to a value of 0. As was the case for the XOR networks described earlier, the minimum squared error to define a "hit" was 0.01. A network that used four hidden units converged to a solution – hits on every training pattern – after 11,643 epochs. The order of pattern presentation was randomized after every epoch. When the network converged, its total sum of squared error was 0.101, which is quite small, considering that this value is summed over 192 different training patterns.

The network that was produced by this training is quite a bit more complicated than the XOR networks that were described above. One cannot simply look at the connection weights to determine how it functions, because with 24 input units, 4 hidden units, and 192 training patterns, there is far too much data to process. A proper interpretation of this network is delayed until Chapter 12. However, there are some core characteristics of this network that might suggest specific avenues that could be explored when the network's structure was investigated.

For example, one wonders if there is any significance to the fact that four hidden units were required by this network to classify the chords. In this training set, the number four is important in more than one way. First, there are four different types of chords. Is it possible that the different hidden units are each capturing a characteristic of one of these chords? Second, four notes define each chord. Perhaps each hidden unit detects the position of a note on a key, and uses this information to help the network to cope with the different inversion. A detailed investigation of such possibilities would require us to examine the responses of the hidden units to different kinds of patterns, the relative values of the connection weights that feed into the hidden units, as well as of the weights that feed into the output units. One of the goals of analyzing such properties would be to discover how the network represented the musical characteristics that defined each type of chord. Is this representation surprising or interesting? Is it possible that people use this representation too? Does the representation reveal anything surprising about the mathematical relationships between different kinds of chords or scales? Once answers to these kind of representational questions are hunted down, one would be in a position to explore whether or not the network's representations change when a different input and/or output encoding is employed.

11.5   A Third Case Study: From Connectionism to Selectionism

Since its birth in the mid-1950s, cognitive science has been guided by the digital computer metaphor, and has developed functionalist theories that have largely (and deliberately) ignored the neural bases of mental phenomena (Calvin, 1996; Clark, 1989; Edelman, 1992). More recently, a strong reaction against this practice has produced two biologically inspired theories of cognition, *instructionism* and *selectionism*. While both of these approaches have emerged as challengers to classical cognitive science, they have also been placed in an unfortunate competition with each other. There is a general view that instructionist and selectionist theories are mutually incompatible (Edelman, 1987; Piattelli-Palmarini, 1989). Below, with the goal of providing another example of how multilayered networks might contribute to synthetic psychology, some computer simulations are described to demonstrate that this is not necessarily the case. These simulations show that it might be possible to incorporate the main ideas of selectionism into an instructionist framework.

11.5.1   *Instructionist versus selectionist theories*

Instructionist theories view cognition as the ultimate product of neuronal growth. In its most extreme form, the developing brain is viewed as initially being a *tabula rasa* (Pinker, 2002). As the result of interactions with an environment, neural structure emerges via the growth and/or strengthening of neurons and synapses. "Many neuroscientists equate learning with the forming of associations, and look for an associative bond in the physiology of neurons and synapses, ignoring other kinds of computation that might implement learning in the brain" (p. 21).

Connectionist networks can easily be cast as examples of instructionism. Prior to training, connections among processing units are essentially structureless, because initial connection weights are usually small and random. During training, connection weights grow in size, structure is "written" by the environment into the network, and the network develops into a system capable of computing a specific function. "The connectionists, of course, do not believe in a blank slate, but they do believe in the closest mechanistic equivalent, a general-purpose learning device" (Pinker, 2002, p. 78).

Instructionist theories have both advantages and disadvantages. On the one hand, they have been highly formalized, and through this formalization have been explored in detail using computer simulation methods and also have been linked to well-established theories of pattern recognition and machine learning (e.g., Pao, 1989; Ripley, 1996). On the other hand, this formalization may have been purchased at the expense of their biological relevance. Many neuroscientists have raised serious questions about the neural plausibility of instructionist theories like PDP networks (e.g., Calvin, 1996; Douglas & Martin, 1991).

In contrast to instructionism, selectionist theories of cognition deny that the brain is a structureless *tabula rasa*. Instead, selectionists assume that the initial stages of brain development involve the generation of a large and varied amount of structure. This structure provides a pre-existing repertoire of responses to be elicited by the environment. The interaction between the environment and pre-existing structure selects some structures as being more appropriate than others, and this in turn modifies the underlying neural architecture. "After initial selection, certain cell groups in the repertoire have a higher probability than others of being selected by a similar or identical signal pattern" (Edelman & Mountcastle, 1978, p. 60).

Selectionist theories are inspired by immunology (e.g., Cziko, 1995). In response to an infection, biological systems produce enormous amounts of antibodies. Any antibody can be considered as a specific three-dimensional label whose shape binds with the shape of an antigen. Once labeled in this fashion, the antigen becomes a target of other mechanisms that will destroy it. Importantly, antibodies can be produced to completely novel artificial substances. This suggests that there is no limit to the range of different antibodies that an organism can create. How is this possible?

One theory was instructionist in nature (Cziko, 1995). Antigens were assumed to serve as physical templates that could be used to create corresponding antibodies because of direct contact with the immune system. However, this theory encountered many difficulties. For example, because of the rapid immune response to an infection, antibodies will quickly outnumber antigens. This seems impossible if antigens are to serve as templates for antibody construction. Furthermore, the immune system has a memory – it will respond more quickly and effectively to an infection that it has faced before than to a novel infection.

Jerne (1967) provided an alternative selectionist theory of the immune response. According to his theory, an animal initially possesses a relatively small number of individual antibodies, but within this small number there is an incredible diversity of different antibody types. Essentially, the animal starts with a repertoire of antibodies that is capable of dealing with *any* possible future infection. When an infection is encountered, a particular (pre-existing) antibody will bind to the antigen. When this binding occurs, the antibody produces a large number of copies of itself. "It follows that an animal cannot be stimulated to make specific antibodies, unless it has already made antibodies of this specificity before the antigen arrives. It can thus be concluded that antibody formation is a selective process and that instructive theories of antibody formation are wrong" (p. 201).

Jerne (1967) first drew the link between selection in immunology and neural adaptation.

> Looking back into the history of biology, it appears that wherever a phenomenon resembles learning, an instructive theory was first proposed to account for the underlying mechanisms. In every case, this was later replaced by a selective theory. . . . Antibody formation that was thought to be based on instruction by the antigen is now found to result from the selection of already existing patterns. It thus remains to be asked if learning by the central nervous system might not also be a selective process; i.e., perhaps learning is not learning either.
>
> *(Jerne, 1967, p. 204)*

Piattelli-Palmarini (1989, p. 2) provides a more modern example of agreement with this sentiment: "I, for one, see no advantage in the preservation of the term learning. We agree with those who maintain that we would gain in clarity if the scientific use of the term were simply discontinued."

Selectionist theories also have both advantages and disadvantages. On the one hand, selectionist theories maintain a high degree of biological plausibility. For instance, they appear to be extremely consistent with measurements of neural development. Several researchers have observed that in the first year of human life there is a dramatic increase in both the number of neurons and in synaptic density, but that this is followed by a longer period of time in which both of these factors demonstrate substantial declines (see Sporns & Tononi, 1994). This is predicted by selectionist theories in which early neuronal growth provides a large repertoire of neural circuits that is later pruned by environmental exposure.

On the other hand, the strong biological nature of selectionist theories has worked against their formalization. While computer simulations have been used to study some selectionist predictions (e.g., Edelman, 1987, 1988, 1989, 1992), they have not successfully modeled some of the higher-order phenomena that PDP models have been used to study. As a result, selectionist theories have not had a strong impact on cognitive science. In their acknowledgement that selectionist theories have not taken advantage of possible modeling strategies, Changeux and Dehaene (1993, p. 384) point out that "the crucial issue remains to find a learning rule coherent with such a Darwinian picture."

Our hypothesis was that the learning rule being sought by selectionist researchers might in fact be the kind of rule that has already been established in instructionist models. Specifically, there is no reason in principle why procedures used to train PDP models, such as the generalized delta rule, cannot be used in a selectionist paradigm. My students and I began to wonder what would happen with connectionist learning if we provided a network with more hidden units than it needed to solve a problem, and if we initialized the connection weights with values that were much more structured than is traditionally the case. We adopted a synthetic approach to explore these musings.

11.5.2   A connectionist formulation of selectionism

Our research began by considering what would have to be done in order for a learning rule to alter a PDP network in accordance with selectionist assumptions. For selectionism to work, systems must possess a great deal of initial structure that can be selected as needed by environmental pressures. If a connectionist network was (1) provided with many more hidden units than would ordinarily be required, and (2) provided with initial connection weights that were not near-zero, but instead were much larger, and exhibited high variability, then it might be possible to use a rule like the generalized delta rule to select useful, pre-existing processing units from a prestructured network.

In the experiments that we report below, one of our independent variables concerned the distribution from which connection weights were randomly sampled prior to the training of the network. This manipulation was used to insert initial structure into the PDP networks prior to training. In the control condition, all of the weights were initialized by randomly sampling values from a rectangular distribution that ranged from −1 to +1. Structure was added to initial weights by changing the variability (but not the mean) of this distribution. This was accomplished by inserting a "gap" in the distribution. In one experimental condition, this gap resulted in weights being selected from the range −2 to −1, and +1 to +2, but *not* from the range −1 to +1. In a second experimental condition, this gap resulted in weights being selected from the range −3 to −2, and +2 to +3, but *not* from the range −2 to +2. The rationale underlying these conditions was that structure would be supplied to the network by ensuring that all weights began at values that were much more extreme than in the control condition. Furthermore, the larger the "gap" in the distribution from which weights were selected, the higher the variability of the weights. High variability is often used as an index of a high degree of structure in such statistical techniques as factor analysis (e.g., Kaiser, 1958).

Our second independent variable was the number of hidden units available in the network prior to training. In one condition, there were as many hidden units as there were input units. For all of the problems that we studied, this would be a sufficient number of units for a network to represent a solution. In a second condition, there were twice as many hidden units as there were input units. In a third condition, there were three times as many hidden units as there were input units. The basic idea behind these manipulations was to increase the repertoire of hidden unit responses prior to training. As the number of hidden units is increased, so is the potential number of different internal responses to stimulus patterns. This is particularly true when this manipulation is combined with one in which the initial connection weights are highly structured.

Our basic assumption was that in networks in which initial connection weights were highly structured, and in which there was a large number of pre-existing hidden units, the application of the generalized delta rule would essentially serve as a selectionist mechanism. In other words, rather than "growing" a network for solving the task – which is the instructionist view of PDP modeling – the learning rule would select the appropriate hidden units from the large number that were available. One consequence of this should be a dramatic increase in learning speed. However, this should only occur under the appropriate combination of the two independent variables. Our first simulations attempted to determine whether this interaction between independent variables would appear.

11.5.3 A case study: The parity problem

11.5.3.1 Defining the problem

The first experiment was designed to test whether the selectionist approach to PDP networks would provide any benefits for the learning of a particularly difficult pattern recognition problem, the parity problem. In the parity problem, a network has a single output unit, and it has N input units. Each input unit is a bit that can either be on or off. The network is trained to detect whether an odd number of its input bits are active. If this is the case, then the network turns its output unit on. If even numbers of input units are active, then the network turns its output unit off.

The parity problem is an extremely difficult benchmark for a PDP network. This is because patterns that are very near one another in the pattern space require the network to make opposite responses. For example, in the five-bit parity problem the points representing the patterns [1, 0, 0, 1, 1] and [1, 0, 0, 1, 0] would be very near to one another in five-dimensional pattern space, because there is only one difference between them (the last bit). However, this tiny difference in the patterns makes a big difference in a network's response, because it must identify the first pattern as having odd parity, and it must identify the second pattern as not having odd parity. Because nearest neighbors require opposite responses, a network must partition a pattern space into a complex set of decision regions in order to solve the parity problem.

As a result, when processors in PDP networks use the logistic activation function, at least N hidden units are required to represent the solution to an N-bit parity problem. In practice, as N reaches the value of seven or eight, we have found that this minimal network has a great deal of difficulty converging (see also Tesauro & Janssens, 1988). We were interested in whether the performance of a standard network on this difficult problem could be improved by training it from a selectionist perspective.

11.5.3.2 Manipulating the number of hidden units

Each network had one output unit, which was trained to activate when an odd parity problem was presented to the input units, and to fail to activate when an even parity problem was presented to the input units. The output unit was a value unit that used the Gaussian activation function.

Three different versions of the parity problem were examined. In the five-parity problem, the network had five input units, and the training set consisted of all of the 32 binary patterns that could be represented by these units. In the seven-parity problem the network had seven input units and a training set of 128 possible binary inputs. In the nine-parity problem, the network had nine input units and a training set of 512 possible binary inputs. For each version of the parity problem, three different sizes of networks were trained. One had the same number of hidden units as there were input units. A second had twice as many hidden units as there were input units. A third had three times as many hidden units as there were input units. In all of these different conditions, all of the hidden units were value units.

11.5.3.3 Manipulating the initial structure of connection weights

For each network trained on a parity problem, three different starting conditions were examined. The first was a "low structure" condition. In this condition, all of the connection weights in the network were initialized by randomly sampling from the range −1 to +1. The second was a "medium structure" condition. In this condition, all of the connection weights were initialized by randomly sampling from the range −2 to −1 and 1 to 2. The third was a "high structure" condition. In this condition, all of the connection weights were initialized by randomly sampling from the range −3 to −2 and 2 to 3. In all three of these conditions, the bias of each processing unit was initialized with a value of 0. With this structure manipulation, the mean of the sampling distribution was held constant, but the variance of the distribution was increased. In general, as structure increased because of changes in the sampling distribution, the initial weights in the to-be-trained network were more extreme.

11.5.3.4 Training the networks

This experiment had a $3 \times 3 \times 3$ factorial design. The first factor was size of problem (five-parity, seven-parity, nine-parity). The second factor was the number of hidden units (N, $2N$, $3N$). The third factor was the structure in the sampling distribution used to initialize connection weights (low structure, medium structure, high structure). In this design, there are 27 different cells. In each cell, 20 different networks were trained, each randomly initialized in accordance with the constraints imposed by the structure manipulation. Each of these different networks (540 in total) represented a different "subject" in the experiment. The dependent measure for the study was the number of training epochs required for a network to solve the parity problem.

Each network was trained with the Dawson and Schopflocher rule (1992). Network connections were updated after every pattern presentation, using a learning rate of 0.001. One epoch involved the presentation of every possible input pattern to the network. The order of pattern presentation was randomized every epoch. Networks were said to have converged on a solution to the problem when a "hit" was recorded for the output unit for every pattern presented during the epoch. A "hit" was defined as output unit activity of 0.9 or greater when the desired output was 1.0, or as output unit activity of 0.1 or less when the desired output was 0.0. If convergence was not achieved after 10,000 epochs, then training was stopped, and the value of 10,000 was entered as the dependent measure.

11.5.3.5 The potential power of selectionism

If connectionist networks can instantiate selectionist principles, then there should be significant interactions between the manipulations of structure and number of hidden units. In particular, fast learning of the parity problems should require a combination of high structure and a high number of hidden units.

This is exactly the kind of pattern that emerges from the results of this first simulation. Table 11.1 provides the results for the nine-bit parity problem; similar patterns of results were observed for the two other versions of the parity problem

Table 11.1 Mean epochs to converge on the nine-bit parity problem, with standard deviations in parentheses. Each cell represents the mean from training 20 different networks.

| | | Structure | | |
		Low	Medium	High
Number of hidden units	N	10,000 (0.00)	9190.90 (2553.26)	10,000 (0.00)
	2N	9887.35 (503.79)	4218.90 (2650.38)	2840.70 (4257.08)
	3N	10,000 (0.00)	849.05 (361.79)	88.75 (44.65)

that were examined. From the table, it can be seen that the slowest learning occurs in situations in which there is a combination of low structure and a small number of hidden units. The fastest learning occurs in the condition for which there was high structure and a large numbers of hidden units. However, even when the number of hidden units is high, this is not by itself enough to guarantee fast learning. Looking across the last row of the table, it can be seen that when the number of hidden units was held constant at 3N (i.e., held at 27 for the nine-bit version of the parity problem), structure is still required. The low structure condition in this row never led to a learned solution (which is why the average sweeps to completion is 10,000 with zero standard deviation). When medium structure is used for this number of hidden units, on average the problem is learned in well under 1,000 epochs. When high structure is used, learning is accomplished in well under 100 epochs.

A statistical analysis of all of the results of this simulation, using analysis of variance on all 27 cells of the experimental design, confirmed the regularities that were revealed in Table 11.1. Most importantly, there was a significant interaction between the number of hidden units and the level of structure. In general, this emerges because the effect of structure is amplified by increasing the number of hidden units, as we saw in Table 11.1. Here, when the number of hidden units is at the minimum, there is essentially no effect of structure. However, as the number of hidden units is increased, the differences between the means of the different structure conditions become quite large.

One concern with the simulation described above is that it could be argued that the increased learning speed observed was not due to selectionist principles. Rather, the fast learning speed might merely be a reflection of the large connection weights that accompanied the large gaps in a high-structured network. Network structure might not have contributed to the improvements in learning the parity problems.

We ran a second simulation to determine whether the results above were indeed due to the amount of initial structure, or were simply due to the presence of large weights. The second simulation was identical to the first, with the exception of how the connection weights were initialized. Instead of imposing a gap (structure) in the sampling range, the random sampling of connection weights in this experiment spanned across the entire sampling distribution (i.e. from −1 to +1, −2 to +2, and −3 to +3), without leaving a gap in the middle.

The results of the second simulation were markedly different from the first. Table 11.2 presents the mean sweeps to convergence for the nine-bit parity problem, and can be compared to Table 11.1. First, learning this particular version of the parity problem proved enormously difficult in this study. In most of the cells, networks reliably failed to converge on a solution after 10,000 epochs. Second, when learning did occur, it did so for conditions in which there were fewer hidden units, and the range from which connection weights were selected was narrow. Clearly having a wider range of connection weights is not sufficient to account for the results of the first simulation, because if this were so, then Tables 11.1 and 11.2 would have been very similar in appearance. Analysis of variance of the full set

Table 11.2   Mean epochs to converge on the nine-bit parity problem in the second
simulation, with standard deviations in parentheses. Each cell represents
the mean from training 20 different networks.

| | | Connection weight range | | |
		Narrow	Medium	Wide
Number of hidden units	N	9983.70 (72.90)	10,000 (0.00)	10,000 (0.00)
	$2N$	9529.25 (1457.69)	10,000 (0.00)	10,000 (0.00)
	$3N$	10,000 (0.00)	10,000 (0.00)	10,000 (0.00)

of data for the second simulation confirmed this interpretation. It would appear that
the results of the first simulation depend upon the presence of structure – a gap
in the sampling distribution. This is consistent with a selectionist perspective.

11.5.3.6   The need for future research

The experimental results above are a first step towards demonstrating that there
exists an interesting possibility for a convergence between selectionism and
connectionism. However, a great deal more research is required before this
convergence is demonstrated conclusively. The simulations above provided a
result that was consistent with the hypothesis that the learning rule was being
used to select pre-existing structure from the network, and that this dramatically
aided the network in finding a solution to the problem. However, this was only
demonstrated with one problem (parity), and with one architecture (value units).
Clearly, more research needs to be conducted to explore whether these results
generalize to other problems and architectures.

As well, the manipulation of structure was very coarse in the above simulations.
Other manipulations are worthy of exploration. For instance, perhaps the networks
could be provided with specific structures or circuits, designed for accomplishing
particular tasks, rather than just a random assortment of connection weights that
are mathematically structured. "A system assembled out of beefed-up subnetworks
could escape all of the criticisms. But then we would no longer be talking about
a generic neural network!" (Pinker, 2002, p. 82). However, rather than viewing
this development as an abandonment of connectionism, we could more positively
view it as an evolution of connectionism into a more powerful, fully formalized,
selectionist theory.

Chapter twelve

From Synthesis to Analysis

The ability to define a training set, and to use something like the generalized delta rule to train a network to respond to it, is not sufficient to define synthetic psychology. This is because if connectionist models are going be informative, they will not be so by merely being brought into existence. Multilayer perceptrons are so powerful in principle that we should *always* be able to train some kind of network to solve a problem, and we should *never* be surprised by the mere creation of a network. Instead, connectionist models will have to surprise and inform us by telling us something new about a problem that they have learned to solve. In order for us to find out this kind of information, we have to analyze the internal structure of a trained network separately. The purpose of this chapter is to provide an introduction to some methods for interpreting the internal structure of connectionist networks.

12.1 Representing Musical Chords in a PDP Network

In Chapter 11, we introduced an example problem in which a connectionist network was trained to classify musical chords. The network that was described had 24 input units, each of which represented a key or note on a minipiano. The network had four output units, each of which was used by the network to represent a different kind of musical chord – major, minor, dominant, or diminished. The network used four hidden units to successfully classify 192 different chords, each of which was defined by four different notes. The network was able to identify chord type independent of what scale the chord was related to, and independent of what inversion was used to represent the order of the notes that made up the chord.

In order to solve this problem, the internal structure of this network must represent some basic information about music. What kind of knowledge does this network have? Does the network pay attention to the same kinds of regularities that are emphasized when a person learns to play piano? Let us seek some answers to questions of this type by analyzing the structure of this network.

12.1.1 Linear analysis of hidden unit responses

The network that learned to classify musical chords did not have any direct connections between its input units and its output units. We saw in Chapter 11 that one way in which to view such a network is that its hidden units transform or fold the pattern space that the network is learning to classify. With respect to the input unit encoding, the pattern space is not linearly separable. However, when the hidden units detect regularities in the input patterns, they transform the input encoding into a new encoding that is simpler, and which (for many problems) is often linearly separable. If the hidden unit representation is linearly separable, or if it is at least simpler than the input layer representation of patterns, then linear models of data can often reveal a great deal of information about how a network functions.

In order to explore this possibility, we performed discriminant analysis on the music chord network. The discriminant analysis of a data set delivers equations that can be used to classify patterns (e.g., Klecka, 1980). These equations take the values of variables as input, and combine them as a weighted linear sum that is similar to the multiple regression method that was discussed in Chapter 3. The result of summing these weighted predictors determines what category an input pattern belongs to. In our discriminant analysis, the input variables were the activation values of the hidden units to the input patterns. In other words, instead of having 192 different patterns defined by 24 input variables (i.e., the original training set), we represented each of the 192 patterns as a vector of four hidden unit activation values. We used these hidden unit activities to predict the type of chord that was being detected.

The results indicated that the hidden units had indeed simplified the pattern space, because discriminant analysis was able to predict chord type with 98 percent accuracy. To be more specific, it generated a set of equations that correctly classified all of the diminished, dominant, and minor chords. These functions also correctly classified 33 of the 36 major chords. The only problem that this analysis had was that three of the major chords were misclassified as being minor chords.

Even more interesting results were obtained when discriminant analysis was performed using a smaller number of predictor variables. When only the activations of hidden units 2 and 4 were used as predictors, discriminant analysis was still extremely successful, classifying the chords with 94 percent accuracy. Again, all of the diminished, dominant, and minor chords were correctly classified, even though only two predictors were being used; 25 of the major chords were also correctly classified. The remaining 11 major chords were misclassified as being minor chords.

How do only two hidden units transform the 192 input patterns in order to provide this high degree of accuracy in classification? Figure 12.1 illustrates how hidden units 2 and 4 organize the input patterns. This graph is a scatterplot of the 192 chords, where the *x*-position of a chord in the graph is provided by the activity of hidden unit 2, and the *y*-position of a chord in the graph is provided by the activity of hidden unit 4. It can be seen from this graph that there are really only four different combinations of hidden unit activity, and that these combinations correspond nearly perfectly with the four different kinds of chords in the training set. If both hidden units are activated with values of near 1.00, then this indicates that the chord is diminished (triangles on the graph). If one of the hidden units has an activation of near 1.00, and the other has an activation of approximately 0.5 or 0.6, then the chord is dominant (+s on the graph). If one of the hidden units has a fairly high activation (0.6 or higher), and the other has near zero activation, then the chord is minor – except for 12 major chords that fall in this region of the graph (Xs on the graph). If both hidden units have near zero activity, then the chord is major (circles on the graph).

Figure 12.1 also shows how the output units could exploit the hidden unit representation of the input patterns. Recall that in this particular network all four of the output units were value units. A value unit carves two parallel slices through a pattern space. If Figure 12.1 was a pattern space for the output units,

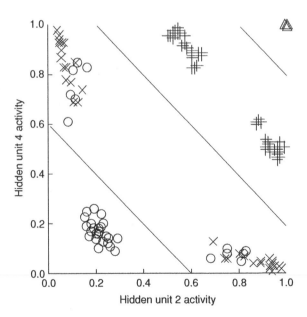

Figure 12.1 Music chords as represented by the activities of hidden units 2 and 4. Circles represent major chords, Xs represent minors, +s represent dominants, and triangles represent diminished chords. The diagonal lines represent cuts that could be made by output units to separate the different chord types from one another

then each of these units could carve this space in such a way that correct responses would be made. This would be accomplished by having each output unit arrange its cuts in a diagonal direction on the graph, going downward from left to right. As can be seen from the diagonal lines that have been added to Figure 12.1, these cuts could be arranged in such a way that only one kind of symbol would fall between them. The only exception to this claim is that in Figure 12.1, 12 of the major chords would incorrectly fall into the region that is occupied by all of the minor chords. Thus this graphical account of how these two hidden units represent musical chords is slightly less accurate than discriminant analysis, because it would make 12 mistakes instead of 11.

Figure 12.1, and the discriminant analysis of hidden unit responses, is interesting and important for two different reasons. First, these analyses raise two interrelated questions about hidden unit representations. What kind of musical regularities do hidden units 2 and 4 detect, such that these two hidden units are able to solve most of the chord problem by themselves? And what is special about the 11 or 12 chords that do not appear to be handled by these two hidden units (and are therefore likely handled by hidden units 1 and 3)? Second, because a two-unit representation can solve most of the problem, these results strongly suggest that we should concentrate our interpretative efforts on hidden units 2 and 4. In the next subsection, we turn to examining the connection weights between these two hidden units and the 24 input units.

12.1.2 Representation of notes by connection weights

In the previous subsection, a general understanding of the chord classification network was provided by the study of one kind of data, hidden unit activities. The values of the connection weights that feed into processors represent a second type of data that can be extremely helpful in the task of network analysis.

For example, consider the two hidden units that appear to be capable of solving most of the chord classification problem. After discriminant analysis had indicated the importance of these two units, we looked at them more closely by examining their connection weights. Recall that each of these units had 24 different incoming connections, each associated with one of the "piano keys" on our imaginary minipiano. In order to solve this particular problem, it seemed reasonable to expect that these connection weights had to represent some property about the different notes that the network was being presented with, and that the hidden units represented the structure of a chord by combining this property from the four notes that could be presented to it by any one of the training patterns.

In examining the connection weights of both hidden units, we observed an extremely regular pattern. For hidden unit 2, the connection weight associated with the lowest A that could be presented was a strong negative. The next connection weight (A#) was a weaker negative value, about half the weight of the first. The third connection weight (B) was a strong positive value, and the

Table 12.1 Correspondence between note names and connection weight values for two hidden units in the chord classification network

Note name	Hidden unit 2	Hidden unit 4
A, C#, F	−0.29	−0.17
A#, D, F#	−0.13	0.31
B, D#, G	0.28	0.14
C, E, G#	0.15	−0.29

fourth connection weight (C) was a positive value that was about half the weight of the third. This same pattern then repeated itself for each set of four notes through to the end of the input units. Hidden unit 4 had exactly the same pattern, but it was shifted one note to the right. The first connection weight was a weak negative, the second a strong positive, the third a weak negative, and the fourth a strong negative. This pattern repeated itself again and again through the input patterns. In both of these patterns, identical notes (i.e., notes that are an octave apart, or separated by 12 keys on the minipiano) were given exactly the same connection weight. Table 12.1 provides the value of the connection weight associated with each note by both of the hidden units.

It is useful to consider the connection weights from Table 12.1 as representing "note names" that are assigned by the hidden units. One interesting property of the table is that it shows that notes for which musicians would provide different names are all given the same name by the hidden units. For example, three notes that we would ordinarily treat as being different are A, C#, and F. However, hidden unit 2 gives all three of these notes the same weight or "name" (−0.29), as does hidden unit 4 (−0.17). An examination of the table shows that there are three other sets of different note names that are treated as being equivalent as far as these two hidden units are concerned.

What is special about these different notes that leads them to be treated in an identical fashion by these hidden units? One important property for each set of three note names in Table 12.1 is that the notes are equally spaced on the keyboard. For instance, C# is four piano keys higher than A, and F is four piano keys higher than C#. This four-key spacing is true of each set of note names in the table. Why is this property important? In all four types of chords, one will never find three different notes that are equally spaced four piano keys apart from one another. What this means is that, for example, the network will never see a pattern in which A, C#, and F are all presented together in the same chord. These three notes are never found together in any major, minor, dominant, or diminished chord. The same is true for the three other sets of three notes in Table 12.1. Thus, in certain respects it makes sense for the network to give each note the same "name." This is because the network will never have to differentiate between all three notes at the same time.

Of course, the network is not presented with single notes as stimuli, but is instead presented with four notes at the same time. Table 12.1 can also be used to provide some insight into why the notes are assigned these particular connection weights, and suggest how the network represents individual chords.

For example, we have already noted that the network will never be presented with the three notes that fall into a single cell in Table 12.1 at the same time. However, it is possible for the network to see a pattern in which one note from each of the four different note groups is presented. For example, one valid stimulus that was presented to the network was B, D, F, and G#. This can be translated into the note "names" of hidden unit 2 as the pattern 0.28, −0.13, −0.29, and 0.15. In terms of the connection weights of hidden unit 4, this chord can also be written as the pattern 0.14, 0.31, −0.17, and −0.29. If one computes the sum of the four names (i.e., connection weights) from hidden unit 2 (as would be the case when the hidden unit calculates its net input function), then the result would be 0.01, which is nearly identical to the bias of −0.01 for that unit. Similarly, if the four values from hidden unit 4 are added together, then the result is −0.01, which is nearly identical to that unit's bias of −0.03. Because for this chord the two net inputs are nearly identical to the respective biases, both hidden units would generate activation values of nearly 1.00. From Figure 12.1, we can see that this would indicate that this chord was diminished. Indeed, all of the diminished chords from the training set can be defined by taking one note from each of the four different groups in Table 12.1. As a result, any diminished chord will result in a near-zero net input for each hidden unit, which will in turn result in a high activation value for both hidden units. This is how these two units represent the fact that a presented chord is diminished in nature.

In general, it appears that the network has selected the connection weights that are listed in Table 12.1 as the "names" for different notes because individual chords are represented as the sum of these names (i.e., when net input is computed), and these particular weight values enable the hidden units to generate unique patterns of net inputs to each chord type. This is illustrated in Table 12.2. It provides the different net input values that are observed in the two hidden units for the different types of chords, including the 12 major chords that are

Table 12.2 Correspondence between chord types and net input values for two hidden units in the chord classification network

Chord type	Hidden unit 2	Hidden unit 4
Major	±0.72	±0.72, ±0.80
Incorrect Major	±0.28, ±0.85	±0.30, ±0.91
Minor	±0.16, ±0.30, ±0.85, ±1.00	±0.13, ±0.30, ±0.90, ±1.05
Dominant	±0.15, ±0.45	±0.14, ±0.45
Diminished	0.01	−0.01

incorrectly classified as being minor. There are several observations that can be made from this table.

First, the net inputs that are calculated fall into a very small number of categories. For example, when hidden unit 2 is presented with a dominant chord, then it will compute one of only four net input values: −0.15, 0.15, −0.45, 0.45. When we note that the symmetric bell shape of the Gaussian activation function essentially ignores the sign of the net input, we can further reduce the number of net input values that are generated to the chord types. For instance, when hidden unit 2 is presented with a dominant chord, it really only generates two net input values, 0.15 and 0.45, because it treats negative and positive values as being identical when they are passed into its activation function.

Second, the fact that the hidden units generate more than one net input to the same kind of chord would indicate that as far as the hidden units are concerned, there is some additional structure within chord type. For example, Table 12.2 suggests that the two hidden units are sensitive to four different subclasses of minor chords. What are these subclasses? This question can be answered simply by inspecting the properties of the different minor chords that are associated with each net input class. Hidden unit 2 generates a net input of ±0.16 to the minor chords that are first and second inversions, and that start with the note A#, D, or F#, or with the note C, E, or G#. These two different sets of notes are the ones that are assigned positive weights or names, as indicated in Table 12.1. It generates a net input of ±1.00 to the minor chords that are first and second inversions, and that start with a note that is assigned a negative weight (i.e., B, D#, or G; A, C, or F). It generates a net input of ±0.30 to minor chords in root position whose starting note is from the group A, C#, or F, or from the other group B, D#, or G. Finally, it generates a net input of ±0.84 to minor chords in root position whose starting note is from the group A#, D, or F#, or from the other group C, E, or G#. In short, by examining the net input calculated by this unit, we can see that it can be used to predict the form of the chord (root position, first inversion, second inversion), as well as the note class (i.e., the row in Table 12.1) from which the chord's starting note is taken. A similar organization of chords is obtained by examining the net inputs of hidden unit 4.

A third observation to make about Table 12.2 is to draw attention to an additional fact that the table does not make explicit. We have seen that the two hidden units each generate four different kinds of net input responses to minor chords. However, it is not the case that we will observe all possible combinations of classes when we examine the relationship between the net inputs of the two hidden units. For example, when hidden unit 2 generates a net input that falls into the class ±0.16, then hidden unit 4 will only generate a net input that falls into the class ±1.05. No other combinations are observed. Such constraints on the combinations of net inputs ultimately result in the highly striated appearance of the transformed pattern space that was graphed in Figure 12.1.

12.1.3 Problems with major chords, and how to solve them

The previous section has detailed how hidden units 2 and 4 represent musical regularities. These hidden units appear to have a very different view. They represent the input patterns using only four different note names, with each note repeated six different times, and with four piano keys separating repeated notes. By representing the individual note "names" with carefully chosen connection weights, these units use the sum of the four note names (i.e., net inputs) to represent whole chords. The net inputs produced by each chord type produce characteristic activity in the two hidden units, which in turn can be used to classify chords (see Figure 12.1). Furthermore, variations in net input (and therefore variations in hidden unit activity) are associated with specific chord structures within a chord class (e.g., type of inversion, type of note upon which the chord begins).

While this representation of musical knowledge is rich and interesting, it is not complete – even for the pattern set that the network was trained to classify. There are a handful of major chords that are not correctly represented by this four-note musical system. Why is this representation unable to deal with these major chords? How do the other two hidden units in the network correct this deficiency?

The first step in answering these two questions involves identifying the major chords that are misclassified by hidden units 2 and 4. When this is done, it becomes clear that the errors made by these two hidden units are extremely systematic. Recall from our description of the chord classification problem in Chapter 11 that our minipiano was based upon a musical system that used 12 different note names (A, A#, B, C and so on up to G#). A major chord in root position could be built upon any one of these 12 different note names, and then this chord could be rearranged to produce its first or second inversion. When hidden unit activities are examined, it becomes clear that the type of representation used by hidden units 2 and 4 only fails for the second inversion of the major chord based on each of these 12 notes (i.e., the second inversion of the major chord based on A, the second inversion of the major chord based on A#, and so on up to the second inversion of the major chord based on G#).

Why does this representation fail for the second inversion of major chords? This can be answered by considering one major chord as an example. Let us take the root position of the major chord based on the note C, which uses the four notes C, E, G, and C. If we used the connection weights for these notes that are assigned by hidden unit 2 (see Table 12.1), this pattern can be represented as the four values 0.15, 0.15, 0.28, and 0.15, which sum to a total of 0.73. Importantly in this root position pattern, three of these connection weights are identical. The first inversion of this major chord is the pattern E, G, C, and E. When represented in terms of hidden unit 2 weights, this pattern uses exactly the same numbers as were observed for the root position version of the chord, but the numbers are arranged in a different order (0.15, 0.28, 0.15, and 0.15). Obviously the sum of weights for the first inversion is identical to the sum that was computed for the root form of the chord, because both chords are defined by the same set of numbers. This is not true for the second inversion of a major chord. The second inversion of the example chord is G, C, E, and G. In this form of the chord, the note that is repeated (G) corresponds to the one connection weight that is different from the others in the previous two examples. As a result, the hidden unit 2 representation of this chord uses the values 0.28, 0.15, 0.15, and 0.28. Because one of the weights is not repeated in this pattern three times, the sum of their values is 0.86 instead of 0.73. This net input value is characteristic of all of the minor chords, and as a result the second inversion of the major chord is misclassified.

It turns out that the properties of this example apply to all of the different major chords that can be presented to the network. Chords in the root position and in the first inversion are represented as three identical weights combined with an additional different weight, and therefore produce the same net input. However, in the second inversion, the representation changes so that the chord is represented as two pairs of different weights. This results in a change in net input, such that the net input is more similar to that produced by a minor chord than that produced by a major chord.

Interestingly, the success of the representation used by hidden units 2 and 4 is so great that when the network learns, it does not abandon this approach, even though it does not work for all of the patterns. What it does instead is maintain this general representation in these two hidden units, and then it customizes the weights of the other two hidden units so that they are extremely specialized, and can handle the exceptions that are not captured by hidden units 2 and 4. In particular, hidden unit 1 only generates an activation of near 1.00 for 11 patterns, which all turn out to be second inversions of major chords. Hidden unit 3 turns on to almost any pattern – except for the one remaining second inversion of a major chord that hidden unit 1's specialized weights cannot capture. By turning off to this one pattern, hidden unit 3 can be used to turn the major chord output unit on, because the output unit's net input is decreased by this one event (or more properly this one absence of an event) by just the right amount to turn the unit on when this one chord is presented to the network.

12.1.4 Implications of the interpretation

The analysis of the chord classification network illustrates two main themes that lie at the heart of network analysis. The first theme is methodological. Ultimately, there are only two kinds of data that are available for network analysis: the responses of processing units to individual patterns, and the values of network connection weights. Network analysis is based on applying different interpretative strategies to these two different sorts of data. This might involve a variety of different approaches, ranging from inspecting particular values of weights or activations, to applying multivariate statistics to find regularities in either type of data. There is likely no single type of analysis that will work for every network.

One reason that no single interpretative technique applies to all networks is that the approach one takes to analyze a network is usually guided by an understanding of the properties of the problem with which the network was presented. In other words, one often uses knowledge about possible regularities in a training set to generate hypotheses about the kinds of properties that a network might be exploiting. For example, in the interpretation of the chord classification network, we realize that different types of chords are based on different intervals or spacing between the notes in the chord. It makes sense to see whether the network is sensitive to this kind of information. It was hypotheses of this sort that led us to realize that individual connection weights could be viewed as being note "names," and that the regular spacing of these names (i.e., four piano keys apart) was a crucial feature of the representations used by hidden units 2 and 4.

The second theme illustrated by the interpretation of this particular network concerns the kinds of information that the analysis might provide. It should be obvious from the preceding pages that network analysis involves a fairly focused treatment of the properties of a particular model. However, the surprises that this treatment reveals are not really properties of the network itself, but rather are properties of the domain about which the network was trained. For example, in the example that we have considered, we learned of a particularly elegant, novel, and compact representation of chord structure – a representation in which one replaced a 12-note system with a different system that used only four notes. While this representation was certainly a property of the network, what it tells us about the network is less important than what it tells us about the structure of music.

This point is particularly important when models are viewed as contributing to synthetic psychology. Network analysis provides us with new and surprising insights about the structure of some domain of knowledge, and about how this structure might be represented. For example, our network analysis indicated that a distributed representation in which two hidden units cooperated could be used to identify almost all of the chord types, and that a small set of special chords (the second inversions of majors) had to be treated as special cases. Furthermore, it revealed a novel set of equivalence classes of notes, where individual notes that we would ordinarily treat as being different could be given the same name (i.e., Table 12.1). Synthetic psychologists can use these sorts of surprises to generate hypotheses that can be studied using the more traditional techniques of experimental psychology. Do humans treat second inversions of major chords as being qualitatively different than any other kind of chord? Is there any evidence to indicate that A, C#, and F are represented as being the same note? There is an old view in empiricist psychology that says that a theory is only as good as the number of new experiments that it points to. The analysis of models that were created by adopting a synthetic approach is certainly a rich source of new hypotheses about domains of interest.

12.2   Interpreting the Internal Structure of Value Unit Networks

It has been argued that connectionism's potential contributions to cognitive science are limited by the fact that these networks are either difficult to interpret, or that interpretations are rarely reported in the literature (e.g., Dawson & Shamanski, 1994; McCloskey, 1991; Mozer & Smolensky, 1989). Connectionists have responded to this kind of challenge by proposing a diverse range of approaches to the interpretation of the internal structure of their networks (e.g., Alexander & Mozer, 1995; Andrews, Diederich & Tickle, 1995; Craven & Shavlik, 1994; Duch, Adamczak, & Grabczewski, 1998; Duch, Adamczak, Grabczewski, Ishikawa & Ueda, 1997; Fu, 1994; Hanson & Burr, 1990; Omlin & Giles, 1996; Thrun, 1995). In recent years in my own laboratory we have been exploring a variety of techniques for interpreting the internal structure of value unit networks. The purpose of this section of the chapter is to introduce these methods.

12.2.1   Identifying trigger features in integration device networks

How does the brain encode our experiences? Many contemporary neuroscientists believe that the brain uses representations that depend upon the signals of large numbers of simultaneously active neurons (for an overview see Pouget, Dayan, & Zemel, 2000).

> A singular neuron for each concept is rendered implausible in most vertebrates by the neurophysiological evidence that has accumulated since 1928, when the first recordings from sensory nerves revealed a broad range of sensitivity. . . . This isn't to say that a particular interneuron might not come to specialize in some unique combination – but it's so hard to find narrow specialists, insensitive to all else.
>
> *(Calvin, 1996, pp. 12,13)*

However, the view that neural representations depend upon the action of large populations of cells is not universal. For well over half a century, neuroscientists have attempted to understand the biology of vision by mapping the receptive fields of individual neurons in the visual system (e.g., Hubel & Wiesel, 1959; Lettvin, Maturana, McCulloch & Pitts, 1959). Their results suggest that it may be possible to describe a neuron as being sensitive to a "trigger feature," which, when detected, produces maximum activity in the cell. Furthermore, the more centrally the neuron is located in the visual system, the more complex and abstract its trigger feature is likely to be (see Kandel, Schwartz & Jessel, 1991, chs. 28–30).

Such results led Barlow (1972) to propose his neuron doctrine for perceptual psychology. "The central proposition is that our perceptions are caused by the activity of a rather small number of neurons selected from a very large population of predominantly silent cells. The activity of each single cell is thus an important perceptual event and it is thought to be related quite simply to our subjective experience" (p. 371). What this central proposition leads to is the view that in order to determine the role of a specific neuron in the visual system, one must find its trigger feature – the stimulus pattern that best matches the cell's receptive field. "A description of that activity of a single nerve cell which is transmitted to and influences other nerve cells, and of a nerve cell's response to such influences from other cells, is a complete enough description for functional understanding of the nervous system" (p. 380).

Whether the neuron doctrine is true of the brain is a controversial issue. However, this issue is independent of the possibility that the neuron doctrine can be usefully applied to connectionist networks. First, these networks are acknowledged to be far simpler than brains (e.g., Douglas & Martin, 1991), and thus might be more amenable to an analysis that tries to identify trigger features. Second, in many cases the training sets that are presented to networks are simple in nature and this too might allow trigger feature identification to be successful.

12.2.1.1 Empirical discovery of trigger features

How would one apply the neuron doctrine to connectionist networks? One approach would be purely empirical in nature. A trained network would be viewed as being no different from a biological system, and would therefore be studied using techniques analogous to those used by neuroscientists to explore the receptive fields of visual neurons.

Moorhead, Haig, and Clement (1989) provided one example of this approach. They used the generalized delta rule to train a multilayer perceptron to detect the presence of horizontal or vertical edges or bars. In other words, the output units in their network were trained to respond as if they were simple cells in the visual cortex. Their network had two independent banks of 25 input units per bank, where one bank represented the "off" signals coming from a 5×5 array of neurons performing a difference of Gaussian filtering, and the other bank represented the "on" signals coming from this same set of filters. These two sets of processors represented the results of filtering a much larger raw image (21×21 pixels), where each raw image was a line or edge that passed through the center of the display at a specific orientation. The question of interest was whether the hidden units developed biologically plausible receptive fields. Moorhead, Haig, and Clement borrowed a technique from neuroscience to answer this question. They spot-mapped the receptive fields of the hidden units by presenting a small 3×3 stimulus, which was either bright or dark, at every possible position in the 21×21 raw image array. Each raw "spot" image was filtered in the same manner as were the original stimuli, and the responses of the hidden units were recorded to each spot. They then graphed the receptive field by plotting hidden unit activity at the coordinates of each spot stimulus. Moorhead et al. had hoped to find that these receptive fields would have a center-surround appearance, but this was not what they observed in most of their hidden units. "There is no direct equivalence between the retinogeniculo striate pathway and a neural network which has been trained to respond in a manner similar to simple cells" (p. 802).

A second example of this empirical approach is found in Zipser and Andersen (1988). They used a network to explore how the location of a target on the retina could be combined with information about gaze direction to transform the coordinates of a target into head-centered space. This kind of task is important because it is one approach to generating a stable representation of the world in which objects maintain a constant position even as we look around, changing the projection of objects on our eyes. The input units encoded the location of targets on a retina that was defined as an 8×8 grid of processors. Each processor was tuned to generate a maximum response when a target spot was presented at its location, but would also generate a weaker response if the target were presented at a neighboring location. A second set of input units encoded eye position information. Signals from these two sets of input units were sent to a set of 25 hidden units, which in turn fed into an array of output units that represented target position in a normalized coordinate system. The network learned to make these transformations very quickly. At the end of training, Zipser and Andersen spot-mapped the hidden units. They did this by presenting a target spot at each of 17 different locations while eye coordinates were held fixed. This procedure was analogous to a study in which the responses of neurons in the parietal cortex of monkeys were measured when the monkeys fixated on one stimulus location while targets were presented to others. After spot-mapping the network, the hidden unit responses were normalized so that the maximum response always was assigned a value of 1; this procedure was also applied to the single-cell recording data taken from the monkeys. Zipser and Andersen found a striking resemblance between the receptive fields of the hidden units and the receptive fields of the neurons, suggesting that these neurons are being used to transform coordinate systems.

12.2.1.2 Analytic discovery of trigger features

A second approach to identifying the trigger features in a connectionist network is analytic, and depends upon the activation function that is used by the hidden units. To be more precise, if a hidden unit uses the logistic activation function (or some similar monotonic activation function), then one can identify the stimulus that best matches the receptive field of the hidden unit simply by inspecting its connection weights.

Assume that a hidden processing unit uses a monotonic activation function like the logistic, and computes its net input by summing the weighted signals that it receives from the input units. The trigger feature for this unit is the input stimulus that produces the maximum activation in the unit. Because the activation function is monotonic, this also means that the trigger feature is the input stimulus that produces the highest net input. What stimulus will do this? If we know what the highest and lowest possible activation values for the input units are, we can inspect the connection weights and define the trigger feature. We simply assign the highest possible input value to each connection that has a positive weight, and the lowest possible input value to each connection that has a negative weight. The resulting pattern of high and low inputs is the trigger feature for that unit.

Dawson, Kremer, and Gannon (1994) used this analytic rule to define the trigger features for a network that was similar in spirit to the vision network studied by Moorhead, Haig, and Clement (1989). Their network was an 11×11 array of input units that could be turned either on or off. These inputs fed into a 9×9 array of hidden units. In one condition, each hidden unit only received input from a small 3×3 window of input units. Dawson, Kremer and Gannon presented horizontal or vertical bars at all possible positions in their input array. Their network had two output units that were trained to be analogous to complex cells in the visual cortex – one unit was trained to turn on to any vertical bar, while the other unit was trained to turn on to any horizontal bar. They inspected the connection weights to identify the trigger features for each hidden unit in accordance with the rule described in the previous paragraph. They discovered a significant number of the hidden units had developed receptive fields that were analogous to those of simple cells. This was not the case in a second network in which every hidden unit was connected to every input unit. Dawson, Kremer and Gannon argued that biologically plausible receptive fields might be obtained by imposing constraints on network connections, and suggested that failure to do so might be one reason that Moorhead, Haig, and Clement did not find the receptive fields that they were interested in.

12.2.2 Families of trigger features in value units

Dawson, Kremer, and Gannon (1994) demonstrated the utility of an analytic definition of the trigger feature of an integration device. Can one define the trigger feature of a value unit in a similar way?

For the sake of simplicity, let us assume that we are working with a value unit with μ set to 0 in its Gaussian activation function. Following Barlow's (1972) neuron doctrine, the trigger feature for this unit will be the feature that produces the maximum activation. For this value unit, this will occur when the net input to the unit is equal to 0 (i.e., equal to the value of μ). When will the net input be equal to 0? Recall that for the kinds of networks that we have been discussing in this book, the net input function is the inner product between a vector that represents a stimulus and a vector that represents the connection weights that fan into the unit. So the net input will be equal to 0 when this inner product is equal to 0. However, when an inner product is equal to 0, this means that the two vectors being combined are orthogonal to one another, with an angle of 90° between them. In other words, the trigger feature for a value unit is an input pattern that is orthogonal to the connection weights of the unit.

This definition has an extremely important implication. In principle, there will not be only one input pattern that is orthogonal to a unit's connection weights. The connection weights of a value unit can be viewed as being analogous to a surface normal in computer vision (e.g., Marr, 1982). A surface normal is a vector that is perpendicular to a plane; the direction in which the surface normal is pointed provides the orientation of the plane in space. What the connection weights of a value unit do is provide the orientation of a hyperplane in hyperspace. Any vector that falls flat along this hyperplane will be perpendicular to the connection weights, and will therefore serve as a trigger feature. Many different vectors can fall along this hyperplane. As a result, we must conclude that a value unit does not have a single trigger feature, but that many different input vectors – each related to one another in a very restricted way – are trigger features for this kind of unit.

One further consequence of this analysis of value unit trigger features is that there will be other families of input patterns as well. These will be patterns that fall into the same hyperplane, but the hyperplane will not be orthogonal to the vector of connection weights. One consequence of this is that all of these patterns will produce identical net inputs, but these net inputs will be some value that is not equal to μ. McCaughan, Medler, and Dawson (1999) discuss the geometry of this observation in more detail.

What are the consequences of this analysis of value units? First, because of their activation function, value units are best thought of as orienting some hyperplane in hyperspace that defines its trigger features. All of the input vectors that fall into this plane will produce the same net input, and will also result in maximum activation in the value unit. Other input patterns will fall into other hyperplanes that are at different orientations. These patterns will also produce identical net inputs, which will lead to identical activations. However, these will have differ-ent values from the net inputs/activations generated by the trigger features. What all of this implies is that if one trains a network of value units, and then measures the responses of its hidden units to all of the members of the training set, the hidden unit activations should be highly organized. Instead of having a rectangular distribution of activation values, one set of patterns will all generate one activation value, another set will generate a different activation value, and so on. This is the basis of the banding phenomenon that was described in Chapter 2. By identifying the sets of patterns that all produce the same levels of activation values in a hidden value unit, and by examining the features that these patterns have in common, we can develop a very rich account of the kinds of features that the hidden units are exploiting (Berkeley, Dawson, Medler, Schopflocher, & Hornsby, 1995). The next subsection provides an example of this kind of interpretation in action.

12.2.3 Identifying local features in a network of value units

12.2.3.1 Problem definition

The monks problems are a set of three different artificial training sets that have been used as a standard benchmark for comparing different machine learning algorithms (Thrun et al., 1991). Six different features define the appearance of each monk in the problem set. They can have one of three possible head shapes and one of three possible body shapes. They can be holding one of three different objects. They can wear a jacket that is one of four different colors. They may or may not be smiling. They may or may not be wearing a tie. The full datasets that define the monks problems can be obtained from the UCI Machine Learning Repository (Blake & Merz, 1998).

In the first monks problem, an input pattern belongs to the target category if it is consistent with the following rule: ((head shape = body shape) or (jacket color = red)). In the training set, half of the patterns belong to the target category. Typically, when this problem is studied a system is first trained on 124 of these patterns, and its performance is then tested on the remaining stimuli. Because our interest was in network interpretation, we did not follow this practice. Instead, we trained a network to correctly classify all 432 monks that can be created by combining the values of the six different features.

12.2.3.2 Network architecture and problem encoding

In this example, a value unit network was trained to solve the first monks problem. It consisted of one output value unit and two hidden value units. The output unit was trained to turn on when the network was presented with a pattern that belonged to the target category, and to turn off to any other pattern. Fifteen input units were used to encode the input patterns using a local coding scheme.

The local coding scheme worked as follows. The first three input units represented head shape. If this shape was round, then only the first input unit was turned on. If this shape was square, then only the second input unit was turned on. If this shape was octagon, then only the third input unit was turned on. The next three input units encoded body shape using exactly the same scheme. The seventh input unit was turned on if the monk was smiling, and was turned off otherwise. The next three input units represented whether the monk was holding a sword, a balloon, or a flag by turning the corresponding unit on, and turning the other two units off. The next four input units represented jacket color (red, yellow, green, or blue) by turning the appropriate unit on, and the other three units off. The final output unit was turned on if the monk wore a tie, and was turned off otherwise.

12.2.3.3   Training the network

The training set consisted of all 432 patterns of the first monks problem, and the network was trained using the Rumelhart software that was discussed in Chapter 11. The network was started in a random state, with each connection weight being randomly selected from the range −0.1 to 0.1. Unit biases were set equal to 0.00 throughout training. The network was trained using Dawson and Schopflocher's (1992a) learning rule for value units, with a learning rate of 0.01. The order of pattern presentation was randomized every epoch. The network generated a "hit" for every pattern after only 22 epochs of training.

After the network converged, we plotted the jittered density plots of its two hidden units. Each point on the jittered density plot represents the hidden unit activity that is produced when one of the training patterns is presented. The x-coordinate of the point represents the activation value. The y-coordinate of the point is a randomly selected value, which is used to minimize the overlap of points that generate the same hidden unit activity. The jittered density plots for the two hidden units in this network were distinctly banded. The first hidden unit had three bands. For this unit, 228 of the patterns generated an activity of 0.00 (band H1 A), 60 of the patterns generated an activity between 0.11 and 0.22 (band H1 B), and the remaining 144 patterns generated an activity of 1.00 (band H1 C). The second hidden unit was also organized into three distinct bands. Ninety-six of the patterns generated an activity of 0.00 (band H2 A), 192 of the patterns generated an activity between 0.06 and 0.13 (band H2 B), and the remaining 144 patterns generated an activity between 0.99 and 1.00 (band H2 C).

12.2.3.4   Identifying definite features associated with bands

How are these bands used to interpret the inner workings of a trained network? Berkeley, Dawson, Medler, Schopflocher, and Hornsby (1995) reasoned that for a subset of training patterns to all fall into the same band, they must share some input features in common. In order to identify what these shared features are, you look at only the subset of patterns that belong to a band of interest. Each of these patterns is defined as a set of input values, and descriptive statistics are performed on these input values. If these statistics show that a property is true of all of the patterns that belong to the band, then this property is called a *definite feature*, and is used to interpret the network. There are two different kinds of definite features that can be discovered in this way.

Berkeley et al. (1995) called the first a *definite unary feature*. A definite unary feature occurs when one of the input units has the same value for all of the patterns that belong to a band. When descriptive statistics are performed, this is revealed when the standard deviation of that feature for the set of patterns is equal to zero. In the monks network, one example of a definite unary feature is found in band H1 C. In this band, input unit 11 is always equal to 0 for each of the 144 patterns in the band. As this unit represents the jacket color red, this feature is important, because it indicates that for these patterns, jacket color is never red, and therefore none of these patterns belong to the target category.

Berkeley et al. (1995) called the second a *definite binary feature*. A definite binary feature occurs when two input units are in a constant relationship for all of the patterns that belong to a band. What this means is that while the individual values of the input units vary in the band, the relationship between the two remains the same. In particular, the two input units will either have identical values, or they will have opposite values, when inputs are encoded in a binary format. A definite binary feature is revealed when one takes all of the patterns that fall into a band, and computes the correlations between the values of the input units. For binary encoding, if a correlation of 1.00 is found between two input units, then this indicates that the two units always have the same value. If a correlation of -1.00 is found then this indicates that the two units always have the opposite value. Band H1 C in the monks network also provides an example of a definite binary feature. For the 144 patterns in this band, the correlation between the values of input unit 3 and input unit 6 is equal to -1.00. This indicates that these two input units never have the same value – when input unit 3 is set to 1, input unit 6 is set to 0; when input unit 3 is set to 0, input unit 6 is set to 1. This feature is important, because input unit 3 represents octagonal head shape, and input unit 6 represents octagonal body shape. If these two units are never equal for all 144 patterns in this band, then head shape and body shape are never the same for any of these patterns. This provides another reason why these 144 patterns do not conform to the rule that defines the patterns that belong to the target category.

Table 12.3 provides the definite features that were identified in all six bands that were observed in this network. One thing that immediately becomes apparent

Table 12.3 Definite features in the bands of the monks network

Unit	Band	Definite Feature	Interpretation	Implication
H1	A	Input 3 = Input 6	Eh?	Eh?
	B	Input 11 = 1 Inputs 12, 13, 14 = 0	Jacket red	In target class
	C	Input 11 = 0 Input 3 ≠ Input 6	Jacket not red Different body and head shapes	Not in target class
H2	A	Input 11 = 1 Inputs 12, 13, 14 = 0	Jacket red	In target class
	B	Input 2 = Input 5	Eh?	Eh?
	C	Input 11 = 0 Input 2 ≠ Input 5	Jacket not red Different body and head shapes	Not in target class

from examining this table is that both hidden units can be seen as devices that respond to properties that rule out the possibility that a pattern belongs to the target class. If a pattern generates high activity in either (or both) hidden units, then it will fall into band C. All of the patterns that belong to band C in either unit have the wrong jacket color, and the wrong relationship between head and body shape, to turn the output unit on. When we examine the connection weights from the two hidden units to the output unit, we find further support for this interpretation. The connection weight from hidden unit 1 is 0.84, and the weight from hidden unit 2 is 0.96, while the bias of the output unit is equal to 0.00. So if one or both of the hidden units activates, the net input will be too high to turn the output unit on. The output unit will only respond if both hidden units have very low activity – that is, if both of them have failed to detect any reason that a pattern should *not* be put into the target category.

Four of the six bands described in Table 12.3 provide definite features that have useful local interpretations. What this means is that by examining these features by themselves, in the context of the input encoding, meaning can be assigned to them. Furthermore, this assigned meaning is relevant for describing how the network generates a correct response. However, the other two bands (H1 A and H2 B) do not appear to have this property. While both bands are associated with definite binary features, these features by themselves do not appear to be sufficient to support a decision about whether a pattern belongs to the target category.

For example, an examination of band H1 A reveals that input units 3 and 6 have the same value. This indicates that for the patterns that fall into this band, head shape and body shape are either both octagonal, or are both not octagonal. In this latter case, it is possible that head and body shape are different – one could be round, the other square, and both would not be octagonal. So, by itself, this definite feature is not completely useful. Exactly the same observation can be made for band H1 B. For the pattern that fall into this band, head shape and body shape are either both square, or are both not square, and this regularity is not by itself a sufficient condition for making an output response.

Why then are these two hidden units detecting these two features? The answer to this question is that these two bands are not being used locally and independently to guide the network's response. Instead, these two bands are detecting two features that can be used in combination to make a judgment about an input pattern. There are some patterns that, when presented, will cause activity that will fall into band H1 A and into band H2 B at the same time. For these patterns, it will be the case that input 3 = input 6, and that input 2 = input 5. If both of these properties are true, then it must follow that head shape and body shape are equal, and that the pattern belongs to the target category. It is impossible to define a pattern in this training set in which both of these equalities hold, but head shape and body shape differ.

These two bands therefore encode a useful and interpretable feature, but the meaning of this feature is distributed over different bands that are found in different hidden units. Thus these bands do not provide local features. Dawson and Piercey (2001) have shown that in many cases the bands found in value units encode distributed features. As a result, the kind of local analysis that was demonstrated in Table 12.3, which was characteristic of my lab's early research on network interpretation (e.g., Berkeley et al., 1995; Dawson, Medler, & Berkeley, 1997), is often not going to be appropriate. A different kind of analysis, which is geared to discovering interpretations that are distributed across hidden units, is required. This alternative approach to network analysis is described in the next subsection.

12.2.4   Identifying distributed features in a network of value units

12.2.4.1   Problem definition

In order to demonstrate the discovery of distributed features in a network of value units, let us consider another classification problem that is used as a benchmark in the machine learning literature. The problem that we will use is the zoo database that is also available from the UCI Machine Learning Repository (Blake & Merz, 1998).

The zoo database consists of 101 different animals, each described by 16 different features. Most of the features are coded as being true or false (hair, feathers, eggs, milk, airborne, aquatic, predator, toothed, backbone, breathes, venomous, fins, tail, domestic, catsize). One of the features (legs) is represented as a number indicating how many legs an animal has.

The task of a system that is presented with the zoo database is to use these 16 features to classify each of the patterns into one of seven different animal types: 41 of the animals belong to the type "mammal," 20 to the type "bird," 5 to the type "reptile," 13 to the type "fish," 4 to the type "amphibians," 8 to the type "insect," and a varied assortment of 10 animals belong to the type "other" (clam, crab, crayfish, lobster, octopus, scorpion, seawasp, slug, starfish, worm).

12.2.4.2   Network architecture

A value unit network was trained to categorize the different animals in the zoo database. It consisted of seven output value units, each of which represented one of the different animal types. When an animal of a particular type was presented, the network's task was to turn on the corresponding output unit, and to turn all of the other output units off. The network also had three hidden value units. Sixteen input units were used to encode the input patterns. Of these units, 15 were turned either on or off to represent the presence or absence of the feature that each unit represented. The 16th unit was assigned a value of 0, 2, 4, 6, or 8 to indicate the number of legs that a particular animal had.

12.2.4.3 Training the network

The network was trained using the Rumelhart software. It was started in a random state, with each connection weight being randomly selected from the range −0.1 to 0.1, and with each unit bias (i.e., μ) being started at 0.00. Unit biases were modified during learning. The network was trained using Dawson and Schopflocher's (1992a) learning rule for value units, with a learning rate of 0.01. The order of pattern presentation was randomized every epoch. The network was trained until a "hit" was obtained for every pattern. Convergence was achieved after 1,101 epochs of training.

The purpose of training this demonstration network was to provide an example of how one might proceed to discover definite features that are not local, but are instead distributed across hidden units. Our favored technique for identifying such features is to use cluster analysis. The next subsection provides a brief introduction to cluster analysis, and in particular identifies one practical problem that is faced whenever any cluster analysis is performed. The subsection that follows offers one solution to this problem that is possible when neural networks are being analyzed. With these two points out of the way, the chapter returns to this network, and demonstrates how cluster analysis can be performed on it.

12.2.4.4 Activations, cluster analysis, and the number of clusters problem

Cluster analysis is a method for dividing a set of n observations into g groups (Ripley, 1996). For example, k-means is the name of a statistical method that partitions data into a prespecified (k) number of groups by minimizing the sum of squared distances from each data point to the center of its assigned cluster (Aldenderfer & Blashfield, 1984). In other words, when clustering is performed by k-means, stimuli that are assigned to the same cluster are nearer to each other than they are to stimuli that are assigned to different clusters.

Cluster analysis would appear to be an ideal approach for taking the activations of hidden units to input patterns, and grouping different patterns into meaningful groups. All of the patterns that are assigned to the same group would be related in the sense that they produced similar patterns of activation across a group of hidden units. After patterns were assigned to groups on this basis, we could search for definite features among all of the patterns that belonged to the same cluster. This would provide a method for discovering features that were distributed across hidden units. The banding of hidden units would still be important, because the more structured the raw data is, the more successful cluster analysis should be.

Given that the primary goal of cluster analysis is to assign data to groups, an obvious question to ask is "How many groups should be used?" Unfortunately, no single method for determining the optimal number of clusters in a data set has been agreed upon (Aldenderfer & Blashfield, 1984; Everitt, 1980; Gorsuch, 1983). This is reflected in the fact that many different methods exist for dealing with this issue.

One approach to the number of clusters problem is to have an objective and automatic decision rule, which typically involves the examination of some quantitative aspect of the clustering algorithm's performance as a function of the number of groups to which data has been assigned. For example, Milligan and Cooper (1985) used Monte Carlo methods to examine the performance of 30 such rules on data sets with known error-free clustering structure. Another approach to the number of components problem is more subjective, often utilizing graphs and requiring the user to make a judgment based on the appearance of a curve. For example, Aldenderfer and Blashfield (1984, pp. 54–6) describe a variant of the scree test (Cattell, 1978) that can be applied to cluster analysis. Other subject-ive methods include deciding on the number of clusters after simply inspecting scatterplots of the raw data (e.g., Ripley, 1996, p. 313). In general, most cluster analysts recommend some combination of formal and graphical methods to arrive at the most reliable solution to the number of clusters problem, although the specific methods are not agreed upon (e.g., Aldenderfer & Blashfield, 1984; Sarle, 1994). Indeed, a variety of different approaches may be applied because in the end any methods used will be "judged by their results; a successful clustering produces groups which can be interpreted by domain experts" (Ripley, 1996, p. 311).

Why has no single solution to the number of clusters problem emerged? Aldenderfer and Blashfield (1984) point out two main difficulties that have not been overcome. The first is the fact that it is extremely difficult to create an appropriate null hypothesis (e.g., an operationalization of "structureless data") against which methods for determining the appropriate number of clusters can be compared. The second is that multivariate data distributions are typically very complex and potentially mixed, and as a result "it is unreasonable to assume that formal tests of clustering ability are likely to be developed" (p. 54).

While these two points provide excellent reasons for the failure to develop a *general* solution to the number of clusters problem, they do not rule out the possibility for identifying a solution to this problem that can be usefully applied to a *specific* domain. The hidden unit activities of a trained connectionist network represent one specific domain in which this problem can be solved. The next subsection will describe a heuristic objective rule for determining how many clusters should be used to organize the data that is obtained when a set of hidden units are wiretapped.

12.2.4.5   Solving the number of clusters problem

Consider a network that has been successfully trained to map each member of a stimulus set to the correct member of a response set. For example, in a moment we will return to an analysis of the value unit network that learned to assign the 101 different animals to seven different categories on the basis of the input features. As was noted earlier, one approach to determining how the network performs this mapping, or to determining the nature of the internal representations used by the network, is to measure hidden unit activities produced in the network by each of the training patterns. This would produce a set of hidden unit activity vectors that could then be examined with k-means cluster analysis. The point of this analysis would be to reduce this potentially large number of vectors into a much smaller number of clusters. Furthermore, these clusters should be interpretable – by examining the properties of each cluster, one should be able to determine how the trained network actually translated input features into an output response.

How many clusters should the set of hidden unit activity vectors be assigned to? The answer depends upon one piece of heuristic information that we have about the domain that is being clustered: there is a correct mapping from hidden unit activity vectors to output responses. We know that this must be true, because if the network has correctly learned the task that it was presented, then the network itself has discovered one such mapping. This knowledge can be used as follows: *we should extract the smallest number of clusters such that every hidden unit activity vector assigned to the same cluster produces the same output response in the network*. In other words, every pattern that is assigned to the same cluster should produce the same output response in the network if all of the patterns in the cluster truly belong together. We should find the smallest number of clusters for which this property is true.

In practice, the following procedure can be followed to implement this rule. Assume that a network has been trained to correctly classify a set of input patterns, and that the hidden unit activity vectors for each of these patterns have been recorded. Perform a k-means cluster analysis of these vectors. Once complete, create a two-way frequency table for the data. This table should record the number of instances in each cluster that correspond to each possible output vector for the network. For example, in the zoo network, this table would indicate how many patterns that fell into cluster *x* were mammals, how many patterns that fell into cluster *x* were birds, and so on. By examining this table, determine whether another k-means analysis is required (an analysis involving partitioning the data into a larger number of clusters). If the cluster analysis is incomplete, then there will be more than one nonzero entry in at least one of its rows, indicating that members of the same cluster map onto two (or more) different network responses. In this case, another cluster analysis should be performed, with patterns being assigned to at least one additional cluster. This process is repeated until each row of the frequency table has only one nonzero entry per row, indicating a unique mapping from clusters of hidden unit activity vectors to network responses. An interpretation of these clusters should indicate the nature of the internal representations used by the network to produce its stimulus/ response mapping.

12.2.4.6   Cluster analysis of the zoo network

We analyzed the zoo network by performing k-means cluster analysis on the set of hidden unit activities that were obtained by wiretapping the network. The results were surprisingly simple – when the hidden unit activities were assigned to seven different clusters, each cluster was "pure" in the sense that every member in a cluster was associated with the same network response. According to the stopping rule that was introduced in the previous subsection, this is the desired number of clusters for our analysis. No additional cluster analysis was required.

It should be pointed out that while this particular analysis worked with the minimum number of clusters possible, this is usually not the case. It is more typical to have to assign hidden unit activities to more clusters than there are types of network responses, because each cluster captures important distinctions between patterns that lead to the same response. For example, in one analysis performed by Dawson, Medler, McCaughan, Willson, and Carbonaro (2000), there were nine different responses that were possible from a network that classified mushrooms as being edible or poisonous, and that also provided a reason for making this judgment. However, hidden unit activities had to be assigned to 13 different clusters before each cluster was "pure." Furthermore, the cluster analysis of the hidden unit activities generated a much simpler solution than does a cluster analysis that classifies animals in terms of the 16 different features that are input to the animal. Even when k-means clustering assigns patterns to 25 different clusters, some of the clusters are not pure. Clearly the hidden units have discovered regularities in the data that are both powerful and simplifying.

After hidden unit activities have been assigned to clusters, the next step is to identify definite features associated with each cluster. We do this by applying the same techniques that were reported in the analysis of the monks network. However, instead of computing descriptive statistics for patterns that fall into a particular band on a hidden unit, we now apply these statistics to the subsets of patterns that all belong to the same cluster. Table 12.4 provides the definite features that were obtained for each cluster.

It is important to note that these definite features only emerge by simultaneously considering the patterns in terms of the activations that they produce in all three hidden units. If the activations of individual units are considered separately, then it is very difficult to grasp the kinds of features that a particular hidden unit is detecting. This is because the units are not working to detect features locally, but are instead working cooperatively to represent distributed features. At the level of individual hidden units, because these units are not working as local feature detectors, very disparate combinations of animal properties can have the same effect on a hidden unit.

For example, let us consider how hidden unit 1 treats birds and insects. From Table 12.4 it can be seen that both of these animal types produce very similar activity in the hidden unit. If we examine the definite features associated with both types of animal, we see that they only differ in terms of three features:

Table 12.4 Feature analysis of the clusters taken from the zoo network. The average activity produced in each hidden unit by the patterns in the cluster is given, along with the definite unary and binary features that were revealed by descriptive statistics

Cluster	Type	H1	H2	H3	Unary features	Binary features
1	Mammal	0.93	0.00	0.87	~feathers, milk, backbone, breathes, ~venomous	eggs ≠ toothed
2	Fish	0.00	1.00	0.88	~hair, ~feathers, eggs, ~milk, ~airborne, aquatic, backbone, ~breathes, fins, 0 legs, tail	
3	Bird	0.94	0.99	0.02	~hair, feathers, eggs, ~milk, backbone, breathes, ~fins, 2 legs, tail	
4	Other	0.17	0.66	0.01	~hair, ~feathers, ~milk, ~airborne, ~toothed, ~backbone, ~fins, ~domestic	eggs ≠ tail
5	Reptile	0.01	0.16	0.98	~hair, ~feathers, ~milk, ~airborne, backbone, ~fins, tail, ~domestic	Aquatic ≠ breathes, predator ≠ catsize, eggs ≠ aquatic, eggs ≠ breathes, predator = toothed, toothed ≠ catsize
6	Insect	0.88	0.22	0.00	~feathers, eggs, ~milk, ~aquatic, ~toothed, ~backbone, breathes, ~fins, 6 legs, ~tail, ~catsize	
7	Amphibian	0.00	0.15	0.33	~hair, ~feathers, eggs, ~milk, ~airborne, aquatic, toothed, backbone, breathes, ~fins, 4 legs, ~domestic, ~catsize	

feathers, backbone, and legs. Birds have feathers, a backbone, and two legs; insects have no feathers and no backbone, but have two legs. How is it possible that these differences in features can still result in having a similar effect on hidden unit 1? An examination of connection weights points to an answer. The weights from these three features that feed into hidden unit 1 are −1.12 for feathers, 0.54 for backbone, and −0.15 for number of legs. Considering these three features alone – the only features that distinguish all birds from all insects in the training set – we can determine that different combinations produce similar contributions to net input. For birds, the contribution to net input is

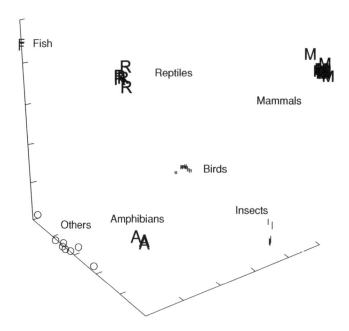

Figure 12.2 The pattern space for the zoo problem after the 16 input features have been transformed into activation values in three hidden units.

$(1 \times (1.12)) + (1 \times 0.54) + (2 \times (-0.15)) = -0.88$. If we take away feathers and backbone, but compensate by adding more legs, we can get nearly exactly the same contribution to net input for insects: $(0 \times (-1.12)) + (0 \times 0.54) + (6 \times (-0.15)) = -0.90$. In other words, extremely different combinations of unrelated features provide the same effect on the hidden unit. For this reason, interpreting the kinds of features represented by individual units is not particularly fruitful for this network. Instead, one can only make sense of the network by interpreting features associated with animals that produce particular effects on all three hidden units.

How, then, does this distributed representation of features by the hidden units get converted into appropriate output unit responses? The activity produced in each hidden unit by a pattern provides three coordinates to locate that pattern as a point in a transformed pattern space. The hidden units work in coordination to place patterns that share the definite features listed in Table 12.4 in very similar locations in this space. This can be seen in Figure 12.2. Because the hidden units geometrically arrange the animals in this neat way, the output units can adjust their hidden units so that a particular cluster of points falls into their receptive fields, and the units will only turn on to one cluster that has been isolated in this fashion.

12.3   Network Interpretation and Synthetic Psychology

In this chapter, we have focused on introducing techniques for interpreting networks of value units. We have seen different approaches demonstrated on three different networks. In this final section, we will briefly review the results of some applications of these approaches that have appeared in the synthetic psychology literature. These examples have been organized into three different categories. First, a network that was interpreted by examining local features associated with bands is discussed. This interpretation is analogous to the monks network analysis that was described above. Second, some networks that were interpreted by examining features distributed across hidden units are reviewed. These networks were explored using the clustering techniques that were demonstrated for the zoo network. Finally, a network that was explored by examining the structure of its connection weights is given a brief overview. The techniques used for this network are most similar to the ones that were used to investigate the chord classification network at the start of this chapter.

12.3.1 Interpretations based on finding local features in bands

12.3.1.1 The Wason card selection problem

One task that is famous in cognitive psychology is Wason's (1966) selection task. In standard form, it consists of presenting a participant with an abstract conditional rule of the form, *if p then q*, and four cards displaying the categories of *p*, *not-p*, *q*, and *not-q*. For example, a subject might be given the rule "If there is a vowel on one side of the card, then there is an even number on the other side of the card," and might see four cards: "E", "K", "4" and "7." Although participants can see only one side of each card, they are told that each card has another category on its flip side. Participants are then instructed to test the truth of the rule by selecting the fewest possible cards from the set of four. In other words, they have to choose the smallest number of cards such that if these cards were flipped over, and their other side examined, this evidence would either prove or falsify the rule. According to formal methods of assessing the truth of a conditional rule, only an instance of a *p* together with a *not-q* can falsify the rule (Garnham & Oakhill, 1994). Hence, participants need to choose the *p* and the *not-q* cards (i.e., "K" and "7" in our example) because only these cards can provide information that disproves the rule.

The Wason selection task appears to be a simple problem, but this simplicity is deceptive, because participants usually get it wrong (for a review see Evans, Newstead, & Byrne, 1993). For this reason, the selection task has been studied extensively since it first appeared in the literature.

In one recent examination of the selection task, Leighton and Dawson (2001) adopted a synthetic approach, and trained connectionist networks to choose relevant cards. Three different networks were created. One generated the correct responses as dictated by logic. A second network generated one of the incorrect responses often observed in humans, and just selected the *p* card. A third simulation generated another common human error, and selected the *p* and the *q* cards. In these networks, the first four input units were used to encode a logical rule in binary notation, and four sets of three input units (for a total of 16 units in all) were used to represent the cards that were presented to the network. Eight different conditional rules were developed, and all combinations of four different types of cards (with two cards per card type) were created, which resulted in a training set of 3,072 different patterns. The networks each had four different output units, one for each card. If an output unit was turned on, then this indicated that the network would flip this card over to test the rule that was presented.

After the networks were trained, the hidden units were wiretapped, and the results of this wiretapping were plotted using jittered density plots. One example of this analysis was performed on the eight hidden units that were used by the network that was trained to generate logically correct responses to the selection task. For this network (as well as the other two described in the paper), the jittered density plots were highly banded. Leighton and Dawson (2001) noted that pairs of hidden units had very similar plots. An examination of definite features associated with correlated pairs of hidden units indicated that pairs of hidden units controlled each output unit. One of the units was highly sensitive to the type of rule that was being presented to the network, and both units were only sensitive to patterns that indicated that a particular output unit should be turned on. In other words, each pair of hidden units used definite features that focused on rule properties that were correlated with turning only one of the cards over.

One interesting question that Leighton and Dawson (2001) also explored with their networks was task complexity. Perhaps human subjects make certain kinds of responses because these involve a smaller computational load. They found that when a network was only required to turn one card over, the problem was simpler – only two hidden units were required. Eight hidden units were required for both networks that had to turn two cards over. However, the one network that turned two cards over to make logically incorrect responses was sensitive to a much simpler set of definite features. The result of all of these analyses and comparisons between networks resulted in an inductive theory of Wason task reasoning, in contrast to more typical deductive theories.

12.3.2   Interpretations based on finding features distributed across hidden units

Many of the early analyses of networks in my laboratory were based on methods that focused on identifying local features associated with bands. For example, this kind of analysis of a network trained to classify logical syllogisms revealed a set of internal rules that were very classical in nature, and which were used to argue for similarities between connectionist and symbolic models of cognition (e.g., Berkeley et al., 1995; Dawson, 1998; Dawson, Medler, & Berkeley, 1997). However, our experiences with network analysis have indicated that the reliable identification of local features is more the exception than the rule. Instead, we have found that we are much more likely to discover distributed features in networks, as is indicated by the case studies that are described below.

12.3.2.1 The mushroom problem

The mushroom problem is another benchmark training set for machine learning (Schlimmer, 1987), and can also be obtained from the UCI Machine Learning Repository (Blake & Merz, 1998). It consists of 8,124 different patterns, each defined as a set of 21 different features. The task is to use these features to decide whether a mushroom is edible or not.

In one study, Dawson, Medler, McCaughan, Willson, and Carbonaro (2000) trained a network of value units to solve the mushroom problem. The network had one output unit, four hidden units, and 21 input units (one for each input feature). After training was successfully completed, they "wiretapped" the responses of the hidden units to each of the training patterns. K-means cluster analysis was then performed. Dawson et al. used the heuristic stopping rule described in this chapter to determine that the data should be assigned to 13 different clusters. They then identified the definite features associated with each cluster.

After identifying definite features, Dawson et al. (2000) proceeded to use them to provide a concise description of how the network was classifying mushrooms. First, they represented the possible feature values associated with each cluster as a vector of 119 entries, because when considering the different values for the 21 different features, 119 different values are possible. If a feature value belonged to the cluster, then it was given a value of 1 in the vector; otherwise it was given a value of –1. Second, they performed a discriminant analysis using these vectors. The 119 features in the vectors were used as predictors, and the predicted variable was networked response – whether the feature vector was associated with mushrooms that were edible or not. They found that a simple discriminant function that used only seven feature values (cap color = cinnamon, odor = anise, gill color = white, stalk color above ring = white, ring type = evanescent, habitat = meadows, habitat = woods) could correctly classify every pattern in the training set. It would appear that the hidden units were collectively representing the presence or absence of these features, and that the output units used this distributed representation to solve the mushroom problem. This analysis resulted in a completely novel account of how the mushroom problem could be solved, and the nature of this account is arguably more psychologically plausible than accounts derived from traditional methods in machine learning, such as decision trees.

12.3.2.2 The mushroom problem with extra outputs

Dawson et al. (2000) also interpreted a network of value units trained on a variation of the mushroom problem. This variation involved extra-output learning, in which the network not only had to use an output unit to represent whether a mushroom was edible or not, but also had to use other output units to represent the reason for this decision. This network used 21 input units, five hidden units, and 10 output units. The first output unit indicated if the mushroom was edible. The remaining nine output units each represented a reason for making a decision, where each reason corresponded to a particular terminal branch in a classical decision tree that was created by applying traditional machine learning techniques to the mushroom problem data set. The purpose of this second network was to determine whether the decision tree could be translated into a network using standard connectionist training techniques.

After training, the responses of the five hidden units to each of the 8,124 patterns were recorded, and k-means cluster analysis was conducted. After applying the heuristic stopping rule it was determined that the patterns of hidden unit activities should be assigned to 12 different clusters. As was the case in the previous analysis, each of these clusters was associated with a definite set of mushroom features. However, this was not the most interesting analysis that could be performed using these clusters. Instead, Dawson et al. (2000) translated the classical decision tree into a set of nine condition-action rules that defined a small production system. They then demonstrated a unique mapping in which all of the patterns that belonged to a particular cluster map directly onto one of these productions. In other words, they were able to show that when the five hidden units had a particular pattern of activity – a pattern that could be assigned to one of the clusters – this could be translated into a claim that the network was executing a specific production rule. Dawson et al. (2000) used this result to argue that connectionist models and classical symbolic models of the type are not only extremely similar, but are identical, at least from the perspective of how some philosophers of science view theories. This claim about theory identity depends on the ability to translate one kind of theory into another. Many would argue that this is not possible if the two theories are fundamentally different.

12.3.3   Interpretations based on other techniques

There may be instances for which the two types of approaches that have been illustrated in the two preceding sections simply don't work. For example, in some cases when a value unit network is dealing with continuous inputs, the jittered density plots do not band (e.g., Dawson, Dobbs, Hooper, McEwan, Triscott, & Cooney, 1994). In other cases, a network of value units might be better viewed as a function approximation network. In this case, distributed features can be hard to find (e.g., Zimmerman, 1999). In situations like this, other interpretative techniques need to be explored. Usually, these techniques involve taking different approaches to discovering regularities that are present in hidden unit activities, connection weights, or both.

We have already seen a detailed account of this final type of analysis in Chapter 8. When Dawson, Boechler, and Valsangkar-Smyth (2000) analyzed a network that had been trained to make spatial judgments, they had to explore specific relationships between geographic distances and connection weights. This required them to view hidden units as occupying particular places on a map, and as a result forced them to use optimization techniques to determine where on the map hidden units could be located. The results of this approach, as was detailed in Chapter 8, were the discovery of a particular type of encoding (coarse allocentric representation of space) that could be related to some theoretical issues in the cognitive map literature. A second implication of this research, in the context of the current chapter, is to emphasize the point that there is no single technique for network analysis. Many different analytic approaches may need to be explored before a network reveals its internal secrets.

Chapter thirteen

From Here to Synthetic Psychology

We have now come to the end of this introduction to the synthetic approach in psychology and cognitive science. Let us take a moment to review some of the main themes that this book has covered, and to consider where one might proceed from here.

Models have had an important role to play in both psychology and cognitive science. In Chapter 2, we saw that the reason for this is that models offer many advantages. They help to provide a rigorous specification of a theory by making terms more precise, by providing new tools for studying concepts, and by revealing hidden assumptions. They permit complex domains to be studied, in some cases providing insights where techniques such as mathematics fail. They also provide a medium in which a researcher can be provided with surprising insights into a phenomenon. While we also saw that all of these advantages do not come without having other potential costs, these advantages make modeling both a plausible and fruitful endeavor.

However, modeling is not a homogenous practice. There are many different kinds of models that are available to researchers, and these were overviewed in Chapters 3 through 5. We identified three different classes of models: models of data, mathematical models, and computer simulations. We compared and contrasted these different types of models in terms of a number of basic properties. Does the model attempt to fit pre-existing measurements? Is the model linear? Does the model depend upon some goodness-of-fit metric? Can the model surprise us? Does the model behave, or does it merely summarize or describe behavior?

As we moved from Chapter 3 to Chapter 5, we saw a transformation in these properties. For example, models of data fit pre-existing measurements, are usually linear, live or die by their goodness of fit to data, do not provide surprises, and do not behave. In contrast, computer simulations need not fit pre-existing data, usually have important nonlinear components, do not depend on fitting data, are designed to surprise us, and actually behave. In short, there is more to modeling than describing some data that has already been collected by some statistical equation.

The implications of this observation were explored in Chapters 6 and 7. Given that we can create models that behave, one approach to modeling is to assume some basic components, and to use these components to construct a behaving system. If the right kinds of components have been selected, then the behavior should be both surprising and interesting. From this synthetic approach, one main purpose of a model is to show how a set of interesting components can behave. The model's behavior becomes the primary data of interest.

Why is this approach to modeling attractive? One of the main reasons is Braitenberg's (1984) law of uphill analysis and downhill synthesis. If an interesting set of nonlinear components are put together, and if these components are placed in a complex or interesting environment, then the expected result is that the synthesized system will generate more complicated behavior than one would have predicted on the basis of the known properties of the components. Furthermore, because the system was constructed, then the expectation is that the researcher who built it will have a ready explanation for these surprises. In short, Braitenberg's position was that synthetic psychology should lead to simpler theories of complex phenomena.

However, Chapter 8 argued that Braitenberg's (1984) position does not seem to be completely correct. In many cases, it is possible to construct a system that surprises, but to also be in a position where an understanding of that system is not readily available. It was then claimed that for synthetic psychology to work, one certainly has to synthesize models that behave. However, it is inevitable that once these models are constructed, researchers will have to adopt an analytic approach to derive theories that explain their performance. While it is likely that this analysis will be immeasurably aided by having built a system, this step is necessary and can be complex. This point was illustrated by an example analysis of a connectionist network that had learned to make spatial judgments about cities in Alberta.

Indeed, connectionism provides one rich medium in which synthetic psychology can be practiced and explored. In Chapters 9, 10, and 11 we discussed connectionist modeling in terms of three general synthetic building blocks. The first was the storing of associations between stimuli and responses in a set of modifiable connection weights. The second was the incorporation of nonlinear activation functions into the processing units from which the networks were constructed. The third was the development of learning rules that were capable of chaining layers of nonlinear processors together to make sequences of decisions. In each chapter, we saw how these different building blocks provided tools that could be applied to psychological problems. We also saw, in Chapter 11, that when these three building blocks were combined together, extremely powerful models were possible.

Nevertheless, once these models are synthesized, they must still be analyzed in order to provide psychological explanations. Chapter 12 illustrated this by discussing some of the general techniques that could be used to interpret the internal structure of one type of connectionist architecture, networks of value units. Three different techniques were explored. The first was the examination of connection weights and hidden unit responses. The second was the discovery of local features associated with bands that are often found in the jittered density plots of wiretapped hidden units. The third was the use of cluster analysis to identify definite features that are distributed across activity patterns in more than one hidden unit.

It is hoped that this discussion of connectionism and synthetic psychology can provide the reader with the inspiration to explore new phenomena by adopting the synthetic approach. Some of this exploration can be conducted with the software that has been developed in my lab during the creation of this manuscript. Other connectionist environments might prove more powerful and useful, particularly as the complexity or size of problems of interest increases. Of course, connectionism is not the only medium in which this kind of exploration can be conducted – symbolic models in artificial intelligence, genetic algorithms, artificial life simulations, and behavior-based robotics are also candidates that have been explored by many researchers. Regardless of the medium, though, the approach will still be the same. Choose some components. Build something with them. Watch your creation behave, searching for emerging surprises. Finally, explain these surprises by performing an analysis of the structure of the system that you built.

References

Adams, B., Breazeal, C., Brooks, R. A., & Scasselati, B. (2000). Humanoid robots: A new kind of tool. *IEEE Intelligent Systems, 15,* 25–31.

Aldenderfer, M. S., & Blashfield, R. K. (1984). *Cluster Analysis* (vol. 07–044). Beverly Hills, CA: Sage Publications.

Alexander, J. A., & Mozer, M. C. (1995). Template-based algorithms for connectionist rule extraction. In G. Tesauro, D. S. Touretzky, & T. K. Leen (eds.), *Advances in Neural Information Processing Systems* (vol. 7, pp. 609–16). Cambridge, MA: MIT Press.

Anderson, J. A., & Rosenfeld, E. (1988). *Neurocomputing: Foundations of Research.* Cambridge, MA: MIT Press.

Anderson, J. A., Silverstein, J. W., Ritz, S. A., & Jones, R. S. (1977). Distinctive features, categorical perception and probability learning: Some applications of a neural model. *Psychological Review, 84,* 413–51.

Anderson, J. R., & Bower, G. H. (1973). *Human Associative Memory.* Hillsdale, NJ: Lawrence Erlbaum Associates.

Andrews, R., Diederich, J., & Tickle, A. B. (1995). A survey and critique of techniques for extracting rules from trained artificial neural networks. *Knowledge-Based Systems, 8,* 373–89.

Ashby, W. R. (1956). *An Introduction to Cybernetics.* London: Chapman & Hall.

Ashby, W. R. (1960). *Design for a Brain* (2nd edn.). New York: John Wiley & Sons.

Ashcraft, M. H. (1989). *Human Memory and Cognition.* Glenview, IL: Scott, Foresman and Co.

Atkinson, R. C., Bower, G. H., & Crothers, E. J. (1965). *An Introduction to Mathematical Learning Theory.* New York: John Wiley & Sons.

Ballard, D. (1986). Cortical structures and parallel processing: Structure and function. *The Behavioral and Brain Sciences, 9,* 67–120.

Bannon, L. J. (1980). An investigation of image scanning. Unpublished doctoral dissertation, University of Western Ontario, London, ON.

Barlow, H. B. (1972). Single units and sensation: A neuron doctrine for perceptual psychology? *Perception, 1,* 371–94.

Bechtel, W. (1985). Contemporary connectionism: Are the new parallel distributed processing models cognitive or associationist? *Behaviorism, 13,* 53–61.

Bechtel, W., & Abrahamsen, A. (1991). *Connectionism and the Mind*. Cambridge, MA: Blackwell.

Berkeley, I. S. N., Dawson, M. R. W., Medler, D. A., Schopflocher, D. P., & Hornsby, L. (1995). Density plots of hidden value unit activations reveal interpretable bands. *Connection Science, 7*, 167–86.

Berlyne, D. E. (1971). *Aesthetics and Psychobiology*. New York: Appleton-Century-Crofts.

Bever, T. G., Fodor, J. A., & Garrett, M. (1968). A formal limitation of associationism. In T. R. Dixon & D. L. Horton (eds.), *Verbal Behavior and General Behavior Theory* (pp. 582–5). Englewood Cliffs, NJ: Prentice-Hall.

Bird, A. (1998). *Philosophy of Science*. Montreal & Kingston: McGill-Queen's University Press.

Blake, C. L., & Merz, C. J. (1998). *UCI Repository of Machine Learning Databases*. Irvine, CA: University of California, Department of Information and Computer Science. Available at <http://www.ics.uci.edu/~mlearn/MLRepository.html>.

Blickhan, R., & Full, R. J. (1993). Similarity in multilegged locomotion: Bouncing like a monopode. *Journal of Comparative Physiology A 173*, 509–7.

Block, N. (1981). *Imagery*. Cambridge, MA: MIT Press.

Blumenthal, L. M. (1953). *Theory and Applications of Distance Geometry*. London: Oxford University Press.

Bock, R. D., & Jones, L. V. (1968). *The Measurement and Prediction of Judgment and Choice*. San Francisco, CA: Holden-Day.

Bodanis, D. (2000). *E = MC2: A Biography of the World's Most Famous Equation*. Toronto, CA: Random House.

Boden, M. (1977). *Artificial Intelligence and Natural Man*. New York: Basic Books.

Boring, E. G. (1950). *A History of Experimental Psychology*. New York: Appleton-Century-Crofts.

Braitenberg, V. (1984). *Vehicles: Explorations in Synthetic Psychology*. Cambridge, MA: MIT Press.

Braithwaite, R. B. (1970). Models in the empirical sciences. In B. A. Brody (ed.), *Readings in the Philosophy of Science* (pp. 268–75). Englewood Cliffs, NJ: Prentice-Hall.

Brooks, R. A. (1989). A robot that walks; emergent behaviours from a carefully evolved network. *Neural Computation, 1*, 253–62.

Brooks, R. A. (1999). *Cambrian Intelligence: The Early History of the New AI*. Cambridge, MA: MIT Press.

Brooks, R. A. (2002). *Flesh and Machines: How Robots Will Change Us*. New York: Pantheon Books.

Brown, T. H. (1990). Hebbian synapses: Biophysical mechanisms and algorithms. *Annual Review of Neuroscience, 13*, 475–511.

Burgess, N., Donnett, J. G., Jeffery, K. I., & O'Keefe, J. (1999). Robotic and neuronal simulation of the hippocampus and rat navigation. In N. Burgess, K. J. Jeffery, & J. O'Keefe (eds.), *The Hippocampal and Parietal Foundations of Spatial Cognition* (pp. 149–66). Oxford: Oxford University Press.

Burgess, N., Recce, M., & O'Keefe, J. (1995). Spatial models of the hippocampus. In M. A. Arbib (ed.), *The Handbook of Brain Theory and Neural Networks* (pp. 468–72). Cambridge, MA: MIT Press.

Caelli, T. (1981). *Visual Perception: Theory and Practice*. Oxford: Pergamon Press.

Calvin, W. H. (1996). *The Cerebral Code*. Cambridge, MA: MIT Press.

Cattell, R. B. (1978). *The Scientific Use of Factor Analysis*. New York: Plenum Press.

Changeux, J.-P., & Dehaene, S. (1993). Neuronal models of cognitive functions. In M. H. Johnson (ed.), *Cognition and Brain Development: A Reader* (pp. 363–402). Oxford: Blackwell.

Cheng, K., & Spetch, M. L. (1998). Mechanisms of landmark use in mammals and birds. In S. Healy (ed.), *Spatial Representation in Animals* (pp. 1–17). Oxford: Oxford University Press.

Chomsky, N. (1959). A review of B. F. Skinner's *Verbal Behavior. Language, 35,* 26–58.

Chomsky, N. (1965). *Aspects of the Theory of Syntax.* Cambridge, MA: MIT Press.

Chomsky, N. (1995). *The Minimalist Program.* Cambridge, MA: MIT Press.

Chomsky, N., & Halle, M. (1991). *The Sound Pattern of English.* Cambridge, MA: MIT Press.

Churchland, P. M., & Churchland, P. S. (1990). Could a machine think? *Scientific American, 262,* 32–7.

Churchland, P. S., Koch, C., & Sejnowski, T. J. (1990). What is computational neuroscience? In E. L. Schwartz (ed.), *Computational Neuroscience* (pp. 46–55). Cambridge, MA: MIT Press.

Churchland, P. S., & Sejnowski, T. J. (1992). *The Computational Brain.* Cambridge, MA: MIT Press.

Clark, A. (1989). *Microcognition.* Cambridge, MA: MIT Press.

Clark, A. (1993). *Associative Engines.* Cambridge, MA: MIT Press.

Coombs, C. H., Dawes, R. M., & Tversky, A. (1970). *Mathematical Psychology: An Elementary Introduction.* Englewood Cliffs, NJ: Prentice-Hall.

Cotman, C. W., Monaghan, D. T., & Ganong, A. H. (1988). Excitatory amino acid neurotransmission: NMDA receptors and Hebb-type synaptic plasticity. *Annual Review of Neuroscience, 11,* 61–80.

Cotter, N. E. (1990). The Stone–Weierstrass theorem and its application to neural networks. *IEEE Transactions on Neural Networks, 1,* 290–5.

Craik, K. J. M. (1943). *The Nature of Explanation.* Cambridge, UK: Cambridge University Press.

Craven, M. W., & Shavlik, J. W. (1994). Using sampling and queries to extract rules from trained neural networks. In W. W. Cohen & H. Hirsh (eds.), *Proceedings of the Eleventh International Conference on Machine Learning* (pp. 37–45). San Francisco, CA: Morgan Kaufmann.

Crick, F., & Asanuma, C. (1986). Certain aspects of the anatomy and physiology of the cerebral cortex. In J. McClelland & D. E. Rumelhart (eds.), *Parallel Distributed Processing* (vol. 2, pp. 333–71). Cambridge, MA: MIT Press.

Cummins, R. (1983). *The Nature of Psychological Explanation.* Cambridge, MA.: MIT Press.

Cybenko, G. (1989). Approximation by superpositions of a sigmoidal function. *Mathematics of Control, Signals, and Systems, 2,* 303–14.

Cziko, G. (1995). *Without Miracles: Universal Selection Theory and the Second Darwinian Revolution.* Cambridge, MA: MIT Press.

Dawson, M. R. W. (1990). Training networks of value units: Learning in PDP systems with nonmonotonicactivation functions. *Canadian Psychology, 31*(4), 391.

Dawson, M. R. W. (1991). The how and why of what went where in apparent motion: Modeling solutions to the motion correspondence process. *Psychological Review, 98,* 569–603.

Dawson, M. R. W. (1998). *Understanding Cognitive Science.* Oxford: Blackwell.

Dawson, M. R. W., Boechler, P. M., & Valsangkar-Smyth, M. (2000). Representing space in a PDP network: Coarse allocentric coding can mediate metric and nonmetric spatial judgements. *Spatial Cognition and Computation, 2,* 181–218.

Dawson, M. R. W., & Di Lollo, V. (1990). Effects of adapting luminance and stimulus contrast on the temporal and spatial limits of short-range motion. *Vision Research, 30,* 415–29.

Dawson, M. R. W., Dobbs, A., Hooper, H. R., McEwan, A. J. B., Triscott, J., & Cooney, J. (1994). Artificial neural networks that use single-photon emision tomography to identify patients with probable Alzheimer's disease. *European Journal of Nuclear Medicine, 21*(12), 1303–11.

Dawson, M. R. W., Kremer, S., & Gannon, T. (1994). Identifying the trigger features for hidden units in a PDP model of the early visual pathway. In R. Elio (ed.), *Tenth Canadian Conference On Artificial Intelligence* (pp. 115–19). San Francisco, CA: Morgan Kaufmann.

Dawson, M. R. W., Medler, D. A., & Berkeley, I. S. N. (1997). PDP networks can provide models that are not mere implementations of classical theories. *Philosophical Psychology, 10,* 25–40.

Dawson, M. R. W., Medler, D. A., McCaughan, D. B., Willson, L., & Carbonaro, M. (2000). Using extra output learning to insert a symbolic theory into a connectionist network. *Minds and Machines, 10,* 171–201.

Dawson, M. R. W., Nevin-Meadows, N., & Wright, R. D. (1994). Polarity matching in the Ternus configuration. *Vision Research, 34,* 3347–59.

Dawson, M. R. W., & Piercey, C. D. (2001). On the subsymbolic nature of a PDP architecture that uses a nonmonotonic activation function. *Minds and Machines, 11,* 197–218.

Dawson, M. R. W., & Pylyshyn, Z. W. (1988). Natural constraints in apparent motion. In Z. W. Pylyshyn (ed.), *Computational Processes in Human Vision: An Interdisciplinary Perspective* (pp. 99–120). Norwood, NJ: Ablex.

Dawson, M. R. W., & Schopflocher, D. P. (1992a). Modifying the generalized delta rule to train networks of nonmonotonic processors for pattern classification. *Connection Science, 4,* 19–31.

Dawson, M. R. W., & Schopflocher, D. P. (1992b). Autonomous processing in PDP networks. *Philosophical Psychology, 5,* 199–219.

Dawson, M. R. W., & Shamanski, K. S. (1994). Connectionism, confusion and cognitive science. *Journal of Intelligent Systems, 4,* 215–62.

Dawson, M. R. W., & Thibodeau, M. H. (1998). The effect of adapting luminance on the latency of visual search. *Acta Psychologica, 99,* 115–39.

Dawson, M. R. W., & Wright, R. D. (1994). Simultaneity in the Ternus configuration: Psychophysical data and a computer model. *Vision Research, 34,* 397–407.

De Wilde, P. (1997). *Neural Network Models* (2nd edn.). London: Springer.

Delamater, A. R., Sosa, W., & Katz, M. (1999). Elemental and configural processes in patterning discrimination learning. *The Quarterly Journal of Experimental Psychology, 52B,* 97–124.

DeYoe, E. A., & van Essen, D. C. (1988). Concurrent processing streams in monkey visual cortex. *Trends in Neuroscience, 11,* 219–26.

Dickinson, M. H., Farley, C. T., Full, R. J., Koehl, M. A. R., Kram, R., & Lehman, S. (2000). How animals move: An integrative view. *Science, 288,* 100–6.

Douglas, R. J., & Martin, K. A. C. (1991). Opening the grey box. *Trends in Neuroscience, 14,* 286–93.

Dreyfus, H. L. (1992). *What Computers Still Can't Do.* Cambridge, MA: MIT Press.

Duch, W., Adamczak, R., & Grabczewski, K. (1998). Extraction of logical rules from training data using backpropagation networks. *Neural Processing Letters, 7,* 211–19.

Duch, W., Adamczak, R., Grabczewski, K., Ishikawa, M., & Ueda, H. (1997). Extraction of crisp logical rules uing constrained backpropagation networks – comparison of two new approaches. Paper presented at the European Symposium on Artificial Neural Networks (ESANN, April '97), Bruge, Belgium.

Duch, W., & Jankowski, N. (1999). Survey of neural transfer functions. *Neural Computing Surveys, 2,* 163–212.

Dutton, J. M., & Briggs, W. G. (1971). Simulation model construction. In J. M. Dutton & W. H. Starbuck (eds.), *Computer Simulation of Human Behavior* (pp. 103–26). New York: John Wiley & Sons.

Dutton, J. M., & Starbuck, W. H. (1971). *Computer Simulation of Human Behavior.* New York: John Wiley & Sons.

Edelman, G. M. (1987). *Neural Darwinism.* New York: Basic Books.

Edelman, G. M. (1988). *Topobiology.* New York: Basic Books.

Edelman, G. M. (1989). *The Remembered Present.* New York: Basic Books.

Edelman, G. M. (1992). *Bright Air, Brilliant fire.* New York: Basic Books.

Edelman, G. M., & Mountcastle, V. B. (1978). *The Mindful Brain.* Cambridge, MA: MIT Press.

Eich, J. M. (1982). A composite holographic associative recall model. *Psychological Review, 89,* 627–61.

Elman, J. L., Bates, E. A., Johnson, M. H., Karmiloff-Smith, A., Parisi, D., & Plunkett, K. (1996). *Rethinking Innateness.* Cambridge, MA: MIT Press.

Ericsson, K. A., & Simon, H. A. (1984). *Protocol Analysis: Verbal Reports as Data.* Cambridge, MA: MIT Press.

Estes, W. K. (1975). Some targets for mathematical psychology. *Journal of Mathematical Psychology, 12,* 263–82.

Evans, J. St. B. T., Newstead, S. E., & Byrne, R. M. (1993). *Human Reasoning: The Psychology Of Deduction.* Hillsdale, NJ: Lawrence Erlbaum Associates.

Everitt, B. (1980). *Cluster Analysis.* New York: Halsted.

Farah, M. J. (1994). Neuropsychological evidence with an interactive brain: A critique of the "locality" assumption. *Behavioral and Brain Sciences, 17,* 43–104.

Farah, M. J., Weisberg, L. L., Monheit, M., & Peronnet, F. (1989). Brain activity underlying mental imagery: Event-related potentials during mental image generation. *Journal of Cognitive Neuroscience, 1,* 302–16.

Feigenbaum, E. A. (1995). The simulation of verbal learning behavior. In E. A. Feigenbaum (ed.), *Computers and Thought* (pp. 297–309). Cambridge, MA: MIT Press.

Feigenbaum, E. A., & Feldman, J. (1995). *Computers and Thought.* Cambridge, MA: MIT Press.

Fodor, J. A. (1968). *Psychological Explanation: An Introduction to the Philosophy of Psychology.* New York: Random House.

Fodor, J. A. (1975). *The Language of Thought.* Cambridge, MA: Harvard University Press.

Fodor, J. A. (1983). *The Modularity of Mind.* Cambridge, MA: MIT Press.

Fodor, J. A., & McLaughlin, B. P. (1990). Connectionism and the problem of systematicity: Why Smolensky's solution doesn't work. *Cognition, 35,* 183–204.

Fodor, J. A., & Pylyshyn, Z. W. (1988). Connectionism and cognitive architecture. *Cognition, 28,* 3–71.

Foster, J., Ainsworth, J., Faratin, P., & Shapiro, J. (1997). Implementing a mathematical model of hippocampal memory function. In M. A. Conway (ed.), *Cognitive Models of Memory* (pp. 275–312). Cambridge, MA: MIT Press.

Fu, L. (1994). Rule generation from neural networks. *IEEE Transactions on Neural Networks, 24*, 1114–24.

Fukushima, K. (1986). A neural network model for selective attention in visual pattern recognition. *Biological Cybernetics, 55*, 5–15.

Full, R. J., & Tu, M. S. (1991). Mechanics of a rapid running insect: two-, four-, and six-legged locomotion. *Journal of Experimental Biology, 156*, 215–31.

Funahashi, K. (1989). On the approximate realization of continuous mappings by neural networks. *Neural Networks, 2*, 183–92.

Furumoto, L. (1980). Mary Whiton Calkins (1863–1930). *Psychology of Women Quarterly, 5*, 55–68.

Gallistel, C. R. (1990). *The Organization of Learning*. Cambridge, MA: MIT Press.

Gardner, H. (1984). *The Mind's New Science*. New York: Basic Books.

Garnham, A., & Oakhill, J. (1994). *Thinking and Reasoning*. Cambridge, MA: Blackwell.

Gerrissen, J. F. (1991). On the network-based emulation of human visual search. *Neural Networks, 4*, 543–64.

Gluck, M. A., & Myers, C. E. (1997). Psychobiological models of hippocampal function in learning and memory. *Annual Review of Psychology, 48*, 481–514.

Goodale, M. A. (1988). Modularity in visuomotor control: From input to output. In Z. W. Pylyshyn (ed.), *Computational Processes in Human Vision: An Interdisciplinary Perspective* (pp. 262–85). Norwood, NJ: Ablex.

Goodale, M. A. (1995). The cortical organization of visual perception and visuomotor control. In S. M. Kosslyn & D. N. Osherson (eds.), *An Invitation to Cognitive Science: Visual Cognition* (vol. 2, pp. 167–213). Cambridge, MA: MIT Press.

Goodale, M. A., & Humphrey, G. K. (1998). The objects of action and perception. *Cognition, 67*, 181–207.

Gorsuch, R. L. (1983). *Factor Analysis* (2nd edn.). Hillsdale, NJ: Lawrence Erlbaum Associates.

Granger, R., Ambros-Ingerson, J., & Lynch, G. (1989). Derivation of encoding characteristics of Layer II cerebral cortex. *Journal of Cognitive Neuroscience, 1*, 61–87.

Graubard, S. (1988). *The Artificial Intelligence Debate*. Cambridge, MA: MIT Press.

Grey Walter, W. (1950). An imitation of life. *Scientific American, 182*(5), 42–5.

Grey Walter, W. (1951). A machine that learns. *Scientific American, 184*(8), 60–3.

Grey Walter, W. (1963). *The Living Brain*. New York: W.W. Norton & Co.

Grossberg, S. (1988). *Neural Networks and Natural Intelligence*. Cambridge, MA: MIT Press.

Grush, R. (2000). Self, world and space: The meaning and mechanisms of ego- and allocentric spatial representation. *Brain and Mind, 1*, 59–92.

Hagan, M. T., Demuth, H. B., & Beale, M. (1996). *Neural Network Design*. Boston, MA: PWS Publishing.

Hallahan, W. L. (1996). DECtalk software: Text-to-speech technology and implementation. *Digital Technical Journal, 7*, 5–19.

Hanson, S. J., & Burr, D. J. (1990). What connectionist models learn: Learning and representation in connectionist networks. *Behavioral and Brain Sciences, 13*, 471–518.

Hanson, S. J., & Olson, C. R. (1991). Neural networks and natural intelligence: Notes from Mudville. *Connection Science, 3*, 332–5.

Hartman, E., Keeler, J. D., & Kowalski, J. M. (1989). Layered neural networks with Gaussian hidden units as universal approximation. *Neural Computation, 2*, 210–15.

Haugeland, J. (1985). *Artificial Intelligence: The Very Idea*. Cambridge, MA: MIT Press.

Hebb, D. O. (1949). *The Organization of Behaviour*. New York: John Wiley and Sons.

Hebb, D. O. (1959). A neuropsychological theory. In S. Koch (ed.), *Psychology: A Study of a Science. Volume 1: Sensory, Perceptual, and Physiological Foundations* (pp. 622–43). New York: McGraw-Hill.

Hille, B. (1990). *Ionic Channels of Excitable Membranes* (2nd edn.). Sunderland, MA: Sinauer.

Hillis, W. D. (1988). Intelligence as emergent behavior, or, the songs of Eden. In S. R. Graubard (ed.), *The Artificial Intelligence Debate* (pp. 175–89). Cambridge, MA: MIT Press.

Hinton, G. E., & Anderson, J. A. (1981). *Parallel Models of Associative Memory*. Hillsdale, NJ: Lawrence Erlbaum Associates.

Hocking, B. (1963). *The Ultimate Science: A Layman's Account of Biology*. Toronto, ON: CBC Publications.

Hodges, A. (1983). *Alan Turing: The Enigma of Intelligence*. London: Unwin Paperbacks.

Holland, J. H. (1992). *Adaptation in Natural and Artificial Systems*. Cambridge, MA: MIT Press.

Holland, J. H. (1998). *Emergence*. Reading, MA: Perseus Books.

Holland, O., & Melhuish, C. (1999). Stigmergy, self-organization, and sorting in collective robotics. *Artificial Life, 5*, 173–202.

Hopcroft, J. E., & Ullman, J. D. (1979). *Introduction to Automata Theory, Languages, and Computation*. Reading, MA: Addison-Wesley.

Hopfield, J. J. (1982). Neural networks and physical systems with emergent collective computational abilities. *Proceedings of the National Academy of Sciences, 79*, 2554–8.

Horgan, J. (1993). The mastermind of artificial intelligence. *Scientific American, 269*(5), 35–8.

Hornik, M., Stinchcombe, M., & White, H. (1989). Multilayer feedforward networks are universal approximators. *Neural Networks, 2*, 359–66.

Hubel, D. H., & Wiesel, T. N. (1959). Receptive fields of single neurones in the cat's striate cortex. *Journal of Physiology, 148*, 574–91.

Hume, D. (1952). *An Enquiry Concerning Human Understanding*. La Salle, IL: Open Court Publishing Company.

Ingle, D. (1973). Two visual systems in the frog. *Science, 181*(4104), 1053–5.

Jackendoff, R. (1992). *Languages of the Mind*. Cambridge, MA: MIT Press.

James, W. (1890). *The Principles of Psychology* (vol. 1). New York: Dover Publications.

Jerne, N. K. (1967). Antibodies and learning: Selection versus instruction. In G. C. Quarton & T. Melnechuk & F. O. Schmitt (eds.), *The Neurosciences: A Study Program* (pp. 200–8). New York: Rockefeller University Press.

Johnson, S. (2001). *Emergence*. New York, NY: Scribner.

Jordan, M. I. (1986). An introduction to linear algebra in parallel distributed processing. In D. Rumelhart & J. McClelland (eds.), *Parallel Distributed Processing* (vol. 1, pp. 365–422). Cambridge, MA: MIT Press.

Jourdain, R. (1997). *Music, the Brain, and Ecstasy*. New York: William Morrow & Co.

Kaiser, H. R. (1958). The VARIMAX criterion for analytic rotation in factor analysis. *Psychometrika, 23*, 187–200.

Kamin, L. J. (1969). Selective association and conditioning. In N. J. Mackintosh & W. K. Honig (eds.), *Fundamental Issues in Associative Learning* (pp. 42–64). Halifax: Dalhousie University Press.

Kandel, E. R., Schwartz, J. H., & Jessell, T. M. (1991). *Principles of Neural Science* (3rd edn.). New York: Elsevier.

Karsai, I. (1999). Decentralized control of construction behavior in paper wasps: An overview of the stigmergy approach. *Artificial Life, 5*, 117–36.

Kasabov, N. K. (1996). *Foundations of Neural Networks, Fuzzy Systems, and Knowledge Engineering.* Cambridge, MA: MIT Press.

Kintsch, W. (1970). *Learning, Memory, and Conceptual Processes.* New York: John Wiley & Sons.

Kitchin, R. M. (1994). Cognitive maps: What are they and why study them? *Journal of Environmental Psychology, 14,* 1–19.

Klecka, W. R. (ed.). (1980). *Discriminant Analysis* (vol. 07–019). Thousand Oaks, CA: Sage.

Klein, R. M. (1999). The Hebb legacy. *Canadian Journal of Experimental Psychology, 53*(1), 1–3.

Koch, C., & Ullman, S. (1985). Shifts in selective visual attention: Towards the underlying neural circuitry. *Human Neurobiology, 4,* 219–27.

Koffka, K. (1935). *Principles of Gestalt Psychology.* New York: Harcourt, Brace & World.

Kohler, W. (1975). *Gestalt Psychology.* New York: New American Library.

Kosslyn, S. M. (1980). *Image and Mind.* Cambridge, MA: Harvard University Press.

Kosslyn, S. M. (1994). *Image and Brain.* Cambridge, MA: MIT Press.

Kosslyn, S. M., Pascual-Leone, A., Felican, O., Camposano, S., Keenan, J. P., Thompson, W. L., Ganis, G., Sukel, K. E., & Alpert, N. M. (1999). The role of area 17 in visual imagery: Convergent evidence from PET and rTMS. *Science, 284,* 167–70.

Kosslyn, S. M., Thompson, W. L., & Alpert, N. M. (1997). Neural systems shared by visual imagery and visual perception: A positron emission tomography study. *Neuroimage, 6,* 320–34.

Kosslyn, S. M., Thompson, W. L., Kim, I. J., & Alpert, N. M. (1995). Topographical representations of mental images in area 17. *Nature, 378,* 496–8.

Krumhansl, C. L. (1978). Concerning the applicability of geometric models to similarity data: The interrelationship between similarity and spatial density. *Psychological Review, 85,* 445–63.

Krumhansl, C. L. (1982). Density versus feature weights as predictors of visual identifications: Comment on Appelman and Mayzner. *Journal of Experimental Psychology: General, 111,* 101–8.

Kruskal, J. B., & Wish, M. (1978). *Multidimensional Scaling.* Beverly Hills, CA: Sage Publications.

Kube, C. R., & Bonabeau, E. (2000). Cooperative transport by ants and robots. *Robotics and Autonomous Systems, 30,* 85–101.

Kube, C. R., & Zhang, H. (1994). Collective robotics: From social insects to robots. *Adaptive Behavior, 2,* 189–218.

Kubow, T. M., & Full, R. J. (1999). The role of the mechanical system in control: A hypothesis of self-stabilization in hexapedal runners. *Philosophical Transactions of the Royal Society B, 354,* 849–61.

Kuffler, S. W., Nicholls, J. G., & Martin, A. R. (1984). *From Neuron to Brain* (2nd edn.). Sunderland, MA: Sinauer Associates.

Kukla, A. (1989). Nonempirical issues in psychology. *American Psychologist, 44*(5), 785–94.

LaBerge, D., Carter, M., & Brown, V. (1992). A network simulation of thalamic circuit operations in selective attention. *Neural Computation, 4,* 318–31.

Langton, C. G. (1995). *Artificial Life: An Overview.* Cambridge, MA: MIT Press.

Leahey, T. H. (1987). *A History of Psychology* (2nd edn.). Englewood Cliffs, NJ: Prentice-Hall.

Lederman, L. (1993). *The God Particle.* New York: Dell Publishing.

Leighton, J. P., & Dawson, M. R. W. (2001). A parallel distributed processing model of Wason's selection task. *Cognitive Systems Research, 2,* 207–31.

Lettvin, J. Y., Maturana, H. R., McCulloch, W. S., & Pitts, W. H. (1959). What the frog's eye tells the frog's brain. *Proceedings of the IRE, 47*(11), 1940–51.

Levitan, I. B., & Kaczmarek, L. K. (1991). *The Neuron: Cell and Molecular Biology.* New York: Oxford University Press.

Levy, S. (1992). *Artificial Life.* New York: Vintage Books.

Lewandowsky, S. (1993). The rewards and hazards of computer simulations. *Psychological Science, 4,* 236–43.

Lewandowsky, S., & Hockley, W. E. (1991). Relating theory and data: Towards an integration. In W. E. Hockley & S. Lewandowsky (eds.), *Relating Theory and Data: Essays on Human Memory in Honor of Bennet B. Murdock* (pp. 3–19). Hillsdale, NJ: Lawrence Erlbaum Associates.

Lippmann, R. P. (1987). An introduction to computing with neural nets. *IEEE ASSP Magazine, April,* 4–22.

Lippmann, R. P. (1989). Pattern classification using neural networks. *IEEE Communications Magazine, November,* 47–64.

Locke, J. (1977). *An Essay Concerning Human Understanding.* London: J.M. Dent & Sons.

Luce, R. D. (1989). Mathematical psychology and the computer revolution. In J. A. Keats, R. Taft, R. A. Heath, & S. H. Lovibond (eds.), *Mathematical and Theoretical Systems* (pp. 123–38). Amsterdam: North-Holland.

Luce, R. D. (1997). Several unresolved conceptual problems of mathematical psychology. *Journal of Mathematical Psychology, 41,* 79–87.

Luce, R. D. (1999). Where is mathematical modeling in psychology headed? *Theory & Psychology, 9,* 723–77.

Lunneborg, C. E. (1994). *Modeling Experimental and Observational Data.* Belmont, CA: Duxbury Press.

Lynch, G. (1986). *Synapses, Circuits, and the Beginnings of Memory.* Cambridge, MA: MIT Press.

Mackenzie, D. (2002). The science of surprise. *Discover, 23*(2), 59–62.

Malgady, R. G., & Johnson, M. G. (1976). Modifiers in metaphor: Effect of constituent phrase similarity on the interpretation of figurative sentences. *Journal Of Psycholinguistic Research, 5,* 43–52.

Marr, D. (1982). *Vision.* San Francisco: W.H. Freeman.

Martinez, J. L., & Derrick, B. E. (1996). Long-term potentiation and learning. *Annual Review of Psychology, 47,* 173–203.

Massaro, D. W. (1988). Some criticisms of connectionist models of human performance. *Journal of Memory and Language, 27,* 213–34.

Matin, L. (1968). Critical duration, the differential luminance threshold, critical flicker frequency, and visual adaptation: A theoretical treatment. *Journal of the Optical Society of America, 58,* 404–15.

McCaughan, D. B., Medler, D. A., & Dawson, M. R. W. (1999). Internal representation in networks of nonmonotonic processing units. Paper presented at the International Joint Conference on Neural Networks, July, Washington, DC.

McClelland, J. L. (1986). Resource requirements of standard and programmable nets. In D. Rumelhart & J. McClelland (eds.), *Parallel Distributed Processing* (vol. 1, pp. 460–87). Cambridge, MA: MIT Press.

McClelland, J. L., & Rumelhart, D. E. (1986). *Parallel Distributed Processing* (vol. 2). Cambridge, MA: MIT Press.

McClelland, J. L., Rumelhart, D. E., & Hinton, G. E. (1986). The appeal of parallel distributed processing. In D. Rumelhart & J. McClelland (eds.), *Parallel Distributed Processing* (vol. 1, pp. 3–44). Cambridge, MA: MIT Press.

McCloskey, M. (1991). Networks and theories: The place of connectionism in cognitive science. *Psychological Science, 2*, 387–95.

McComb, G. (1987). *The Robot Builder's Bonanza: 99 Inexpensive Robotics Projects*. Blue Ridge Summit, PA: TAB Books.

McCorduck, P. (1988). Artificial intelligence: An apercu. In S. Graubard (ed.), *The Artificial Intelligence Debate* (pp. 65–84). Cambridge, MA: MIT Press.

McCorduck, P. (1991). *Aaron's Code: Meta-Art, Artificial Intelligence, and the Work of Harold Cohen*. New York: W.H. Freeman.

McCulloch, W. S. (1988). What is a number, that a man may know it, and a man, that he may know a number? In W. S. McCulloch (ed.), *Embodiments of Mind* (pp. 1–18). Cambridge, MA: MIT Press.

McCulloch, W. S., & Pitts, W. (1943). A logical calculus of the ideas immanent in nervous activity. *Bulletin of Mathematical Biophysics, 5*, 115–33.

McCulloch, W. S., & Pitts, W. H. (1988). A logical calculus of the ideas immanent in nervous activity. In W. S. McCulloch (ed.), *Embodiments of Mind* (pp. 19–39). Cambridge, MA: MIT Press.

McNaughton, B., Barnes, C. A., Gerrard, J. L., Gothard, K., Jung, M. W., Knierim, J. J., Kudrimoti, H., Qin, Y., Skaggs, W. E., Suster, M., & Weaver, K. L. (1996). Deciphering the hippocampal polyglot: The hippocampus as a path integration system. *The Journal of Experimental Biology, 199*, 173–85.

Medin, D. L., Goldstone, R. L., & Gentner, D. (1993). Respects for similarity. *Psychological Review, 100*(2), 254–78.

Medler, D. A. (1998). A brief history of connectionism. *Neural Computing Surveys, 1*, 18–72.

Medler, D. A., McCaughan, D. B., Dawson, M. R. W., & Willson, L. (1999). When local isn't enough: Extracting distributed rules from networks. *Proceedings of the 1999 International Joint Conference on Neural Network* (pp. 305i-vi), Washington, DC.

Mellet, E., Petit, L., Mazoyer, B., Denis, M., & Tzourio, N. (1998). Reopening the mental imagery debate: Lessons from functional anatomy. *Neuroimage, 8*, 129–39.

Miller, R. R., Barnet, R. C., & Grahame, N. J. (1995). Assessment of the Rescorla–Wagner model. *Psychological Bulletin, 117*, 363–86.

Milligan, G. W., & Cooper, M. C. (1985). An examination of procedures for determining the number of clusters in a data set. *Psychometrika, 50*, 159–79.

Milner, P. M. (1957). The cell assembly: Mark II. *Psychological Review, 64*(4), 242–52.

Minsky, M. (1963). Steps toward artificial intelligence. In E. A. Feigenbaum & J. Feldman (eds.), *Computers and Thought* (pp. 406–50). New York, NY: McGraw-Hill.

Minsky, M. (1972). *Computation: finite and Infinite Machines*. London: Prentice-Hall International.

Minsky, M., & Papert, S. (1988). *Perceptrons* (3rd edn.). Cambridge, MA: MIT Press.

Mitchell, M. (1996). *An Introduction to Genetic Algorithms*. Cambridge, MA: MIT Press.

Moorhead, I. R., Haig, N. D., & Clement, R. A. (1989). An investigation of trained neural networks from a neurophysiological perspective. *Perception, 18*, 793–803.

Moravec, H. (1999). *Robot*. New York: Oxford University Press.

Mozer, M. C., & Smolensky, P. (1989). Using relevance to reduce network size automatically. *Connection Science, 1*, 3–16.

Murdock, B. B. (1982). A theory for the storage and retrieval of item and associative information. *Psychological Review, 89*, 609–26.

Murdock, B. B. (1985). Convolution and matrix systems: A reply to Pike. *Psychological Review, 92*, 130–32.

Murdock, B. B. (1997). Context and mediators in a theory of distributed associative memory (TODAM2). *Psychological Review, 104*, 839–62.

Newell, A. (1973). Production systems: Models of control structures. In W. G. Chase (ed.), *Visual Information Processing* (pp. 463–526). New York: Academic Press.

Newell, A. (1980). Physical symbol systems. *Cognitive Science, 4*, 135–83.

Newell, A. (1990). *Unified Theories of Cognition*. Cambridge, MA: Harvard University Press.

Newell, A., & Simon, H. A. (1972). *Human Problem Solving*. Englewood Cliffs, NJ: Prentice-Hall.

O'Keefe, J., & Burgess, N. (1996). Geometric determinants of the place fields of hippocampal neurones. *Nature, 381*, 425–8.

O'Keefe, J., & Dostrovsky, J. (1971). The hippocampus as a spatial map: Preliminary evidence from unit activity in the freely moving rat. *Brain Research, 34*, 171–5.

O'Keefe, J., & Nadel, L. (1978). *The Hippocampus as a Cognitive Map*. Oxford: Clarendon Press.

Omlin, C. W., & Giles, C. L. (1996). Extraction of rules from discrete-time recurrent neural networks. *Neural Networks, 9*, 41–52.

Oreskes, N., Shrader-Frechette, K., & Belitz, K. (1994). Verification, validation, and confirmation of numerical models in the earth sciences. *Science, 263*, 641–6.

Ortony, A. (1979). Beyond literal similarity. *Psychological Review, 86*, 161–80.

Paivio, A. (1969). Mental imagery in associative learning and memory. *Psychological Review, 76*, 241–63.

Paivio, A. (1971). *Imagery and Verbal Processes*. New York: Holt, Rinehart & Winston.

Paivio, A. (1986). *Mental Representations: A Dual-Coding Approach*. New York: Oxford University Press.

Pao, Y.-H. (1989). *Adaptive Pattern Recognition and Neural Networks*. Reading, MA: Addison-Wesley.

Pavlov, I. P. (1927). *Conditioned Reflexes*. New York: Oxford University Press.

Pearce, J. M. (1997). *Animal Learning and Cognition: An Introduction*. Hove, UK: Psychology Press.

Pearce, J. M., & Bouton, M. E. (2001). Theories of associative learning in animals. *Annual Review of Psychology, 52*, 111–39.

Pedhazur, E. J. (1982). *Multiple Regression in Behavioral Research* (2nd edn.). New York: Holt, Rinehart and Winston.

Pfeifer, R., & Scheier, C. (1999). *Understanding Intelligence*. Cambridge, MA: MIT Press.

Piattelli-Palmarini, M. (1989). Evolution, selection and cognition: From "learning" to parameter setting in biology and in the study of language. *Cognition, 31*, 1–44.

Pike, R. (1984). Comparison of convolution and matrix distributed memory systems for associative recall and recognition. *Psychological Review, 91*, 281–94.

Pinker, S. (2002). *The Blank Slate*. New York: Viking.

Popper, K. R. (1979). *Objective Knowledge*. London: Oxford University Press.

Pouget, A., Dayan, P., & Zemel, R. S. (2000). Information processing with population codes. *Nature Review Neuroscience, 1*, 125–32.

Pylyshyn, Z. W. (1979a). Metaphorical imprecision and the "top-down" research strategy. In A. Ortony (ed.), *Metaphor and Thought* (pp. 420–36). Cambridge, UK: Cambridge University Press.

Pylyshyn, Z. W. (1979b). The rate of "mental rotation" of images: A test of a holistic analogue hypothesis. *Memory and Cognition, 7,* 19–28.

Pylyshyn, Z. W. (1980). Computation and cognition: Issues in the foundations of cognitive science. *Behavioral and Brain Sciences, 3,* 111–69.

Pylyshyn, Z. W. (1981). The imagery debate: Analogue media versus tacit knowledge. *Psychological Review, 88*(1), 16–45.

Pylyshyn, Z. W. (1984). *Computation and Cognition.* Cambridge, MA.: MIT Press.

Pylyshyn, Z. W. (1991). The role of cognitive architectures in theories of cognition. In K. VanLehn (ed.), *Architectures for Intelligence* (pp. 189–223). Hillsdale, NJ: Lawrence Erlbaum Associates.

Quinlan, J. R. (1986). Induction of decision trees. *Machine Learning, 1,* 81–106.

Quinlan, P. (1991). *Connectionism and Psychology.* Chicago: University of Chicago Press.

Redish, A. D., & Touretzky, D. S. (1999). Separating hippocampal maps. In B. N. Jeffery, K. J. Jeffery, & J. O'Keefe (eds.), *The Hippocampal and Parietal Foundations of Spatial Cognition* (pp. 203–19). Oxford: Oxford University Press.

Rescorla, R. A., & Wagner, A. R. (1972). A theory of Pavlovian conditioning: Variations in the effectiveness of reinforcement and nonreinforcement. In A. H. Black & W. F. Prokasy (eds.), *Classical Conditioning II: Current Research and Theory* (pp. 64–99). New York: Appleton-Century-Crofts.

Restle, F. (1971). *Mathematical Models in Psychology: An Introduction.* Baltimore, MD: Penguin Books.

Restle, F., & Greeno, J. G. (1970). *Introduction to Mathematical Psychology.* Reading, MA: Addison-Wesley.

Ripley, B. D. (1996). *Pattern Recognition and Neural Networks.* Cambridge, UK: Cambridge University Press.

Rochester, N., Holland, J. H., Haibt, L. H., & Duda, W. L. (1956). Tests on a cell assembly theory of the action of the brain, using a large digital computer. *IRE Transactions on Information Theory, IT, 2,* 80–93.

Rojas, R. (1996). *Neural Networks: A Systematic Exploration.* Berlin: Springer.

Rollins, M. (2001). The strategic eye: Kosslyn's theory of imagery and perception. *Minds and Machines, 11,* 267–86.

Romney, A. K., Shepard, R. N., & Nerlove, S. B. (1972). *Multidimensional Scaling: Theory and Applications in the Behavioral Sciences. Volume II: Applications.* New York, NY: Seminar Press.

Rosenblatt, F. (1962). *Principles of Neurodynamics.* Washington: Spartan Books.

Roufs, J. A. J. (1972). Dynamic properties of vision. I. Experimental relationships between flicker and flash thresholds. *Vision Research, 12,* 261–78.

Royce, J. R. (1970). The present situation in theoretical psychology. In J. R. Royce (ed.), *Toward Unification in Psychology.* Toronto: University of Toronto Press.

Rumelhart, D. E., & Abrahamson, A. A. (1973). A model for analogical reasoning. *Cognitive Psychology, 5,* 1–28.

Rumelhart, D. E., Hinton, G. E., & Williams, R. J. (1986a). Learning internal representations by error backpropagation. In D. E. Rumelhart & J. McClelland (eds.), *Parallel Distributed Processing* (vol. 1, pp. 318–62). Cambridge, MA: MIT Press.

Rumelhart, D. E., Hinton, G. E., & Williams, R. J. (1986b). Learning representations by back-propagating errors. *Nature, 323,* 533–36.

Rumelhart, D. E., & McClelland, J. (1986a). On learning the past tenses of English verbs. In J. McClelland & D. E. Rumelhart (eds.), *Parallel Distributed Processing. Volume 2: Psychological and Biological Models* (pp. 216–71). Cambridge, MA: MIT Press.

Rumelhart, D. E., & McClelland, J. L. (1986b). *Parallel Distributed Processing* (vol. 1). Cambridge, MA: MIT Press.

Sandon, P. A. (1992). Simulating visual attention. *Journal of Cognitive Neuroscience, 2,* 213–31.

Sarle, W. S. (1994). Neural networks and statistical models. Paper presented at the Nineteenth Annual SAS Users Group International Conference, April.

Schlimmer, J. S. (1987). Concept acquisition through representational adjustment. Unpublished doctoral dissertation, University of California Irvine, Irvine, CA.

Searle, J. R. (1980). Minds, brains, and programs. *Behavioral and Brain Sciences, 3,* 417–24.

Searle, J. R. (1984). *Minds, Brains, and Science.* Cambridge, MA: Harvard University Press.

Searle, J. R. (1990). Is the brain's mind a computer program? *Scientific American, 262,* 26–31.

Searle, J. R. (1992). *The Rediscovery of the Mind.* Cambridge, MA: MIT Press.

Seidenberg, M. (1993). Connectionist models and cognitive theory. *Psychological Science, 4,* 228–35.

Seidenberg, M., & McClelland, J. (1989). A distributed, developmental model of word recognition and naming. *Psychological Review, 97,* 447–52.

Sejnowski, T. J., & Rosenberg, C. R. (1988). NETtalk: A parallel network that learns to read aloud. In J. A. Anderson & E. Rosenfeld (eds.), *Neurocomputing: Foundations of Research* (pp. 663–72). Cambridge, MA: MIT Press.

Selfridge, O. G. (1956). Pattern cognition and learning. In C. Cherry (ed.), *Information Theory* (pp. 345–53). London: Butterworths Scientific Publications.

Shanks, D. R. (1995). *The Psychology of Associative Learning.* Cambridge, UK: Cambridge University Press.

Shanks, D. R. (1997). Representation of categories and concepts in memory. In M. A. Conway (ed.), *Cognitive Models of Memory* (pp. 111–46). Cambridge, MA: MIT Press.

Shepard, R. N. (1972). A taxonomy of some principal types of data and of multidimensional methods for their analysis. In R. N. Shepard, A. K. Romney, & S. B. Nerlove (eds.), *Multidimensional Scaling: Theory and Applications in the Behavioral Sciences. Vol 1: Theory* (pp. 21–47). New York: Seminar Press.

Shepard, R. N., & Cooper, L. A. (1982). *Mental Images and their Transformations.* Cambridge, MA: MIT Press.

Shepard, R. N., Romney, A. K., & Nerlove, S. B. (1972). *Multidimensional Scaling: Theory and Applications in the Behavioral Sciences. Vol. I: Theory.* New York: Seminar Press.

Shepherd, A. J. (1997). *Second-Order Methods for Neural Networks.* London: Springer.

Sherry, D., & Healy, S. (1998). Neural mechanisms of spatial representation. In S. Healy (ed.), *Spatial Representation in Animals* (pp. 133–57). Oxford: Oxford University Press.

Siegelmann, H. T. (1999). *Neural Networks and Analog Computation: Beyond the Turing Limit.* Boston, MA: Birkhauser.

Simon, H. A. (1996). *The Sciences of the Artificial* (3rd edn.). Cambridge, MA: MIT Press.

Skinner, B. F. (1957). *Verbal Behavior.* New York: Appleton-Century-Crofts.

Smolensky, P. (1988). On the proper treatment of connectionism. *Behavioral and Brain Sciences, 11,* 1–74.

Sorabji, R. (1972). *Aristotle on Memory.* Worcester, UK: Ebenezer Baylis and Son.

Sporns, O., & Tononi, G. (1994). *Selectionism and the Brain.* San Diego, CA: Academic Press.

Steinbuch, K. (1961). Die lernmatrix. *Kybernetik, 1,* 36–45.

Sternberg, S. (1969). Memory-scanning: Mental processes revealed by reaction-time experiments. *American Scientist, 4,* 421–57.

Stone, G. O. (1986). An analysis of the delta rule and the learning of statistical associations. In D. E. Rumelhart & J. McClelland (eds.), *Parallel Distributed Processing* (vol. 1, pp. 444–59). Cambridge, MA: MIT Press.

Sutton, R. S., & Barto, A. G. (1981). Toward a modern theory of adaptive networks: Expectation and prediction. *Psychological Review, 88*(2), 135–70.

Taylor, W. K. (1956). Electrical simulation of some nervous system functional activities. In C. Cherry (ed.), *Information Theory* (pp. 314–28). London: Butterworths Scientific Publications.

Tesauro, G., & Janssens, B. (1988). Scaling relationships in backpropagation learning. *Complex Systems, 2*, 39–44.

Theraulaz, G., & Bonabeau, E. (1999). A brief history of stigmergy. *Artificial Life, 5*, 97–116.

Thompson, W. L., Kosslyn, S. M., Sukel, K. E., & Alpert, N. M. (2001). Mental imagery of high- and low-resolution gratings activates Area 17. *Neuroimage, 14*, 454–64.

Thrun, S. (1995). Extracting rules from artificial neural networks with distributed representations. In G. Tesauro, D. S. Touretzky, & T. K. Leen (eds.), *Advances in Neural Information Processing Systems* (vol. 7, pp. 505–12). Cambridge, MA: MIT Press.

Thrun, S. B., Bala, J., Bloedorn, E., Bratko, I., Cestnik, B., Cheng, J., De Jong, K., Dzeroski, S., Fahlman, S. E., Fisher, D., Hamann, R., Kaufman, K., Keller, S., Kononenko, I., Kreuziger, J., Michalski, R. S., Mitchell, T., Pachowicz, P., Reich, Y., Vafaie, H., Van de Welde, W., Wenzel, W., Wnek, J., & Zhang, J. (1991). *The MONK's Problems – A Performance Comparison of Different Learning Algorithms* (Technical Report CS-CMU-91-197). Pittsburgh: Carnegie Mellon University.

Tolman, E. C. (1932). *Purposive Behavior in Animals and Men*. New York: Century Books.

Tolman, E. C. (1948). Cognitive maps in rats and men. *Psychological review, 55*, 189–208.

Tourangeau, R., & Sternberg, R. J. (1981). Aptness in metaphor. *Cognitive psychology, 13*, 27–55.

Tourangeau, R., & Sternberg, R. J. (1982). Understanding and appreciating metaphors. *Cognition, 11*, 203–44.

Touretzky, D. S., Wan, H. S., & Redish, A. D. (1994). Neural representation of space in rats and robots. In J. M. Zurada, R. J. Marks, & C. J. Robinson (eds.), *Computational Intelligence: Imitating Life*. New York: IEEE Press.

Turing, A. M. (1936). On computable numbers, with an application to the Entscheidungsproblem. *Proceedings of the London Mathematical Society, Series 2h, 42*, 230–65.

Turing, A. M. (1950). Computing machinery and intelligence. *Mind, 59*, 433–60.

Tversky, A. (1977). Features of similarity. *Psychological Review, 84*, 327–52.

Tversky, A., & Gati, I. (1982). Similarity, separability, and the triangle inequality. *Psychological Review, 89*, 123–54.

Ungerleider, L. G., & Mishkin, M. (1982). Two cortical visual systems. In D. Ingle, M. A. Goodale, & R. J. W. Mansfield (eds.), *Analysis of Visual Behavior* (pp. 549–86). Cambridge, MA: MIT Press.

VanLehn, K. (1991). *Architectures for Intelligence*. Hillsdale, NJ: Lawrence Erlbaum Associates.

von Neumann, J. (1973). First draft of a report on the EDVAC. In B. Randell (ed.), *The Origins of Digital Computers: Selected Papers* (pp. 355–64). Berlin: Springer-Verlag.

Waldrop, M. M. (1992). *Complexity: The Emerging Science at the Edge of Order and Chaos*. New York: Simon & Schuster.

Warren, H. C. (1921). *A History of the Association Psychology*. New York: Charles Scribner's Sons.

Wason, P. C. (1966). *Reasoning*. New York: Penguin.

Wasserman, E. A., & Miller, R. R. (1997). What's elementary about associative learning? *Annual Review of Psychology, 48*, 573–607.

Watkins, M. J. (1990). Mediationism and the obfuscation of memory. *American Psychologist, 45*, 328–35.

Watson, J. B. (1913). Psychology as the behaviorist views it. *Psychological Review, 20*, 158–77.

Watson, J. D. (1968). *The Double Helix*. New York: New American Library.

Webb, B. (1996). A cricket robot. *Scientific American, 275*, 94–9.

Webb, B. (2000). What does robotics offer animal behaviour? *Animal Behaviour, 60*, 545–58.

Whitten, D. N., & Brown, K. T. (1973). Slowed decay of the monkey's cone receptor potential by intense stimuli, and protection from this effect by light adaptation. *Vision Research, 13*, 1659–67.

Wickens, T. D. (1982). *Models for Behavior: Stochastic Processes in Psychology*. San Francisco: W. H. Freeman.

Widrow, B., & Hoff, M. E. (1960). Adaptive switching circuits. *Institute of Radio Enginners, Wester Electronic Show and Convention, Convention Record, Part 4*, 96–104.

Wiener, N. (1948). *Cybernetics: Or Control and Communciation in the Animal and the Machine*. Cambridge, MA: MIT Press.

Williams, M. R. (1997). *A History of Computing Technology* (2nd edn.). Los Alamitos, CA: IEEE Computer Society Press.

Winer, B. J. (1971). *Statistical Principles in Experimental Design* (2nd edn.). New York: McGraw-Hill.

Wittgenstein, L. (1953). *Philosophical Investigations* (G. E. M. Anscombe, trans.). Oxford: Blackwell.

Zeigler, B. P. (1976). *Theory of Modelling and Simulation*. New York: John Wiley & Sons.

Zimmerman, C. L. (1999). A network interpretation approach to the balance scale task. Unpublished Ph.D., University of Alberta, Edmonton.

Zipser, D., & Andersen, R. A. (1988). A back-propagation programmed network that simulates response properties of a subset of posterior parietal neurons. *Nature, 331*, 679–84.

Name Index

Subject Index

Printed and bound by CPI Group (UK) Ltd, Croydon, CR0 4YY

16/04/2025

14658550-0005